IOLO MORGANWG AND THE ROMANTIC TRADITION IN WALES

General Editor: Geraint H. Jenkins

William Owen Pughe, *Iolo Morganwg 1798*, watercolour.
Reproduced by kind permission of the National Library of Wales.

Bard of Liberty:
The Political Radicalism of Iolo Morganwg

GERAINT H. JENKINS

UNIVERSITY OF WALES PRESS
CARDIFF
2012

© Geraint H. Jenkins, 2012

All rights reserved. No part of this book may be reproduced, stored in a retrieval system, or transmitted in any form or by any means, electronic, mechanical, photo-copying, recording or otherwise, without clearance from the University of Wales Press, 10 Columbus Walk, Brigantine Place, Cardiff CF10 4UP.

www.uwp.co.uk

British Library Cataloguing-in-Publication Data
A catalogue record for this book is available from the British Library.

ISBN   978-0-7083-2498-1 (hardback)
           978-0-7083-2499-8 (paperback)
e-ISBN 978-0-7083-2500-1

The right of Geraint H. Jenkins to be identified as the author of this work has been asserted by him in accordance with sections 77 and 79 of the Copyright, Designs and Patents Act 1988.

Typeset in Wales by Eira Fenn Gaunt, Cardiff
Printed in Great Britain by CPI Antony Rowe, Chippenham, Wiltshire

*For Gareth Elwyn Jones
the bravest of Welsh historians*

IOLO MORGANWG AND THE ROMANTIC TRADITION IN WALES

Other volumes already published in the series:

A Rattleskull Genius: The Many Faces of Iolo Morganwg, edited by Geraint H. Jenkins (University of Wales Press, 2005; paperback edn., 2009)

The Truth against the World: Iolo Morganwg and Romantic Forgery, by Mary-Ann Constantine (University of Wales Press, 2007)

Bardic Circles: National, Regional and Personal Identity in the Bardic Vision of Iolo Morganwg, by Cathryn A. Charnell-White (University of Wales Press, 2007)

The Correspondence of Iolo Morganwg, edited by Geraint H. Jenkins, Ffion Mair Jones and David Ceri Jones (3 volumes, University of Wales Press, 2007)

The Literary and Historical Legacy of Iolo Morganwg 1826–1926, by Marion Löffler (University of Wales Press, 2007)

'The Bard is a Very Singular Character': Iolo Morganwg, Marginalia and Print Culture, by Ffion Mair Jones (University of Wales Press, 2010)

Contents

Preface		ix
List of Abbreviations		xi
1.	'On the Banks of the Daw'	1
2.	'I was always pushing forward'	29
3.	'When he nobly for Liberty stood'	47
4.	'The Unparalleled Eventfulness of this Age'	79
5.	'[He] is now a seller of seditious Books and will be planting Treason wherever he goes'	123
6.	'I have as much Cimbric patriotism as any man living'	163
7.	'I am what I am, and I most fervently thank God that I am what I am'	209
Select Bibliography		245
Index		267

Preface

This volume, the last in the series, is devoted to the development and expression of politics in the tempestuous life of Iolo Morganwg. In Victorian times Iolo was depicted as a benign, even saintly, figure, while twentieth-century Welsh scholars for the most part dwelt largely on his so-called malign gifts as a literary forger. Here he is portrayed as a political animal who kept abreast of current affairs, gloried in the ideals of the Atlantic revolutions, and made it his business to make life as difficult as possible for upholders of the *ancien régime*. A contrarian by nature, Iolo was no stranger to conflicts and dust-ups. A combination of ill-luck, misadventures, personal slights and his own politico-religious convictions drove him into the arms of champions of reason, toleration and justice. He became one of the founders of the Unitarian movement in Wales and, inspired by Tom Paine's *Rights of Man*, he joined the republican cause and came to be known as the 'Bard of Liberty'. He took up the cause of the 'swinish multitude' – poor, downtrodden people – and used his gift for satire to express his healthy disrespect for the ruling classes. He campaigned passionately against war and the slave trade and did his utmost on behalf of victims of socio-economic change and political oppression. As a citizen of the world, he understood the importance of establishing cultural institutions which would enrich and sustain the native Welsh culture, and he can justly be considered a shrewd and far-seeing nation-builder. Iolo never abandoned his radical political stance or his commitment to Rational Dissent. He remained true to his values to the very last and deserves an honoured place in the historical annals as a humanitarian and a friend of liberty.

The overwhelming bulk of material relating to Iolo Morganwg is to be found in the National Library of Wales, an institution which is very close to my heart. I heartily salute and thank its staff for giving me unstinting support during the course of my researches into this complex and fascinating collection of manuscripts. I also readily acknowledge my debt to the staff of the British Library, Bristol Record Office, Cardiff Central Library, Dr Williams's Library, Gwent Record Office, Glamorgan Archives and West Glamorgan Archives Service. I have benefited immensely from the knowledge and friendship of several of my former colleagues at the University of Wales Centre for Advanced Welsh and Celtic Studies who contributed to the Arts and Humanities Research Council-funded project on Iolo Morganwg. These include Mary-Ann Constantine, Cathryn A. Charnell-White, Andrew Davies, David Ceri Jones, Ffion Mair Jones and Marion Löffler. I also record my thanks for the financial support I received at different stages from the British Academy and the Leverhulme Trust. The following scholars have helped in a variety of ways, not least in sharing their insights with me in correspondence or private conversation: John Barrell, Hywel M. Davies, Chris Evans, Robert Evans, Martin Fitzpatrick, Ronald Hutton, Brian Ll. James, E. Wyn James, Prys Morgan, Geraint Phillips, Richard Suggett, Huw Walters and David Wykes. All errors which remain are my own.

I am especially grateful to Glenys Howells for scanning the text with an eagle eye and making many invaluable corrections and suggestions, to Nia Davies for processing the work with exceptional care, and to Dafydd Johnston, my successor as Director of the University of Wales Centre for Advanced Welsh and Celtic Studies, for his part in bringing this multi-volume series to a successful conclusion. William Howells kindly spared me the chore of compiling the index. I gladly acknowledge my debt of thanks to the staff of the University of Wales Press, especially Sarah Lewis and Siân Chapman, for their generous advice and support in the preparation of this book. Most of all, I thank my wife Ann from the bottom of my heart for living with Iolo for so long and for praising and cursing him as often as did Peggy, his own equally redoubtable wife.

October 2011   Geraint H. Jenkins

Abbreviations

ALMA	Hugh Owen (ed.), *Additional Letters of the Morrises of Anglesey (1735–1786)* (2 vols., London, 1947–9)
Bardic Circles	Cathryn A. Charnell-White, *Bardic Circles: National, Regional and Personal Identity in the Bardic Vision of Iolo Morganwg* (Cardiff, 2007)
BBCS	*Bulletin of the Board of Celtic Studies*
BIHR	*Bulletin of the Institute of Historical Research*
CA	*The Carmarthen[shire] Antiquary*
CIM	Geraint H. Jenkins, Ffion Mair Jones and David Ceri Jones (eds.), *The Correspondence of Iolo Morganwg* (3 vols., Cardiff, 2007)
CMCS	*Cambridge Medieval Celtic Studies*
CRhIM	P. J. Donovan (ed.), *Cerddi Rhydd Iolo Morganwg* (Caerdydd, 1980)
DWB	*The Dictionary of Welsh Biography down to 1940* (London, 1959)
EHR	*English Historical Review*
FHSJ	*Flintshire Historical Society Journal*
GCH IV	Glanmor Williams (ed.), *Glamorgan County History, Volume IV: Early Modern Glamorgan from the Act of Union to the Industrial Revolution* (Cardiff, 1974)
GCH V	A. H. John and Glanmor Williams (eds.), *Glamorgan County History, Volume V: Industrial Glamorgan from 1700 to 1970* (Cardiff, 1980)
HGB	Geraint and Zonia Bowen, *Hanes Gorsedd y Beirdd* (Cyhoeddiadau Barddas, 1991)

HHSC	R. T. Jenkins and Helen M. Ramage, *A History of the Honourable Society of Cymmrodorion and of the Gwyneddigion and Cynreigyddion Societies (1751–1951)* (London, 1951)
IMChY	G. J. Williams, *Iolo Morganwg a Chywyddau'r Ychwanegiad* (Llundain, 1926)
Iolo Manuscripts	Taliesin Williams (ed.), *Iolo Manuscripts: A Selection of Ancient Welsh Manuscripts* (Llandovery, 1848)
JMHRS	*Journal of the Merioneth Historical and Record Society*
JWBS	*Journal of the Welsh Bibliographical Society*
Lewis: IM	Ceri W. Lewis, *Iolo Morganwg* (Caernarfon, 1995)
Literary and Historical Legacy	Marion Löffler, *The Literary and Historical Legacy of Iolo Morganwg 1826–1926* (Cardiff, 2007)
LlC	*Llên Cymru*
MAW	Owen Jones, Iolo Morganwg and William Owen Pughe, *The Myvyrian Archaiology of Wales* (3 vols., London, 1801–7)
MC	*Montgomeryshire Collections*
MH	*Merthyr Historian*
NLW	National Library of Wales
NLWJ	*National Library of Wales Journal*
ODNB	*Oxford Dictionary of National Biography*
OED	*Oxford English Dictionary*
RAEW	Elijah Waring, *Recollections and Anecdotes of Edward Williams, the Bard of Glamorgan; or, Iolo Morganwg, B.B.D.* (London, 1850)
Rattleskull Genius	Geraint H. Jenkins (ed.), *A Rattleskull Genius: The Many Faces of Iolo Morganwg* (Cardiff, 2005)
TCHBC	*Trafodion Cymdeithas Hanes Bedyddwyr Cymru*

'The Bard is a Very Singular Character'	Ffion Mair Jones, *'The Bard is a Very Singular Character': Iolo Morganwg, Marginalia and Print Culture* (Cardiff, 2010)
THSC	*Transactions of the Honourable Society of Cymmrodorion*
TLlM	G. J. Williams, *Traddodiad Llenyddol Morgannwg* (Caerdydd, 1948)
TRS	*Transactions of the Radnorshire Society*
Truth against the World	Mary-Ann Constantine, *The Truth against the World: Iolo Morganwg and Romantic Forgery* (Cardiff, 2007)
WHR	*Welsh History Review*
Williams: *IM*	G. J. Williams, *Iolo Morganwg – Y Gyfrol Gyntaf* (Caerdydd, 1956)
Williams: *PLP*	Edward Williams, *Poems, Lyric and Pastoral* (2 vols., London, 1794)
WJRH	*Welsh Journal of Religious History*

1
'On the Banks of the Daw'

In July 1793 William Winterbotham, a thirty-year-old assistant minister at How's Lane Particular Baptist Church, Plymouth, was plucked from relative obscurity and thrust into the public limelight when he was sentenced at the Exeter assizes to a fine of £200 and four years in prison for preaching sedition in his sermons.[1] This unlikely standard-bearer of civil liberties was bundled off to Newgate prison, the most notorious gaol in Britain. Dubbed 'a prototype of hell'[2] by Henry Fielding, Newgate was regarded as the English equivalent of the Bastille. Yet, by greasing the palm of the gaoler, visitors were allowed to attend to some of the needs of imprisoned radicals. Winterbotham's fellow prisoners included twelve leaders of the London Corresponding Society, an artisan society reckoned to be the mouthpiece of sans-culottism, and whenever poets, rationalists and Unitarians like William Godwin, Theophilus Lindsey, Robert Southey and Gilbert Wakefield visited incarcerated dissidents there was much talk of liberty, natural rights and justice.[3] Letters, papers and books were exchanged, poems were read aloud, and the name of William Pitt was taken in vain very loudly.

Among Winterbotham's regular visitors early in 1795 was a Rational Dissenter from the Vale of Glamorgan who, in Welsh-speaking circles, went by the pseudonym Iolo Morganwg (Edward of Glamorgan). Born Edward Williams, and known by that name by the radical intelligentsia of London, he had built for himself from 1791 onwards a reputation as a fiery Welsh Painite whose much-vaunted suffix BBD (Bardd wrth Fraint a Defod Beirdd Ynys Prydain / Bard by the Privilege and Rite of the Bards of the Island of Britain) lent him

---
[1] *The Trial of Wm. Winterbotham . . . at Exeter; On the 25th. of July, 1793* (London, 1794); Michael R. Watts, *The Dissenters. Volume II. The Expansion of Evangelical Nonconformity* (Oxford, 1995), p. 354; Michael Durey, 'William Winterbotham's Trumpet of Sedition: Religious Dissent and Political Radicalism in the 1790s', *Journal of Religious History*, 19, no. 2 (1995), 141–57; *ODNB* s.v. William Winterbotham.
[2] Stephen Halliday, *Newgate: London's Prototype of Hell* (Stroud, 2006), p. 190.
[3] Michael T. Davis, Iain McCalman and Christina Parolin (eds.), *Newgate in Revolution: An Anthology of Radical Prison Literature in the Age of Revolution* (London, 2005), pp. xiii, xvi.

an air of authority and mystery.⁴ By publicly defying 'church and king' mobs, fulminating against kingcraft and priestcraft, and publicizing – in Welsh and English – the cause of anti-slavery and peace, he had become a marked man. It took courage to be a free-born Welshman and to disseminate the principles of his 'politicized Bardic system'⁵ in the 'hell, commonly called London',⁶ but Iolo admired kindred spirits who dared to flout the repressive legislation of the times. Since William Winterbotham was of artisan stock, an autodidact and a man of hard-hitting views – and thus a mirror image of Iolo himself – he was glad to visit the Baptist pastor at Newgate. On arrival he regularly used to append the self-styled title 'Bard of Liberty' to his name and address in the visitors' book. Eventually he was rumbled and accosted by the irate gaoler:

> 'So!' said the official, 'you are *the Bard of Liberty*, are you?'
> 'Yes, sir, I am.'
> 'Then, Mr. Bard of Liberty, you are to understand that the only liberty allowed you here, will be to walk out the way you came in.'
> 'O, very well, Mr. Gaoler, by all means; and I wish no Bard of Liberty may ever meet with worse treatment, than being told to walk *out of* a prison.'⁷

Having been sent packing, but still confident that he had held his ground during this heated exchange, Iolo returned to his lodgings that evening and turned to the odes of Horace, one of his favourite lyric poets. Inspired by reading the ode beginning 'Integer vitae', which enunciates the principle that no man 'who is pure of heart and innocent of evil' should fear misfortune,⁸ he composed, in the manner of Horace, seven verses entitled 'The Newgate Stanzas',⁹ a blistering attack on loyalist mobs, tyrannical monarchs and placemen, and a passionate defence of 'bright Liberty' and the inalienable rights of man:

> Dear Liberty, thy sacred name
> O! Let me to the world proclaim
>   Thy dauntless ardor sing;
> Known as thy son, nor Knaves of State,
> Nor Spies, I fear, nor placeman's hate,
>   Nor Mobs of Church and King.

---

[4] *RAEW*, p. 52.
[5] Damian Walford Davies, *Presences that Disturb: Models of Romantic Identity in the Literature and Culture of the 1790s* (Cardiff, 2002), p. 167.
[6] *CIM*, I, p. 600, Iolo Morganwg to Margaret (Peggy) Williams, 20 September 1793.
[7] *RAEW*, pp. 47–8.
[8] *Horace: The Complete Odes and Epodes*, translated by David West (Oxford, 1997), pp. 43–4, Book I, no. XXII. For a transcription of this Latin ode by Iolo, see NLW 13159A, pp. 151–2. For other Welsh-language verses by him, based on Horace's work, see NLW 13148A, pp. 260–1. See also V. G. Kiernan, *Horace: Poetics and Politics* (Basingstoke, 1999).
[9] NLW 21334B, pp. 24–6; NLW 21335B, pp. 12–14.

> Nor jails I dread, nor venal Court,
> And where belorded fools resort,
> > I scare them with a frown;
> J. Reeves, and all his gang, defeat;
> And if a Tyrant King I meet,
> > Clench fist and knock him down.

Such bravado was characteristic of Iolo in his contempt for John Reeves's Association for the Preservation of Liberty and Property against Republicans and Levellers, and during the so-called 'reign of terror' he sailed close to the wind on several occasions by reminding everyone who chose to listen that 'there is very warm blood in my heart, and every drop of it solemnly dedicated to the cause of Truth'.[10]

In spite of what some previous writers have claimed, it is impossible to believe that Iolo Morganwg was not a political animal. Anyone who has delved into his rich and engrossing archive will know that his creative genius was enmeshed in a cultural, historical and political context which meant that he could not, even had he wanted to, insulate himself from the campaign for religious and civil liberties which stemmed from Enlightenment thought and the Atlantic Revolutions. Even before the excitement generated by the events in France in 1789 Iolo had embarked on an unconventional path, and the story of his early life is essential to the understanding of his views on religion and politics. His own temperament and habits of mind, the driving ambitions of his mother, the class barriers he faced, the cultural and intellectual food he imbibed from inspiring mentors, and the rugged independence and self-improvement which his trade as a stonecutter encouraged, were critical influences in his development as an unorthodox young man.

First of all, however, a note of caution must be sounded regarding Iolo's handling of evidence and his veracity. As in the case of holy matrimony, entering Iolo's voluminous archive should on no account be undertaken lightly. He is an intensely controversial figure because, as G. J. Williams and Mary-Ann Constantine have shown, he clearly shaped, moulded and distorted historical and literary evidence.[11] If, as is patently the case, his creative imagination was almost always at work in association with cultural 'truths' and if, as is even more certain, his material is seriously compromised and flawed according to scholarly standards, it is perfectly legitimate to question whether his references to his upbringing and private life are just as devious and misleading. His

---

[10] NLW 21396E, no. 12.
[11] The best literary analysis of Iolo's fabrications may be found in *Truth against the World*, while the exposure of Iolo's fraudulent Dafydd ap Gwilym poems by Griffith John Williams is contained in *IMChY*.

autobiographical preface to *Poems, Lyric and Pastoral* (1794), and other unpublished drafts of his memoirs, reveal that he was a pastmaster at making and remaking narratives of his life. At times one is left with the impression that Iolo was not only a multi-layered figure but also someone who lived a multiplicity of lives. His recollections, suffused as they are with the Romantic emphasis on self-exploration and self-identity, battling against alarming obstacles and demons, and satisfying an insatiable craving for knowledge, are peppered with a variety of misrepresentations and half-truths. It is very clear that Iolo told fibs about himself and others, smeared his enemies, betrayed many of his friends, and harboured grudges until his dying day. If his sources were often suspect, so too were his judgements on others. It is also worth bearing in mind that most of Iolo's manuscripts are undated. Although a good many of them correspond to different handwriting styles which he deployed over time, it is still extraordinarily difficult to date individual items within his self-confessed 'vast heap of crude papers'.[12] We simply cannot be wholly sure about when he wrote what or whether, for instance, the dates he attributed to certain poems, essays or personal associations are accurate. As the years rolled by, too, his memory became more fallible and on one revealing occasion he conceded that 'there is a wide difference between the memory, let it be ever so perfect, of what is past, and an actual . . . experience of it'.[13] All writers, of course, have selective memories, but in Iolo's brooding mind personal prejudices and obsessions clouded his judgement and made him susceptible to factual errors. It would be unwise, therefore, to take everything that he wrote at face value. Some parts ring truer than others and identifying these is a matter of judgement.

Although his papers contain characteristically conflicting versions, Edward Williams alias Iolo Morganwg was probably born on Wednesday, 11 March 1747 and was baptized two days later.[14] In one engaging account he claimed that he had drawn his first breath as the sun began to rise, as if some divine portent had occurred.[15] He was born in the tiny hamlet of Pennon in the parish of Llancarfan in the Vale of Glamorgan, a parish which he described as 'a kind of mountaineous Country in min[i]ature' and in which Pennon was 'a little obscure village, where the welsh only is spoken'.[16] According to tradition, St Cadog founded a monastery in the parish in the sixth century, and its most famous chronicler was Caradog of Llancarfan, the eleventh-century author of several Lives of the Saints. Both men figured prominently in Iolo's extraordinary store of local legend and history, and as late as Iolo's final year in 1826 a poignant

---

[12] *CIM*, II, p. 469, Iolo Morganwg to William Owen Pughe, 15 February 1803.
[13] NLW 21387E, no. 27.
[14] NLW 21426A, no. 6; NLW 13141A, p. 111; Glamorgan Archives, Llancarfan PR.
[15] NLW 21319A, p. 11.
[16] NLW 13141A, pp. 141–2; NLW 21387E, no. 22.

piece of marginalia by him celebrated the role of Catwg Ddoeth, Caradog and Taliesin Tir Iarll in nurturing wisdom, learning and virtue:

> Yn Llancarfan bu'r [?gâ]n gynt
> Yn [?ei] chwŷl, iawn ei helynt;
> Er mael yn leufer miloedd.
>
> (The beautiful Muse was formerly at Llancarfan
> Upon [?her] course, her journey fitting;
> The source of light for the benefit of thousands.)[17]

Iolo was thus a native of the Vale of Glamorgan, commonly reckoned to be the most gentrified, wealthy and populous part of the county during Iolo's youth and early manhood. Iolo himself calculated that the Vale was 'about 30 miles in length, its breadth between the mountains and the Sea is various, in some places nearly 15 miles, in its western extremity not more than three if so much, but 8 miles at least may be considered as a fair average'.[18] Over his life he acquired an intimate and unrivalled knowledge of the geology, agriculture, architecture, archaeology and social customs of the Vale and delighted in what he passionately believed to be an enchanting tale of castles, churches, mansions and cottages. Growing numbers of antiquaries, clergymen and gentlemen of leisure were being attracted by the picturesque beauty of the region and whoever encountered Iolo were assured by him that the temperate climate, tranquillity, teeming orchards and gardens, whitewashed cottages and literate peasantry that characterized the 'garden of Wales'[19] lent it a special, even unique, charm.

Iolo's parents were also of the Vale. Edward William(s) senior (b. 1715) and Ann Matthew (b. 1713) were married in the parish church of Llan-maes on 8 November 1744.[20] Having lost a precious ten-month-old daughter, they were then blessed with four sons – Edward, Miles, John and Thomas – who were born in that order between 1747 and 1755. All of them followed in the footsteps of their father by becoming stonemasons, but only one of them – Iolo – stayed in Glamorgan. Miles and John emigrated to Jamaica in 1778, prospered as stonemasons, and acquired substantial properties and slaves. Iolo's youngest brother Thomas shared Iolo's literary tastes, but he, too, eventually

---

[17] NLW 21284E, letter no. 699, Taliesin Williams to Iolo Morganwg, 12 February 1826. For this *cywydd* and a translation, see *'The Bard is a Very Singular Character'*, pp. 208–9.

[18] NLW 13114B, p. 21. See also Brian Ll. James, 'The Vale of Glamorgan, 1780–1850: A Study in Social History, with special reference to the ownership and occupation of land' (unpublished University of Wales MA thesis, 1971); Donald Moore, 'Visions of the Vale', *Morgannwg*, L (2006), 77–119.

[19] NLW 13116B, p. 384.

[20] NLW Ll8/129; Glamorgan Archives, St Athan PR, 1744.

pulled up his roots by travelling to Jamaica in 1785 and, much to Iolo's disapproval, helped to sustain the profitable economy, based on colonial slavery, of the island.[21]

Iolo Morganwg was born into a land of around half a million people, most of whom were dependent for their livelihood on the land and its associated crafts and trades. The lot of many was to undertake grindingly hard labour for little reward. Political and social power lay in the hands of a small number of wealthy families that had for the most part managed to displace the native gentry who had fallen victim to mystifying failures in the male line, crippling debts, mortgages and encumbrances. Estate after estate, notably in Glamorgan, had been snapped up by a new ruling class who believed that they had a God-given right to their superior wealth, privileges and status.[22] A manifestly unfair – at least to our eyes – and corrupt political system was dominated by this landed interest and, according to Peter Thomas, the total Welsh electorate, at around 25,000, was lamentably small.[23] The right to vote was restricted to adult males who possessed suitable property qualifications and the electoral dominance of the landed Titans owed as much to their coercive clout as to the deeply ingrained habits of deference which prevailed among the enfranchised few. Political feelings seldom ran high and even by-elections provoked little sense of excitement. It was hard to distinguish between Whig and Tory activists, and a combination of apathy and lack of political awareness sustained the prevailing regime. Protestantism, overwhelmingly represented by members of the established church and popularly regarded as 'y fam eglwys' (the mother church), was deeply entrenched, and support for Catholicism and its associated political cause, Jacobitism, was at best tepid even in the critical year of 1745 when the cause of the exiled Charles Edward Stuart was largely ignored. Iolo would say many derogatory things about Catholics and be just as censorious about the soul-stirring Methodist enthusiasts who, venturing out from mid-Wales, had taken root in the Vale by the time of his birth. By contrast, advances in Welsh-language schooling and literacy, promoted by a network of circulating schools sponsored by Madam Bridget Bevan and administered by Griffith Jones, Llanddowror, were judged by Iolo to be a more palatable result of the evangelical revival, not least because it enhanced a native tongue spoken by nine-tenths of the population. A distinctly smaller minority of worshippers were loath to

---

[21] NLW 21319A, pp. 11–13; NLW 21387E, no. 8; Clare Taylor, 'Edward Williams ('Iolo Morganwg') and his Brothers: A Jamaican Inheritance', *THSC* (1980), 35–43; Andrew Davies, '"Uncontaminated with Human Gore"? Iolo Morganwg, Slavery and the Jamaican Inheritance' in *Rattleskull Genius*, pp. 293–313.

[22] Philip Jenkins, *The Making of a Ruling Class: The Glamorgan Gentry 1640–1790* (Cambridge, 1983); idem, 'The Creation of an "Ancient Gentry": Glamorgan 1760–1840', *WHR*, 12, no. 1 (1984), 29–49.

[23] Peter D. G. Thomas, *Politics in Eighteenth-Century Wales* (Cardiff, 1998), pp. 1–7.

elevate the passions above the intellect, and these thoughtful people generally preferred to throw in their lot with Dissent, which admittedly provoked only sporadic interest. Its supporters, barred from public office and the universities, were still second-class citizens.

Nevertheless, profound changes occurred during Iolo's lifetime, changes which, for a radically-minded, book-loving craftsman, proved to be both testing and exhilarating. Demographic growth (the total population of Wales had more than doubled by the time of his death), intense industrialization (notably in the uplands of Glamorgan, but also in Swansea and its environs), striking gains in rates of literacy among intelligent and progressive groups of middling sorts, widespread evangelization, largely but not exclusively promoted by Calvinistic Methodists, and the emergence of a small but robust Enlightenment intelligentsia within Dissenting academies and elsewhere – all of these were transforming Wales.[24] Even a cursory appraisal of Iolo's papers will convince the reader that he was acutely aware that the world around him was changing swiftly and that the seismic effects of the Atlantic Revolutions were bound to create new ideologies and discourses that would inevitably lead to a fairer society. The old world, he once wrote, 'is truly old, grey and quite worn out to the stump with wickedness'.[25]

In 1754 Iolo's family moved to the village of Flemingston, also in the Vale, close to the river Thaw (or Daw, as Iolo often referred to it in his poems). The parish probably took its name from the Fleming family, who resided as lords of the manor between the thirteenth and the seventeenth centuries.[26] His father had built a small thatched cottage, containing one living room and two bedrooms, on the site of a ruined house.[27] The cottage and garden were leased for three lives from Lady Charlotte Edwin of Llanmihangel, and it was here from the age of seven, with a few sojourns elsewhere, that Iolo lived until his death in his eightieth year.[28] On the ground floor the ceilings were so low that only in the middle of the living room was it possible to stand upright, and even after Iolo's mother had died and his brothers had emigrated he ensured that space was at a premium by cramming the cottage to bursting point with books, manuscripts, letters and notebooks. This small rural parish of 673 acres had a

---

[24] For an introduction to these themes, see Geraint H. Jenkins, *The Foundations of Modern Wales: Wales 1642–1780* (Oxford, 1987); idem, 'Wales in the Eighteenth Century' in H. T. Dickinson (ed.), *A Companion to Eighteenth-Century Britain* (Oxford, 2002), pp. 392–402. For the last point, see the questions raised in R. J. W. Evans, 'Was there a Welsh Enlightenment?' in R. R. Davies and Geraint H. Jenkins (eds.), *From Medieval to Modern Wales: Historical Essays in Honour of Kenneth O. Morgan and Ralph A. Griffiths* (Cardiff, 2004), pp. 142–59.
[25] *CIM*, I, p. 450, Iolo Morganwg to Hannah More, [?1792].
[26] J. Barry Davies, 'Flemingston Court: One of the Greater Houses of the Vale', *Meisgyn and Glynrhondda Local History Newsletter*, 118 (1997), 1–10.
[27] NLW 21410E, no. 53.
[28] Ibid., no. 4.

population of 66 in the first official census,[29] and throughout his long and eventful life Iolo's name was inextricably associated with Flemingston, or Flimston as it was often called (Trefflemin in Welsh). To Iolo, it was a blissful, idyllic place. He developed a strong affinity with it and derived considerable pleasure from strolling solitarily along the winding banks of the Thaw which, he proudly claimed, passed through 'the richest soil in the Country'.[30] With the unabashed pride of a local patriot, he declared in 1796 that 'Flimston is in the best part of the Vale of Glamorgan, and its Land esteemed the best of the best part'.[31] Closely identifying with animals in the fields and relishing the songs of the blackbird, cuckoo and thrush, he loved this place like no other:

> Enslav'd by no passion, secluded from pride,
>   A rustic, inglorious, I dwell in this vale:
> Let fools, lovely Nature, thy dictates deride,
>   I know thy sweet voice, and attend to thy tale;
> And here may my moments glide peaceful along,
>   No conscience upbraiding my bosom to gnaw;
> Thou, too, shall partake of thy Bard's humble song,
>   My dear native cot on the *Banks of the Daw*.[32]

Iolo's enjoyment of nature was matched by his strong appreciation of the history of the parish or, to be more precise, the history as he imagined it to be. He convinced himself that the most notable self-educated person from the Vale was Edward Pritchard, a former rector of the parish, who died at the ripe age of ninety-eight in 1742.[33] Pritchard had been a remarkably multifaceted figure who had mastered all the 'mechanic Trades', fashioned a vertical dial on the parish church, and developed such skills in mathematics and astronomy that it was said that even the great Isaac Newton was moved to visit him on several occasions.[34] Iolo evidently saw something of himself in Pritchard and regarded him as a model from whom he could learn how to improve himself as a self-taught, versatile artisan. There is of course a degree of absurdity in the claims Iolo made about the former rector, but they may have been based on tales he heard on the hearth during his childhood. What is certain is that Iolo was determined to put his Flemingston cottage on the map. His home became so heavily strewn with transcripts, notes, jottings, lists, books, scraps of paper and all kinds of curios and ephemera that it seemed to pulse with life and passion. Its disorderly condition often caused Iolo considerable torment, but it was also his

---

[29] James, 'The Vale of Glamorgan, 1780–1850', p. 211.
[30] NLW 13116B, p. 387.
[31] NLW 13115B, p. 1.
[32] Williams: *PLP*, I, p. 44.
[33] NLW 13157A, p. 158.
[34] NLW 13152A, pp. 447–50.

pride and joy. During his latter years Iolo became a celebrity. Antiquaries, travellers and artists flocked to his home to pay homage, seek information and ask for assistance. An audience with Iolo was a special event because, as his first biographer Elijah Waring put it, 'his memory was literally heaped up with materials both curious and multiform'.[35]

Had Iolo's cottage survived – it was allowed to fall into disrepair after his death and had been demolished by 1850 – it might have become a place of pilgrimage as important to the Welsh as the 'Auld Clay Biggin' in Alloway is to devotees of Burns and Dove Cottage in Grasmere to Wordsworthians. As it is, the only memorial to him in the parish is a bilingual wall tablet in the north-west corner of the nave of the Church of St Michael in which Iolo was buried.[36] Erected in 1855 by Caroline, Countess of Dunraven, and other wealthy admirers of the Welsh bard, the memorial became an attraction to patriotic pilgrims during the Victorian and Edwardian period. 'A good many people come here fussing about old Iolo', claimed an English-speaking labourer derisively as the mythical depiction of Iolo as an innocent, saintly sage took root.[37] Even in the absence of a gravestone, it was widely believed that 'there is no danger . . . that [Iolo's] memory will not be kept alive and evergreen for many ages' ('nid oes berygl . . . na ddeil ei goffadwriaeth yn fyw ac yn wyrddlas am oesau lawer').[38] While all this lay in the future, there is no doubt that, from an early age, 'my Flimston house', as Iolo described it in one of his sketches of the building,[39] was a special, even inspirational, place.

Iolo's parents clearly exerted a profound influence on his upbringing and affected his cast of mind. In his preface to *Poems, Lyric and Pastoral* in 1794 his mother looms large, while there is scarcely any mention of his father. In Waring's biography, which was based on Iolo's reminiscences, the reverse is true. Under the circumstances it might be prudent to accept that he owed them both a debt. Iolo evidently inherited his father's temperament. Edward William(s) senior was a plain-speaking man, quick to take offence and prone to fly into sudden rages.[40] 'Poor fellow,' wrote Iolo on hearing news of his death

---

[35] *RAEW*, p. 11.
[36] Geoffrey R. Orrin, *Medieval Churches of the Vale of Glamorgan* (Cowbridge, 1988), pp. 161–5.
[37] Quoted in *Literary and Historical Legacy*, p. 155.
[38] The assertion was made by Isaac Foulkes in *Geirlyfr Bywgraffiadol o Enwogion Cymru* (Liverpool, 1870), p. 992. Quoted in Hywel Gethin Rhys, *'A Wayward Cymric Genius': Celebrating the Centenary of the Death of Iolo Morganwg* (Aberystwyth, 2007), p. 30.
[39] NLW 21416E, no. 14. The sketch is reproduced, together with an undated drawing of the cottage after it was modernized, in Geraint H. Jenkins, 'On the Trail of a "Rattleskull Genius": Introduction' in *Rattleskull Genius*, p. 6.
[40] Note, however, that Rhys Davies, one of his apprentices, described him as 'a quiet unsentimental man'. *RAEW*, p. 9.

in 1795, 'his unfortunate temper has been too cruelly resented.'[41] This very human failing also entered Iolo's bloodstream. As we shall see, Iolo himself found it difficult to control his feelings and seems to have taken delight in raising hackles wherever he went. If the father was indeed like his son, he must also have derived satisfaction from the family tree which Iolo painstakingly assembled during the late 1780s. He traced his paternal ancestry not only to the eleventh-century Welsh prince Bleddyn ap Cynfyn but also even further back to Cadwaladr the Blessed (d. 664/682), who was such an influential figure in Welsh bardic lore and especially in vaticinatory poetry.[42] To this illustrious lineage Iolo added the astonishing, though not entirely inconceivable, assertion that, through a collateral branch of the Williamses of Whitchurch and Llanishen, no less a figure than Oliver Cromwell was among his ancestors.[43] By the time of the French Revolution Iolo was strongly veering towards the libertarian ideals of Dissent and wearing the Cromwellian association like a badge of honour. And whenever he launched furious assaults against kingcraft he happily dredged up the memory of how his illustrious forebear had taken the King of England to the block. He had no qualms about informing the prim evangelical Hannah More that he had inherited 'much of the enterprizing spirit of my famous, or rather infamous, uncle Oliver Cromwel, for I am of the family'.[44]

A farmer's son from Llandough, Edward William(s) senior had completed his apprenticeship as a stonemason and builder in 1738.[45] Iolo described his father as a mason, stonecutter, tiler, plasterer, carpenter and joiner; intensely proud of these skills, it gave him great satisfaction to pass them on to each of his four sons.[46] Iolo claimed to have mastered the alphabet by watching him inscribing tombs and gravestones, and by the age of nine he was carving stones himself.[47] Having learned all the branches of the trade of the journeyman mason at his father's elbow, at fourteen he completed his apprenticeship. Thereafter, a mallet and a chisel, as well as a pen and pencil, were never far from the hands of Nedi (or Neti in the local dialect) Williams junior. As a mason, Iolo thus gained much greater freedom of movement than, say, a tenant farmer or a labourer would have had, and a much wider range of opportunities beckoned

---

[41] *CIM*, I, p. 758, Iolo Morganwg to Margaret (Peggy) Williams, 2 May 1795. It was Iolo who fashioned and inscribed his father's gravestone. NLW 21418E, no. 2.
[42] NLW 13130A, p. 280; NLW 21319A, pp. 16–17.
[43] NLW 21387E, no. 10; *RAEW*, pp. 162–3; Williams: *IM*, pp. 83–5.
[44] *CIM*, I, p. 452, Iolo Morganwg to Hannah More, [?1792].
[45] NLW 21410E, no. 2.
[46] NLW 21319A, p. 11.
[47] NLW 21387E, no. 2.

as his gifts as a stonecutter matured.[48] Even masons of humble station, as Iolo was, were subjected to fewer inhibitions and restraints than workers who were tied to the soil. They were also more likely as itinerant artisans to encounter new ideas and become familiar with signs of political disaffection or religious turmoil. By working alongside his father in the mansions and farms of local landed gentry families of modest wealth like Jones of Fonmon, Edwin of Llanmihangel and Dunraven, Bassett of Llaneley or Nicholls of the Ham, for instance, Iolo might well have learned some deep and lasting lessons about the advantages of having landowners who were an organic part of the community.[49] Robert Jones (d. 1793) of Fonmon, at whose home the Williams family worked regularly, was a member of the Society of Gentlemen Supporters of the Bill of Rights which was set up in 1769 to promote the radical cause of John Wilkes.[50] Opposition to affluent absentee magnates was already emerging in Glamorgan in the early 1770s at precisely the time when Iolo was becoming something of a free spirit. In due course Iolo would act as cheerleader for the gentry families who championed the cause of the 'Independence of Glamorgan' in the celebrated by-election of 1789.[51]

Iolo's relatively matter-of-fact references to his father contrast sharply with his melodramatic and possibly semi-fictionalized depiction of his mother in the preface to *Poems, Lyric and Pastoral*, a portrayal which was largely dictated by his determination to persuade a genteel reading public to subscribe to his anthology and also to enable him to achieve metropolitan fame. But even the vividness of Iolo's imagination cannot alter the fact that Ann Matthew was a remarkable woman and that she was his most intimate companion during his childhood. Born in 1713, she was a descendant of the decayed branch of the illustrious Matthew family of Llandaf and Radyr. Either through profligacy or misfortune, her father, Edward Matthew, had lost his property at Ty'nycaeau, Coychurch, and his daughter never truly recovered from the loss of social status caused by the wholly unexpected downturn in the economic fortunes of her family.[52] As a child she was placed in the care of her aunt, Elizabeth Blades (née Seys), mistress of the Elizabethan mansion at Boverton, near Llantwit Major, and was educated at a boarding school.[53] When she married the stonemason Edward William(s) in 1744 it was not a match which a once respectable family could have wished for, but, as Iolo put it theatrically, it was 'her lot to

---

[48] The best account of Iolo the stonemason is by Richard Suggett, 'Iolo Morganwg: Stonecutter, Builder, and Antiquary' in *Rattleskull Genius*, pp. 197–226.
[49] NLW 21325A, nos. 3–7.
[50] Thomas, *Politics in Eighteenth-Century Wales*, p. 219.
[51] Jenkins, *The Making of a Ruling Class*, p. 187.
[52] Williams: *PLP*, I, p. xv; Williams: *IM*, p. 86.
[53] I am indebted to Dr Moira Dearnley for allowing me to read her unpublished paper, '"Lost Superiority": Iolo Morganwg's connections with the Seys family of Boverton'.

marry a mason',[54] thereby juxtaposing the lady of noble descent with the low-born peasant, a popular literary device in eighteenth-century literature.[55] Despite these reverses, Ann William(s) continued to believe herself to be a woman of superior worth and maintained 'a dignity of mind which kept [her] aloof from many'.[56] Her self-conceit also presumably arose from her descent from an ancient family of outstanding Welsh master-poets (*penceirddiaid*) of Tir Iarll (the Earl's Land) in the uplands of Glamorgan, a prestigious lineage which the young Iolo was never to forget. Indeed, he attributed several of his own Welsh poems to his grandfather on his mother's side in order to associate himself in the public domain with the great medieval poets of Glamorgan.[57] This highly intelligent, well-read woman, weighed down by old torments, channelled into her eldest son some of her own cultural tastes and ambitions. She was determined that he should make something of himself and, as Gwyn A. Williams has claimed, 'something of the demon which was to drive Edward Williams came from her'.[58]

We know very little about Iolo's childhood. There are no likenesses of him as a child or a young man and all the portraits which have come down to us – by Colonel Taynton, William Owen Pughe and Robert Cruikshank – depict him either in middle age or old age when the stresses and strains of being a stonemason and the effects of opium had ravaged his features and body. He claims to have been a sickly child and throughout his life he was troubled by nervous disorders and respiratory ailments. Yet he was solidly built and, as his foot-slogging feats reveal, he was blessed with extraordinary reserves of stamina. The relative peace and calm of the Flemingston countryside was an ideal place for four siblings to appreciate nature, get up to mischief and look forward to occasional visits to the nearby bustling town of Cowbridge. Years later Iolo recalled some dramatic, even terrifying, events which persuaded him that in some mysterious way his life had been spared for good reasons:

> Snake sprung at me when about 3 or 4 years of age. I was not hurt – took it up and cut it to pieces. Sow ran away with me. Yet I escaped unhurt. Ran out of bed in the small Pox into the Beans. Cow tossed me with her horns, two or 3 times, but I escaped unhurt.[59]

---

[54] NLW 21319A, no. 10.
[55] Cathryn A. Charnell-White, 'Women and Gender in the Private and Social Relationships of Iolo Morganwg' in *Rattleskull Genius*, p. 366.
[56] NLW 21387E, no. 10.
[57] See the examples in *CRhIM*, pp. 62–3.
[58] Gwyn A. Williams, *Madoc: The Making of a Myth* (London, 1979), p. 99.
[59] NLW 21387E, no. 31.

The above passage may well represent what Waring called 'his vivid fancy'[60] and also his growing sense of self-regard by the 1790s.

Iolo's strong imagination and thirst for knowledge were apparent even in his childhood. He confessed to being 'sullen and stubbornly silent'[61] when he was sent to school and he refused to be taught by anyone but his doting mother. English was the language of the household and Iolo's mother not only taught him to read, spell, write and sing, but also showered him with books, periodicals and magazines. A sweet singer herself, she sang songs to him, talked about poetry and music, and about how the art of the bards had nurtured literary tastes and genuine morality. His first reading book was *The Vocal Miscellany* (1733), a two-volume compendium of over four hundred English songs, 'from which I probably received the first poetical Bias, being of the opinion that Poetry, like all other sciences, is a mere acquisition and no supernatural talent'.[62] On many occasions he went to some pains to emphasize how poetry and song had provoked his imagination from an early age:

> Warm from a child I lov'd the Bardic Muse,
> My worlds of bliss all center'd in her views.[63]

In due course poetry came to give coherence to Iolo's thinking, and its perennial vitality, duly expressed in odes, pastorals, ballads, *cywyddau*, *tribannau* and hymns, enabled him later in life to express his outrage against tyranny, cruelty and injustice. His mother also taught him to play the flute, an accomplishment which brought him much solace during his incarceration in a debtors' gaol in 1786–7.

While some of the early creative inspiration came from songs and ballads, both oral and printed, Iolo also discovered through his mother works which made an even more lasting impression. Looking back over his life he admitted to being particularly 'fond of religious books'.[64] Pride of place went to the English Bible, which he came to admire enormously. From the outset he appreciated the literary quality of the Bible and his correspondence and papers are replete with scriptural images and references. Indeed, he was 'more pleased with the Bible than with any other book'.[65] To him – again in retrospect – one of

---

[60] *RAEW*, p. 148.
[61] NLW 21283E, letter no. 600, marginal note; 'The Bard is a Very Singular Character', Appendix V: Literature, no. 5(b), pp. 289–91.
[62] *The Vocal Miscellany: A Collection of above Four Hundred Celebrated Songs* (2 vols., London, 1733); NLW 21387E, no. 2.
[63] Williams: *PLP*, I, p. xxiii; NLW 13151A, p. 41; NLW 21424E, no. 19.
[64] NLW 21283E, no. 600, marginal note; 'The Bard is a Very Singular Character', Appendix V: Literature, no. 5(b), p. 290.
[65] NLW 21387E, no. 2.

the great virtues of the Bible was that it had 'gradually emancipated mankind' from the Reformation period onwards.[66] Its ubiquitous quality also appealed to him. Acutely aware that the scriptures were often used as 'a Nose of Wax'[67] to justify a theological or political stance, he did so himself in illuminating the mysteries of metempsychosis, or in sustaining his perpetual search for 'Truth', or even in decrying 'northwalian braggings' over the literary qualities of William Morgan's first Welsh Bible of 1588.[68] Used properly, he claimed from the 1790s onwards, the Bible was an indispensable exemplar of social justice and humanity. During those years it amused him to tell of the occasion during Pitt's 'Reign of Terror' when he affixed the label 'The Rights of Man' to a Bible in his bookseller's shop at Cowbridge and sold it to a government spy who, until the truth dawned on him, was convinced that he had nailed Iolo as a purveyor of seditious material.[69] The Bible-reading Iolo knew as well as anyone that politics were intimately bound up with religion, and he consistently emphasized the importance of placing the scriptures within the reach of common readers. His own early grounding in the Bible taught him that there was no substitute for an intimate knowledge of God's Word.

Ann William(s) also plied her youthful prodigy with the works of English poets. At a time when the Bard of Avon's works were reaching readers of all classes in England and were being freely quoted in printed anthologies,[70] she steeped him in Shakespeare's works and filled him with genuine enthusiasm for the poet's imaginative power. In Shakespeare, Iolo discovered the most sublime artistic imagination, a gift which could detect and illuminate the deepest truths of nature. He often marvelled at how someone of humble origins could possess such glowing sparks of natural genius and, as one who was himself sensitive and responsive to nature, it is not surprising that he admired Shakespeare as the one who had 'flung widely open the gates of Nature's School'.[71] In May 1802, while braving wretched weather, he went out of his way on his return from London to visit Stratford-upon-Avon in order to pay homage to the Bard. Having visited every nook and cranny of the town, he wrote: 'I feel something like magic in every thing that relates to Shakespeare.'[72]

---

[66] NLW 21396E, no. 3.
[67] NLW 21433E, nos. 1, 7. See also NLW 21432E, nos. 2, 3, 5.
[68] NLW 13144A, p. 217; NLW 13145A, pp. 13–151; NLW 13123B, p. 54; NLW 13121B, p. 427; NLW 13160A, p. 365; NLW 21426E, no. 68.
[69] *RAEW*, pp. 108–9.
[70] William St Clair, *The Reading Nation in the Romantic Period* (Cambridge, 2004), pp. 148–9, 156–7. See also Thomas F. Bonnell, *The Most Disreputable Trade: Publishing the Classics of English Poetry 1765–1810* (Oxford, 2008).
[71] NLW 13103B, p. 48.
[72] *CIM*, II, p. 416, Iolo Morganwg to Walter Davies (Gwallter Mechain), 1 June 1802; NLW 13174A, ff. 11^{r-v}, 17^r.

Another canonical figure to whom Iolo was introduced by his mother and who became an animating presence in his life was Milton. Milton's poetry, of course, was heavily influenced by the Bible, and *Paradise Lost* was a particular favourite in Iolo's home.[73] He was less interested, however, in the allegorical and mythological aspects of Milton's epic – 'wherever he appears as a learned mythologist, he is disgustingly absurd'[74] – than in the humanistic and political values found therein. Milton's work was embraced by Romantic poets and early political radicals alike, and Iolo especially identified with the dramatization of the struggle for liberty in *Paradise Lost*. Moreover, among the works in his possession in the mid-1790s was a copy of the English translation of *Defensio pro Populo Anglicano* (1651), which combined a defence of regicide government with a good deal of scurrilous invective.[75] From Milton, Iolo learned that knowledge and truth were a force for good in the daily battle against obscurantism and intolerance, and his poetry and other writings endowed him with a natural suspicion of self-perpetuating institutions which suppressed individual freedom. His fellow anti-trinitarian Thomas Evans (Tomos Glyn Cothi) famously dubbed him a 'second Milton' ('Ail Miltwn') on the strength of his willingness in the 1790s to challenge ecclesiastical and secular authority.[76] It should not go unnoticed, moreover, that Milton's greatest epic produced Iolo's most unforgettable put-down: on reading *Coll Gwynfa*, William Owen Pughe's laborious Welsh translation of *Paradise Lost*, he declared loftily: 'alas how truly lost'![77]

Other influential writers recommended to him by his mother and others helped him to mature as a poet and a political satirist. Arthur Golding's translation of Ovid's *Metamorphoses* (1565–7) offered wit and sensuality, and illuminated the work of Dafydd ap Gwilym. Pope's *Works*, published in revised versions in the 1760s, were heavily thumbed by Iolo, and his powers of invective and political satires, especially *The Dunciad*, provided valuable models for the future: 'Now Satire came, with fi'ry pow'rs; / Engag'd my thoughts; employ'd my hours.'[78] Another firm favourite was Sir Thomas Browne's *Religio Medici* (1635–6), which offered a perceptive guide to the role of faith and the power

---

[73] NLW 21387E, no. 10; NLW 13091E, p. 291; NLW 13107B, p. 23; NLW 21407C, nos. 1, 5.
[74] NLW 21419E, no. 24.
[75] NLW 13136A, pp. 137–63. Milton had been commissioned to rebut the charges made by Salmasius in his Latin work *Defensio Regia pro Carolo I* (1649).
[76] NLW 6238A, pp. 281–2.
[77] *CIM*, III, p. 520, Iolo Morganwg to Evan Williams, 12 May 1819. He went on to claim that in this 'down-melted Milton', Pughe had 'fallen away from Milton as much or more than Adam fell from God'. Ibid., pp. 520–1. For the background to this animosity, see Glenda Carr, 'An Uneasy Partnership: Iolo Morganwg and William Owen Pughe' in *Rattleskull Genius*, pp. 443–60.
[78] Williams: *PLP*, I, p. 32. See also Iolo's memorandum 'from Pope's letters' in NLW 21419E, no. 14, and NLW 13098B, p. 103.

of reason. Iolo claimed that it 'gave me first an inquisitive and free turn of thinking'.[79] His reading of the massively popular *Robinson Crusoe* also encouraged his independent-mindedness: 'I derive[d] some singular, but, I believe, beneficial Ideas.'[80] This gripping adventure story evidently appealed to the romantic within him and also may have led him to reflect on government and kingship. If he read it as a political fable, which is conceivable, Crusoe's role as a slave trader, as well as his sense of social and spiritual alienation, may have coloured his attitude towards institutions.[81] Such books certainly excited his imagination and, by borrowing from friends and picking up bargains at local sales, he read everything that came his way. He developed mechanical and scientific interests, and turned to Francis Bacon's *Advancement of Learning* (1605) for an interpretation of natural and experimental histories, and to Conyers Purshall's *An Essay on the Mechanical Fabrick of the Universe* (1707) for data on gravitation, motion, reflection and refraction. And since, from an early age, he showed signs of becoming an irremediable hypochondriac, it is hardly surprising that he warmed to Gideon Harvey's *The Vanities of Philosophy and Physick* (1699), a work which purported to contain guidance on how to preserve health and prolong life.[82]

Doubtless this extensive reading was matched by a good deal of practical experimentation. Iolo was good with his hands and was always ready to branch out into different fields of expertise. There was also a special place in his formative years for widely-read journals, periodicals and magazines. He regularly sampled issues of three influential Whig periodicals – the *Tatler*, the *Guardian* and the *Spectator*, whose letters, essays and satires helped to shape his literary taste and development as a political writer.[83] Iolo's nose was always in a book and his early grounding in the above publications served him in good stead as he formulated his ideas and struggled to find his voice. Writing to the celebrated philosopher David Williams in 1811, he acknowledged his debt to those, most notably his mother, who had set him on his way: 'Every kind of genius is actually made or created by circumstances which, making strong and indellible impression on the mind of early infancy, too early perhaps to be remembered, strongly determine it to certain pursuits.'[84]

In several of his reminiscences Iolo portrayed himself in his teens as a cissified mother's pet, a day-dreamer and a 'booby' who, others feared, was in

---

[79] NLW 21387E, no. 9. See also NLW 21407C, no. 1.
[80] NLW 21387E, no. 2. See Iolo's list of books in his possession in NLW 21407C, no. 1.
[81] Manuel Schonhorn, *Defoe's Politics: Parliament, Power, Kingship, and Robinson Crusoe* (Cambridge, 1991).
[82] NLW 13106B, pp. 175–7; NLW 21387E, nos. 2, 9.
[83] NLW 21387E, no. 2.
[84] *CIM*, III, p. 39, Iolo Morganwg to David Williams, 8 January 1811.

danger of reading his 'senses away'.[85] He supposedly moped in corners and fretted over his fragile health. But this version of a gawky, asthmatic ugly duckling is hardly convincing. Bookish he most certainly was, and he had his share of ailments, but he was also a stubborn and rebellious youngster. At the age of twelve he changed his mind about sampling conventional schooling, but his father, having invested in his future as a stonemason and builder, refused to send him to school. To his credit, for once in his life Iolo bore no grudges: 'Necessity has no law: my father was not blameable.'[86] But there were tantrums when his mother flatly refused to allow her favourite son to waste his talents by going to sea.[87] Iolo was not afraid to speak his mind and jealousy between him and his brothers must have provoked domestic tensions. Strong-willed and restless, Iolo was no 'booby'. The teenager who regularly earned a few shillings by cutting down elm and ash trees in order to provide bandy players with durable bats became a hot-blooded youth who courted local girls with amorous songs and stanzas[88] and was addressed by the poet Dafydd ap Rhisiart as an 'affectionate rascal, swift, alert and brilliant' ('Walch curwydd hylwydd hoywlathr').[89] Drafts of his strict-metre love poems, which he composed under the pseudonyms Iorwerth Gwilim, Iorwerth Morganwg or 'Prydydd bychan morganwg' (the little poet of Glamorgan) were multiplying swiftly from the late 1760s.[90] Moreover, his English-language pastorals were suffused with references to lovers with wistful eyes, rosy lips and snow-white breasts whom he presumably seduced either in his imagination or 'under tree and branch in that hollow in the woodland'.[91] Although it is impossible to tell, one suspects that he had a reputation as a bit of a rogue among local girls. What is certain is that his own depiction of himself as an unconvivial recluse is a caricature.

Thanks largely to his mother's influence, English was Iolo's first language and, as we have seen, his stock of books and magazines were also in English. But even as he worked his way through the demanding literary fare supplied by his mother and others, he also became intoxicated by Wales's senior tongue.

---

[85] NLW 21387E, no. 9; Williams: *PLP*, I, p. xvi. The *OED* defines a 'booby' as a silly fellow or a namby-pamby.
[86] NLW 21283E, no. 600, marginal note; *'The Bard is a Very Singular Character'*, Appendix V: Literature, no. 5(b), p. 290.
[87] NLW 21387E, no. 10.
[88] NLW 13089E, p. 169. He charged 3d. or 6d. for each bat; NLW 21423E, nos. 13, 14. For bandy playing and other popular customs, see G. J. Williams, 'Glamorgan Customs in the Eighteenth Century', *Gwerin*, 1 (1957), 102–3; Allan James, *Diwylliant Gwerin Morgannwg* (Llandysul, 2002).
[89] *CIM*, I, pp. 45, 46 (trans.), Dafydd ap Rhisiart to Iolo Morganwg, 9 May 1770.
[90] NLW 13087E, pp. 289–98, 299–310, 319–22, 351–4, 356–7.
[91] NLW 13170B, pp. 31, 89, 93, 170; NLW 21392F, nos. 22, 23, 30ᵛ, 45, 49; NLW 21420E, nos. 8, 15, 20, 21; NLW 21424E, nos. 22, 35; Williams: *PLP*, I, *passim*; Prys Morgan, *Iolo Morganwg* (Cardiff, 1975), pp. 28–30.

During the latter half of the 1760s he came to admire the Welsh-language poetic tradition and immerse himself in things Welsh at a stage when cultural patriots were convinced that a linguistic and literary crisis was looming.[92] Articulate middling sorts, who voiced this sense of foreboding, believed that the 'natural' leaders of society were being found wanting. Absentee landowners – often reviled as 'Great Leviathans' – were swallowing up native estates at an alarming rate and casting scorn on the cultural aspirations of 'clownish' Welsh speakers. Not a whit better, and perhaps a good deal worse, were 'yr Esgyb Eingl', non-Welsh bishops who, as political appointees, disfigured their sees by championing the English language at the expense of the vernacular and by rewarding their own monoglot English-speaking favourites.[93] This inglorious ruling clique, so it was believed, were so intent on distancing themselves from the language, literature and history of the Welsh people that they were blissfully unaware of the barrage of hostile criticism levelled against them by almanackers, ballad-mongers, poets, prose writers and social commentators. Many other social and cultural handicaps conspired against Welsh speakers and English speakers in Wales at this time. The lack of formal, accredited centres of learning was a palpable defect. While Scotland had four universities and England two, Wales had none. There was no recognizable public sphere or civil society. The largest towns – Wrexham, Carmarthen, Swansea – were dwarfed by cities like London, Dublin and Edinburgh, and there were no national institutions such as a library or a conservatory to preserve the literary and musical treasures which were mouldering in scattered private libraries on country estates. No clubs or societies with a distinctive cultural agenda existed in Wales and there was no national newspaper press to broach and analyse political issues. There were no monuments to Welsh patriots, and historiographical trends, in both languages, were strongly integrationist.[94] The long-standing political union of England and Wales, dating from 1536–43, had embedded itself in the psyche and affections of the Welsh and, at times of war, patriotic chest-beating in support of the British cause was not uncommon. According to Iolo's friend Walter Davies (Gwallter Mechain), it was too much to expect a country bereft of institutions of statehood and a metropolitan culture to breed 'a philosophic Bacon, an experimental Boyle, or an historic Gibbon'.[95]

Iolo, however, did not share this complacent, even defeatist, stance. He understood of course the social handicaps which bedevilled the Welsh but, in his

---

[92] Geraint H. Jenkins, 'The Cultural Uses of the Welsh Language 1660–1800' in idem (ed.), *The Welsh Language before the Industrial Revolution* (Cardiff, 1997), pp. 369–406.
[93] NLW 2532B, f. 27ᵛ; Evan Evans, *Casgliad o Bregethau* (2 vols., Y Mwythig, 1776), I, sig. B2ᵛ.
[94] Geraint H. Jenkins, 'Historical Writing in the Eighteenth Century' in Branwen Jarvis (ed.), *A Guide to Welsh Literature c. 1700–1800* (Cardiff, 2000), pp. 23–44.
[95] *Cambrian Register*, I (1796), 282.

own case at least, he was not prepared to grin and bear it. He fervently believed that it was possible for farmers, artisans and craftsmen – people with innate gifts as well as a hunger for knowledge and self-improvement – to express their individuality, enter the literary sphere, and voice their cultural and political disaffection. He gloried in his lack of formal education and, like many eighteenth-century autodidacts of a Romantic bent, he expressed particular hostility towards the traditional universities. He loathed the fact that privilege and wealth meant more than brains and opportunity. To him, universities were 'schools of pedantry'[96] whose undemanding syllabuses stifled the imagination, independent judgement and radical thought. In 'The Learned Ignorants', a poem written in 1772, he deplored the inability of university-trained English scholars to appreciate the aesthetics of the Welsh pastoral tradition. Neither the 'tatter'd *Oxonian*'[97] nor the writers of Grub Street knew anything of 'the wheat's golden curls'.[98] He mocked the pomposity of the 'Double-mill'd Dunce[s]' – those with doctorates in divinity – upon whom the vulgar stared with 'stupid admiration':[99]

> See stalking audaciously, full of himself,
>   Yon proud Academic appears.
> Well versed in the science of prowling for pelf,
>   It's black, a true symbol, he wears.
> Upstilting his name (DD, MA, DL) with nonsensical sound
>   In the knowledge of Nature untried,
> His soul is immersed in the deepest profound
>   Of Error, and insolent Pride.[100]

There was no doubt an element of inverted snobbery here, but even in his own neck of the woods he saw how universities fostered division and inequality. The steady stream of well-to-do boys from Cowbridge Grammar School who went up to Jesus College, Oxford, were subsequently able to establish an 'unjust ascendancy over those whose fortune in life never enabled them to reside there'.[101] Worse still, the University of Oxford – 'a filthy puddle of iniquity' – did Wales a disservice by spewing out clerics with 'superlative vices' who proved a drain on the slender financial resources of their parishioners, scoffed at the Welsh tongue, and consumed alcohol to excess.[102]

---

[96] NLW 13115B, p. 346.
[97] Williams: *PLP*, I, p. 86.
[98] See 'The Reapers: A Pastoral (Inscribed to Glamorgan Agricultural Society)'. Ibid., p. 60.
[99] NLW 21387E, no. 38.
[100] NLW 21335B, p. 40.
[101] Iolo Davies, *'A Certaine Schoole': A History of the Grammar School at Cowbridge, Glamorgan* (Cowbridge, 1967), p. 49; NLW 13089E, p. 288.
[102] NLW 13174A, ff. 2ᵛ, 3ᵛ, 4ʳ.

Perhaps to prove his point, in his youth Iolo mixed with groups of artisans and craftsmen who were fiercely independent and whose literary interests owed nothing to public schools or universities. He not only benefited from, but also took part in, a significant Welsh-language socio-cultural revival in south Wales from the late 1760s onwards. By that stage the Welsh language had made appreciable advances within hitherto monoglot English and bilingual zones within the Vale of Glamorgan. Iolo himself attributed the transformation to the influence of Griffith Jones's circulating schools and the growth of Dissent, and had he been more warmly disposed towards Calvinistic Methodists he might also have acknowledged the presence of Welsh religious revivalists as Cymricizing agents.[103] Nonetheless, during these years he became enchanted by the Welsh language. Edward Williams of Middle Hill, Llancarfan, one of Iolo's godfathers, took him in hand at the age of fifteen, taught him the rudiments of Welsh verse, and opened his eyes to the glories of the bardic past which his mother had hinted at. He was so impressed by his young pupil's quick and enquiring mind that he encouraged his versifying and supplied him with helpful Welsh grammars.[104] Thereafter the study of Welsh poetry became an intensely pleasurable and edifying experience for Iolo, and whenever his godfather invited local poets to eat, drink and carouse at his home he participated wholeheartedly:

> At Edward William's dwelling house,
> (By Jove we'll have a good carouse,)
> To eat Roast beef and weather mutton,
> Well dress'd to please the greatest glutton,
> To drink strong ale and bottled beer,
> And Crown the day with noble cheer.
> Attend good folks I'll have ye know it
> The Jolly Landlord is a poet.
> He'll stir his noddle all day long
> To please you with a merry song.[105]

When the gossipy diarist William Thomas of Michaelston-super-Ely described Edward Williams, Middle Hill, as 'a smart, lettered man',[106] he recognized that it was possible for literate, bookish men to shape the values and careers of others. In this convivial world Iolo also developed links with lively, hard-

---

[103] Brian Ll. James, 'The Welsh Language in the Vale of Glamorgan', *Morgannwg*, XVI (1972), 16–36; Eryn M. White, 'The Established Church, Dissent and the Welsh Language *c.* 1660–1811' in Jenkins (ed.), *The Welsh Language before the Industrial Revolution*, pp. 257–8.
[104] NLW 21387E, no. 10.
[105] NLW 13089E, p. 147.
[106] R. T. W. Denning (ed.), *The Diary of William Thomas of Michaelston-super-Ely, near St Fagans Glamorgan, 1762–1795* (Cardiff, 1995), p. 92.

drinking carpenters, nailers and maltsters who composed songs at the Old Globe in Cardiff, and by organizing eisteddfodau at Llantrisant, Aber-cwm-y-fuwch and presumably elsewhere, such groups took on the responsibility, abandoned by the gentry, of reviving dormant literary traditions in the county.[107] Eager to ensure that his poetic aspirations were more widely recognized, at the age of twenty-three Iolo expressed his delight at the publishing plans of the newly launched fortnightly magazine *Trysorfa Gwybodaeth, neu, Eurgrawn Cymraeg* (1770) by sending to the editor Josiah Rees a dozen *englynion* expressing the hope that the venture would 'give a great deal of joy to all those who love the ancient Welsh tongue' ('y rhydd ef lawer o ddywenydd i bawb ag sydd yn caru'r hen iaith Gymraeg').[108]

Just as, and perhaps more, important to Iolo the budding poet and the independent man were the links he and his Vale-based colleagues established with kindred spirits in the *Blaenau* (Uplands), the hill country of Glamorgan. There were striking contrasts in Iolo's day between the fertile and affluent lowland Vale and the rugged rural uplands where soils were too infertile to persuade any farmer to invest spare capital in improvements and where wheeled traffic moved at a snail's pace during inclement weather. On the other hand, the uplands were swiftly laying claim to be the birthplace of modern Wales. During Iolo's early manhood the parish and emerging ironworks town of Merthyr Tydfil were already becoming celebrated for their 'flaming labyrinths',[109] a cluster of productive ironworks located along the northern rim of the South Wales Coalfield and financed by the capital of powerful families like the Bacons, the Guests and the Crawshays, whose wealth was closely associated with the stimulus provided by successive wars and the burgeoning slave trade. The environmentally-conscious Iolo always found something to please his eye in this often inhospitable terrain. In one marginal note he maintained that the craggy uplands were just as inviting to the Romantic poet as were the fertile lowlands:

> The Mountains which Tower in our northern parts display nature in all her beauty of wild and romantic Grandeur. The plain sumits cover'd over with numerous flocks and herds, the sides either cultivated fields, or fine woods, thro frequently peep a craggy rock whiten'd over with moss, its grey hairs of antiquity. Wild torrents & cascades wildly foaming over precipices often tumble down those lofty hills.[110]

---

[107] *CIM*, I, pp. 71–3, 73–5 (trans.), James Turberville (Iaco Twrbil) to Iolo Morganwg, 10 January 1773; NLW 21309D; NLW 21311A.
[108] *CIM*, I, pp. 38–40, 40–2 (trans.), Iolo Morganwg to the publishers of *Trysorfa Gwybodaeth*, 25 February 1770; G. J. Williams, 'Josiah Rees a'r *Eurgrawn Cymraeg*', *LIC*, 3, no. 2 (1954), 119.
[109] See Chris Evans, *'The Labyrinth of Flames': Work and Social Conflict in Early Industrial Merthyr Tydfil* (Cardiff, 1993).
[110] NLW 21285E, no. 787, marginal note.

Iolo's kindred spirits were not the powerful industrial barons but rather the small groups of freeholders, artisans and craftsmen who had a reputation for poetical expertise and independence of thought, a combination which he found irresistible. As far as Iolo was concerned there were three versatile poets who ensured that the *Blaenau*, supposedly the home of the authentic Welsh bardic tradition and mythology, never lost its aura of romance and mystery. Lewis Hopkin of Hendre Ifan Goch, Llandyfodwg, was a gifted poet and writer who had an excellent network of contacts in the world of Welsh- and English-language publishing. A good-natured, generous and exceptionally versatile man, he was at different stages in his career a joiner, carpenter, glazier, stonecutter, wireworker, shopkeeper, surveyor and farmer. This was a man who could build a house, furnish it on his own, and fill it with books.[111] His son described him as 'a man of universal genius both for literature and mechanics'.[112] Iolo called him 'my splendid teacher' ('fy Athraw godidog') and when Hopkin died in November 1771 he showed his affectionate regard for him by publishing an elegy of 278 lines in his honour.[113] On Hopkin's death, John Bradford, a weaver, fuller and dyer of Betws Tir Iarll, became Iolo's chief bardic mentor and in one of his manuscripts he traced the line of the principal poets of Glamorgan from Dafydd ap Gwilym in the fourteenth century to Bradford and his disciples in late eighteenth-century Wales.[114] The third associate was Edward Evan(s), a weaver's son from Aberdare who served an apprenticeship as a glazier and carpenter under Lewis Hopkin's benevolent eye before eventually becoming a farmer and a Dissenting minister at Aberdare. His posthumously-published collection of Welsh poetry, *Afalau'r Awen*, which appeared in 1816 and was reprinted in 1837 and 1874, inspired several generations of Glamorgan poets.[115] As we shall see, these many-sided men were fond of unorthodox theological and political ideas, to which Iolo warmed. For the moment, however, their principal role was to provide Iolo with detailed knowledge of the poetic tradition and its arcane secrets and to encourage him to demonstrate verve and ingenuity in his compositions. Nothing gave Iolo greater pleasure in the early 1770s than dispatching poems, stanzas and songs from 'the pure, luscious Vale' ('|y| Fro bûr frâs') to colleagues in the 'bare frosty' uplands

---

[111] NLW 13141A, pp. 129–31; *TLlM*, pp. 231–6; Lewis: *IM*, pp. 31–3; Ceri W. Lewis, 'The Literary History of Glamorgan from 1550 to 1770' in *GCH IV*, pp. 612–14.

[112] Lemuel James, *Hopkiniaid Morganwg: Being a Genealogical Biography of the Hopkin Family of Glamorgan with the Works of Hopkin Thomas Philip and Lewis Hopkin* (Bangor, 1909), p. 115.

[113] NLW 13141A, p. 129; NLW 13087E, pp. 361–4; Edward Williams (Iorwerth Gwilim), *Dagrau yr Awen neu Farwnad Lewis Hopcin Fardd, o Landyfodwg ym Morganwg* (Pont-y-fon, 1772). For a printed and annotated copy of this elegy in Iolo's papers, see NLW 21317A.

[114] NLW 13116B, pp. 373–4; NLW 13141A, p. 131; *TLlM*, pp. 237–40; Lewis: *IM*, pp. 31–3; Lewis in *GCH IV*, pp. 614–16.

[115] NLW 13141A, p. 131; R. T. Jenkins, 'Bardd a'i Gefndir (Edward Ifan o'r Ton Coch)', *THSC* (1946–7), 97–149; *TLlM*, pp. 245–51; Lewis in *GCH IV*, pp. 618–19.

('noethrew naws') of Glamorgan for critical appraisal.[116] In turn, impressed by his razor-edge intelligence and turn of phrase, they counted him among the brightest lights on the literary horizon.

Iolo, of course, was an Anglican by upbringing, but the fact that he co-operated with avowed Dissenters reveals a readiness to pull together to promote cultural interests. At this early stage in his life he was still presumably frequenting church services and he was certainly consorting with literary-minded parsons, two of whom left their mark on him by making him believe profoundly in the value of words to both prose and poetry. From 1770–1 Iolo began accumulating an appreciable corpus of linguistic and dialectal data which convinced him that the Welsh language could boast its 'own native terms of perfect elegance, propriety, and force of expression'[117] and that the Gwentian (or Silurian) dialect was second to none. One of the thorniest issues facing Welsh scholars from the mid-eighteenth century onwards was how to convince their own people, let alone English critics and especially satirists, that the Welsh language was not only a copious tongue but that it was also sufficiently flexible and fashionable to accommodate new words.[118] As the pace of bilingualism quickened, the demand for Welsh–English and English–Welsh dictionaries increased markedly. Iolo was fortunate, therefore, to find himself rubbing shoulders in his locality with two outstanding lexicographers who improved and enriched their mother tongue by rescuing old words and minting new ones, a habit which Iolo cultivated for most of his adult life.

The first was Thomas Richards, a native of Carmarthenshire who served as the conscientious (though poorly paid) perpetual curate of Coychurch from 1738 to 1790.[119] Like Iolo, Richards was largely self-educated and since Iolo's mother was the daughter of Edward Matthew of Ty'nycaeau, Coychurch, he must have come to know Richards through his mother or other relatives. Harshly described by Goronwy Owen of Anglesey as 'poor plodding Richards',[120] the curate of Coychurch had made his reputation as a man of letters by publishing *Antiquae Linguae Britannicae Thesaurus* – a Welsh–English dictionary – in 1753. Made possible by an impressive list of 681 subscribers, which included the future George III, the dictionary was based on the path-

---

[116] *CIM*, I, pp. 53–4, 54–5 (trans.), John Bradford (Siôn Bradford or Iorwerth Tir Iarll) to Iolo Morganwg, 10 June 1771. See also Ffion M. Jones, '"Gydwladwr Godi[d]og . . .": Gohebiaeth Gymraeg Gynnar Iolo Morganwg', *LlC*, 27 (2004), 140–52.

[117] NLW 13089E, p. 426.

[118] See the discussion in Caryl Davies, *Adfeilion Babel: Agweddau ar Syniadaeth Ieithyddol y Ddeunawfed Ganrif* (Caerdydd, 2000).

[119] Brian Ll. James, *Thomas Richards 1710–1790: Curate of Coychurch, Scholar and Lexicographer* (Coychurch, [1989]); Lewis in *GCH IV*, pp. 630–3; Richard M. Crowe, 'Thomas Richards a John Walters: Athrawon Geiriadurol Iolo Morganwg' in Hywel Teifi Edwards (ed.), *Llynfi ac Afan, Garw ac Ogwr* (Llandysul, 1998), pp. 227–51; *ODNB*.

[120] J. H. Davies (ed.), *The Letters of Goronwy Owen (1723–1769)* (Cardiff, 1924), p. 68.

breaking work of Dr John Davies, Mallwyd, in the early Stuart period, but it also revealed that Richards was steeped in the works of distinguished wordsmiths like William Salesbury, Thomas Wiliems and Edward Lhuyd. Iolo got on famously with Richards, who found him a clever and attentive young scholar, and he spent long hours poring over books and manuscripts in the lexicographer's well-stocked library at Coychurch.[121] Richards urged him to extend and improve his Welsh and English vocabulary, reflect upon etymology, and master spelling, syntax and punctuation. As their mutual respect and friendship ripened, Iolo's lists of words grew by the hour, and there can be no doubting the sincerity of his particular attachment to words from Glamorgan and to the Gwentian dialect.

From around 1769 Iolo also fell under the spell of another Carmarthenshire-born cleric and lexicographer. A timber-merchant's son, John Walters was the rector of Llandough and lived some two miles from Iolo's home.[122] Over the course of the best part of thirty years – Walters died in 1797 – Iolo depended heavily on his advice and guidance. Admiringly, he once referred to Walters as 'the very best Critic in the Welsh language living',[123] and it was at his feet that he learned Latin, French and a smattering of Greek. Whereas Thomas Richards was modest and self-effacing, Walters was self-assertive and candid in his views. He shaped Iolo's mind in several ways. First, he taught him to cherish one of the oldest living languages in the world. In a fulsome paean to his native tongue, published in Cowbridge in 1771, Walters maintained: 'I prefer *this* to any of the languages ancient or modern, that I have any acquaintance with.'[124] He also pilloried those who publicly declared their aversion to the Welsh tongue and who displayed 'a tameness of spirit' and 'a servility of disposition' when it came to defending the vernacular tradition.[125] Sentiments such as these touched Iolo profoundly. Secondly, Walters urged him to enrich his vocabulary by collecting, classifying and minting Welsh words. In so doing, he gave his young pupil's career some much-needed direction and discipline. In 1770 Walters had launched a mammoth literary enterprise: *An English–Welsh Dictionary*, published in fourteen parts at Cowbridge between 1770 and 1783, and in a further two substantial volumes in London in 1794, was the most successful long-term cultural project of the age.[126] It made Walters's reputation as a distinguished wordsmith and Iolo played his part by

---

[121] NLW 21387E, nos. 10, 16.
[122] Lewis in *GCH IV*, pp. 633–5; Crowe, 'Thomas Richards a John Walters', pp. 227–51; *ODNB*.
[123] NLW 21387E, no. 10.
[124] John Walters, *A Dissertation on the Welsh Language* (Cowbridge, 1771), p. 63.
[125] Ibid., p. 60.
[126] Brian Ll. James, 'The Cowbridge Printers' in Stewart Williams (ed.), *Glamorgan Historian, 4* (Cowbridge, 1967), pp. 231–44.

submitting contributions. He was gratified, thrilled even, to be associated with such a prestigious undertaking.

At the outset, however, master and pupil were extremely wary of each other. Iolo was sensitive to criticism and fearful of Walters's caustic tongue. Walters believed that Iolo was impulsive and unreliable, and he took a dim view of some of his wilder etymological presumptions.[127] Yet, he recognized the young stonemason's exceptional promise and his individuality. 'The Bard', he informed Owen Jones (Owain Myfyr) cryptically, 'is a very singular character . . . almost as unsteady as poor Ieuan Fardd.'[128] Stubborn and unsteady Iolo may have been, but his enthusiasm was never in doubt. He pillaged the works of Welsh bards and transcribed many of the works of the Poets of the Princes and *cywyddwyr* like Dafydd ap Gwilym. He was so confident in his ability that by 1770 he was contemplating publishing a collection of his poems under the title 'Blaendardd yr Awenydd' (Shoots of the Muse).[129] He keenly listened to local words and dialects, and regularly jotted down unfamiliar or striking idioms and expressions. By 1776 he had collected around 9,000 Welsh words and the best part of a thousand dialectal forms.[130] According to the fine Cardiganshire-born scholar Evan Evans (Ieuan Fardd), Iolo was 'of great use to Mr Walters, who often consults him'.[131]

Clearly anxious to please his mentor and impress him with the extent of his knowledge, Iolo filled his letters to Walters with poetic and etymological data. But Walters's austere, patrician manner and his brusqueries increasingly annoyed Iolo, and he resented having his creative powers reined in by someone whose eye was 'more microscopic than Telescopic'.[132] In 1781 he complained that Walters was envious of his abilities and had become 'more than half an enemy to me' ('yn fwy na hanner gelyn imi'),[133] but he continued to draw on his extensive learning and share his obsession with words. Ironically, Walters's great dictionary reflected Iolo's restless desire to discover and define himself. Many of the Welsh words coined in the early stages were associated with individuality and self-awareness, among them *hunander* (egoism, 1771), *teimladrwydd* (sentiment, 1773), *dynoliaeth* (humanity, 1774), *gwladgarwch* (love of country, 1776), and *myfiaeth* (egotism, 1777).[134] Anyone who knew the young

---

[127] See *CIM*, I, pp. 51–2, 65–70, 80–8, 91–100.
[128] BL Add. 15024, ff. 185–6, John Walters to Owen Jones (Owain Myfyr), 29 January 1779.
[129] NLW 21388E, no. 14; Williams: *IM*, p. 133.
[130] *CIM*, I, pp. 111–12, Iolo Morganwg to Owen Jones (Owain Myfyr), 25 January 1776. For the background, see Richard M. Crowe, 'Diddordebau Ieithyddol Iolo Morganwg' (unpublished University of Wales Ph.D. thesis, 1988).
[131] NLW 31B, p. 96.
[132] NLW 13123B, p. 26.
[133] *CIM*, I, p. 176, Iolo Morganwg to Owen Jones (Owain Myfyr), 23 February 1781.
[134] *Geiriadur Prifysgol Cymru* (4 vols., Caerdydd, 1950–2002); Prys Morgan, 'Dyro Olau ar dy Eiriau', *Taliesin*, 70 (1990), 38–45.

Iolo well might have concluded that such words epitomized him. In 1773 the dictionary included for the first time the word *athrylithfawr*, a rather convoluted Welsh equivalent for *genius*. Iolo was fond of celebrating 'natural genius' and, given his own ambitions in that direction, there may well be grounds for believing that he coined the Welsh equivalent and forwarded it to Walters.[135] What can be said with certainty is that Walters taught Iolo to respect and cherish words, both Welsh and English, learned and vernacular. The quality of Iolo's prose style, as reflected in his correspondence, improved markedly from the early 1770s onwards, and Walters's tutelage stood him in good stead when he came to write a large number of forthright essays, satires and poems in the 1790s and thereafter. Walters made Iolo a more nimble as well as rigorous writer, and much more capable, when the opportunity came, of challenging men in authority.

In the summer of 1773 Iolo packed his bags and set off for London. In his memoirs he claimed to have cast off his moorings because his mother's death had been such an unbearable blow: 'I endeavoured to fly from sorrow by flying from home.'[136] There is no reason to disbelieve his claim that his bereavement was a profound emotional upheaval in his life. As we have seen, his veneration of his mother is well attested, and some of his poems convey this deep sense of loss. A decade after she had passed away, probably of tubercular illness, the 'tide of grief' felt by Iolo still flowed strongly:

> Ten years are past, since she, from pinching grief,
> Fled to that place where anguish finds relief.
> Yet still for her the spring of sorrow flows
> And memory awakens all my woes.[137]

'Still I weep for thee', he wrote in a sonnet composed in memory of his mother in 1790,[138] and the preface to *Poems, Lyric and Pastoral* in 1794 is haunted by her presence. But Ann William(s) had died, aged fifty-seven, in August 1770,[139] three years before Iolo trudged to London to pursue his trade as a stonemason.

It is hard to believe that Iolo left home for no motive other than brokenhearted despair over the demise of a mother who, however devoted he was to her, had lain buried long since. Other pressing reasons were clearly involved. One strong possibility is that his departure was linked indirectly to the impending

---

[135] Prys Morgan, 'A Private Space: Autobiography and Individuality in Eighteenth- and Early Nineteenth-Century Wales' in Davies and Jenkins (eds.), *From Medieval to Modern Wales*, pp. 171–4.
[136] NLW 13106B, pp. 175–7.
[137] NLW 21422E, no. 2.
[138] Williams: *PLP*, II, p. 97.
[139] NLW 21318A, p. 100; NLW 21418E, no. 1.

marriage of Kitty Deere, the daughter of Matthew Deere of Ash Hall, Ystradowen, a former sheriff of Glamorgan, to the Revd William Church, rector of Flemingston, Michaelston-juxta-Cowbridge and Llanilid.[140] Kitty Deere's beauty and intelligence had stirred Iolo's fancy and he once claimed that she – 'Sun of the muse and star of love' ('Haul awen a seren serch') – had turned him into a poet.[141] But her higher social status probably meant that this was a case of unrequited or forbidden love. Having wooed her in vain from afar, the lovesick Iolo could not bear to be in the vicinity when his beloved Kitty walked down the aisle of Llandough parish church on 14 October 1773.[142]

A second, much stronger, possibility is that Iolo was forced to flee in haste as a result of his own reckless behaviour. Sometime in 1770–1 his swagger and hasty temper drew him into a violent affray with a certain John Charles.[143] Iolo's sharp tongue and satirical songs, exemplified by stanzas to a 'William the Cowardly Wretch' from Flemingston (Gwilim Gachadur o Drefflemin),[144] had earned him an unenviable reputation in the locality as a sower of strife, and the fracas with John Charles might have occurred following an ill-tempered verbal exchange. Iolo claimed that he was the injured party but, following a civil case, of which no details have survived, damages and costs were awarded to Charles and his solicitor Thomas Williams. Still protesting his innocence, Iolo maintained (not for the last time in his life) that he was a victim of the 'rascalities of Persons of no Consciences',[145] but even William Bassett, his own solicitor, knew that Iolo had confessed his guilt in a letter to a bailiff.[146] One can imagine that his father was furious at his eldest son's youthful indiscretion, not least because the verdict was potentially ruinous to a family of stonemasons. Iolo's reputation plummeted still further when rumours spread of his alleged unscrupulous behaviour while collecting subscriptions in north Wales in 1772 for a proposed anthology of Glamorgan poetry entitled 'Diddanwch y Cymru' (Entertainment for the Welsh), a substantial volume priced at four shillings for subscribers.[147] In the event, the work never materialized and in the summer of 1773 Iolo fled like a thief in the night from the clutches of the law and the fury of duped subscribers, with the harsh words of John Charles's attorney ringing in his ears and the shillings of subscribers and well-wishers

---

[140] Patricia Moore (ed.), *Glamorgan Sheriffs* (Cardiff, 1995), p. 92; Jenkins, *The Making of a Ruling Class*, pp. 32, 93, 184.
[141] NLW 13087E, pp. 335–6; NLW 21388E, no. 38; *CIM*, I, pp. 66–7, 67–8 (trans.), Iolo Morganwg to John Walters, 1 November 1772.
[142] Glamorgan Archives, Llandough PR, 1773. Iolo vented his despair in a *cywydd* composed in London on 13 August 1773. NLW 21388E, no. 13.
[143] Williams: *IM*, pp. 188–9.
[144] Ibid., pp. 131–2.
[145] NLW 21319A, pp. 12–13.
[146] *CIM*, I, pp. 48–9, William Bassett to Iolo Morganwg, 22 January 1771.
[147] NLW 21390E, no. 4; Williams: *IM*, pp. 168–75; *CIM*, I, pp. 65–8, Iolo Morganwg to John Walters, 1 November 1772.

from Gwynedd tinkling in his pockets. Freed from his mother's suffocating grip, the young unruly stonemason had brought disgrace upon himself and his family.

For the moment, then, Iolo Morganwg turned his back on 'Davona's Vale' and headed east on foot to the teeming city of London. He was now twenty-six and on his own. Leaving behind his private sorrows and other misfortunes, he was forced for the first time in his life to find work as an independent stonecutter, look after his own interests and, if possible, satisfy his growing literary ambitions. Fully bilingual and remarkably versatile, he delighted in words, was fully capable of composing captivating strict-metre and free-metre Welsh poetry, and had established himself as a competent writer of English poetry and prose. As he strode jauntily eastward, more adventures awaited this touchy, headstrong but gifted young man.

2

'I was always pushing forward'

There are several passages in Iolo's drafts of his memoirs or correspondence, especially those written for the benefit of well-born people in England in the 1790s, which stretch credulity to snapping point. Among them are his claim that he had lived the life of a hermit in an 'obscure part of the kingdom . . . a very sequestered corner of Wales'.¹ The truth is, however, that Glamorgan became the most productive, commercialized and progressive county in Wales during the second half of the eighteenth century. The localism of the past was being undermined by the traffic in goods, people and ideas, and the large-scale industrialization of the *Blaenau* had a profound effect on the whole economy of the county. Even in the Vale of Glamorgan, a major granary for south Wales, there was an air of change and excitement. As Philip Jenkins has shown, the Vale had become 'a crossroads rather than a backwater'.² At this southern-most point in Wales, highland, lowland and Atlantic Britain converged,³ and its strategic advantages made it susceptible to socio-cultural influences from many directions. The bustling town of Cowbridge, a couple of miles from Iolo's home, was most certainly not an out-of-the-way place.⁴ Far from it. Located on the major coaching route which ran from London through Bristol and Cardiff and on to Swansea, it was well used to accommodating the many stage-coaches, horses and travellers in its hospitable inns. The river Thaw, so close to Iolo's heart, reached the sea at nearby Aberthaw where all kinds of vessels plied their trade daily with ports in Gloucestershire, Somerset and Devon, as well as more distant destinations. The proximity of the new industrial enterprises, the development of turnpike roads and the availability of cross-channel ferries meant

---

1. *CIM*, I, p. 439, Iolo Morganwg to George, Prince of Wales, [?1792]; ibid., II, p. 49, Iolo Morganwg to Mary Barker, 26 March [1798].
2. Philip Jenkins, *The Making of a Ruling Class: The Glamorgan Gentry 1640–1790* (Cambridge, 1983), p. 10.
3. This point is well made by Brian Ll. James in 'The Welsh Language in the Vale of Glamorgan', *Morgannwg*, XVI (1972), 16.
4. Idem, 'Cowbridge' in Stewart Williams (ed.), *South Glamorgan: A County History* (Barry, 1975), pp. 225–41.

that Iolo, even in his youth, was not hermetically sealed from the outside world. Thanks to the turnpike roads, the flying machines and the mail-coaches, from the 1770s Iolo entered the age of speed. He may have shunned carriages and habitually chosen to walk rather than ride on horseback, but he was fully aware that a new spirit was abroad in the world of communications and transport.

The summer of 1773 opened a new phase in Iolo's life, one of nomadic endeavour and the broadening of horizons and experiences. His antennae bristling as he tramped eastwards, he was determined to 'remain inde[pe]ndent of all the world',[5] keep abreast of cultural developments, and face the world with confidence. Even if misfortune happened to dog his 'thorn obstructed way', he resolved never to show anything less than 'bold fortitude'.[6] Already known for his lack of caution, he would now become ever more restless. There were always places to see, people to meet, books to read, and all aspects of human knowledge to explore. As prickly as he was resilient, even at this stage he had an over-inflated sense of his own importance.

From the early Tudor period onwards the Welsh had never been able to ignore the presence and attractions of London. Its bright and alluring lights drew them like moths. By the time of the first census in 1801 London was nearly twice as populous as the whole of Wales, and its size, shape and mythical reputation captured the imagination of many Welsh people. To William Owen Pughe, who became (at least for a time) one of Iolo's firmest friends in London, it was the epicentre of the world.[7] A playground for the rich, a centre of consumption and a cultural focus, it offered a mouth-watering array of amenities and opportunities for young and ambitious people. The pulling power of the metropolis was well-nigh irresistible to rootless rural labourers and footloose artisans and craftsmen who were prepared to risk having their morals corrupted by living close to thieves, harlots, rakes and pickpockets, and their health adversely affected by squalor, dirt and disease. Although the Welsh language figured among the Babel of tongues heard in London, Welsh in-migrants were too small in number to crystallize as an independent and easily identifiable group. At this time around 20,000 of its inhabitants were of Welsh origin, but since they did not settle in distinctive enclaves they did not constitute a powerful critical mass within society.[8] Nevertheless, Welsh birds of a feather certainly flocked to convivial London-Welsh society meetings, and it was here that Iolo would leave his mark.

---

[5] NLW 21387E, no. 9.
[6] NLW 21392F, no. 74.
[7] William Owen Pughe, *A Dictionary of the Welsh Language* (2 vols., London, 1803), I, sig. b3^r.
[8] Emrys Jones, 'The Welsh in London in the Seventeenth and Eighteenth Centuries', *WHR*, 10, no. 4 (1981), 473; idem (ed.), *The Welsh in London 1500–2000* (Cardiff, 2001), p. 55.

No letters from Iolo have survived for the twelve months from August 1773, but he was evidently greatly impressed by London's handsome public buildings, elegant squares and terraces, and sophisticated town houses. As an artisan, he could hardly pose as a man about town, but he made himself known to a variety of social groups, mostly Welsh, and he may have found work with statuaries at Piccadilly. When his stonemason brothers followed him to London, he chastised Thomas, the youngest sibling, for forsaking the metropolis at an early stage:

> I think it savours somthing of indiscreation, that near a kin to madness, for you to entertain such romantic notions of the pleasures of the country, when you had (one should think) more experience than the poets and novel writers that very often turn your brains. The countrey, it is true, has pleasures and realy superior to those of the town. But the hardships that a working man must necessarily bear there are far more than an equiavalent to them. Though it was very indiscreet in you to come to London at first, it was ten times more so for you [to] leave it. You had acquired a tolerable proficiency in a very good trade which, if you had followed for a few years in London, would be greatly to your advantage.[9]

The underlying message here is that Iolo himself, in spite of indifferent health which forced him to rely on the soothing powers of opium,[10] had found regular and lucrative work in London, and that his skills in carving, pointing, moulding, smoothing, dressing and painting had been enhanced. 'In my trade I was always pushing forward',[11] he wrote, and he duly noted and learned from the extraordinarily diverse range of architectural patterns which characterized the city's landscape. At this stage in his life he does not appear to have detested the 'Great Wen' in the way that he would in the 1790s. Work opportunities must have been available and he was probably employed by one of the statuary workshops in Westminster.[12] He may have worked on Waterloo Bridge and, given that he penned 'The Stonecut[t]er's Song' at Westminster, it is not inconceivable that he spent some time carrying out repairs to the notorious structural defects of the old Westminster Bridge which was immortalized in the paintings of Canaletto and in Wordsworth's paean 'Earth has not anything to show more fair'.[13]

---

[9] *CIM*, I, p. 79, Iolo Morganwg to Thomas Williams, 26 August 1774.
[10] NLW 21387E, no. 10.
[11] Ibid., no. 35.
[12] Richard Suggett, 'Iolo Morganwg: Stonecutter, Builder, and Antiquary' in *Rattleskull Genius*, p. 200.
[13] NLW 21421E, no. 2a; NLW 21392F, no. 73; R. J. B. Walker, *Old Westminster Bridge: The Bridge of Fools* (Newton Abbot, 1979), chapter 6.

In later years Iolo prided himself on epitomizing the old proverb about the rolling stone which gathered no moss.[14] Within a year of arriving in London the high road beckoned once more. Although he made intermittent visits back to London, the next three years were spent working in Kentish towns like Margate, Deal, Dover, Sandwich and Faversham. His asthmatic complaint may have prompted him to move, but Kent also offered new economic opportunities as well as a more congenial climate. By 1801 Kent had become the fifth largest county in England and its array of dockyard towns and ports, as well as its thriving agricultural and industrial activities, offered an appreciable range of employment opportunities.[15] In late August 1774, on the recommendation of a foreman of a gang of stonemasons at Margate, Iolo was taken on by John Deveson, a stonecutter at Sandwich, who initially offered him free lodgings at his home.[16] Sandwich had a population of 2,259 in 1776 and its civic leaders were anxious to improve the appearance of the town by providing timber-framed buildings with neo-classical architectural façades and other enhancing features.[17] How far this impinged on Iolo's daily work is impossible to tell, but by February 1775 he was complaining bitterly that, in spite of his many promises, Deveson had not paid him fully for his labours.[18] His colleagues found Iolo hot-tempered and opinionated, and presumably no tears were shed when he moved on once more, this time to Faversham, a market town between Canterbury and Sittingbourne, close to the flatlands of the north Kent marshes where sailing barges on Faversham Creek plied in timber, bricks and flint.[19] He spent the best part of 1776 working for Charles Drayson, a stonemason and bricklayer at Faversham,[20] and found life there more conducive to reading and writing, even though he was often assailed by gloomy doubts and forebodings.[21]

How far did Iolo's experiences in south-east England deepen his natural aversion to authority, sharpen his wit and colour his view of others? First of all, he gained a good deal from his association with the London Welsh. The propensity of Welsh in-migrants to form cultural and patriotic societies meant

---

[14] NLW 21428E, no. 2.
[15] Alan Armstrong (ed.), *The Economy of Kent 1640–1914* (Woodbridge, 1995), pp. 12–14.
[16] *CIM*, I, p. 79, Iolo Morganwg to Thomas Williams, 26 August 1774. John Deveson (c. 1722–1809) was a freeman of Sandwich and lived in Strand Street. Centre for Kentish Studies, Maidstone, SA/RF 1–14, 17, 22, 24.
[17] E. Martin, *Occupations of the People of Sandwich* (Sandwich, 1978), pp. 23–7; T. L. Richardson, *Historic Sandwich and its Region 1500–1900* (Sandwich Local History Society, 2006), pp. 85, 97.
[18] *CIM*, I, p. 101, Iolo Morganwg to Edward William(s), 3 February 1775.
[19] See Arthur Percival, *Old Faversham* (Rainham, 1988) and Anthony Swaine, *Faversham: Its History, its Present Role and the Pattern for its Future* (Faversham, 1970).
[20] See *CIM*, I, p. 109, Iolo Morganwg to Owen Jones (Owain Myfyr), 25 January 1776; ibid., I, p. 118, Iolo Morganwg to Edward William(s), [?8 February 1776].
[21] He claimed that during his days in Kent 'my passion for poetry revived'. NLW 13106B, p. 176.

that London gained a reputation as the surrogate capital of Wales during the eighteenth century. The Honourable and Loyal Society of Ancient Britons, founded in 1715, had established a well-regarded Welsh school in the city, and in 1751 Lewis Morris, the Anglesey-born polymath, had provided further cultural stimulus by setting up the Society of Cymmrodorion, whose aim was to encourage 'the Cultivation of the *British* Language, and a Search into Antiquities'.[22] By the time of his death in 1765, however, Morris was resigned to the fact that the motley crew of brandy-makers, chocolate-makers, peruke-makers and gentry who frequented meetings were unlikely to fulfil his ambition of creating a Welsh equivalent to the Society of Antiquaries or even the Royal Society. His brother Richard, an overly conscientious clerk in the Navy Office, devoted his leisure hours to persuading toffy-nosed or philistine members of the Society to assist him in discovering, transcribing and publishing Welsh manuscripts, only to find that they preferred wine, women and song to the study of medieval literature. Iolo deplored their passivity: 'Ai ydynt yn cyfarfod i rywbeth amgen nag i fwyta ag i yfed a syfrdanu?' ('Do they meet for any reason other than to eat and drink and be delirious?')[23] Not surprisingly, the Cymmrodorion Society was wound up, pro tem, in 1787, having failed to set its house in order following the death of Richard Morris eight years earlier.[24]

Three years before Iolo first set foot in London a third Welsh society, dubbed the Gwyneddigion (Men of Gwynedd), was established in December 1770. This more welcoming and jolly band of young men, almost all of whom hailed from north Wales, were more in tune with Iolo's cultural interests. 'Hir oes i'r iaith Gymraeg' (Long life to the Welsh language) was one of their favourite toasts and they set their minds to enhancing the future prospects of the native tongue by publishing Welsh books and reviving the moribund eisteddfodic tradition. The Gwyneddigion usually met on the first Monday of each month in taverns like the George and Vulture in Lombard Street and more especially at the Bull's Head in Walbrook, otherwise known as 'Y Crindy' in recognition of its witty and voluble host Evan Roberts alias 'Y Crin'.[25] It was Iolo's

---

[22] 'Constitutions of the Honourable Society of Cymmrodorion', *Y Cymmrodor*, I (1877), 15. For the background, see *HHSC* and Emrys Jones and Dewi Watkin Powell, *The Honourable Society of Cymmrodorion: A Concise History 1751–2001* ([London], [2004]).

[23] *CIM*, I, pp. 265, 268 (trans.), Iolo Morganwg to John Edwards (Siôn Ceiriog), 13 September 1784.

[24] For Iolo's elegy to Richard Morris, see A. Cynfael Lake (ed.), *Blodeugerdd Barddas o Ganu Caeth y Ddeunawfed Ganrif* (Cyhoeddiadau Barddas, 1993), pp. 215–22, 252. An English translation, together with the original *cywydd*, may be found in *CIM*, I, pp. 204–10, 211–17 (trans.), Iolo Morganwg to Owen Jones (Owain Myfyr), 2 September 1782.

[25] G. J. Williams, 'Bywyd Cymreig Llundain yng Nghyfnod Owain Myfyr', *Y Llenor*, XVIII (1939), 73–82, 218–32; Glenda Carr, 'Bwrlwm Bywyd y Cymry yn Llundain yn y Ddeunawfed Ganrif' in Geraint H. Jenkins (ed.), *Cof Cenedl XI: Ysgrifau ar Hanes Cymru* (Llandysul, 1996), pp. 59–87.

good fortune to strike up a friendship with Owen Jones (Owain Myfyr), one of the founding fathers and the first president of the Society.[26] A Denbighshire man, he had settled in London in the mid-1760s as an apprentice with a company of skinners. Aged thirty-two in 1773, he was not yet the rotund, prosperous furrier of the late 1780s, but he had a gift for talent-spotting and an insatiable desire to bring Welsh texts into the public domain. Iolo made an enormous impression on him and he swiftly came to believe that the Glamorgan stonemason had no equal as an authority on the Welsh poetic tradition.[27] Owain Myfyr dispensed gifts and financial support on a generous scale and by the 1790s Iolo's family was so beholden to him that he was referred to as 'the good man of London'.[28] He was certainly instrumental in promoting Iolo's literary career and his protégé was also pleased to find many kindred spirits who shared his cultural interests, not least his growing obsession with the poetry of Dafydd ap Gwilym, the greatest of the Welsh medieval *cywyddwyr*. The wittiest of orators was John Edwards (Siôn Ceiriog), who served as secretary of the Society in 1779 and later as its president.[29] The same posts were also held by Robert Hughes (Robin Ddu yr Ail o Fôn), a lawyer's clerk from Anglesey.[30] Both were around the same age as Iolo; he took to them immediately, and was devastated when they died in their mid-forties in 1792 and 1785 respectively. Throughout his life Iolo was especially attracted to those who took risks and lived life to the full. He enjoyed lively company in which he could talk freely and outrageously, and also bask in the attention and recognition he received. Joining the Gwyneddigion therefore offered this fast-talking Glamorgan stonemason the opportunity to promote his literary and (later) political initiatives, to network freely, and gain a degree of social credibility.

As we have seen, several claims made by Iolo as he rewrote the narratives of his life in later years must always be treated with a hefty degree of scepticism. One of them – made publicly in a letter to the Prime Minister, William Pitt, in December 1796 – was that he had always been a stranger to alcoholic beverages.[31] By that stage, it is true, he had become an irremediable tea-drinker, but until probably the age of forty-five he was an enthusiastic toper. Alcohol ran freely in all of the 3,000 or so clubs and societies located in late eighteenth-

---

[26] Geraint Phillips, 'Bywyd a Chysylltiadau Llenyddol Owain Myfyr (Owen Jones, 1741–1814)' (unpublished University of Wales Ph.D. thesis, 2006); idem, 'Forgery and Patronage: Iolo Morganwg and Owain Myfyr' in *Rattleskull Genius*, pp. 403–23; idem, *Dyn heb ei Gyffelyb yn y Byd: Owain Myfyr a'i Gysylltiadau Llenyddol* (Caerdydd, 2010).
[27] NLW 15415E, p. 11, Owen Jones (Owain Myfyr) to John Walters, 9 January 1777.
[28] *CIM*, I, p. 363, Iolo Morganwg to Owen Jones (Owain Myfyr), 10 October 179[0].
[29] *HHSC*, pp. 101–1; *DWB*.
[30] *HHSC*, pp. 97–9; *DWB*.
[31] *CIM*, I, p. 844, Iolo Morganwg to William Pitt, 16 December 1796. See also NLW 21387E, no. 7.

century London,[32] and Gwyneddigion meetings were no exception. As Roy Porter has noted, 'oceans [of alcohol] were swallowed, and not just during the gin craze',[33] and since the Bull in Walbrook was 'well stored with brandy, beer, and gin'[34] prolonged bingeing was not uncommon among young Welshmen who reckoned that hard drinking and ritual smoking betokened manliness. The London Welsh jostled to sit at the table of Iorwerth Morganwg (as he was known to them), for there was rarely a dull moment when he was in his cups. Joining in the fun, he sang songs, recited poetry, played the flute, told tall stories, and bombarded listeners with his prejudices. Amid the noisy pranks and laddish rituals, Iolo was often the star turn.

Nor was Iolo abstemious in the company of the stonemasons of London and Kent. Chisellers who raised clouds of dust which filled their lungs and dried their throats all day long needed no excuse to abuse their livers in the evening. In inns, alehouses and taverns the temperance cause was unknown, and even as he yearned for his native patch Iolo dominated the drinking table, as songs like 'Devilish Good Thing', composed and sung with gusto at the meetings of the 'Drive away Care Club' at Faversham, reveal all too clearly:

> Good liquor, my boys
> Is the source of our joys
> And in the muse that inspires me to sing,
> Push the glass briskly round,
> Let good humour abound,
> For you know that's a devilish good thing.
>
> . . .
>
> This bumper shall pass
> To my favourite lass,
> Her charms make the wild welkin ring,
> To the fair we'll be just
> Honour tells us we must,
> A sweet girl is a dev'lish good thing.[35]

Such boisterous occasions offered not only copious supplies of liquor, companionship and humour, but also the opportunity to sing bawdy songs and make salacious jokes at the expense of women.

---

[32] Peter Clark, *British Clubs and Societies 1580–1800: The Origins of an Associational World* (Oxford, 2000), p. 131.
[33] Roy Porter, *Flesh in the Age of Reason* (London, 2003), p. 236.
[34] William Ll. Davies, 'David Samwell's Poem – "The Padouca Hunt"', *NLWJ*, II, nos. 3 and 4 (1942), 144.
[35] NLW 21424E, nos. 13, 13a.

There are many references to Bacchanalian delights and lusty bawdiness in Iolo's papers, and it bears repeating that in pre-Nonconformist Wales many males of Iolo's generation believed that sexual pleasure was a civilizing force. The eighteenth century was the age of sexually-charged novels like *Moll Flanders*, *Tom Jones* and *Fanny Hill*, and the uncensored correspondence of the celebrated Morris brothers provides abundant testimony that Welshmen were more than capable of behaving badly.[36] Libidinous males in Georgian London were never short of whores. There were up to 30,000 public streetwalkers in London[37] and a wide range of enticing bawdy-houses and bordellos where harlots like Polly Peacham and Sarah Frome were vigorously impregnated by the likes of Lewis Morris,[38] whom Iolo despised as 'an infidel, a Debauchee and a most abominable lyar and imposter'.[39] Another prominent figure with whom he became associated was George, Prince of Wales, to whom Iolo, with great misgivings, dedicated his anthology of English poems in 1794.[40] This royal scamp was not only a wilful spendthrift but also a regular frequenter of a flagellation house in Covent Garden. 'It is not known', claimed one observer waspishly, 'whether the Royal Wrist wielded the whip or whether the Royal Buttocks submitted to it.'[41] Pleasure-seeking and what neo-classicists called 'low cheerfulness' were thus integral parts of London life, and many of the poems, satires, squibs and lampoons which Iolo composed, mostly from the 1790s onwards, are foreshadowed in his early writings which were based on his experiences in rumbustious Gwyneddigion meetings and as a beguiling entertainer in drinking clubs favoured by stonecutters.[42]

[36] For some examples of this material in its original form, see NLW 600E, letters dated 23 October 1753, 24 November, 19 December 1754, 3 October 1755, 18 June, 13, 18 September, 11 October, 1 November 1757. See also Martin Davis, 'Hanes Cymdeithasol Meirionnydd 1750–1859' (unpublished University of Wales MA thesis, 1987), pp. 187–90; Rhiannon Thomas, 'William Vaughan: Carwr Llên a Maswedd', *Taliesin*, 70 (1990), 69–76; Alun R. Jones, 'Lewis Morris and "Honest Mr Vaughan" of Nannau and Corsygedol', *JMHRS*, XIII, part 1 (1998), 31–42.

[37] Roy Porter, 'Material Pleasures in the Consumer Society' in Roy Porter and Marie Mulvey Roberts (eds.), *Pleasure in the Eighteenth Century* (Basingstoke, 1996), p. 34.

[38] BL Add. 14929, pp. 18, 152; BL Add. 14937, p. 286; Huw Jones, *Diddanwch Teuluaidd* (Llundain, 1763), pp. 150–2, 179–83; *ALMA*, I, pp. 201–2; ibid., II, p. 935; Bedwyr Lewis Jones, 'Rhyddiaith y Morrisiaid' in Geraint Bowen (ed.), *Y Traddodiad Rhyddiaith* (Llandysul, 1970), p. 281.

[39] Hugh Owen, *The Life and Works of Lewis Morris (Llewelyn Ddu o Fôn) 1701–1765* (Anglesey Antiquarian Society and Field Club, 1951), p. civ. Iolo believed that Morris was a literary pygmy: 'Is not Lewis Morris, think you, one of these diminutive beings?' *CIM*, I, p. 553, Iolo Morganwg to Walter Davies (Gwallter Mechain), 12 March 1793.

[40] Williams: *PLP*, I, p. [v]; *CIM*, I, pp. 491–4, Iolo Morganwg to George, Prince of Wales, [?June 1792].

[41] Ephraim J. Burford, *Wits, Wenchers and Wantons. London's Low Life: Covent Garden in the Eighteenth Century* (London, 1986), p. 230.

[42] Bedwyr Lewis Jones, 'Lewis Morris a Goronwy Owen: "Digrifwch Llawen" a "Sobrwydd Synhwyrol"' in J. E. Caerwyn Williams (ed.), *Ysgrifau Beirniadol*, X (Dinbych, 1977), pp. 290–308.

Iolo once described the Bull in Walbrook as 'a very creditable bawdy house'[43] and, although it was not as seedy as he made out, it often rang to the sounds of Rabelaisian bawdiness and obscenity. Lewis Morris, a bon viveur who delighted in carnal indiscretions, believed that the poets, wags and humorists who frequented clubs, societies and eisteddfodau were 'inclined to buffoonry, dirty language, and indecent expressions'.[44] When testosterone raged mightily among its young bucks, the Gwyneddigion Society had a reputation for bawdy sexual bravado. Relatively lax censorship laws by this time meant that a wide range of erotic books was available at booksellers,[45] titillating images of the female body abounded, and lustful young men in clubs and societies spiced poems and songs with sexually explicit material. This did not necessarily mean that Welshmen were required to visit the metropolis to avail themselves of what Welsh writers called *digrifwch* (amusement). Welsh-language interludes and ballads were drenched with sexual innuendo, raffish gentlemen and aspiring middling sorts derived sexual gratification from coarse verse and prose declaimed in drinking parties and bardic contests, and some supposedly strait-laced Calvinistic Methodists were thought to be susceptible to carnal lusts.[46] Even the Enlightenment, by exalting the body, stimulated a 'hedonistic liberation of the libido'.[47]

Well aware of Iolo's penchant for racy anecdotes and jokes, the high-spirited Gwyneddigion, led by Siôn Ceiriog and Robin Ddu yr Ail o Fôn, encouraged him to brag about his and their sexual exploits. He obliged with a few lines in the *cywydd* metre praising Siôn Ceiriog for his sexual prowess:

> Bwch ydyw iw ryw a'i rin,
> Diawlig am ledu deulin;
> Marchaidd ymhlîth y merched.
>
> (He is a buck by nature and a buck to his sex,
> A devilish one for spreading two knees;
> A stallion amongst the girls.)[48]

Iolo was familiar with Dafydd ap Gwilym's 'Cywydd y Gal' (A *cywydd* to the penis) and, to his friends' great delight, he responded with a bawdy song entitled

---

[43] *CIM*, I, p. 447, Iolo Morganwg to William Meyler, [?1792].
[44] *ALMA*, II, p. 525.
[45] Karen Harvey, *Reading Sex in the Eighteenth Century: Bodies and Gender in English Erotic Culture* (Cambridge, 2004), p. 41.
[46] NLW 67A, pp. 57–68; Geraint H. Jenkins, '"Peth Erchyll Iawn" oedd Methodistiaeth', *LlC*, 17, nos. 3 and 4 (1993), 199–201.
[47] Roy Porter, 'Mixed Feelings: The Enlightenment and Sexuality in Eighteenth-Century Britain' in Paul-Gabriel Boucé (ed.), *Sexuality in Eighteenth-Century Britain* (Manchester, 1982), p. 5.
[48] *CIM*, I, pp. 133–4, 137 (trans.), Iolo Morganwg to Owen Jones (Owain Myfyr), 6 March 1779; ibid., I, pp. 143, 144–5 (trans.), John Edwards (Siôn Ceiriog) to Iolo Morganwg, 10 July 1779.

'Cân Morfydd i'r Gyllell gîg' (Morfydd's song to the meat knife) in which the fair Morfudd (Dafydd ap Gwilym's lover of yore) extolled the pleasures of the 'wondrous' blade deployed by the young Gwyneddigion stags as they tumbled into her bed.[49] Manly good fellowship and sexual conquests were celebrated in these circles and also wherever journeymen masons assembled. Iolo was evidently deeply immersed in this culture and he often spiced his songs with lewd or misogynistic references.[50]

One striking example is 'The Stonecut[t]er's Song', to be sung to the tune 'a cobbler there was and he lived in his stall', which Iolo composed while working in a statuary workshop in Westminster.[51] This drinking song-cum-sexual fantasy begins as follows:

> A young stonecutter once did in Westminster dwell
> Who for mirth and good humour did many excell
> No lad more expert wielded chizel and mallet
> He could sing a good song and eke make a good ballet
> . . . Dery Down

and is notable for the deft way in which Iolo deploys the tools of his trade as euphemisms for vigorous fornication. The song is replete with double entendres ('drill', 'tool', 'work'd') as the young stonemason eventually has his way and 'works' his lover with 'a well-tempered Tool'. Perhaps emboldened by the reception this song received, Iolo also composed a more raunchy eulogy to the stonecutter in a Welsh *cywydd*.[52] Here the central erotic metaphor was more explicit:

> naddwr maen yn ddewr a maith
> a naddwr awenyddiaith
> a chwyraidd wyf a chywrain
> yn naddu serch ar ferch fain
> . . .
> myn Dyn da naddu mun deg
> a gyrri arni garreg.

---

[49] NLW 21390E, nos. 22, 23; NLW 21388E, no. 26; *CIM*, I, pp. 134–5, 138–9 (trans.), Iolo Morganwg to Owen Jones (Owain Myfyr), 6 March 1779.

[50] NLW 21390E, no. 31; NLW 21391E, nos. 6, 10.

[51] NLW 21392F, pp. 73–4. Parts of the poem are either illegible or have faded away completely. With the aid of an ultraviolet lamp Mary-Ann Constantine has produced a text, with an analysis of the content, in 'Songs and Stones: Iolo Morganwg (1747–1826), Mason and Bard', *The Eighteenth Century: Theory and Interpretation*, 47, nos. 2–3 (2006), 242–7.

[52] NLW 21391E, no. 40. See also his jollier 'Cân y Maensaer' (The mason's song) in NLW 21391E, no. 41; *CRhIM*, pp. 45–7. Journeymen had a reputation for singing ribald songs and practising crude rituals. See Anna Clark, *The Struggle for the Breeches: Gender and the Making of the British Working Class* (London, 1995), p. 33.

> (a hewer of stone brave and long-lasting
> and a hewer of poesy
> and I am accomplished and skilful
> in hewing lust on a slender girl
> . . .
>
> a good Man will hew a fair maiden
> and drive his stone into her.)

One suspects that Iolo and his friends practised and perhaps relished the ribaldry more than the sex, and these defiant and amusingly vulgar works can be seen as an early foretaste of Iolo's unconventional way of writing. In the eyes of the pious, he was a disruptive and amoral presence, while those who knew of his taste for the satires of Pope and Swift were quite possibly aware that such a skilful purveyor of lewd poems might also begin to turn his hand to singing prurient or even seditious songs about kings and priests.

Iolo also discovered that venturing out of Wales pushed him towards publications that otherwise he might never have been able to buy or read. In order to exaggerate his attainments as a young autodidact he liked to give the impression that Wales lagged behind in the enormous surge in the demand for, and supply of, books.[53] But the impact of the London-generated urban culture was deeply felt in Glamorgan. Here the gentry and middling sorts avidly embraced new leisure and cultural forms, as well as the fashions and tastes of the metropolis.[54] Moreover, thanks to the proliferation of printing presses and bookshops, subscription ventures, book clubs, circulating schools and libraries, as well as the upsurge in religious revivalism, an explosion of reading occurred throughout Wales during Iolo's lifetime.[55] By the end of the eighteenth century nearly every town of consequence in Wales had at least one printing press[56] and this stimulated a striking take-off in the output of publications. In Iolo's own backyard Cowbridge could boast a diocesan library and a flourishing book club. In 1769–70 Rhys Thomas, Iolo's friend and an experienced printer, brought his press at Llandovery to the town and guided most of John Walters's celebrated Welsh dictionary through each stage of publication.[57]

Yet, in terms of access to diverse reading matter, leaving Wales, even for four years only, was a boon to someone who was determined to improve his mind

---

[53] NLW 21387E, no. 9.
[54] Jenkins, *The Making of a Ruling Class*, chapter 9.
[55] Geraint H. Jenkins, 'The Eighteenth Century' in Philip Henry Jones and Eiluned Rees (eds.), *A Nation and its Books: A History of the Book in Wales* (Aberystwyth, 1998), pp. 109–22.
[56] Eiluned Rees, 'Developments in the Book Trade in Eighteenth-Century Wales', *The Library*, 5th series, 24 (1969), 33.
[57] Brian Ll. James, 'The Cowbridge Printers' in Stewart Williams (ed.), *Glamorgan Historian, 4* (Cowbridge, 1967), pp. 231–44.

and get on in life. On his travels Iolo 'picked up a little superficial knowledge of many things'[58] and his sojourn in London was clearly decisive. By frequenting coffee-houses, taverns and clubs – ideal places for reading as well as conversation – he kept in close touch with the world of English letters and affairs of the realm. Grub Street hacks and sages kept him on his toes, and there were dozens of daily and weekly newspapers to pore over. Most of all, there was a bewildering range and quantity of printed books begging to be bought by bibliophiles like Iolo. A fourfold increase in printed output occurred in the quarter following the end of extra-statutory perpetual copyright in 1774,[59] and Iolo could not but gawp at the array of cheap books, reprints, anthologies, adaptations and books published in parts, which caught his eye as he wandered through the streets and alleys where booksellers sold and auctioned their wares.[60] Through the London Welsh, more especially the good offices of Richard Morris and Owain Myfyr, Iolo gained access to critically important Welsh manuscripts and books, among them the poems of Dafydd ap Gwilym and Lewis Morris's ill-fated compendium 'Celtic Remains'. He read Ellis Wynne's *Gweledigaetheu y Bardd Cwsc* (The Visions of the Sleeping Bard) and Theophilus Evans's *Drych y Prif Oesoedd* (Mirror of the Early Ages), both early eighteenth-century classics, in London, and had the temerity to instruct his father to forward to him no less bulky a tome than Edward Lhuyd's magisterial *Archaeologia Britannica*,[61] a quarto volume which weighed in at 440 pages.

Most of all, Iolo enjoyed the opportunity and the freedom to enhance his powers of understanding by reading books on the philosophy of knowledge. His normally eclectic mind now focused on the notion of benevolence. Like many 'natural geniuses' of the age, Iolo immersed himself in the 'cult of feeling'.[62] His starting-point was Locke, from whom he learned that people's knowledge of the world around them is founded on perception. He moved on to Hume's *A Treatise of Human Nature* (1739–40), which taught him that opening up our sensitive faculties – feeling and perception – enriches the imagination, thereby raising the intriguing question of whether the authority of experience might

---

[58] NLW 21387E, no. 9.
[59] William St Clair, *The Reading Nation in the Romantic Period* (Cambridge, 2004), p. 118.
[60] Terry Belanger, 'Publishers and Writers in Eighteenth-Century England' in Isabel Rivers (ed.), *Books and Their Readers in Eighteenth-Century England* (Leicester, 1982), pp. 18–20; James Raven, 'The Book Trades' in Isabel Rivers (ed.), *Books and Their Readers in Eighteenth-Century England: New Essays* (London, 2001), pp. 1–34.
[61] *CIM*, I, p. 111, Iolo Morganwg to Owen Jones (Owain Myfyr), 25 January 1776; ibid., I, p. 118, Iolo Morganwg to Edward William(s), [?8 February 1776].
[62] Thomas A. Roberts, *The Concept of Benevolence: Aspects of Eighteenth-Century Moral Philosophy* (London, 1973); Janet Todd, *Sensibility: An Introduction* (London, 1986); John Mullan, *Sentiment and Sociability: The Language of Feeling in the Eighteenth Century* (Oxford, 1988); G. J. Barker-Benfield, *The Culture of Sensibility: Sex and Society in Eighteenth-Century Britain* (London, 1992).

itself be construed as being no more than fiction.[63] He then turned to works of sentimental fiction, like Rousseau's *Julie, ou la nouvelle Héloïse* (1761), a sentimental love story, based on the intense emotional experiences of the ill-fated heroine who fell in love with her tutor, Saint-Preux. Both in French and English, the novel was a bestseller and Iolo was clearly drawn to it by its epistolary form and the new emphasis on benevolent paternalism and natural affection, ideas which were assuming greater prominence in the religious discourse of the period.[64]

Iolo's own Romantic persona, as well as his ability to internalize the sufferings of others and empathize with them, was also enriched by the works of Henry Mackenzie, the Anglo-Scot lawyer and man of letters who was one of Burns's bosom favourites. Iolo's admiration for Burns came later,[65] but he bought a copy of Mackenzie's remarkably influential novel *The Man of Feeling* (1771), a work which helped him to develop a language of feeling and, as he read profusely in a freezing garret in London or a foul-smelling cowhouse on the outskirts, to understand the workings of the human mind.[66] He was so taken by Mackenzie's third and last novel, *Julia de Roubigné* (1777) – a work suffused with tear-laden accounts of the shocking treatment suffered by slaves – that he transcribed excerpts from it.[67] *Julia de Roubigné* was written in the form of unanswered letters and it is significant, too, that Iolo transcribed some of the letters of Clement XIV (Ganganelli), a virtuous, humble and peace-loving man who was Pope from 1769 to 1774 and who was considered a shining example of a compassionate benevolist who had shown 'sparks of genius' from an early age.[68]

Thus did Iolo become a devotee of the cult of sensibility. Benevolence was an affection or a passion which prompted individuals to be compassionate towards others, to shed tears on behalf of the underprivileged and the oppressed, and to promote their well-being and happiness. Marilyn Butler has noted that 'humanitarian feeling for the real-life underdog is a strong vein from the 1760s to the 1790s, often echoing real-life campaigns for reform'.[69] As one of the

---

[63] NLW 21407C, nos. 2, 5; NLW 13136A, pp. 137–63.
[64] NLW 21326A, unpaginated; Jean-Jacques Rousseau, *Eloisa: or, a Series of Original Letters, translated by William Kenrick, 1803* (facsimile repr., 2 vols., Oxford, 1989); Jane Rendall, 'Feminizing the Enlightenment: The Problem of Sensibility' in Martin Fitzpatrick, Peter Jones, Christa Knellwolf and Iain McCalman (eds.), *The Enlightenment World* (London, 2004), pp. 258–9.
[65] *Truth against the World*, pp. 70–1.
[66] NLW 21407C, no. 1; NLW 21422E, no. 1.
[67] Henry Mackenzie, *Julia de Roubigné*, ed. Susan Manning (East Linton, 1999); NLW 21428E, no. 4; NLW 21326A.
[68] *Interesting Letters of Pope Clement XIV (Ganganelli)* (3 vols., London, 1777), I, pp. ii–iii; NLW 21428E, no. 5.
[69] Marilyn Butler, *Romantics, Rebels and Reactionaries: English Literature and its Background 1760–1830* (Oxford, 1981), p. 31.

Welsh underdogs himself, Iolo was well placed to embrace these sensibilities and in his first published English poem, 'On first hearing the Cuckoo', in July 1775, he cried:

> Let me employ the present hour,
> In works of sweet benevolence.[70]

A few months later, under the pen-name 'Flimstoniensis', he published 'Ode to Benevolence' in the *Kentish Gazette* in which he maintained that a Welsh bard was singularly well equipped to express sympathy towards the victims of poverty, wars and slavery:

> The Bard can feel. Touch'd by thy rankling smart,
> Sore feel th'envenomed edge that rends thy bleeding heart.[71]

On occasions he voiced a combination of sentimentalism and Enlightenment rationalism:

> The pupil of *Innocence*, *Friendship*, and *Peace*,
> My soul with *Benevolence* fraught;
> This life I will spend, and in *Wisdom* increase,
> And *Reason* shall govern my thought.
>
> The victims of *Sorrow* shall call me their friend,
> I feel, and partake, of their woe;
> To the whole human race my *good-will* shall extend,
> And I'll wish I had *more* to bestow.[72]

In his pastorals, 'Ideal Grief or modern fine feelings'[73] surfaced on many occasions as he increasingly advocated the view that humanity entailed benevolence, morality and justice. Thereafter, during his journey through life, Iolo remained inspired by the ethic of benevolence and its implications for mankind. Writing in the early 1790s, and drawing by that stage on the outcome of the Atlantic revolutions, he emphasized the utmost importance of 'ideas of morality, of Benevolence, Justice, Liberty, Peace. In short of all those sublimely benign virtues that constitute the transcendently lovely Christian Religion'.[74]

---

[70] *The Town and Country Magazine*, VII (July, 1775), 382. See also 'To the Cuckoo', Williams: *PLP*, I, pp. 49–53, for a 'considerably altered' version.
[71] *Kentish Gazette*, 31 January–3 February 1776; NLW 13170B, p. 65.
[72] Williams: *PLP*, I, p. 107.
[73] NLW 13170B, pp. 42–4.
[74] NLW 21387E, no. 23.

Many of the pastorals composed by Iolo during his sojourn in south-east England bear the influence of the works of Shenstone and Collins and reflect a genre dismissed by E. P. Thompson as 'effete pastoral idealizations'.[75] They evoke familiar rural images – harmonious harvest-making, seclusion from urban strife, the joys of courtship – and were, unwittingly perhaps, supportive of the 'anaesthetising tradition'[76] which prevailed under Old Arrogance. Yet, some of Iolo's poems, while not overtly political in their focus, posed questions in a general way about the misuse of power and wealth, about violence and war (he refers to 'intestine broils' and 'mangled hides'),[77] and the possibility that seeing oppressors swinging from a gibbet might count as a 'devilish good thing'.[78] There is nothing, however, to suggest that Iolo was actively concerned with contemporary politics at this time. He does not appear to have associated himself with extra-parliamentary associations like the Society for Constitutional Information or the Society of Gentlemen Supporters of the Bill of Rights and, although he later came to know Robert Morris, the first secretary of the latter Society, he took no part in the Wilkes controversy.

As the most passive of the Celtic nations, Wales was 'perhaps less excited by the conflict [i. e. the American War of Independence] than any other country in the British Isles'.[79] Living in London and Kent, however, Iolo was better placed than most of his countrymen to keep abreast of the constitutional dispute and the hostilities which broke out in April 1775. London newspapers kept him informed of events and he may well have been struck by rousing accounts – 'the cry of young and old is liberty or death' – published in the *Kentish Gazette* or the *Canterbury Journal*.[80] Never a champion of things military, he penned a Welsh ode calling for conciliation and peace,[81] and during the lengthy period of heavy snow and granite-like frosts in January and February 1776 he dreaded the prospect of atrocities and human losses: 'There is a vengance plainly attending this affair, the blood-thirsty villains will not percieve this till it is too late.'[82] By this stage, too, he was deeply interested (and moved) by the longstanding legend, maintained in print and word of mouth, that Madog (or Madoc) ab Owain Gwynedd had discovered America during a voyage from Wales in 1170 and that a tribe of Mandans, Madoc's lost descendants, were

---

[75] E. P. Thompson, *The Romantics: England in a Revolutionary Age* (Woodbridge, 1997), p. 12.
[76] John Goodridge, *Rural Life in Eighteenth-Century English Poetry* (Cambridge, 1995), p. 87. See also Carl Woodring, *Politics in English Romantic Poetry* (Cambridge, Mass., 1970).
[77] 'Extract from the Head of the Rock. A Poem', *The Town and Country Magazine*, VII (December, 1775), 663.
[78] NLW 21328A, pp. 135–6.
[79] Stephen Conway, *The British Isles and the War of American Independence* (Oxford, 2000), p. 135.
[80] *Kentish Gazette*, no. 811, 10–14 February 1776.
[81] NLW 13122B, pp. 39–43. See also J. H. Davies, *A Bibliography of Welsh Ballads printed in the 18th Century* (London, 1911), pp. xvi, xvii–xviii, 100–1.
[82] *CIM*, I, p. 117, Iolo Morganwg to Edward William(s), [?8 February 1776].

still inhabiting the upper reaches of the Missouri.[83] As we shall see, the Madoc controversy later acquired a palpable political edge, one which Iolo did not hesitate to exploit as he gained a greater awareness of events in the New World.

Although life in London and Kent thus offered Iolo a broader view on life in general – a greater selection of books, magazines and newspapers to read, convivial drinking parties as well as the pleasures of the flesh, an opportunity to hone his skills as a poet, and an introduction to hotly-debated political issues – he was never entirely content with his lot during what he later referred to as 'useless rambles'.[84] He often sank into melancholy and pined for 'Old Cambria', especially his 'native cot' in Glamorgan.[85] Urban life – its fogs, mists and smells – aggravated his asthma and he feared that his manners and morals were being undermined by living among such 'a vile debauched race of men'.[86] A less than streetwise young stonemason like Iolo was often at the mercy of unscrupulous employers like Deveson as well as roguish customers. Although hostile characterizations of the Welsh were in decline by the latter half of the eighteenth century, 'poor Taff' still figured as a penurious, ignorant, self-despising creature in prints and cartoons. The image of *Saint-David for Wales* (1781) portrays Taffy, complete with leeks, cheese, ale and a fish strapped to the saddle of his goat, as a thief,[87] and the fact that Welsh people like Iolo were able to avail themselves of job opportunities in England was the cause of considerable resentment. Vulnerable to racist prejudice, the Welsh were often depicted by the English as lesser beings to be pitied or derided.[88] Iolo was plainly taken aback by the 'opprobrious epithets'[89] showered on him by English stonemasons, especially by that 'ignorant set of blockheads' at Sandwich who had no intention of obeying the commands of the Welsh 'Taffy' placed at their head by John Deveson.[90] Unnerved by this barrage of anti-Welshness, Iolo launched his own aggressive counterblast in Welsh verse:

> Y Saeson cochion cuchiog, – wff iddynt!
>   Hyll ydynt a llidiog;
> Hîl Rhonwen felen foliog,
> Dyna ddiawl! a'i dannedd ôg.

---

[83] Ibid.; Gwyn A. Williams, *Madoc: The Making of a Myth* (London, 1979), chapter 2.
[84] NLW 21387E, no. 9.
[85] NLW 21422E, no. 1; NLW 21423E, nos. 65, 75; NLW 21424, no. 35; NLW 21328A, pp. 169–78.
[86] *CIM*, I, pp. 101–2, Iolo Morganwg to Edward William(s), 3 February 1775; NLW 21428E, no. 2.
[87] Michael Duffy, *The Englishman and the Foreigner* (Cambridge, 1986), pp. 258–9. See also Peter Lord, *Words with Pictures: Welsh Images and Images of Wales in the Popular Press, 1640–1860* (Aberystwyth, 1995).
[88] Paul Langford, *Englishness Identified: Manners and Character 1650–1850* (Oxford, 2000), p. 314.
[89] NLW 21422E, no. 1.
[90] *CIM*, I, p. 107, Iolo Morganwg to Edward William(s), 13 September 1775.

Ni feidr y Sais brwysglais brwnt,
Na gwawd y tafawd na'r tant,
Eithr aml twrf a chwrf a ch–nt
Ymhlith meibion cochion Cent.

(The scowling, red-headed English be damned!
They are ugly and vicious;
The race of sallow, big-bellied Rhonwen,
– There's a devil! – with teeth like a harrow.

The foul Englishman with his impetuous voice
Knows not how to praise with poetry nor with music,
Yet there is often commotion and beer and c–nt
Among the red-headed sons of Kent.)[91]

Having read Joseph Cradock's outpouring of anti-Welsh sentiment in *Letters from Snowdon* (1770),[92] Iolo was in no mood to pull his punches. Smarting under these humiliations, his animosity towards the English ran deep.

Iolo was also deeply wounded by some of the brushes he had with writers in Grub Street. Easily needled by anti-Welsh gibes, he was fair game for those who amused themselves by goading or belittling young writers. On one occasion, while browsing in a bookseller's shop, he espied the famous Samuel Johnson, a man who never warmed to the Celts and who, according to his latest biographer, prided himself on his 'rough rudeness'.[93] Undaunted, Iolo approached him to seek his advice about which of three English grammars he should choose to buy. The great man scowled at him and gruffly replied: '*Either of them* will do for *you*, young man.' Iolo immediately felt his blood rising, and muttered: '*Then, Sir, to make sure of having the best, I will buy them all.*'[94] Thereafter he found little good to say of Johnson. At various times, he maintained that many of Johnson's ideas were 'truly ridiculous', that he was a proud, vain brute, and that he 'had always thought him mad'.[95] Iolo never forgot a slight or a snub, and bore grudges religiously.

If Iolo was outraged by the overbearing arrogance of the English, so too was he offended by repeated ridicule at the hands of people from north Wales. Although he found Owain Myfyr, Siôn Ceiriog and Robin Ddu yr Ail o Fôn extremely good company, he was not altogether at ease in the Venedotian-dominated environs of the London Welsh. Some members of

---

[91] Ibid., pp. 108–9.
[92] Ibid., I, p. 112, Iolo Morganwg to Owen Jones (Owain Myfyr), 25 January 1776.
[93] Peter Martin, *Samuel Johnson: A Biography* (London, 2008), p. 57.
[94] *RAEW*, pp. 27–8.
[95] NLW 21387E, nos. 9, 11; NLW 13144A, pp. 436–7; NLW 21401E, no. 3.

the Gwyneddigion Society found him an intensely irritating and boastful young man.[96] Iolo used to bridle whenever his Silurian accent and stubborn provincialism were held up to scorn: 'The north-Wales poets hav[e] always taken a liberty, bordering on unwarrantable licentiousness, of use[ing] their local words and phrases in their works; certainly a Silurian write[r] must be allowed the same priviledge.'[97] Obsessed by what he believed to be the jealousy and conceit of northerners, he even convinced himself that Richard Morris thoroughly disapproved of his criticisms of his brother Lewis's work, 'Celtic Remains': 'many times I have discovered the most malignant envy in his countenance; indeed he and many other great pretenders to uncommon skill in the Welsh Language I find fall greatly short of my expectations.'[98] This painful and disturbing experience stayed with him, so much so that he could never let such slights or expressions of disapproval pass without reacting furiously. Thin-skinned to the extreme, this Glamorgan mason, 'unborn to title or estate' and contemptuous of 'book-poring pedants' as well as insufferable north Walians, now yearned for 'Glamorgan's happy Land' and especially his 'native cot' in 'fair Davona's vale'.[99]

By 1777 the hue and cry over the John Charles affair had died down and Iolo decided to forsake the tainted air and 'tinsel charms'[100] of urban life in England for the comforting banks of the Thaw. Escaping from 'the silly Cit[y]'s malignant sneer / the coxcombs hissing cry',[101] he nursed deep-seated grievances against those who had ignored, patronized or derided him. His heightened sense of the self was reflected in his position as a 'man of feeling' in what seemed to him to be an unfeeling world. The spring in the prodigal son's step in 1773 had disappeared as he renewed his search for a fixed and regular income as a stonemason which would help him to blossom as a writer and as a custodian of Glamorgan's past.

---

[96] NLW 13140A, p. vii.
[97] *CIM*, I, p. 110, Iolo Morganwg to Owen Jones (Owain Myfyr), 25 January 1776.
[98] NLW 21285E, draft letter no. 779, Iolo Morganwg to John Walters, [?February 1775].
[99] Williams: *PLP*, I, pp. 24–36, 85–90; NLW 21328A, pp. 96, 177.
[100] NLW 21328A, p. 173.
[101] Ibid., p. 99.

3

'When he nobly for Liberty stood'

The period between Iolo's return to Glamorgan in 1777 and the outbreak of the French Revolution marked a decisive turning-point in his career. These were turbulent years, packed with many unhappy personal incidents, misadventures and misfortunes, not all of which were of his own making but which nevertheless left him deeply embittered. He took a wife, who bore him three children in this period, but his hopes of pursuing a lucrative career as a stonecutter were dashed by his chronic inability to handle his wife's debt-ridden inheritance and his own personal finances. Marital life brought 'too many cares and anxieties, too much bustle and business',[1] from which he often took refuge in his literary work. Still smarting from the gibes of some of the more malevolent Gwyneddigion, he found the works of Dafydd ap Gwilym a potent inspiration, so much so that he fashioned brilliant imitations of his *cywyddau*, a piece of literary deception which deceived the London Welsh and remained undetected until the early twentieth century. Studying Glamorgan's historical and literary traditions became 'the love of my heart' ('hoffder fy nghalon')[2] and, as he began to find poetry more congenial than chiselling stone, his debts mounted exponentially. By the mid-1780s his life was spiralling out of control and, following angry exchanges with creditors and lawyers, he was dispatched to the debtors' prison in Cardiff for twelve months. Although he used the time to read and write profusely, the whole experience proved to be a crushing psychological blow to such a self-absorbed and ambitious man. Prison changed him. He became prone to morbid depressions and irrational fears, and there is no mistaking his disenchantment with the established church and the politics of oligarchy. By 1789 he had emerged as the poet laureate[3] of the 'independent' cause in Glamorgan and, although he had not yet become politicized in the sense

---

[1] *CIM*, I, p. 234, Iolo Morganwg to Owen Jones (Owain Myfyr), 20 September 1783.
[2] Ibid., I, pp. 174, 175 (trans.), Iolo Morganwg to Owen Jones (Owain Myfyr), 15 February 1781.
[3] J. Philip Jenkins, 'Jacobites and Freemasons in Eighteenth-Century Wales', *WHR*, 9, no. 4 (1979), 404.

that French revolutionaries would have recognized, he was veering strongly towards Rational Dissent.

Iolo was barely thirty when he returned from London. He took a circuitous route in order to sample the archaeological delights of Avebury and to beg for stonecutting commissions from statuaries in Bath and Bristol. Henry Marsh of Bristol took him on as an assistant for several months, during which Iolo helped him to fashion the famous monument in Ross parish church to John Kyrle, the philanthropist and landscape designer who was eulogized by Pope as 'the Man of Ross'.[4] Such a prestigious undertaking was a feather in his cap and he must have expected similar commissions when he reached the Vale of Glamorgan in the summer of 1777. He at least hoped to be able to find regular work and that his previous misdemeanours had been forgotten, but he soon discovered that all was far from well. The gossipy denizens of Cowbridge, where 'so many love to pry and prate',[5] had long memories and were still suspicious of him, especially since he displayed no signs of contrition. He threw all his energy into finding work, but he and his brothers became increasingly cash-strapped. Miles and John were so disillusioned that they set sail for Jamaica in 1778, and Iolo was forced to resume his peripatetic ways, this time in the West Country, where he gained further experience as a stone- and marble-mason, and had several brushes with death on sloops which ferried him from port to port.[6]

By this stage his days as a bachelor were numbered. Sometime in 1778 he fell passionately in love with Margaret (or Peggy, as he always called her), the only daughter of Rees and Elinor Roberts of St Mary Church.[7] He found in 'my dearest dear, my Peggy, my love, my angel . . . every thing that warms my heart or pleases my taste . . . your sensibility, innocent simplicity, delicate modesty and unaffected sweetness of temper are the very beauties which my soul can taste'.[8] He sent this beloved 'Euron' (golden one) – his poetic name for her – supplies of sugar and kept a lock of her hair among his most treasured possessions.[9] A sceptic might suggest that Iolo was in such straitened circumstances that he urgently needed a wife of some means, but he was clearly smitten by Peggy. He pined for her when he was away and delighted in her company on his return. In a bid to return permanently to Glamorgan and be

---

[4] *RAEW*, p. 107n. For John Kyrle, see *ODNB*. The memorial was funded by Lady Constantia Dupplin.

[5] Iolo Davies, *'A Certaine Schoole': A History of the Grammar School at Cowbridge, Glamorgan* (Cowbridge, 1967), p. 376.

[6] *CIM*, I, pp. 172–3, Iolo Morganwg to Margaret (Peggy) Williams, 14 September [1780]; ibid., I, pp. 234–5, Iolo Morganwg to Owen Jones (Owain Myfyr), 20 September 1783.

[7] NLW 13141A, p. 111.

[8] *CIM*, I, pp. 127–8, Iolo Morganwg to Margaret (Peggy) Williams, [?1778].

[9] Ibid., p. 129; ibid., I, p. 149, Iolo Morganwg to [Margaret (Peggy) Williams], [?April 1780].

recognized as an experienced master craftsman, he arranged for printed handbills publicizing his skills to be distributed in the Cowbridge area. Capitalizing on his experience of having mastered his craft under the aegis of distinguished statuaries in London and elsewhere, he pronounced himself capable of making 'all sorts of *Chimney-pieces, Monuments, Tombs, Head-stones,* and every other Article in the Marble and Freestone-Masonry, in the newest and neatest Manner, and on the most reasonable Terms'.[10] What shines through very clearly in Iolo's papers is his deep pride in his occupational skills, the steadiness of his hand, the sharpness of his eye and the sureness of his touch.[11] In his songs, notably 'Cân y Maensaer' (The mason's song),[12] he trumpeted the character, skills and expertise of the stonecutter, and in one of his self-aggrandizing aphorisms he maintained that a mason was a greater asset to society than a judge.[13]

A class-driven element emerged in his writings as he struggled to find regular work. In his 'rational drinking-song', composed for the benefit of journeymen masons, he deplored the fact that such highly skilled and intelligent craftsmen were 'not always treated as they should be by those who, it is not very well known for what reason, assume the title of superiors'.[14] Iolo could speak with authority on the properties of various stones, marbles and other raw material, and as he assimilated the visual evidence of stone craftsmanship he began to fashion far-fetched anecdotes about fellow stonecutters like Richard and William Twrch, whom he claimed were descended from the celebrated poet Iorwerth Fynglwyd and who had supposedly designed and built the porch at Beaupré Castle.[15] Desperate for work, and bursting with grandiose plans, he urged Thomas Mansel Talbot of Margam Abbey to transform his estate into 'a kind of earthly paradise' characterized by an elegant round tower up to 500 feet high, sturdy farmhouses, whitewashed cottages, a school, and a wide variety of trees, orchards and gardens. Such an organic community, he maintained, would not only add lustre to Talbot's reputation as an aesthete, but would also offer artisans, craftsmen and freeholders the opportunity to exhibit their skills. Iolo argued – in shrewd political terms – that by retaining freehold leases within this community Talbot would 'thus obtain a considerable number of voices in your interest at any future election'. To clinch his argument he assured him that 'Benevolence joined to fortune and a fine taste are able to

---

[10] NLW 21420E, nos. 1–2.
[11] See, for instance, NLW 21431E, no. 29; NLW 13116E, pp. 346–59. See also Paul Joyner, *Artists in Wales c.1740–c.1851* (Aberystwyth, 1997), pp. 127–8, and Richard Suggett, 'Iolo Morganwg: Stonecutter, Builder, and Antiquary' in *Rattleskull Genius*, pp. 200–16.
[12] NLW 13146A, pp. 424–5.
[13] NLW 13137A, p. 202. See also NLW 21431E, no. 29.
[14] Williams: *PLP*, II, p. 80.
[15] NLW 13116E, pp. 131–42.

secure to their possessors all the glory this world can afford'.[16] His pleas, however, fell on deaf ears, and the elaborate plan he prepared for a proposed extension to Cowbridge town hall to accommodate the Courts of the Great Sessions was no more successful.[17] Once more Iolo was forced to look elsewhere – to Devon and Cornwall – for work. As his debts mounted, there was evidently much toil and trouble behind the scenes. Just as Robert Burns saw the prospect of an Excise appointment as a means of stabilizing his finances, so did Iolo contemplate a career change. Early in 1781 he sought support from local luminaries – Sir Humphrey Mackworth and the Revd Gervase Powell among them – for an application for the post of custom-house officer or tide waiter at Aberthaw, a post which commanded an annual salary of £30.[18] Since Iolo was more in the poacher than the gamekeeper mould, it is unlikely that he would ever have been appointed, but the fact that he was willing to consider abandoning his cherished vocation indicates that his finances were parlous.

But when Iolo was married by his mentor, the Revd John Walters, to his sweetheart Peggy Roberts at St Mary Church on 18 July 1781, he had every reason to believe that his fortunes would improve.[19] For one thing, she suited him admirably. A shrewd, level-headed woman, she was the perfect foil for her passionate and wayward husband. Her spelling and grammar may have been shaky, but she nursed her own literary aspirations and Iolo appreciated that she had 'a literary, even a philosophic, turn'.[20] She was well placed to pass judgement on his poems and to discuss philosophy and politics with him. Moreover, she would display extraordinary personal strength in coping with her husband's quirks of behaviour, unworldly ways and especially his penchant for 'bilding castels in the ayre'.[21] Often hurt and bewildered by his behaviour, and increasingly disconcerted by his unorthodox views, she stood by him through thick and thin. Iolo and Peggy remained together for forty-five years. Only death separated them, and Peggy outlived Iolo by just a matter of months.

Having slipped further and further into debt, Iolo also hoped that his marriage would improve his finances. Some months earlier his wife had inherited a twenty-eight acre farm in the parish of Rumney (known today as Pen y Pill farm) in Monmouthshire, and Iolo was convinced that this windfall would

---

[16] *CIM*, I, pp. 168–71, Iolo Morganwg to Thomas Mansel Talbot, 23 August 1780.
[17] NLW 21416E, nos. 27–9, 31.
[18] *CIM*, I, p. 178, Iolo Morganwg to Gervase Powell, 28 February 1781; ibid., I, pp. 179–80, Iolo Morganwg to Sir Herbert Mackworth, 1 March 1781.
[19] Glamorgan Archives, St Mary Church PR.
[20] *CIM*, II, p. 65, Iolo Morganwg to Mary Barker, 26 March [1798].
[21] Ibid., I, p. 713, Margaret (Peggy) Williams to Iolo Morganwg, 10 December 1794. Iolo had originally planned to call his anthology of English poems 'Castles in the Air'. NLW 21328A, title-page.

solve his financial worries at a stroke.[22] But the inheritance proved to be an encumbrance rather than a blessing. The property was in a poor state and was heavily mortgaged. Iolo had no head for business and he entrusted the task of settling his affairs and paying creditors to a solicitor, William Rees of Court Colman, and forwarded the relevant deeds and papers to him. According to Iolo, Rees prevaricated for two years and then refused to proceed with the matter or return the deeds.[23] In the meantime, Iolo overreached himself by embarking on a series of ill-judged ventures designed to raise money. To the dismay of his wife, he let land at favourable annual rents, tried his hand at farming, rented workshops in Cardiff and Wells for his trade as a mason, and took out a licence to sell tea, coffee and chocolate at his Flemingston home, thereby becoming, as he self-deprecatingly put it, 'a Jack of all trades'.[24] To add to this comedy of errors he bought a fifteen-ton sloop – which he grandly called the *Lion* – that shortly sank to the bottom of the Bristol Channel.[25] He turned his hand to too many things and everything he touched in the world of business seemed to turn to dust. Characteristically, rather than accept the responsibility for his plight, he blamed others for his run of misfortune and for the 'cares and anxieties . . . daily attendant on me'.[26] Tied to the marriage post, as he indelicately put it, he also became a father from July 1782 onwards. The birth of Margaret (also known as Peggy) was followed by that of Ann (known as Nancy) in January 1786.[27] Two infants to feed and worry over deepened his melancholy and the stresses and strains of keeping creditors at bay proved well-nigh intolerable.

Although to some degree Iolo was a victim of circumstances, he was also evidently poorly equipped to cope with his personal finances. To the detriment of his economic interests and domestic responsibilities, he devoted far too much of his time and creative energies to the pursuit of knowledge and especially his own literary passions. He was full of plans (many of them half-baked) and ambitions. He embarked on several small-scale schemes of horticultural improvements, acquired a deep knowledge of trees, flowers and animals, designed scientific experiments, and tinkered with ingenious inventions based

---

[22] NLW 21389E, 98/8; *CIM*, I, pp. 295–7, Iolo Morganwg to [George Hardinge], [?August 1787].
[23] Writing sometime in the late 1780s, Iolo said of Rees: 'Mr Rees has had in his hands this three year mortgage Deeds to the amount of £100 principal & interest which he promised to recover for me verbally & by Letters which I have but of late he has thrown off the mark refuses either to proceed or restore me the papers.' NLW 21387E, no. 16.
[24] *CIM*, I, p. 234, Iolo Morganwg to Owen Jones (Owain Myfyr), 20 September 1783; NLW 21410E, no. 20.
[25] NLW 21410E, no. 17; NLW 21422E, no. 12; NLW 21389E, 98/9.
[26] *CIM*, I, p. 235, Iolo Morganwg to Owen Jones (Owain Myfyr), 20 September 1783.
[27] Glamorgan Archives, Flemingston PR.

on 'true mathematical principles'.[28] His affection for Glamorgan increased by the day and nothing gave him greater ease and delight than studying its literary and historical past. As a searcher for, and an embellisher of, the truth, he delighted in fresh ideas and approaches. But while he mulled over the prospect of increasing the fecundity of salmon and trout in local rivers, of growing melons and dates, and of mastering the Japanese method of making paper,[29] his creditors were closing in. Even as he fathered his splendidly forged *cywyddau* on Dafydd ap Gwilym, collected data on dialects and speech-forms, and transcribed a mass of historical material, insolvency was looming.

One major cause of Iolo's abstraction from his financial affairs was his relationship with the Revd John Walters's two eldest sons, John and Daniel who, while drinking tea or punch in his company in Beaupré woods or simply by corresponding regularly, bolstered Iolo's self-esteem by convincing him that he should take heart at the prospect of becoming a major poet. John Walters junior served as headmaster of Cowbridge Grammar School and some of his publications, notably *Poems with Notes* (1780) and *Translated Specimens of Welsh Poetry* (1782), reveal him to have been an unusually gifted young man. When he took up a similar post at Ruthin, his brother Daniel succeeded him at Cowbridge.[30] Although Iolo was a good bit older than them, they became firm friends from 1778 onwards. More gullible than their father, the Walters brothers were not only sympathetic to Iolo's claims to rustic authenticity and natural genius but were also deeply impressed by the grandeur of his vision. Daniel Walters in particular was captivated by the 'ingenious . . . great Bard' and pandered to his vanity by claiming that his poems would honour any pen.[31] When Iolo claimed that the Muse had perished following his marriage, Daniel Walters chastised him for his lethargy and urged him to recant 'by weeping and gnashing of teeth, by fasting . . . by disciplining and mortifying, at least three times a day, your Jesuitical carcase and, lastly, by writing a poem entitled "The Muse's Resurrection after having been buried during the honeymoon in the marriage-bed".'[32] The three poets discussed the authenticity of Macpherson's ancient Scottish poems and the Chatterton controversy, and when Iolo dispatched drafts of his English poems to John Walters junior he was invited to use 'a judicious pencil' to soften the asperities in his 'Hymn to

---

[28] NLW 13138A, pp. 310–11; NLW 13143A, pp. 270–1; NLW 13149A, pp. 5–6.
[29] NLW 21414E, no. 19.
[30] Davies, *'A Certaine Schoole'*, pp. 375–9; G. J. Williams, 'Daniel Walters', *Y Llenor*, XX (1941), 176–82; idem, 'Daniel Walters: A Poet of the Vale' in Stewart Williams (ed.), *Glamorgan Historian, 3* (Cowbridge, 1966), pp. 238–43; *ODNB* s.v. John Walters.
[31] NLW 6514E, p. 18, Daniel Walters to John Walters, jun., 16 April 1783; *CIM*, I, pp. 192–3, Daniel Walters to Iolo Morganwg, 23 October 1781.
[32] *CIM*, I, p. 221, Daniel Walters to Iolo Morganwg, 1 October 1782.

the Devil'.[33] The premature death from consumption of these young brothers – Daniel in 1787 and John in 1789 – was a grievous blow to Iolo. Deprived of his most ardent cheerleaders in Glamorgan, he was forced to rely even more heavily on his association with luminaries among the London Welsh, notably Owen Jones (Owain Myfyr) but also the Merioneth-born grammarian William Owen Pughe. Without them, it promised to be a struggle to be noticed and heard.

In the meantime Iolo owed money to a great many professional people in Cowbridge and elsewhere.[34] Tiring of his empty promises, these creditors were losing patience by 1783–4. The leader of the pack was John Walton, a Cowbridge surgeon who, over a five-year period, had supplied Iolo with a variety of medicines, powders and nostrums, including pearl barley, julaps, bark, emetics, tinctures and oils, and who now believed it was 'high time our matters sho[uld] be settled'.[35] John Llewellin of Coedrhiglan, John Wood, a prominent Cardiff attorney, William Rees of Court Colman and Dr Morgan, a Llandaf surgeon, joined in the chorus of the aggrieved, and at one point Iolo and his wife and daughter fled across the Bristol Channel to avoid them.[36] Sullen and resentful, Iolo did not endear himself to some of his neighbours by tarnishing their reputations in verse. He came to believe that some of them were stirring up mischief by spreading rumours and lies about his creditworthiness. Driven by fury, he resorted to verbal abuse. Sometime around 1786 he was accused by one Watkin Lloyd of writing a scurrilous song about his wife Gwenllian and of distributing copies of it in Flemingston.[37] Iolo strenuously denied the charge, but his penchant for composing bawdy misogynist songs and the fact that two copies of 'Cân Gwenn' figure in his papers strongly suggests that he was the culprit.[38] It was an ill-advised poem; intemperate in tone, it depicted Gwenllian Lloyd as a mendacious gossip who deserved to be strung up or burned to a cinder. Heated exchanges followed, and matters came to a head when Iolo was confronted by Gwenllian Lloyd, her daughter Cati and her sister-in-law who collectively showered him with abuse, pelted his four-year-old daughter Margaret with stones and then, with the help of Watkin Lloyd and a henchman, seized him, knocked him down and kicked him repeatedly. 'I will murder you now', cried Watkin Lloyd, and had not

---

[33] Ibid., I, p. 189, John Walters, jun., to Iolo Morganwg, 13 April 1781.
[34] NLW 21389E, 99, nos. 16, 20, 27, 47.
[35] *CIM*, I, pp. 249–51, John Walton to Iolo Morganwg, 22 October 1783.
[36] Ibid., I, pp. 277–8, Thomas Williams to Iolo Morganwg and Margaret (Peggy) Williams, 9 [October] 1785.
[37] NLW 21410E, no. 23.
[38] NLW 21388E, no. 28; NLW 21414E, no. 18. For the general context, see Bernard Capp, *When Gossips Meet: Women, Family, and Neighbourhood in Early Modern England* (Oxford, 2003) and Richard Suggett, 'Slander in Early-Modern Wales', *BBCS*, XXXIX (1992), 119–53.

Iolo's mother-in-law intervened he might have suffered a worse fate than heavy bruising.[39] Edgy and unpredictable, Iolo was especially scornful of scolding women and malicious gossips. 'Nani foul feat of Wentloog Marsh' ('Nani Gamp aflan o Forfa Gwaunllwg') and 'wry-mouthed Bessy' ('Bessi fingam') were just two obstreperous women who felt the rough edge of Iolo's tongue.[40]

Matters came to a head in the summer of 1786. It is safe to assume that at this point his stock had never been lower among the petite bourgeoisie of Cowbridge and the plebeian inhabitants of Flemingston.[41] Saddled with debts which were increasing daily and unable to control his foul temper, he had made many enemies and antagonists. Once cajoling, pleading and dunning had failed, his major creditors turned to the courts. At the suit of John Walton and Evan Griffith of Pen-llin, Iolo was arrested on 6 August 1786 and bundled off to the debtors' prison in Cardiff with just threepence in his pocket.[42] Over the course of the eighteenth century the expansion of commercial culture and the proliferation of petty credit transactions had carried serious financial risks for vulnerable borrowers and consumers.[43] As far as Iolo was concerned, his post-marital financial encumbrances, not to mention his disorderly way of life, had compounded these problems. His case was by no means unique. The fictional works of Fielding, Smollett and especially Dickens are littered with examples of the vagaries of credit and of how people who had fallen on hard times became ensnared by a host of petty debts.[44] John Howard's famous survey of English and Welsh gaols, *The State of the Prisons in England and Wales* (1777), reveals that overall about half of all the inmates were debtors, but that in Wales the total number of debtors was more

---

[39] NLW 21410E, no. 23.
[40] NLW 21391E, no. 6; NLW 13091E, p. 95. See also his unlovely epitaph to an old maid in NLW 21392F, no. 48ᵛ. Cf. *CRhIM*, pp. 62–3.
[41] See the verses, composed by Iolo in the late 1780s and copied on to a letter from John Walters, regarding a supposed visit by a farmer's son from the *Blaenau* who was shocked to discover how abusive Flemingston people were when he visited his girlfriend. NLW 21283E, no. 520.
[42] NLW 21389E, 98, nos. 12–13.
[43] Margot C. Finn, *The Character of Credit: Personal Debt in English Culture, 1740–1914* (Cambridge, 2003).
[44] Joanna Innes, 'The King's Bench Prison in the Later Eighteenth Century: Law, Authority and Order in a London Debtors' Prison' in John Brewer and John Styles (eds.), *An Ungovernable People: The English and their Law in the Seventeenth and Eighteenth Centuries* (London, 1980), pp. 250–98; Margaret DeLacy, *Prison Reform in Lancashire, 1700–1850: A Study in Local Administration* (Manchester, 1986); Norval Morris and David J. Rothman (eds.), *The Oxford History of the Prison* (Oxford, 1995); Philip Woodfine, 'Debtors, Prisons, and Petitions in Eighteenth-Century England', *Eighteenth-Century Life*, 30, no. 2 (2006), 1–31. For conditions in Swansea and Carmarthen prisons, see Roger Lee Brown, 'Swansea Debtors' Gaol in the Nineteenth Century', *Morgannwg*, XVII (1973), 10–24, and Richard W. Ireland, *'A Want of Order and Good Discipline': Rules, Discretion and the Victorian Prison* (Cardiff, 2007).

than double that of felons.[45] Creditors were entitled to seize and imprison debtors and ensure that they were held in gaol until they redeemed their debts. A person's body, in effect, was retained in surety for his estate. So long as the prisoner remained incarcerated, no creditor could touch his estate. But although the law for recovery of debt did not permit creditors to secure the lands or funds of a defaulter, they were able to determine the length a debtor spent in gaol by prolonging negotiations for a settlement. In Iolo's case, twelve months passed before he was released.

Although Iolo often bemoaned his penal experience, Cardiff prison was clearly not a Pentonville or a Bastille. True, it was wretched, even ruinous, in appearance, and calls for improvements became increasingly clamorous from the 1770s,[46] but its lax and disorderly routine meant that the lot of a debtor was nowhere near as harsh as that suffered by a hardened convicted felon or by some of the early Protestant Dissenters whose history Iolo had come to know well. John Howard, who was painfully aware that the gaol was unfit for purpose, called on the commissioners of peace for Glamorgan to bestir themselves and expedite the building of a new prison for felons and debtors:

> The New Gaol, not finished, is to consist of three separate Houses, with Courtyards between them. The Old Gaol to be taken down; and in Front (where it now stands) is to be the House for Debtors: a Court behind it – Then the Gaoler's House: this is built; two rooms on a floor. Behind it, the Felons Court-yard; and beyond that, their House or Wards; which are also built: on the ground-floor, a small room for the Turnkey; and three vaulted rooms: above them three chambers, twelve feet and a half by ten.[47]

In the event, however, few major improvements were effected and the building of a new county gaol was delayed until 1832–3. Already convinced that he had been both wronged and demeaned, Iolo was thus forced to serve his sentence in an unreformed debtors' prison.

It was nevertheless of some comfort to him that civil prisoners enjoyed certain freedoms and privileges denied to hardened criminals. Relatives and friends of debtors were able to visit freely and bring clothes, food, drink, books, letters and paper with them. The law required that debtors and criminals be afforded separate sleeping quarters, and cohabitation between husband and wife was often permitted. We know that Iolo's room in Cardiff gaol included two tables, a bed, two chairs, a pair of shelves, a bellows, a pair of tongs, a poker, a teapot, two cups and saucers, a knife and fork, a pewter spoon and a

---

[45] John Howard, *The State of the Prisons in England and Wales* (Warrington, 1777), pp. 453–75.
[46] William Rees, *Cardiff: A History of the City* (2nd edn., Cardiff, 1969), pp. 152–3.
[47] Howard, *The State of the Prisons in England and Wales*, p. 474.

teaspoon, two chipped plates, a jug and a saucepan.[48] His wife supplied him with copious reading matter and writing paper, and his confinement proved extremely productive in terms of his intellectual development. Over the year his bardo-druidic vision began to crystallize and he managed to complete the bulk of his favourite manuscript, 'Cyfrinach Beirdd Ynys Prydain' (The Secret of the Bards of the Isle of Britain), a work which, not for the want of trying, he was never able to publish during his lifetime.[49] His wife also spent many nights sleeping with him and it was here that Iolo's only son, Taliesin (baptized 16 September 1787), was conceived.[50] Such arrangements, often haphazard and casual, provided consolations which helped to alleviate the misery of being surrounded by unfriendly felons and morose debtors.

To a considerable degree the nature of the regime was determined by the willingness of a prisoner to ingratiate himself with the gaoler and the turnkey, pay the required entry and subsistence fees promptly, and submit himself to prison etiquette. As long as a prisoner paid up with a smile and behaved himself, he was treated as a dependable customer by the gaoler. Any other course of action invited retribution. A gaoler could make the life of an imprisoned debtor extremely uncomfortable, even to the extent of denying him privileges to which he was legally entitled. Most persons in Iolo's position would have kept their head down, obeyed the rules and prayed for early release. But Iolo's instinctive reaction was to challenge authority, question rules and regulations, and rage at the injustices heaped upon him. On his arrival in August 1786 he immediately raised the hackles of the gaoler Thomas Morgan by sending a letter of complaint to the Chief Justices of the Courts of the Great Sessions regarding the exorbitant entry fee of half a crown. Once he got wind of this, Morgan loudly abused him and bruised his ribs by thrusting him against the rails of a staircase.[51] On another occasion, after Iolo had agreed to pay Morgan half a crown for permission to complete carving a monument in the prison's brewhouse, the gaoler reneged on the agreement by allowing another prisoner to set up a distillery in the brewhouse, thereby depriving Iolo of sufficient space to use his chisel and mallet.[52]

As an avowed man of feeling, Iolo was deeply affected by the plight of fellow debtors, many of whom were much poorer than him. As far back as the mid-seventeenth century radical groups like the Levellers and the Diggers had waged a sustained campaign against unjust confinement for debt, and during Iolo's day their radical rhetoric was revived by Wilkite supporters. Indeed, it

---

[48] NLW, Great Sessions P: Glamorgan Prothonotary Papers Post-1660, 2751 (August 1787).
[49] Taliesin Williams (ed.), *Cyfrinach Beirdd Ynys Prydain* (Abertawy, 1829); Williams: *IM*, pp. 375–8, 443.
[50] Glamorgan Archives, Flemingston PR.
[51] NLW 21389E, 98, no. 12.
[52] Ibid.

became fashionable for articulate prisoners with a grievance to set themselves up as enemies to the arbitrary and tyrannical nature of the law. Joanna Innes has described the growing protests against imprisonment for debt from the 1770s onwards as reflecting the ideas and rhetoric of resurgent political radicalism,[53] and during his captivity Iolo unquestionably steeped himself in the rights of debtors and underprivileged people and paraded himself as a champion of oppressed debtors. To the great irritation of the authorities, including the gaoler, Iolo employed his poetic gifts in the service of genuine victims of economic distress. In a clever, trenchant satire, entitled 'A Callendar of all the Debtors now Confined in Cardiff Gaol, who in the Creditor's opinion deserve to be hanged',[54] he held up to censure a legal system which instilled within impoverished, unfortunate people a profound hatred of authority and of the prison cell:

> Come read my new Ballad and here you shall find
> A list of poor Debtors in Cardiff Confined,
> Convicted of poverty, what a vile thing,
> And doom'd by their Creditors shortly to swing.
>
> Ned Williams a mason, whose case is not rare,
> Stands indicted for build[ing] huge Castles in air,
> And also for trespass, a scandalous crime,
> On the grounds of Parnassus by scribbling a Rhime.
>
> The next William Freme, one well known thro' the land,
> As a Mason of note, but he built on the sand,
> Hard blew the fierce tempest, high swell'd the rude stream,
> And down came the building of poor William Freme.
>
> The third Evan Smith, one unmindful of Pelf,
> Convicted of proving a Rogue with himself.
> We know that where sense and good nature prevail
> These heineous offences well merit a Jail.
>
> William Meyrick, alas! brought his neck to the noose
> As wise men well know for he chased a wild goose,
> Some strongly suspect that his skull had a flaw
> When he tangled himself in the snares of the Law.
>
> Ah! poor Sandy Wilson, such whims to persue,
> In thinking attorneys were honest and true,
> Thou art punish'd severe for that error profound,
> In seeking for Justice where none was e'er found.

---

[53] Innes, 'The King's Bench Prison in the Later Eighteenth Century', pp. 290–8.
[54] NLW 21389E, 98, no. 4.

James Jacob must hang for not knowing a Bee,
From the foot of a Bull, as we plainly may see,
He took a horn Button, and this was high fun,
In stead of a shilling as sure as a gun.

Now comes David William, he'll surely be hang'd,
Or at least with a good Cat of nine tails be bang'd,
For minding too much, if the truth shall be shown,
Another man's business, neglecting his own.

Again Philip Edmund, a wild mountaineer,
Is indicted, and soon at the Bar must appear,
He now lies in Jail, and is closely confined,
For not knowing half the vile tricks of mankind.

The ninth William Evans, attend to the Rhime,
Over-reaching himself is his Capital crime,
Dear Judge shew thy mercy, Release him from Jail,
But Confine him for life in a Butt of good Ale.

The Tenth is John Griffiths who fiercely can fight,
He drub'd a Bum bailiff, a thing very right,
And sure out of prison he never shall come,
Whilst Lawyers deserve a good kick in the Bum.

There is poor David Morgan, his Creditors hope,
With his Brother Llewelin condemn'd to the rope,
For striving, alas! 'tis no subject of mirth,
To break a brass pot with a pipkin of earth.

The last Henry Prosser a whimsical Chap,
He gave his rich Creditor's knuckles a rap.
That was a great Crime as we very well know,
[?   ][55] hide they're all rogues of the Row.

While such verses might well have proved inspiring to imprisoned debtors, they provoked fury and outrage among the authorities. Undeterred, Iolo sought further legal advice and urged his father to send him a copy of *The Gentleman, Merchant, Tradesman, Lawyer, and Debtor's Pocket Guide, in cases of Arrest* (1785),[56] from which he learned a good deal about the law of debt and especially the inadequacies of the Insolvency Acts, nine of which had been passed between 1755 and 1781. Under the terms of an insolvency act an imprisoned debtor

---

[55] Even with the aid of an ultraviolet lamp, the first part of this line is indecipherable.
[56] *CIM*, I, p. 294, Iolo Morganwg to [Edward William(s)], [?July 1787].

was able to regain his freedom by submitting an application for release in the form of a schedule of his assets. No insolvency acts, however, were passed by Parliament between 1781 and 1793, which meant that debtors like Iolo were incarcerated for longer periods. Iolo did not endear himself to the Cardiff gaoler and his superiors by preparing a petition to the House of Commons in January 1787 as part of a general campaign for an insolvency act and revised regulations relating to arrest and imprisonment for debt. Iolo claimed to be championing the just cause of industrious farmers, penurious labourers and journeymen tradesmen who, having through no fault of their own fallen into debt and been dispatched to 'the loathsome appartments of a prison', had left impoverished families behind them.[57] In a devastating indictment of current legislation, which strongly echoed the strictures of Samuel Johnson in *The Idler* in 1758–9, Iolo exposed the arbitrary nature of the debt law, the injustice of allowing attorneys to delay proceedings against debtors in custody, and the folly of allowing the latter to associate with felons, sharpers and rogues who taught them new tricks and tempted them to commit far worse crimes on their release. Cruelly separated for long periods from their wives and children, debtors were forgotten men whose sighs 'resound thro the woeful cells':

> How is the Lot of those who are exiled to the antipodes, doomed to traverse the unhospitable wilds of Botany bay to be envied, and even those who still more severely condemned to swelter in the Torrid climes of Affrica to contend with Lions and Tygers, when compared with the Lot of a poor debtor in custody for more than £200?[58]

Iolo urged members of the House of Commons to arrange for county magistrates to assemble once a month to receive schedules and tender the necessary oaths to free debtors in custody. The petition as a whole not only constituted a brave and doughty defence of the rights of poor debtors but also a personal *cri de cœur* by the beleaguered Flemingston stonemason.

Not surprisingly, Iolo was increasingly harassed and maltreated by the Cardiff gaoler. On 25 May 1787 his beloved German flute was stolen, perhaps in a bid to silence one of his ways of expressing disaffection and anger. But his harsh and insistent voice still rang out. On 15 June, a time when Iolo was recovering from a prolonged bout of fever and was dependent on the ministrations of his wife, the gaoler Thomas Morgan ordered her to leave the prison lest she, heavily pregnant with her third child, give birth prematurely. Unwilling to allow his wife to walk twelve miles in her condition at night, Iolo furiously remonstrated with Morgan who, with the help of the turnkey, responded by

---

[57] NLW 21389E, 98, no. 7.
[58] Ibid.

dragging him by the hair into the courtyard and beating him severely. Crying 'murder' loudly, Iolo (so he claimed) did not strike back and by the time the fracas ended he was nursing severe bruises to his head and chest. His wife Peggy was unceremoniously bundled into the street without her stays, hat and cloak, and thereafter she was forced to take lodgings in the town whenever she visited Iolo. A week later Morgan exacted further revenge by transferring Iolo from the civilian quarters to a common cell peopled by condemned convicts.[59] Whilst licking his wounds over the summer, on 15 August 1787 Iolo petitioned George Hardinge and Abel Moysey, Chief Justices of the Courts of the Great Sessions, for redress for the gross ill-treatment and abuse he had suffered at the hands of the Cardiff gaoler.[60] It is hard to believe his claim that he had behaved with the utmost propriety over the preceding year, but in exposing and ridiculing the inconsistencies and failings of legislation associated with debt he eloquently expressed the pain and suffering of his fellow prisoners. Even at this stage he was filled with an overriding urge to expose man's inhumanity to man.

Being locked up in prison proved to be a humiliating experience for Iolo. It scarred him deeply, making him bitter and resentful, especially towards the likes of John Walton who had consigned him to the fate of an imprisoned debtor. As his scathing mock epitaph to Walton reveals, the loss of respect and the degradation he had suffered behind bars had turned him into a vengeful enemy:

> Here lies Jack Walton, one who plied
> The costly pill, grew rich and died;
> Enquire no more, for who can tell –
> Go search the registers of Hell.[61]

Iolo found it hard to live with the disgrace and deliberately kept news of his plight from the London Welsh, several of whom might have intervened on his behalf had they known.[62] But during these troubled years no one in his native patch came to the rescue of this 'storm-bird' ('aderyn y ddrycin'), as G. J. Williams depicted him,[63] and he sought refuge in the study of the Romantic

---

[59] NLW 21389E, no. 12.
[60] *CIM*, I, pp. 295–7, Iolo Morganwg to [George Hardinge], [?August 1787].
[61] NLW 21424E, no. 63. He also referred elsewhere to 'Dr Walton with his pill murd'ring skill'. Ibid., no. 14.
[62] See *CIM*, I, pp. 309, 311 (trans.), William Owen Pughe to Iolo Morganwg, 28 March 1788. Pughe informed Iolo that Owain Myfyr had told him: 'Be buaswn yn gwybod fod felly ar Iorwerth mi fuaswn i yn ei wneud yn rhydd.' ('If I had known that it was thus with Iorwerth I would have made him free.')
[63] Williams: *IM*, p. 450n.

literary past of Glamorgan, in the radical Enlightenment of Rational Dissent, and in county politics. Paradoxically, by doing so he achieved a much higher public profile as a poet, a creative writer and a political campaigner.

Much of this stemmed from his deep sense of personal disenchantment. Many social obstacles and personal animosities had adversely affected his career and preyed on his mind, including his relative poverty and lack of social connections, the racial slurs of Johnson and others, the provincial hauteur of some members of the London-Welsh societies, the snobbery of university graduates and the priestly caste, the mean-spiritedness of the Cowbridge middling sorts and, to cap it all, the indignities of prison life. That the forces of the establishment – lay and ecclesiastical – had done nothing to protect him, rankled deeply:

> I have hitherto been an enthusiastic lover of my native Isle of Britain, but undeserved I have experienced in it such injuries as almost entirely ruined me. I could not cringe to insolent wealth who assumed an authority which I could not possibly respect. This, and from another quarter the silent paced foot of the most designing knavery, deprived me, and that in a manner the most glaringly inhuman and equally illegal of what I had once hoped would have been competent for the calls of an uncomonly abstemious life. A decent sufficiency was wrestled from me by the hand of overpowering wealth, in defiance of Justice, Law, and I would have said, of shame, had shame been still active in this debased Island.[64]

He began by rejecting not only the Whiggish version of liberty but also by deploring the notion that the independent spirit of freeborn Welsh (or Britons) had manifested itself most clearly in north Wales. While deeply impressed by the deeds of medieval heroes who had 'stain'd their lances red with hostile blood'[65] and by how the works of Welsh bards had been infused with 'sentiments of freedom and of glory',[66] the location of such valour had been wrongly ascribed to Gwynedd.

To Iolo, the natural home of bardo-druidism was Glamorgan, and the literary and historical heritage of his beloved county took cultural and moral precedence over all others. His most influential mentor in the provenance of

---

[64] NLW 21387E, no. 36.
[65] D. Silvan Evans (ed.), *Gwaith y Parchedig Evan Evans (Ieuan Brydydd Hir)* (Caernarfon, 1876), p. 136.
[66] William Warrington, *The History of Wales* (London, 1786), pp. 527–36. Iolo was so taken with Warrington's preface, however, that he transcribed it. NLW 21414E, no. 11. For the background to notions of 'British' independence, see Sam Smiles, *The Image of Antiquity: Ancient Britain and the Romantic Imagination* (London, 1994), p. 136, and David H. Solkin, *Richard Wilson: The Landscape of Reaction* (London, 1982), pp. 99–101.

what modern scholars like to call 'bardic nationalism'[67] was Evan Evans (Ieuan Fardd), the unusually tall 'Longobardus' whose seminal *Specimens of the Antient Poetry of the Welsh Bards* (1764) had marked him out as the finest Welsh scholar of his generation. No mean poet himself, Evans was steeped in the finest early Welsh poetry from the days of Aneirin to the Poets of the Princes. He was convinced that the Welsh language was not only the oldest and most copious tongue in Europe but also the vehicle of some of the most memorable verse ever written.[68] Iolo had visited this impoverished and disorderly curate at Tywyn in Merioneth during his journey to north Wales in 1772,[69] and had come to realize how bardism and druidism could form the centrepiece of a programme of cultural renewal. In that year Evans published *The Love of our Country*, an extraordinary nationalist poem which celebrated the courage of those princes, warriors, law-makers and bards who had stoutly defended the integrity of Wales over the ages. Thereafter, whenever Iolo was able to track down Evans, he interrogated him closely about the ancient British past and the whereabouts of Welsh-language literary treasures. Evans was never happier than when he had 'got his nose in some vellum MS.',[70] and doubtless he and Iolo scornfully discarded 'the wretched rhymes of the English'.[71] Iolo borrowed or purchased Welsh manuscripts from him and annotated them with approving marginal remarks such as 'Dalier Sylw!' (Take heed!) and 'hynod!' (remarkable!).[72] He claimed to have been with Evans in 1780 when he visited the ruins of the court of Ifor Hael (Ifor the Generous, or Ifor ap Llywelyn), the medieval patron who had dispensed lavish hospitality on the renowned poet Dafydd ap Gwilym at Gwernyclepa, Basaleg, in Monmouthshire.[73] Scholars in our day would give their eye teeth to have witnessed the conversation between these two flawed geniuses as they threaded their way through the brambles and imagined the glories of the past. Evans was inspired to compose the famous lament which begins: 'Llys Ifor Hael, gwael yw'r gwedd – yn garnau / Mewn gwerni mae'n gorwedd' ('Ifor Hael's hall, poorly it looks, / A cairn it lies in the meadow').[74] Iolo was captivated not only by these stanzas

---

[67] Katie Trumpener, *Bardic Nationalism: The Romantic Novel and the British Empire* (Princeton, NJ, 1997); *Bardic Circles, passim*; Sarah Prescott, '"Gray's Pale Spectre": Evan Evans, Translation and the Rise of Welsh Bardic Nationalism' in eadem, *Eighteenth-Century Writing from Wales: Bards and Britons* (Cardiff, 2008), pp. 57–83.
[68] Evans (ed.), *Gwaith y Parchedig Evan Evans, passim*.
[69] *CIM*, I, pp. 65–8, Iolo Morganwg to John Walters, 1 November 1772.
[70] *ALMA*, II, p. 492.
[71] Evans (ed.), *Gwaith y Parchedig Evan Evans*, pp. 131–2.
[72] NLW 21287B; NLW 21313B.
[73] NLW 21390E, f. 24ᵛ; Evans (ed.), *Gwaith y Parchedig Evan Evans*, p. 52.
[74] Thomas Parry (ed.), *The Oxford Book of Welsh Verse* (Oxford, 1962), pp. 322–3; Gwyn Jones, *The Oxford Book of Welsh Verse in English* (Oxford, 1977), p. 137; Prys Morgan, '"A Kind of Sacred Land": Iolo Morganwg and Monmouthshire', *The Monmouthshire Antiquary*, XXVII (2011), 127–33.

but also by Evans's profound knowledge of, and respect for, bardic learning.

Another salient influence on Iolo was his visit to Avebury in 1777.[75] Astonished by the 'very stupendous' druidical stones and monuments he examined on Silbury Hill, he was determined to discover archaeological remains of similar interest, if not size, in Glamorgan, not least in order to pour further scorn on the 'exceeding pitiful monuments' he had seen earlier in Anglesey and which made a mockery of Henry Rowlands's claim that the 'Mother of Wales' was the principal seat of druidism.[76] Iolo set about assembling a mass of data about the ancient monuments, landscape and archaeology of Glamorgan, and in letters sent to the *Gentleman's Magazine* he not only paraded his antiquarian learning but also announced that he and Edward Evan(s) of Aberdare were 'the only legitimate descendants of the so-long-celebrated *Ancient British Bards*'.[77] All other versions of the bardic past, he insisted, were spurious. Gray's *The Bard* was judged 'a very inferior thing'[78] and Iolo's withering response to Macpherson's attempts to put *Ossian* on the map was 'Bravo, O! Bravo, O! Well said, mon!'[79] Only in Glamorgan, he insisted, had authentic bardic and druidic teachings been preserved intact, and no county was better able to illustrate the glories of the past. Moreover, he made it plain that the genuine bardic secrets preserved in the upland fastnesses of Glamorgan had always been associated with 'those who ranked not with the higher classes'.[80] By embodying and preserving the literary secrets of the past, a penurious Glamorgan stonemason was thus able to project himself as the guardian of cultural elitism and exclusiveness. It amused him to turn the tables in this way.

While studying the past, gazing at the landscape and exercising his creative genius, Iolo became especially obsessed with the literary inheritance of Glamorgan. He became increasingly convinced that everything of any consequence had its origins in the county, and he was prepared to shape, mould and distort evidence to prove that its heritage excelled that of the rest of Wales. Iolo lived in the golden age of literary forgery and thought nothing of

---

[75] Jon Cannon and Mary-Ann Constantine, 'A Welsh Bard in Wiltshire: Iolo Morganwg, Silbury and the Sarsens', *Wiltshire Studies*, 97 (2004), 78–88.

[76] *CIM*, I, pp. 123–6, Iolo Morganwg to Owen Jones (Owain Myfyr), 12 January 1777; NLW 13130A, p. 292.

[77] *Gentleman's Magazine*, LIX, part 2 (1789), 976–7. For valuable background material, see Prys Morgan, 'From a Death to a View: The Hunt for the Welsh Past in the Romantic Period' in Eric Hobsbawm and Terence Ranger (eds.), *The Invention of Tradition* (new edn., Cambridge, 1992), pp. 43–100; Smiles, *The Image of Antiquity*; Ronald Hutton, *The Druids* (London, 2007). For depictions of Welsh Druids and bards, see Peter Lord, *The Visual Culture of Wales: Imaging the Nation* (Cardiff, 2000), chapter 4.

[78] NLW 13159A, pp. 156–7; Prescott, *Eighteenth-Century Writing from Wales*, pp. 70–82.

[79] *CIM*, I, p. 85, Iolo Morganwg to John Walters, 18 September 1774; *Truth against the World*, Part II, pp. 85–142.

[80] Williams: *PLP*, II, p. 161.

tampering with original poems by amending, emending or mimicking them. Extremely adept in covering his tracks, from the mid-1770s he began transcribing the poems of Dafydd ap Gwilym and also brilliantly executing *cywyddau* in the manner of his hero.[81] Convinced that Dafydd ap Gwilym was 'infinitely superior in genius' to any other Welsh poet,[82] he plied the London Welsh, especially Owain Myfyr and William Owen Pughe, with bogus poems which were duly published as an appendix to Dafydd ap Gwilym's works in 1789.[83] Right up until the final stages of printing and thereafter, Owain Myfyr and Pughe were taken in by Iolo's plausible charm, his quickness of mind and his undoubted mastery of late medieval Welsh poetry. No blame lies with them. Iolo's sparkling poems were far from being pale imitations of the original. Modern scholars reckon some of them to be every bit as good as the authentic poems and Iolo's forgeries were so compellingly attractive that their authenticity lay unquestioned among scholars until the foundation of the University of Wales a hundred years later.[84]

To secretly adopt the persona of Dafydd ap Gwilym was one thing, but to turn him into a Glamorgan man was even more subversive. Iolo claimed that Morgan Llywelyn of Neath had passed on to him the tale of how Ardudful, wife of Gwilym Gam, had given birth to Dafydd ap Gwilym, 'our famous, melodious poet', under a hedge in Glamorgan during a violent hailstorm and of how the infant had then been christened on his dead mother's coffin at Llandaf.[85] But even William Owen Pughe refused to countenance the idea that Dafydd ap Gwilym was a native of Glamorgan and, much to Iolo's disapproval, he chose not to incorporate suspect biographical material in *Barddoniaeth Dafydd ab Gwilym* (1789), and Iolo's transcripts of purported poems by the great medieval poet, many of which were dispatched to London at the eleventh hour, were included in an appendix. Yet Iolo continued to maintain that the prince of Welsh *cywyddwyr* had drawn his first breath in Glamorgan and, at the very least, that he had spent nearly the whole of his career as a poet living in Glamorgan where his final, corrected drafts had been preserved and, by chance, had come into his possession.[86] How he must have chuckled as he assured Pughe that Dafydd ap Gwilym seemed to have been 'the inventor of a truly original species of poetry'.[87]

---

[81] NLW 13090E, pp. 209–454; *IMChY*, pp, 3, 7; Williams: *IM*, p. 213.
[82] NLW 21419E, no. 23.
[83] Owen Jones and William Owen (eds.), *Barddoniaeth Dafydd ab Gwilym* (Llundain, 1789); Thomas Parry, '*Barddoniaeth Dafydd ab Gwilym*, 1789', *JWBS*, VIII, no. 4 (1957), 189–99.
[84] *Literary and Historical Legacy*, pp. 137–46.
[85] *CIM*, I, pp. 338–41, 341–6 (trans.), Iolo Morganwg to William Owen Pughe, 15 October 1788; *Iolo Manuscripts*, pp. 484–7.
[86] NLW 6609D, f. 27ᵛ; NLW 13138A, p. 137; NLW 13158A, p. 334; NLW 21419E, no. 23.
[87] *CIM*, I, p. 306, Iolo Morganwg to William Owen Pughe, 12 March 1788.

Having put his own stamp of genius on the work of Dafydd ap Gwilym and turned him into a Bard of Glamorgan, Iolo also provoked men of letters in Gwynedd by casting serious doubts on their primary claim on the Welsh literary tradition. As early as 1780 he had contemplated publishing a monthly or a quarterly magazine entitled 'Dywenydd Morganwg' (The happiness of Glamorgan) in which he planned to publish a diverse range of prose and verse which would allow readers to bask in the glory of Glamorgan's literary heritage, steep themselves in the old bardic grammars and especially in what he dubbed the 'Glamorgan Measures' ('Mesurau Morgannwg') or the 'Old Classification' ('Dosbarth Morgannwg').[88] Iolo insisted that this ingenious (but spurious) metrical system was much older and also infinitely superior to the hackneyed system of twenty-four strict metres codified by the poet Dafydd ab Edmwnd at the Carmarthen eisteddfod, held under the patronage of Gruffudd ap Nicolas, at Carmarthen c.1453.[89] Iolo's metrical system was highlighted in 'Cyfrinach Beirdd Ynys Prydain', the manuscript on bardic secrets which he prepared during his sojourn in Cardiff prison, and although he was aware that poets in Gwynedd disparaged it as the 'Dogs' Classification' ('Dosparth y Cwn') and the 'Pigs' Classification' ('Dosparth y Moch'),[90] this served only to rouse 'his indignant spirit'[91] and provoke further expressions of faith in the authentic metrical system of his forefathers in Glamorgan. To underpin his argument, moreover, from around 1785 he began composing essays on 'Cadair Morgannwg' (the Chair of Glamorgan) designed to enhance the authority and credibility of Glamorgan poets.[92]

Just as unsettling to the natives of north Wales was Iolo's determination to prove that the Silurian or Gwentian dialect, which Iolo habitually spoke and celebrated, was the most effective means of articulating the literary secrets of the past. The fact that he spoke with what was considered a 'vulgar' or even 'barbarous' dialect made him a curiosity in metropolitan circles. This in itself prompted him to tilt against notions of 'proper speech'[93] and especially the prescriptive tradition which favoured the inhabitants of north Wales. Ever the local patriot, he believed that the Gwentian dialect had been the first standard literary language of Wales and that it had held its authority until the dawn of

---

[88] NLW 13089E, pp. 134–7; *CIM*, I, pp. 150–7, Iolo Morganwg [and Thomas Williams] to the readers of 'Dywenydd Morganwg', [?May 1780]; ibid., I, pp. 159–64, Iolo Morganwg to Owen Jones (Owain Myfyr), 10 July 1780; *TLIM*, p. 47.
[89] Ceri W. Lewis, 'Iolo Morganwg' in Branwen Jarvis (ed.), *A Guide to Welsh Literature c. 1700–1800* (Cardiff, 2000), pp. 141–2.
[90] Williams (ed.), *Cyfrinach Beirdd Ynys Prydain*, p. 4.
[91] *RAEW*, p. 18.
[92] *TLIM*, pp. 5, 101, 252; Williams: *IM*, p. 280.
[93] Lynda Mugglestone, *'Talking Proper': The Rise of Accent as Social Symbol* (2nd edn., Oxford, 2003), chapter 1.

the fourteenth century.[94] Utterly convinced of the rightness of his cause, he raged against those north Walians who had mocked his accent and disparaged his heritage: 'Some Deudneudians arrogate to themselves the modern Literary dialect. I say arrogate, for it is arrogance.'[95] He was acutely conscious of the way in which writers, past and present, in Gwynedd had derided the alleged 'Hottentotish' Welsh spoken in south Wales and who had viewed it as symptomatic of a region bereft of literary achievement and ambition. Iolo longed to remove that egregious slur.

In several intriguing ways, therefore, Iolo developed a strikingly radical critique of received opinion about the Welsh cultural heritage. The past became a radical linguistic and cultural tool in his hands, and Gwyneth Lewis has rightly drawn attention to the strong political dimension associated with his forgeries and his determination to redirect history in favour of his native Glamorgan.[96] If Glamorgan was the authentic headquarters of liberty and morality, then Iolo's bardo-druidic pronouncements unquestionably carried political significance. Since his forebears had proved to be chivalrous defenders of ancient freedoms, he believed that he had a responsibility to follow in their footsteps. Everything appears to suggest that he thoroughly enjoyed publicly rejecting the hidebound pieties of the poets and writers of Gwynedd in favour of a more challenging cultural programme based on bardo-druidism whose roots lay deep in the county of his birth. By refashioning the past, he served what he believed to be the political needs of the present.

Iolo's second response to conventional ways was to repudiate his Anglican upbringing and throw in his lot with religious heterodoxy. Religion stood at the heart of Iolo's development as a radical figure and although we still need to develop a deeper understanding of the nature of his religious thought he unquestionably became an influential and vigorous orchestrator of anti-trinitarian values in south Wales. At this stage, however, the established church still held pride of place throughout Wales. Fondly referred to as the 'mother church', its services, though not as regularly attended as some have supposed, as well as the images, rituals and symbols associated with them, remained the principal focus of ecclesiastical and social life. By at least the early 1780s, however, Iolo harboured grave reservations about the validity and the mission of the established church. His conversations and correspondence with Evan Evans proved to be decisive in this respect. A manic depressive, often awash with alcohol,

---

[94] Richard M. Crowe, 'Diddordebau Ieithyddol Iolo Morganwg' (unpublished University of Wales Ph.D. thesis, 1988); idem, 'Iolo Morganwg and the Dialects of Welsh' in *Rattleskull Genius*, pp. 315–31.

[95] NLW 13138A, p. 129.

[96] Gwyneth Lewis, 'Eighteenth-Century Literary Forgeries, with Special Reference to the Work of Iolo Morganwg' (unpublished University of Oxford D.Phil. thesis, 1991), pp. 148, 156.

Evans flitted to and from eighteen different curacies during his chequered career. With no prospect of reward, he was scathingly blunt about those whom he dubbed the 'Anglo Bishops' ('Esgyb Eingl'), those birds of passage who had no compunction about placing English bounty-hunters in key ecclesiastical posts and remained blind to the linguistic and spiritual needs of their flocks. Convinced that the established church in Wales had been betrayed, he denounced its leaders with fierce passion. In both published and unpublished works he railed against the 'predatory wolves' who had turned the mother church into 'a den of thieves'.[97] Iolo's papers reveal that he owned a copy of Evans's *The Love of our Country*, a critique of the Anglican cause which glowed with indignation and anger,[98] and also material relating to the groundswell of resentment in north Wales when Thomas Egerton, bishop of Bangor, unwisely appointed a monoglot English-speaking octogenarian to minister to the needs of monoglot Welsh parishioners at Trefdraeth and Llangwyfan in Anglesey.[99] Evans was quite certain that bishops looked upon him 'with an evil eye'[100] and Iolo was shocked to witness his impoverished condition and the deterioration in his health during his twilight years.[101] 'Poor Evans!', he wrote, 'He spent the last years of his life in want.'[102] Like Evans, he came to believe that non-Welsh prelates were a disgrace to the memory of their cultured, Welsh-speaking forebears in Elizabethan times. Any reader of Milton, as Iolo was, would have known that the established church was populated by tyrants and there can be little doubt that Evan Evans's forthright views on church government helped to drive Iolo into the arms of Dissent.

But Iolo's own brand of anticlericalism also played its part. By the 1780s he was composing poems designed to mock and demystify the clerical order, and this material clearly prefigures his more politicized assaults on 'priestcraft' in the 1790s. 'Parson Pot' and 'Parson Gravelocks' were a common target[103] and it is not surprising that he was prone to fall foul of local clerics. On one occasion, probably in the spring of 1786, he had a violent altercation with the Revd James Evans, vicar of Marshfield in Monmouthshire. As he walked to his home in St Mellons late one evening, Iolo encountered Evans and his servant who brazenly sought to know his business. Since he proved to be characteristically

---

[97] See, in particular, NLW 2009B and Evan Evans, *Casgliad o Bregethau* (2 vols., Y Mwythig, 1776), I, sig. a3ʳ–b6ʳ. For the background, see Geraint H. Jenkins, 'Yr Eglwys "Wiwlwys Olau" a'i Beirniaid', *Ceredigion*, X, no. 2 (1985), 131–46; Gerald Morgan, 'Ieuan Fardd (1731–1788): "Traethawd ar yr Esgyb Eingl"', ibid., XI, no. 2 (1990), 135–45.
[98] NLW 2595C.
[99] NLW 13159A, pp. 204–5, 210–11; Geraint H. Jenkins, '"Horrid Unintelligible Jargon": The Case of Dr Thomas Bowles', *WHR*, 15, no. 4 (1991), 494–523.
[100] *ALMA*, II, p. 620.
[101] *CIM*, I, pp. 161, 163 (trans.), Iolo Morganwg to Owen Jones (Owain Myfyr), 10 July 1780.
[102] NLW 13112B, p. 16. See also NLW 13141A, p. 206.
[103] NLW 13170B, pp. 232–4; NLW 21392F, no. 16.

guarded and sullen in his replies, he was immediately stopped in his tracks and maltreated:

> . . . could not pass went up little lane ordered Tom to go on to Jack ye weaver. At M Rowlands Struck at me with the whip struck hat to ye court I calld M Rowland up. to save my Life he got up & Edw. Rowland. threw the lash of the whip under my arm and drag'd me by that & the hair of my head etc, along the green I fell and the horse went over me one, and very narrowly escaped it several times.[104]

To what extent the acid-tongued Iolo had provoked Evans and his servant is impossible to tell – only Iolo's version of events has survived – but it is more than likely that he bitterly resented being interrogated by a cleric and probably said so in the most forthright terms. Iolo never forgot this violent whipping and duly penned a satirical poem entitled 'The Marshfield Parson, or Parson of Parsons', to be sung to the tune 'The Devil and Bishop of Canterbury', in which he recounted the 'black deeds' of James Evans, the 'prince of oppressors'.[105] Still in high dudgeon, he then granted him a cameo role in his 'Hymn to the Devil':

> Here lies a wight that knowst him well
> Thy marshfield parson proud as hell
> The gifted Evans in whose mind
> Thy deepest arts are well combined.
> Tutor'd by thee th'obedient elf
> Is a true picture of thy self.
> Thro all thy vast infernal round
> To him no equal can be found.
> Each vice that can the soul disgrace
> That human feeling can efface.
> In his black heart securely dwell,
> Clad in their native hues of hell,
> The God he piously adores
> In countless wealth and worldly stores . . .[106]

It is unlikely that someone like Iolo – who was genuinely poor, and outspoken to boot – would have seen any merit in clerics with fat incomes and little appetite for pastoral care. His fierce outbursts in support of Evan Evans

---

[104] NLW 21392F, f. 26ᵛ. Evans was vicar of Marshfield between 1742 and 1788. John R. Guy (ed.), *The Diocese of Llandaff in 1763: The Primary Visitation of Bishop Ewer* (Cardiff, 1991), pp. 128–9.
[105] NLW 21335B, pp. 6–9.
[106] NLW 21424E, no 17. For James Evans's will, proved 4 February 1789, see NLW Ll/1789/88.

and in condemnation of James Evans strongly suggest that he could no longer be counted a loyal son of the Church.

Why, it might be asked, did Iolo not choose to throw in his lot with the Methodists? After all, the new enthusiasts had injected considerable vigour into the established church and, thanks to the zealous preaching of David Jones, Llan-gan, made inroads in the Vale of Glamorgan by setting up lively society meetings.[107] But Iolo held them in low esteem. The doctrine of predestination offended his liberal instincts and sense of fair play, and, as his 'Jumper's Hymn' reveals, the wild emotionalism of such tub-thumpers was not to his taste.[108] In his view, Methodists lacked intellectual muscle, tolerance towards others and a sense of humour. Uncritical admirers of king, church and country, they did not reach out to the politically disenfranchised or encourage them to voice their grievances. As the years rolled by, Iolo's anti-evangelical animus deepened and, as a self-appointed champion of reason and truth, he made it his business to deride their doctrines and behaviour.

Iolo found much greater affinity with the doctrines and intellectual traditions of Dissent. Baptist and Congregationalist causes expanded in numbers and influence from the 1770s and Iolo was familiar with Joshua Thomas's magisterial *Hanes y Bedyddwyr, ymhlith y Cymry* (History of the Baptists among the Welsh) (1778),[109] a work which displayed a far greater degree of impartiality and magnanimity than that found in one-dimensional Methodist hagiographies. He was also well-versed in the travails of Puritan saints during the Cromwellian years and the persecution suffered by the likes of Vavasor Powell.[110] He was therefore willing to rub along with their descendants so long as they did not share the insensitive arrogance and solemnity of their Methodist rivals. Iolo also flirted with Quakerism, even though its numbers had dwindled almost to nothing in Wales, and he read works by George Fox and William Penn.[111]

Yet it was the cause of Rational Dissent which, in Iolo's eyes, held out most promise for the future of mankind. From around the 1720s the bracing winds of anti-trinitarianism had been blowing vigorously, notably in south-west

---

[107] For David Jones, see *ODNB*. William Williams, Pantycelyn, maintained that Jones could 'make the stoutest oak bend as easily as rushes' ('[gwneuthur] i'r derw mwyaf caled / Blygu'n ystwyth fel y brwyn'). Quoted by Branwen Jarvis, 'Iolo Morganwg and the Welsh Cultural Background' in *Rattleskull Genius*, p. 40.

[108] NLW 13170B, pp. 184–6; NLW 21328A, pp. 196–7.

[109] *CIM*, I, pp. 258, 261 (trans.), Iolo Morganwg to Owen Jones (Owain Myfyr), 8 August 1784.

[110] NLW 13114B, p. 239; NLW 13122B, pp. 140–50; *CIM*, I, pp. 354–5, 355–7 (trans.), Iolo Morganwg to the Protestant Dissenters of Glamorgan, [?June 1789].

[111] NLW 13121B, pp. 335–8; Williams: *PLP*, I, pp. 43–5, 136–42, 186; Richard C. Allen, *Quaker Communities in Early Modern Wales: From Resistance to Respectability* (Cardiff, 2007), pp. 190–1.

Wales where Dissenting academies at Carmarthen and Llan-non encouraged students to think for themselves.[112] In 1733 Llwynrhydowen in south Cardiganshire became the mother church of Arminianism and gave birth to six daughter churches within a decade. The modest gentry, farmers and craftsmen who worshipped in anti-Calvinistic churches believed that Methodism was 'a heap of Absurdities',[113] a charge which prompted their adversaries to demonize their 'heretical' hunting grounds as 'y Smotyn Du' (the Black Spot). This alleged blot on the landscape, however, nurtured an array of gifted Arian and subsequently Unitarian ministers, several of whom served churches in Warwickshire and Worcestershire with great distinction.[114] Arianism swiftly took root in south-west Wales. When the greatest of their pastors, David Davis ('Dafis Castellhywel'), an Arian minister, schoolmaster and poet whom Iolo held in the highest regard, was ordained under an old oak tree near Efail-y-gof, Llwynrhydowen in July 1773, most of the sixteen ministers present were Arians. Unusually cultivated and pugnacious men, they deployed their arguments in favour of free will, toleration and social justice with such vigour that leading Methodists avoided engaging with them in public disputes. Soon, their message spread even further southwards.

Iolo's questioning nature and habitual stubbornness, not to mention his regard for the rational writings of Locke, Hume and Rousseau, meant that he found anti-trinitarianism a much more congenial alternative to Anglicanism than Calvinistic Methodism or Old Dissent. One of his earliest correspondents was Josiah Rees, who was ordained minister of Gellionnen church in the parish of Llan-giwg, Glamorgan, in 1767. Rees was the editor of *Trysorfa Gwybodaeth* (1770), to which Iolo contributed poems, and was not only a key influence in the dissemination of Arian theology in Carmarthenshire and Glamorgan but also, in 1802, one of the founders of the Unitarian Society of South Wales.[115] Further east in Glamorgan a series of splits and secessions strengthened the Arminian/Arian cause in the *Blaenau*, notably in the parishes of Merthyr and Aberdare.[116] As early as 1763 the rector of Merthyr regretfully reported that the bulk of the worshippers in the Merthyr area were Arminians, Anabaptists

---

[112] D. Elwyn Davies, *'They Thought for Themselves': A Brief Look at the Story of Unitarianism and the Liberal Tradition in Wales and Beyond its Borders* (Llandysul, 1982). For short biographies of leading Welsh anti-trinitarians, see idem, *Cewri'r Ffydd: Bywgraffiadur y Mudiad Undodaidd yng Nghymru* ([Aberdâr], 1999).

[113] George Eyre Evans (ed.), *Lloyd Letters (1754–1796), being extant letters of David Lloyd, Minister of Llwynrhydowen* (Aberystwyth, 1908), p. 29.

[114] Idem, *Midland Churches: A History of the Congregations on the Roll of the Midland Christian Union* (Dudley, 1899), pp. 12–13, 57, 125, 127.

[115] G. J. Williams, 'Josiah Rees a'r *Eurgrawn Cymraeg* (1770)', *LlC*, 3, no. 2 (1954), 119; W. J. Phillips, 'Iolo Morganwg and the Rees Family of Gelligron', *NLWJ*, XIV, no. 2 (1965), 227–36.

[116] Glanmor Williams, 'The Earliest Non-conformists in Merthyr Tydfil', *MH*, I (1976), 93.

and Deists,[117] and within a couple of decades these abrasive rationalists had begun to form 'a strong and increasingly combative radical bloc'.[118]

Following the death of Lewis Hopkin in 1771, Iolo had increasingly fallen under the influence of the remarkably well-read fuller and dyer John Bradford of Betws Tir Iarll. With typical hyperbole, he once described Bradford as 'the most learned man that had for more than 200 years appeared in the Principality'[119] and he was certainly proud to acknowledge publicly his debt to him as a bardic mentor and spiritual guide. In one of his notebooks, his son Taliesin wrote: 'a Iolo Morganwg yn ddisgybl i Sion Bradford a minnau (Ab Iolo) yn ddisgybl i fynhad Iolo Morganwg' (and Iolo Morganwg a disciple to John Bradford and I (Ab Iolo) a disciple to my father Iolo Morganwg).[120] The diarist William Thomas remembered Bradford as a disputatious free-thinker and Iolo readily confessed that being in his company gave 'a powerful jolt' ('ysgydwiad nerthol') to his views on the trinity.[121] In referring to his association with the likes of Bradford and Edward Evan(s) (who abandoned his Calvinistic upbringing for Arianism and, as pastor of the Old Meeting House at Trecynon, Aberdare, became sufficiently heterodox for Iolo to embrace him as a genuine druidic-bard),[122] Iolo was not loath to add a little varnish to oral testimony about the forebears of the poets, grammarians, dissidents and anti-trinitarians who assembled in the uplands of Glamorgan. Tales about 'Gwŷr Cwm y Felin' (the Men of Cwm y Felin) haunted his imagination and deepened his commitment to religious scepticism and free inquiry.[123] In an interesting passage in his papers, entitled 'Detached Thoughts [on] Christianity and Religion', and probably dating from the late 1780s, Iolo conceded that his views were highly unfashionable:

> The precepts of Christ are intended to purify the soul, mend the heart, and in short to make men happy. Even in this world the precepts of men conduce rather to fill the head with Systematic notions of Religion, morality etc and rather to believe the doctrines conducive to the advantages of Tyrants, priests, hypocrites, knaves & fools (for they are all of the same class with but a very few exceptions) than those which conduce to the spiritual happiness of Christians; we are seemingly to the eyes of the generality of the world more imediately conected with men than with God. Hence it is a greater crime to disbelieve the Tenets of the Churches of Rome, England, Geneva etc etc than those of the Gospel, and a man will sooner acquire

---

[117] NLW, Ll/QA/1.
[118] Chris Evans, *'The Labyrinth of Flames': Work and Social Conflict in Early Industrial Merthyr Tydfil* (Cardiff, 1993), p. 185.
[119] *TLlM*, pp. 237–9; Williams: *IM*, pp. 119–20.
[120] NLW 13130A, p. 34.
[121] NLW 13121B, p. 338.
[122] NLW 13159A, pp. 142–5; *Gentleman's Magazine*, LIX, part 2 (1789), 976–7.
[123] NLW 13121B, pp. 335–8; NLW 13138A, pp. 104–8; NLW 13141A, pp. 127–33.

the opprobrious title of heretic, infidel & other Charitable appelations for dissenting from the opinions of Calvin, Arminius, Rowland Hill, Monsieur Toplady and Pope Ioan than from those of St Paul and other Gospel authorities.[124]

That the cause of Rational Dissent was numerically small and was treated with suspicion did not trouble Iolo. For the thinking man and the underdog, it was a natural home.

By committing himself to Rational Dissent, Iolo was duty-bound to campaign for universal toleration, free speech, and the abolition of war, slavery and the slave trade. Being branded a second-class citizen rankled. The Test and Corporation Acts, which remained unrepealed until 1828, imposed humiliating civil and political disabilities on all Dissenters, and opponents of the doctrine of the trinity were excluded from the terms of the Toleration Act of 1689.[125] During the famous Glamorgan by-election of 1789 Iolo published an open letter to the Dissenting minority in the county, urging them to recall that lords and bishops had always sought to 'oppress and crush you' ('ich gorthrymu ach dirwasgu') and could not be expected to reveal 'the smallest amount of mercy or clemency' ('y dim lleiaf o drugaredd nag hynawsder') towards them.[126] Likewise, he deplored the bellicosity of British society. Patriotic militarism set his teeth on edge and although he exaggerated when he wrote that 'from an early period of my youth I have been clearly convinced that it is impossible for a Warrior to be a Christian',[127] by the late 1770s his English poems certainly reflected his horror of war and bloodshed. Championing the unstrung bow and the broken sword, he let others 'delight in blood':[128]

> Go Tom, if blood can thus delight
> Go serve mad Kings, Court fame, and fight
> with well directed Cannon Balls
> Knock down ten thousand harmless Gauls.
> Drink human Gore, and laugh thy fill
> At him 'who said thou shall not kill'.[129]

In a review of one of Gibbon's works, published in the *Monthly Review* in 1788, he heartily approved of the comment that 'the History of letters is far more

---

[124] NLW 21414E, no. 9.
[125] Grayson M. Ditchfield, 'The Parliamentary Struggle over the Repeal of the Test and Corporation Acts, 1787–1790', *EHR*, LXXXIX, no. 352 (1974), 551–77.
[126] *CIM*, I, pp. 354, 356 (trans.), Iolo Morganwg to the Protestant Dissenters of Glamorgan, [?June 1789].
[127] NLW 6575E, p. [iii].
[128] NLW 21392F, no. 74.
[129] NLW 21328A, p. 241.

interesting and agreeable than the History of Blood'.[130] His humanitarian conscience – 'soft compassion'[131] as he called it – led him to believe that the slave trade could no longer be condoned. From 1787, the year in which the Quaker-led Society for Effecting the Abolition of the Slave Trade began its campaign in earnest, Iolo became one of the most passionate anti-slavery activists in south Wales. During his confinement in prison he referred sorrowfully to the plight of slaves in Africa and the Caribbean,[132] and in 1789 he condemned human bondage as the very antithesis of benevolent Christianity:

> Behold, on *Afric's* beach, alone,
> Yon sire that weeps with bitter moan;
> She, that his life once truly bless'd,
> Is torn for ever from his breast,
> And, *scourged*, where *British Monarchs* reign,
> Calls for his aid, but calls in vain;
> His sons, on *Slav'ry's* shameless land,
> Now bleed beneath a *Villain's* hand;
> Their writhing frames how sorely gall'd!
> Still *Britons* must be *Christians* call'd –
> Their groans the wide horizon fill!
> Vile *Britons!* 'tis your *Senate's* will –
> I cease – those cruelties affright
> A Muse that shudders at the sight.[133]

The fact that his three brothers were now thriving in the sugar colonies and presumably supporting the view that the slave trade was vital to the interests of the British Empire added poignancy to his abolitionist stance. He deeply admired William Wilberforce's tireless campaign in the House of Commons to end the slave trade and listened with mounting horror to tales told in the taverns of Bristol and Cardiff of the terrible sufferings endured by black captives.

Not surprisingly, therefore, by 1789 Iolo Morganwg was more than ready to enter the public sphere of politics. His reading of Locke had shown him that all men had natural rights, that no one could govern without popular consent, and that the abuse of power could be resisted by peaceful means. Immersed in the culture of sensibility and himself a victim of consumerism and injustice, Iolo had become an enemy of political corruption, religious oppression, militarism, the slave trade and slavery, and imprisonment for debt. As one who had suffered and who remained highly vulnerable to severe

---

[130] NLW 21327A, p. [22].
[131] Williams: *PLP*, I, p. 127.
[132] NLW 21389E, 98, nos. 6–7.
[133] Williams: *PLP*, I, p. 145.

hardship and discrimination, he was well placed to become a political polemicist during the electioneering which preceded the filling of the county seat in 1789. Between 1734 and 1832 only four contested elections were held in Glamorgan and the tussle for supremacy in 1789 attracted considerable interest.[134] During the early part of the eighteenth century there had always been a strong preference for a local candidate, but thereafter, as a new breed of powerful absentee landowners snapped up the properties of the native gentry, naked wealth and political chicanery became far more important than Welsh ancestry or local connections. The alien Titans – dubbed the new parasites by radicals[135] – were determined to exercise tight control over county and borough seats. Ferocious electoral storms were few and far between because their stranglehold over property and privileges remained unchallenged.

By the mid-1780s, however, an 'Independent' interest, a loosely-based caucus of local gentlemen, freeholders and clergymen, began to emerge in opposition to the oligarchic power of the Duke of Beaufort, Lord Mountstuart, Lord Vernon and the Earl of Plymouth, all of whom were absentees.[136] In 1789 Charles Wyndham Edwin, a Gloucestershire man who had inherited the Llanmihangel estate in the Vale of Glamorgan, and who had been elected MP for the county nine years earlier, retired from his seat. Edwin had hoped that his son Thomas would fill the vacancy, but Lord Mountstuart (who later became the first Marquess of Bute in 1796) intervened by nominating an unknown carpet-bagger, Thomas Windsor, a naval captain and the brother of the Earl of Plymouth. His fellow Tory grandees rallied to his support amid cries of outrage by the 'independent' gentry and freeholders of the shire. An electoral storm followed which 'blew up into a veritable whirlwind'.[137] Inevitably, Iolo took part in the tempest.

There were two storm-centres – Cowbridge and Swansea – where vocal 'independents' whipped up enthusiasm for their cause. Cowbridge was an important political focus at that time. From 1767 to 1787 the Courts of the Great Sessions were held there, and the likes of Iolo paid close attention to the political pronouncements of judges and to the fate of prisoners. The first masonic lodge in the county was established in Cowbridge and the diarist

---

[134] Raymond Grant, *The Parliamentary History of Glamorgan 1542–1976* (Swansea, 1978), p. 10.
[135] For local studies of these socio-economic trends, see Peter R. Roberts, 'The Decline of the Welsh Squires in the Eighteenth Century', *NLWJ*, XIII, no. 2 (1963), 157–73; J. Glyn Parry, 'Stability and Change in Mid-Eighteenth Century Caernarfonshire' (unpublished University of Wales MA thesis, 1978); J. Philip Jenkins, 'The Demographic Decline of the Landed Gentry in the Eighteenth Century: A South Wales Study', *WHR*, 11, no. 1 (1982), 31–49; David W. Howell, *Patriarchs and Parasites: The Gentry of South-West Wales in the Eighteenth Century* (Cardiff, 1986).
[136] Llewelyn B. John, 'The Parliamentary Representation of Glamorgan, 1536 to 1832' (unpublished University of Wales MA thesis, 1934), p. 96.
[137] Peter D. G. Thomas, 'Glamorgan Politics, 1688–1790' in *GCH IV*, p. 425.

William Thomas described the scene on St David's Day 1765 (when Iolo was seventeen) when two dozen local Freemasons, dressed in their finery and carrying the tools of their trade, marched to Cowbridge parish church to listen to a sermon preached by the Revd John Williams.[138] As a working stone-cutter, Iolo was interested in masonic organization and terminology, and he knew perfectly well that Freemasonry throughout Europe disseminated the Enlightenment values – reason, tolerance, fraternity – which he cherished. Freemasonry was a fashionable concept among radicals and some of the more prominent Glamorgan gentry such as Jones of Fonmon, Bassett of Bonvilston and Matthews of Llandaf, on whose estates Iolo worked, met regularly at the Bear Inn in Cowbridge.[139] It is not at all clear how closely involved Iolo was in their lively discussions and drinking sessions, but he certainly expressed his sympathy for those journeymen masons in a song intended 'to blunt and soften that irritability of mind, which, from their condition in life, must necessarily be often experienced by those who form the great majority of mankind, persons that subsist by manual labour'.[140] For Iolo in 1789, the priority was to elect a candidate who, even if he could not boast a distinguished Welsh lineage, lived in the county, graced important social functions, considered the needs of the poor as well as the new commercial interests, and recognized the validity of Welsh-language culture.

During the second half of the eighteenth century Swansea had made striking advances as an industrial town, a literary centre, a focus for Dissent and a holiday resort. The first part of Wales to experience truly large-scale industrial development, it was widely known as Copperopolis as well as 'the Brighton of Wales'.[141] Despite the tyrannical and obstructive behaviour of Gabriel Powell, steward to the Duke of Beaufort and derisively known as the 'King of Swansea',[142] disaffected industrialists and freeholders led a spirited campaign to prevent Lord Mountstuart and the Duke of Beaufort from denying them tenurial rights and the opportunity to carry out necessary social and economic

---

[138] R. T. W. Denning (ed.), *The Diary of William Thomas of Michaelston-super-Ely, near St Fagans Glamorgan, 1762–1795* (Cardiff, 1995), p. 133.

[139] Jenkins, 'Jacobites and Freemasons in Eighteenth-Century Wales', 397.

[140] Williams: *PLP*, II, p. 80.

[141] Philip Jenkins, 'Tory Industrialism and Town Politics: Swansea in the Eighteenth Century', *Historical Journal*, 28, no. 1 (1985), 103–23; Rosemary Sweet, 'Stability and Continuity: Swansea Politics and Reform, 1780–1820', *WHR*, 18, no. 1 (1996), 14–39; Stephen Hughes, *Copperopolis: Landscapes of the Early Industrial Period in Swansea* (Aberystwyth, 2000); C. Robert Anthony, 'Seaport, Society and Smoke: Swansea as a Place of Resort and Industry, c.1700–c.1840' (unpublished University of Leicester Ph.D. thesis, 2002); idem, '"A Very Thriving Place": The Peopling of Swansea in the Eighteenth Century', *Urban History*, 32, no. 1 (2005), 68–87; Louise Miskell, *'Intelligent Town': An Urban History of Swansea, 1780–1855* (Cardiff, 2006), chapter 1.

[142] Tom Ridd, 'Gabriel Powell: The Uncrowned King of Swansea' in Stewart Williams (ed.), *Glamorgan Historian*, 5 (Cowbridge, 1968), pp. 152–60.

improvements in the town and the harbour. Their leader, Robert Morris of Clasemont, a volatile Oxford-trained barrister, set himself the task of rescuing the 'Independent' interest from the clutches of Tory tyrants. The son of a wealthy copper industrialist in Swansea, Morris was a strong Wilkite who, in 1772, tarnished his reputation by furtively eloping to the Continent with Fanny Harford, a twelve-year-old heiress, and marrying her, an ill-starred union which was pronounced void in 1784. The disgraced Morris then married a farmer's daughter from Llangyfelach in 1785, inherited a family estate at Tredegar Fawr, near Swansea, and resumed his role as a political gadfly.[143] 'I do love bustle, variety and disturbance to my very soul',[144] he once admitted, and Iolo doubtless espied a kindred spirit. Both men, however, worked independently of each other in the campaign to unseat the Tory grandees.

While Robert Morris orchestrated the publication of flinty printed broadsides under pseudonyms such as 'A Friend to the Independence of Glamorgan' and 'A Supporter of Rights', and disseminated satires of Thomas Windsor which contained a woodcut of the hapless naval commander in a capsized boat in the streets of Swansea,[145] Iolo furiously composed lampoons and open letters in both Welsh and English. The old adage 'Trech gwlad nag arglwydd' (A country is mightier than a lord) figured prominently as he castigated alien oppressors.[146] Writing under the pen name 'Christopher Crabstick', he sardonically congratulated Captain Windsor on graciously accepting the invitation to be 'the tool of a few tyrannical noblemen', even though he was a complete stranger to the county and possessed 'not an inch of land' within its boundaries, and expressed the fervent hope that the freeholders of Glamorgan would make 'a proper use of their feet and football you back to the place from whence you came'.[147] In rousing songs such as 'Wyndham for Ever', sung to the tune 'Obstinate Daughter', and 'Wyndham, Peace, and Liberty', sung to 'Britons never will be Slaves', he maintained that Glamorgan's soul, which had lain dormant for so long, was reawakening:

---

[143] J. E. Ross (ed.), *Radical Adventurer: The Diaries of Robert Morris 1772–1774* (Bath, 1971).

[144] Peter D. G. Thomas, '"Bill of Rights Morris": A Welsh Wilkite Radical and Rogue – Robert Morris (1743–1793)' in Stephen Taylor, Richard Connors and Clyve Jones (eds.), *Hanoverian Britain and Empire: Essays in Memory of Philip Lawson* (Woodbridge, 1998), pp. 267–87.

[145] For this voluminous material, see NLW, Tredegar 53/58, 72/76, 72/78, 72/79, 72/80, 72/81, 72/82; Swansea Museum, SM 1989.539; West Glamorgan Archive Service, 'Broadsides relating to Swansea and Glamorgan', GGF B6, nos. 13, 15, 16, 18. For a printed pamphlet directed against tyrannical aristocrats, penned by Robert Morris and included in Iolo's papers, see NLW 6575, no. 2.

[146] West Glamorgan Archive Service, GGF B6, nos. 27–8; NLW 21388E, no. 42; *CIM*, I, pp. 354–5, 355–7 (trans.), Iolo Morganwg to the Protestant Dissenters of Glamorgan, [?June 1789].

[147] NLW 13091E, pp. 315–16, 324; NLW 21401E, no. 13.

> And venal *Windsor* shall return
> To *Slav'ry's Land*, from whence he came;
> Shall in Oblivion sadly mourn,
> And pine in Shades unknown to Fame.
>   'Rise, GLAMORGAN, sing with me,
>   WYNDHAM, PEACE, and LIBERTY'.[148]

A glorious public struggle was expected, but the Tories ducked the challenge. When Edwin's son, Thomas Wyndham, was nominated at a meeting (which Iolo attended) in Cowbridge town hall on 21 July, Captain Windsor was conspicuous by his absence.[149] A writ for a by-election was issued on 10 August but, to the chagrin of the 'Independents', who were by this stage spoiling for a fight, the absentee magnates withdrew their candidature. Wyndham was thus returned unopposed on 4 September and retained his seat until his death in 1814. But the balance of power remained unchanged. Thomas Wyndham was neither a commoner nor an advocate of the principles of the French Revolution. The 1789 county by-election did not represent the spirit which toppled the Bastille, even if, as Iolo fervently sang, it showed that some fire still existed in the bellies of the 'Ancient Britons'. Yet, in a new song, entitled 'The Champions of Liberty',[150] to mark the occasion, Iolo praised the county families who had stood up to 'Slav'ry's vile Band':

> Such Heroes were those,
> They conquer'd our Foes,
> Undaunted as fam'd *Robin Hood*,
> And WYNDHAM we find
> Was the Man to their Mind,
> When he nobly for Liberty stood.
>   *My brave Boys*,
> *When he nobly for Liberty stood.*

By the time of the 1789 by-election Iolo had become increasingly alienated from the institutions and practices of the established order. By temperament and precept, he preferred to defy convention, row against the tide, and court controversy. He believed that the dictates of reason entitled him to question everything and the diverse selection of books, as well as the 'prodigeous heap of loose paper rubbish'[151] in his cottage, bore witness to his intellectual development. His command of language (especially in English) and flexibility of style

---

[148] NLW 13094E, pp. 74–6; NLW 21402F, nos. 1–6; NLW Tredegar 72/74.
[149] John, 'The Parliamentary Representation of Glamorgan', pp. 118–19.
[150] NLW 21329F, no. 12; NLW 21402F, no. 4; NLW, Tredegar 72/75.
[151] *CIM*, I, p. 364, Iolo Morganwg to Owen Jones (Owain Myfyr), 10 October 179[0].

had improved appreciably, and he had developed a wider range of expression in prose and verse. By allying himself with small groups of intelligent activists, mostly Dissenters, he had immersed himself in the 'politics of oppression',[152] which meant the traffic in human beings, colonial enslavement, warmongering, the persecution of anti-trinitarians, and the provocative essays of racists like John Pinkerton[153] were utterly repugnant to him. The vigorous bilingual culture of Glamorgan had provided a platform for his cultural and political agenda, and he now strongly believed that by committing himself to the cause of justice, humanity and peace he might yet emulate the feats of those 'manly' druidic bards who had embodied 'Liberty's undaunted soul / That fears no Tyrants' rude controul'.[154] Tumultuous times lay ahead.

---

[152] Helen Braithwaite, 'From the See of St Davids to St Paul's Churchyard: Joseph Johnson's Cross-Border Connections' in Damian Walford Davies and Lynda Pratt (eds.), *Wales and the Romantic Imagination* (Cardiff, 2007), p. 48.

[153] NLW 21419E, nos. 3, 6, 12; *CIM*, I, pp. 352–3, Iolo Morganwg to Sylvanus Urban, [?1789].

[154] NLW 21424E, no. 87.

4

'The Unparalleled Eventfulness of this Age'

The year 1789 has a twofold significance in the history of humankind: the federal constitution of the United States of America came into being in the First Congress, and the storming of the Bastille signalled the outbreak of revolution in France. Having already relished promoting the cause of local liberties in Glamorgan, Iolo Morganwg now began to immerse himself in international political debate and draw inspiration from dramatic events which offered new and attractive models of government to those who had tired of the *ancien régime*. Both Atlantic revolutions embodied similar principles, including popular sovereignty, republicanism and the rights of man, all of which made a profound impression on Iolo. He was delighted to discover that American legislators had set the mind of man free by establishing a republic 'as good as, or better than any thing of this kind that has ever yet been established [on] this earth'.[1] Likewise, the founding principles of the French Revolution had made the French 'Glorious Champions of Liberty'.[2] Thereafter he plunged himself, with passion and energy, into the reformist campaign. As he turned himself into an active political participant on a wider stage, his papers became suffused with the language, images and slogans of 'those energetic sons of Liberty'.[3]

It is worth emphasizing that the county of Glamorgan was the most receptive to radical ideas in the whole of Wales. It had become a 'nursery of democratic sentiments'[4] and several exceptional men were keenly alive to the implications of republican democracy and the sovereignty of the people. Pride of place went to Richard Price, the Arian philosopher from Ty'n ton, Bridgend. Having played a critical role in preparing the American people for revolution

---

[1] NLW 13123B, p. 56.
[2] NLW 21392F, no. 62.
[3] NLW 13144A, p. 259. See also John Dunn, *Setting the People Free: The Story of Democracy* (London, 2005); John Keane, *The Life and Death of Democracy* (London, 2009); Ben Wilson, *What Price Liberty?* (London, 2009).
[4] Gwyn A. Williams, 'South Wales Radicalism: The First Phase' in Stewart Williams (ed.), *Glamorgan Historian*, 2 (Cowbridge, 1965), p. 38.

by implanting the notion of 'the sacred blessing of liberty',[5] he then startled upholders of the old order in Europe by heaping praise on the revolutionaries in France for orchestrating 'an event wonderful and unparalleled'. Price's trailblazing sermon *Discourse on the Love of Our Country* (1789) left a deep imprint on Iolo and its sentiments were echoed in a marginal note by him in which he rejoiced in the 'unparalleled eventfulness of this age'.[6] Iolo almost certainly knew the great man personally. During the last three years of his life (he died in 1791), Price took vacations at Bridgend and Southerndown where he rode freely, visited relatives and renewed friendships with active Dissenters and radicals.[7] Iolo also knew his nephew George Cadogan Morgan. Seven years younger than him, Morgan was head of school at Cowbridge Grammar School, a graduate of Jesus College, Oxford, and briefly co-pastor with his uncle at the Old Gravel Pit Meeting House in Hackney, a place of worship which Iolo knew well. Morgan witnessed the fall of the Bastille and, in his *Address to the Jacobine and other Patriotic Societies of the French* (1792), he advocated full-blown republican government.[8]

Iolo also drew inspiration from the career of David Williams, another Welsh philosopher who derived 'sincere Admiration and Joy' from events in Paris.[9] Nine years older than Iolo, he was born at Waunwaelod on Caerffili Mountain in 1738. Academy-trained, he developed heterodox views, moved to London and opened the first Deist chapel in Europe in Cavendish Square in 1776, an initiative which was warmly praised by Voltaire and Rousseau. His most extraordinary work was *Letters on Political Liberty* (1782). Iolo encountered this genteel, rather foppish, figure in the capital in the early 1790s and received subventions from the Royal Literary Fund, a benevolent society founded by Williams to provide financial support for needy authors.[10] Then there was Morgan John Rhys, a native of Llanfabon who served as Baptist minister at Pen-y-garn, near Pontypool, from 1787 to 1791 whereupon he travelled to France and joyously stood on the ruins of the Bastille. Not quite in the league of the Enlightenment intelligentsia of Glamorgan, he was nonetheless a brave and intrepid figure who emigrated to America in 1794, loosened his fiery

---

[5] D. O. Thomas and W. Bernard Peach (eds.), *The Correspondence of Richard Price. Volume I: July 1748–March 1778* (Cardiff, 1983), p. 189.
[6] D. O. Thomas, 'Richard Price's Journal', *NLWJ*, XXI, no. 4 (1980), 393; NLW 21420E, no. 38.
[7] Thomas, 'Richard Price's Journal', 375, 387.
[8] Idem, 'George Cadogan Morgan', *The Price-Priestley Newsletter*, 3 (1979), 53–70; *ODNB*.
[9] James Dybikowski, 'David Williams (1738–1816) and Jacques-Pierre Brissot: Their Correspondence', *NLWJ*, XXV, no. 1 (1987), 95.
[10] Whitney R. D. Jones, *David Williams: The Anvil and the Hammer* (Cardiff, 1986), pp. 171–2; James Dybikowski, *On Burning Ground: An Examination of the Ideas, Projects and Life of David Williams* (Oxford, 1993), p. 239.

tongue in the company of slave-owners and generals,[11] and urged his timid countrymen to forsake their 'little despotic island' for the New World 'where liberty dwells'.[12] While Rhys was editor of the short-lived Welsh-language political quarterly *Cylch-grawn Cymraeg* (1793–4), Iolo corresponded with him and also had plans to translate into English one of his tracts on emigration to America.[13] In their very different ways, these four Glamorgan democrats envisaged a new order of things, but in order to plant the liberty tree and change the world they were required to leave Glamorgan. And from 1791 Iolo followed in their footsteps in his own quest to promote radical ideals.

During the course of the Glamorgan by-election of 1789 Iolo had earned a reputation as a wordsmith and a polemicist, and long before then he had been assembling drafts of his early pastoral poems and selections of songs on political and religious themes. Since stone-cutting brought in little money, he now set his heart on making a living through his pen. Initially, he had thought of calling an anthology of his poems 'Castles in the Air',[14] but then wisely decided that *Poems, Lyric and Pastoral* was a more apt title. But in order to fulfil his ambition of bringing his poems into the public domain and make the venture a viable commercial proposition he required several hundred subscribers. He published an eye-catching prospectus and served notice of his talents by printing in Bath five hundred copies of a sixpenny poem entitled *The Fair Pilgrim* (a translation of a *cywydd* by Dafydd ap Gwilym), a work which ran to three editions.[15] Affluent patrons in Georgian Bath indulged his literary interests and Iolo avidly grasped every opportunity for self-promotion as he made his way to London in 1791. Aware that the ploughman-poet Robert Burns had achieved sensational literary success, he believed that there was no good reason why an untutored Welsh stonemason could not thrive in the literary marketplace and express his opposition to the injustices meted out to plebeian reformists, black slaves, anti-trinitarians and friends of peace.[16] But not even he could have imagined how, in this city of seemingly endless attractions, clamour and change, he would find his political voice.

Iolo spent the best part of five years living in London, largely because the process of acquiring subscribers and guiding his anthology of poems through the press took much longer than he had anticipated, but also because he became so heavily involved in the political tumult of the times. Since Wales

[11] Gwyn A. Williams, *The Search for Beulah Land* (London, 1980); E. Wyn James, '"Seren Wib Olau": Gweledigaeth a Chenhadaeth Morgan John Rhys (1760–1804)', *TCHBC* (2007), 5–37.
[12] John T. Griffith, *Rev. Morgan John Rhys* (2nd edn., Carmarthen, 1910), pp. 232–3.
[13] *CIM*, I, pp. 585–9, 589–93 (trans.), Iolo Morganwg to the publisher of *Cylch-grawn Cymraeg: neu Drysorfa Gwybodaeth*, 27 July 1793; NLW 13123B, p. 61.
[14] See the unpublished draft in two volumes in NLW 21328A.
[15] NLW 21392F, nos. 64, 65, 66; NLW 21420E, no. 33.
[16] NLW 21400C, no. 23.

still had no national metropolis to provide a distinctive public sphere, Iolo used his sojourn in London as a means of broadening his horizons and improving his mind. A city of close to a million inhabitants, London in the 1790s was an exciting and challenging place for a Welsh stonemason who lived life on the edge. It offered a diverse range of communal entertainment, diversion and edification. There were museums (the British Museum was Iolo's favourite), theatres, lectures, operas, pantomimes, puppet shows, burlesques, revels and other festivities.[17] Even a quirky Welsh bard would have wondered at such a range of curiosities, absurdities and amusements. Where but in London could he have encountered General William Augustus Bowles, a plausible rogue whom Iolo described as 'Generalissimo of the Creek Nation',[18] or met Mark Lonsdale, an impresario who specialized in magic-lantern illusionism and phantasmagoric apparitions?[19] These were rich, full and eventful years for him. In taverns, coffee-houses, salons and printing houses, Iolo made himself known by crossing social boundaries, forging alliances, interrogating friends and strangers, and becoming irresistibly caught up in the reformist tide which swept through the streets of London. He rubbed shoulders with poets and writers, preachers and philosophers, democrats and Jacobins, abolitionists and Friends of Peace, Rational Dissenters and Spenceans, millenarians and antinomians, and many others who sharpened his mind. There were always books at hand, and by May 1794 he had well over two hundred books in his lodgings, including works on archaeology, classics, history, druidism, poetry, religion, music and politics.[20] Steeped in romantic poetry and Druidry, he was also well versed in the wonders of the East, the strategic implications of colonial rivalries, and rapidly unfolding events in America and France.

Although Iolo was no great thinker, he was fiendishly clever at cobbling together his own bricolage. As Peter Jones has reminded us, 'everyone learns and absorbs ideas from other people',[21] and Iolo certainly assimilated a wide range of information and ideas before remoulding them to suit his own aspirations. His eclecticism and chaotic working patterns add to his appeal. A myriad topics, influences and prejudices jostled in his mind and he regularly

---

[17] For this profusion of attractions, see James Chandler and Kevin Gilmartin (eds.), *Romantic Metropolis: The Urban Scene of British Culture, 1780–1840* (Cambridge, 2005); Vic Gatrell, *City of Laughter: Sex and Satire in Eighteenth-Century London* (London, 2006); David Worrall, *Theatric Revolution: Drama, Censorship, and Romantic Period Subcultures 1773–1832* (Oxford, 2006).

[18] Williams: *PLP*, I, p. xxvi; Glenda Carr, *William Owen Pughe* (Caerdydd, 1983), pp. 37–8.

[19] *CIM*, I, p. 643, David Pugh to Iolo Morganwg, 20 January 1794; Terry Castle, *The Female Thermometer: Eighteenth-Century Culture and the Invention of the Uncanny* (Oxford, 1995), p. 150.

[20] NLW 13136A, pp. 137–63.

[21] Peter Jones, 'Intellectual Origins of Enlightenment: Introduction' in Martin Fitzpatrick, Peter Jones, Christa Knellwolf and Iain McCalman (eds.), *The Enlightenment World* (London, 2004), p. 8.

bombarded people with them. Increasingly, his writings became suffused with the language, images and slogans of politics. The 1790s were famous for producing 'highly individual and eclectic intellectual responses'[22] to the political travails and challenges of the times, and no one was more intoxicated by the bubbling radicalisms of the decade than Iolo Morganwg.

On his arrival in London in the summer of 1791 he was warmly welcomed back by the London Welsh, notably by William Owen Pughe, whose fierce enthusiasm for the Madoc legend had already captivated him.[23] Although the notion of the Welsh prince Madoc as the discoverer and colonizer of America was a vivid and dramatic tale, it was also shot through with intriguing political implications which appealed to Iolo. The legend itself had first been mooted in print by John Dee in 'Title Royal', a work presented to Elizabeth I in 1580. Thereafter, by a variety of means, the legend had taken root and changed its identity as successive generations adapted it to their own circumstances and needs.[24] It became extremely popular among Welsh-language readers following the publication of Theophilus Evans's best-selling historical epic, *Drych y Prif Oesoedd* (1716; 1740), a work which Iolo read with avid interest, especially the seductive tale that a tribe, possibly tribes, of white-skinned, Welsh-speaking native Indians, the descendants of Madoc's twelfth-century colony, had survived and were living somewhere in the upper reaches of the Missouri. Iolo himself fuelled the 'Madoc fever' among the London Welsh by writing to the *Gentleman's Magazine*, drawing attention to intelligence received from Welsh Dissenters in America and from interviews he had conducted with traders and explorers who claimed to have first-hand evidence of the existence of the Welsh Madogwys (Padoucas) and who were men of 'exemplary veracity, honesty, and piety'.[25] Among those whom he interrogated closely were William Binon (Beynon), a Coety-born Indian trader in Philadelphia, Sir John Colville, a naval man who had served in North America during the War of Independence, and William Pritchard, a Welsh bookseller in Philadelphia.[26] He read key texts on

---

[22] Mark Philp, 'The Fragmented Ideology of Reform' in idem (ed.), *The French Revolution and British Popular Politics* (Cambridge, 1991), p. 54. For Welsh reactions, see Damian Walford Davies, *Presences that Disturb: Models of Romantic Identity in the Literature and Culture of the 1790s* (Cardiff, 2002), chapter 4; Geraint H. Jenkins, 'The Bard of Liberty during William Pitt's Reign of Terror' in Joseph F. Nagy and Leslie E. Jones (eds.), *Heroic Poets and Poetic Heroes in Celtic Tradition: A Festschrift for Patrick K. Ford. CSANA Yearbook 3–4* (Dublin, 2005), pp. 183–206.

[23] *CIM*, I, pp. 365–8, 381–3, William Owen Pughe to Iolo Morganwg, 12 November [1790], 28 March 1791; Carr, *William Owen Pughe*, pp. 36–9.

[24] Gwyn A. Williams, *Madoc: The Making of a Myth* (London, 1979).

[25] *CIM*, I, pp. 386–9, 403–5, Iolo Morganwg to the *Gentleman's Magazine*, 16 June 1791, 14 August 1791; NLW 21322C, p. 8.

[26] *CIM*, I, p. 386, Iolo Morganwg to the *Gentleman's Magazine*, 16 June 1791; ibid., I, p. 462, Iolo Morganwg to William Owen Pughe, 9 January 1792; ibid., I, pp. 517–18, Iolo Morganwg to William Pritchard, 15 August 1792.

the Madoc theme by Dr John Williams, a Welsh Dissenting minister at Sydenham in Kent, and treated the evidence given to William Owen Pughe by the colourful Indian chief William Bowles with deadly seriousness.[27] Those 'most amiably benevolent Ladies',[28] the writer Elizabeth Stuart Bowdler and her daughter, the literary editor Henrietta (Harriet) Maria Bowdler, were bewitched by Iolo's tales of the unAmericanized Indians, so much so that they donated generous subventions to his literary project, *Poems, Lyric and Pastoral*, and provided him with letters of recommendation to the likes of Elizabeth Montagu, queen of the bluestockings, whose literary breakfasts and conversation parties in her lavish home in Mayfair were ideal venues for a Welsh 'labouring' poet seeking converts to the Madoc legend.[29] Some of these well-born women did not know what to make of him, but most of them were bowled over by his wealth of arcane knowledge and titivating tales.

It is easy to mock Iolo and his colleagues for their uncritical acceptance of such a patently spurious tale. More pertinent, however, are the political implications of Iolo's interventions. In many ways, this was a call to action. Prince Madoc became a talisman for his beleaguered fellow Dissenters. Just as Madoc had escaped from 'the horrors of intestine wars' and Norman oppression, and found a 'land of refuge' in the New World, so was it now possible for Iolo's persecuted countrymen to travel to the 'Madocian plains' of America to savour the delights of being in a land which cherished 'the true principles of *Liberty, Justice*, and the *Rights of Humanity*'.[30] He found a kindred spirit in David Samwell, a 'black-eye-brow'd',[31] pockmarked naval surgeon from Denbighshire who, like Iolo, enjoyed riding hobby-horses, making wild and unsubstantiated statements, and consuming large quantities of laudanum. A Rabelaisian figure, Samwell was best known for his vivid account of the death of Captain Cook in the South Seas, but his mock-epic 'The Padouca Hunt' was also a depiction of America as a glorious haven for eloquent,

---

[27] John Williams, *An Enquiry into the Truth of the Tradition concerning the Discovery of America by Prince Madog ab Owen Gwynedd, about the year 1170* (London, 1791); idem, *Farther Observations on the Discovery of America by Prince Madog ab Owen Gwynedd, about the year 1170* (London, 1792); *CIM*, I, pp. 381–3, William Owen Pughe to Iolo Morganwg, 28 March 1791.

[28] Williams: *PLP*, I, p. xiii. For the Bowdler family, see *ODNB*.

[29] *CIM*, I, pp. 416–18, Henrietta Maria Bowdler to Iolo Morganwg, 25 September 1791. Elizabeth Montagu subscribed for twelve sets of *Poems, Lyric and Pastoral*. Williams: *PLP*, I, p. xxxii.

[30] NLW 21322C, pp. 1–2; Williams: *PLP*, II, pp. 212–13; Hywel M. Davies, *Transatlantic Brethren: Rev. Samuel Jones (1735–1814) and His Friends* (London, 1995).

[31] *CIM*, I, p. 419, David Samwell (Dafydd Ddu Feddyg) to Iolo Morganwg, 27 September 1791.

liberty-loving Welshmen.[32] Glad of this support, Iolo spent considerable time collecting evidence, poring over maps and pestering American ambassadors as he prepared a remarkable unpublished compendium entitled 'Padouca Gazette Extraordinary', which he hoped to present in an address to the Royal Society and the Society of Antiquaries.[33]

In admitting to being 'rebelliously partial to the Americans',[34] Iolo also sought to convince those with 'brainless heads' and 'indolent minds' of the significant political and economic benefits of protecting the interests of those whom he affectionately described as 'our Brethren'.[35] In his eyes, the strategic value of Nootka Sound, an inlet on the Pacific coast of Vancouver Island, was paramount during the years from 1789 to 1794. A crisis had blown up when the Spanish navy seized a British vessel which had impudently sought to establish a base for the fur trade at Nootka Sound in direct contravention of the Papal Bull *Inter Caetera* (1493), the Treaty of Tordesillas and other agreements.[36] Outraged by this, on 30 April 1790 the British Cabinet mobilized the Navy and warned Spain of its determination to wage war if required in defence of the right of British subjects to trade and settle on the Pacific Coast of North America. Faced by this threat, Spain surrendered its claims. Aware of these circumstances, Iolo wrote to the prime minister, William Pitt, urging him to establish a perpetual alliance or treaty with Spain which would bring lasting economic and political benefits to Britain.[37] He was also mindful of the advantages of establishing an overland connection between Nootka Sound and the state of Mississippi wherein the Madogwys lived: 'Will it be of any advantage to Government? To Trade and Commerce? Will it put some tens of thousands into the purses of avaricious individuals? Aye, there's the rub. Yes it will.'[38] But whatever qualms Iolo had about promoting commercial links, these paled by comparison with the benefits of rediscovering the Welsh colony. Long after the 'Madoc fever' had abated, Nootka Sound continued to resonate in Iolo's mind. In a mock epitaph to himself, he wrote an inscription

---

[32] William Ll. Davies, 'David Samwell (1751–1798): Surgeon of the "Discovery", London-Welshman and Poet', *THSC* (1926–7), 70–133; idem, 'David Samwell's Poem – "The Padouca Hunt"', *NLWJ*, II, nos. 3–4 (1942), 142–52; Martin Fitzpatrick, 'The "Cultivated Understanding" and Chaotic Genius of David Samwell' in *Rattleskull Genius*, pp. 383–402; Martin Fitzpatrick, Nicholas Thomas and Jennifer Newell (eds.), *The Death of Captain Cook and Other Writings by David Samwell* (Cardiff, 2007). For correspondence between Samwell and Iolo in 1791–2, see *CIM*, I, p. 389–90, 401–3, 410–12, 419–21, 458–60.
[33] NLW 21322C, pp. 1–28. See also NLW 13104B; NLW 21393C; NLW 21394D, nos. 1, 13, 15.
[34] *CIM*, I, p. 518, Iolo Morganwg to William Pritchard, 15 August 1792.
[35] NLW 21393C, p. 24.
[36] John M. Norris, 'The Policy of the British Cabinet in the Nootka Crisis', *EHR*, LXX, no. 277 (1955), 562–80.
[37] *CIM*, I, pp. 548–50, Iolo Morganwg to William Pitt, 4 February 1793.
[38] NLW 21394D, no. 1.

for his own gravestone: 'he died and lies buried here (at Nootka Sound) June 00th 1795, aged 48.'[39]

By the early months of 1792 Iolo was seriously considering embarking on an expedition to the Land of the Free. Discovering the Madogwys was a major incentive, but he also viewed it as an errand of benevolence. He was conscious that many Indian tribes had not only fallen innocent victims to plundering merchants and pseudo-priests, who had robbed them of their lands and possessions, but had also been deprived of the Christian gospel. He informed startled patrons like the Bowdlers and Hannah More that venturing into the 'deepest wilds' of America would prepare the way for a Christianizing mission.[40] He embarked on a rigorous programme of physical exercise in readiness for the Atlantic crossing, but domestic crises, poor health and perhaps a loss of nerve thwarted his plans, and it was left to John Evans, the ill-fated young Methodist from Caernarfonshire, to embark on an epic, but ultimately fruitless, mission in search of the Lost Brothers.[41] Yet, as the injuries done to him and his persecuted brethren continued to mount, Iolo still dreamed of emigrating to the New World. He concocted a 'Plan of a Welsh Colony'. For the sum of £5, exclusive of travelling expenses, a select band of around a hundred Welsh-speaking emigrants (the bulk of whom would be masons, carpenters, smiths, miners, fullers, potters and braziers – men of Iolo's stock and skills) would sail with their families to set up a colony close to the Mississippi river between Ohio and Illinois. The official language of this settlement would be Welsh and its government based on 'the purest principles of Justice, Peace and Liberty'.[42] Such plans penetrated the English literary world and rivals soon appeared. Robert Southey began composing his epic *Madoc* in spring 1795, a poem which remained unpublished until 1805. During the summer of 1794, Southey and Samuel Taylor Coleridge had resolved to set up an egalitarian community – a Pantisocracy – in which liberty, equality, peace and harmony would prevail. The initial aim was to settle on the banks of the Susquehanna river, but when the two English poets clashed over the appropriate site – America or Wales – the scheme was abandoned amid bitter recrimination.[43] For at least ten more years,

---

[39] NLW 13141A, p. 111.
[40] *CIM*, I, pp. 450–1, Iolo Morganwg to Hannah More, [?1792]; NLW 21394D, no. 7.
[41] David Williams, *John Evans and the Legend of Madoc 1770–1799* (Cardiff, 1963); Gwyn A. Williams, 'John Evans's Mission to the Madogwys, 1792–1799', *BBCS*, XXVII, part 4 (1978), 569–601.
[42] NLW 13104B, pp. 255–8.
[43] Paul Jarman, '*Madoc*, 1795: Robert Southey's Misdated Manuscript', *Review of English Studies*, 55, no. 220 (2004), 355–73; Caroline Franklin, 'The Welsh American Dream: Iolo Morganwg, Robert Southey and the Madoc Legend' in Gerard Carruthers and Alan Rawes (eds.), *English Romanticism and the Celtic World* (Cambridge, 2003), pp. 69–84; Tim Fulford, *Romantic Indians: Native Americans, British Literature, and Transatlantic Culture 1756–1830* (Oxford, 2006), chapter 7.

however, Iolo yearned to be free of tyrants, placemen and priests by fleeing westwards:

> O let us to some desert wild
> Haste o'er the stern atlantic wave
> There live with freedom self exiled
> From realms where bloody Tyrants rave
> And thanking heav'n, there shall we thus
> In strains of joy together sing
> 'Good Lord! thou hast deliver'd us
> From Pitt and spies, from
> Church and King.'[44]

Like many Romantics, however, Iolo was also deeply interested in the culture and religion of India and the Far East. India was reckoned to be 'the richest jewel in the imperial crown',[45] and Iolo was keenly aware of the massive territorial empire which the East India Company had acquired by the late eighteenth century and of some of the products – sugar, opium, spices, indigo, muslin – which were on public display in the shops of London. But his passionate interest in the Orient was probably kindled by one of the most eminent subscribers to his anthology of English poems. The son of a brilliant mathematician from Anglesey, Sir William Jones was unquestionably the finest Oriental scholar of his generation in Europe. Known as 'Persian Jones' or 'Bengal Jones' in fashionable and scholarly circles, his learning inspired Iolo's awe and astonishment. But he was also familiar with Jones's reformist credentials. The latter's *Principles of Government in a Dialogue between a Scholar and a Peasant* (1782), a work composed in Ben Franklin's home, was a manifesto for parliamentary reform which was greatly admired by the Society for Constitutional Information. Its message, so appealing to the likes of Iolo, was that peasants 'can comprehend more than you imagine', and Michael Franklin has argued that, in tearing 'the Burkean veil of baroque mystery', Jones anticipated the later works of Paine, Priestley and Godwin.[46]

But to Iolo, Jones's Oriental literature was the principal attraction. It appealed to his dreamy imagination and taste for exotic and dramatic events. Jones not only caught his eye as an advocate of social justice but also as a purveyor of the enormous intellectual resources of the Orient, its natural wonders, customs, laws and manners. He devoted long hours to reading *Asiatick Researches*,

---

[44] NLW 21401E, no. 7.
[45] Huw V. Bowen, *The Business of Empire: The East India Company and Imperial Britain, 1756–1833* (Cambridge, 2006), p. 1.
[46] Michael J. Franklin (ed.), *Sir William Jones: Selected Poetical and Prose Works* (Cardiff, 1995), p. 396.

the house journal of the Asiatic Society of Bengal which Jones had founded in 1784, and became especially enraptured by the translation of Kalidāsa's *Śacontalá*, which depicted the Brahman as 'ascetic and erotic, priest and poet, guardian of hermetic and esoteric wisdom' and which enriched his understanding of the role of the Welsh druidic bards.[47] Iolo's profound respect and admiration for the culture of India was reflected in his papers and collection of books. He transcribed part of the introduction of Charles Wilkins's translation of the *Bhăgvăt-gēētā* and derived a good deal of knowledge of the Hindu doctrine of metempsychosis from his reading of Holwell's *Interesting Historical Events: Relative to the Provinces of Bengal, and the Empire of Indostan* (1766). He also steeped himself in the role of Indian mythologizers and legislators by reading Jones's last published work, *Institutes of Hindu Law; or, the Ordinances of Menu* (1796), a digest of Hindu law in which Iolo identified points of contact with the legal tradition in medieval Wales.[48] Nor were Sir William Jones's extraordinary findings in the field of modern comparative philology lost on Iolo, though he feared that the history of the genesis of the ancient languages of the world and their well being were distinctly unfashionable in a Europe riven by avarice, pride and war.[49] Although he was not naive enough to believe that the Orient was untainted by luxury and corruption, he was greatly taken by the Hindu doctrine of reincarnation and, as we shall see, he underpinned his interpretation of Druid theology with such ideas.[50] Indeed, the more he read about Hinduism and Brahminism, the more he interested himself in what he called 'innovations at least if not reformations' in the history of religion.[51] He delved into Jewish mysticism and theosophy, the origins of the Illuminati of Constantinople and the Theophilanthropists of France, and the 'singularities' (as Elijah Waring put it)[52] of the Deist chapel opened by David Williams in Margaret Street, London. Such forays deepened his understanding of religious faiths and the workings of the human soul, and also coloured his views on imperialism, colonialism and race.

Even as he immersed himself in the attractions of the Atlantic and Asia, Iolo was becoming increasingly preoccupied with political and human rights. According to Elijah Waring, in later life Iolo never tired of recounting his conversations with leading radicals, including Tom Paine, the greatest of his

---

[47] Idem, *Sir William Jones* (Cardiff, 1995), p. 102. See also idem, 'Sir William Jones, the Celtic Revival and the Oriental Renaissance' in Carruthers and Rawes (eds.), *English Romanticism and the Celtic World*, pp. 20–37.
[48] NLW 13089E, p. 468; NLW 13123B, p. 141; NLW 21407C.
[49] NLW 13121B, pp. 481–2.
[50] Ronald Hutton, *Blood and Mistletoe: The History of the Druids in Britain* (London, 2009), pp. 156–7.
[51] NLW 13146A, pp. 102–4.
[52] *RAEW*, p. 49.

age: 'the Bard, who was well acquainted with this clever incendiary, met with a few severe rubs'.[53] Iolo liked nothing better than discussing the liberty of the individual with apostles of freedom. Paine subscribed to his *Poems, Lyric and Pastoral* and Iolo often referred to him as his friend and even nursed hopes of becoming the Welsh Tom Paine.[54] Both men had a good deal in common. The son of a Quaker, Paine had served an apprenticeship as a stay-maker, been poorly educated and at one stage been forced to flee from his creditors. He had reached middle age before his gifts as a writer were recognized. His remarkably successful political pamphlet *Common Sense* (1776) inspired the American colonists and, on his return to England in 1787, he was often referred to by the pen name 'Common Sense'.[55] He soon became engaged in hotly disputed political and ideological issues, especially when Edmund Burke's conservative classic *Reflections on the Revolution in France* (1790) – a riposte to Richard Price – declared that societies should be bound together by due respect for hierarchy, tradition and order. Deeply shocked by Burke's impassioned attack on the French Revolution, Paine published the most popular political pamphlet of the age, *Rights of Man*, in two parts in February 1791 and January 1792. These works outsold other radical literature by a considerable distance: by the end of 1792 both parts had combined sales of around 200,000 copies. The crux of Paine's argument was that God had created man free and equal, and that people had a right to govern their own affairs. Democratic republics such as America were the models to follow since they encouraged citizens to elect governments accountable to the people, thereby freeing them from the curse of despotism, war and bloodshed.[56] In Iolo's case, *Rights of Man* came as a breath of fresh air. His writings became suffused with Paine's radical ideology and bitter denunciations of 'bilious' Burke and his depictions of the 'swinish multitude'.[57] Championing the right of the common man to articulate his contempt for kingcraft, priestcraft and injustice of all kinds, he often relied on dramatic irony:

> What right has a Staymaker, a Cobler, a Welsh mason, Ploughmen, milkmaids, etc. in short any mechanic handicraftsmen or one of any description amongst the said

---

[53] Ibid., p. 46.
[54] Williams: *PLP*, I, p. xxxiv; NLW 21392F, no. 9.
[55] Thomas Paine, *Rights of Man, Common Sense, and Other Political Writings*, ed. Mark Philp (Oxford, 1995; new edn. 2008); Ian Dyck (ed.), *Citizen of the World: Essays on Thomas Paine* (London, 1987).
[56] For Paine's radicalism, see Thomas Paine, *Rights of Man*, ed. Gregory Claeys (Indianapolis, Ind., 1992); John Keane, *Tom Paine: A Political Life* (London, 1995); Eric Foner, *Tom Paine and Revolutionary America* (Oxford, 2005); Edward Larkin, *Thomas Paine and the Literature of Revolution* (Cambridge, 2005); Christopher Hitchens, *Thomas Paine's Rights of Man: A Biography* (London, 2006).
[57] See, for instance, NLW 13121B, p. 448; NLW 21396E, no. 5; NLW 21401E, no. 1.

Swinish Multitude, to pee[r] [into] the Arcanum Imperium, to acquaint themselves with those m[eans] by which the Trade and mystery of a King, or the craft of [a] Priest is carried on. What impudence to think for themselves and their fellow Swine in general, to look at the abuses of the French or any other Government under which they might s[erve]. In short how dare they talk of their own Rights, or in oth[er] king-detested worlds, the Rights of Man, when it is well known that the said Rights are diametrically opposite to the Rights of Kings and utterly subversive of the Rights of Priests.[58]

From Paine, Iolo derived confirmation of his view that monarchs were warmongers and that the monarchy itself, propped up by the ecclesiastical establishment, was a specious, oppressive and contemptible thing. Although, as we shall see, Iolo was not an uncritical admirer of Paine's view on religion, he espoused the cause of the rights of man for the rest of his life.

With these ideas swirling in his head, this proud Welshman was thirsting for the opportunity to publicize his version of druido-bardism in the light of current political circumstances. As early as 1789 Owen Jones (Owain Myfyr) had already nailed the aims of the Gwyneddigion Society to the mast of the French Revolution by declaring that 'Liberty in Church and State' ('Rhyddid mewn Gwlad ac Eglwys') was its goal,[59] but Iolo soon discovered that few London Welshmen had adopted this as an article of faith or committed themselves to libertarianism. Although he readily acknowledged the generous hospitality and support he received from Owain Myfyr and William Owen Pughe, he suspected that the former was too self-important and the latter too timid to promote Painite republicanism. Moreover, he was exasperated by the loyalism of poets from north Wales and their reluctance to respond enthusiastically to the revolution in France. When the Gwyneddigion Society began to sponsor the newly-revived annual eisteddfod in 1789, its hopes of promoting radical works were swiftly dashed. Poets were more interested in drinking heavily and pursuing private feuds than celebrating international events or denouncing injustice.[60] When the 1790 eisteddfod was held in St Asaph a silver chair and a silver medal were offered as prizes for the best poem and prose work. The subject was 'Liberty' ('Rhyddid') and the medal was specially engraved by Augustin Dupré, who was soon to acquire international fame as the engraver-general of coins under the First French Republic.[61] Unhappily,

---

[58] NLW 21396E, no. 14.
[59] NLW 1806E, f. 665, Owen Jones (Owain Myfyr) to Walter Davies (Gwallter Mechain), 31 October 1789.
[60] Iolo believed that eisteddfodau were viewed by the public as an excuse for 'drinking, singing and brawling'. NLW 13158A, p. 189.
[61] Carl Zigrosser, 'The Medallic Sketches of Augustin Dupré in American Collections', *Proceedings of the American Philosophical Society*, 101, no. 6 (1957), 535–50.

however, two diehard loyalists – David Thomas (Dafydd Ddu Eryri) and Walter Davies (Gwallter Mechain) – were rewarded for literary works which were hostile rather than sympathetic to democratic principles. Dafydd Ddu Eryri derived great satisfaction from humming 'Rule Britannia' and berating Tom Paine, while Gwallter Mechain was far too busy hobnobbing with grandees and fawning on bishops to support the suspicious activities of the Glamorgan stonemason.[62] By the early months of 1792, therefore, Iolo no longer frequented the Gwyneddigion Society meetings in London as often as before. The old-style Whiggism or stubborn conservatism of some of its members offended him and he despaired of the inability of 'knaves and fools of every class' to assess literature critically and espouse politically radical values. 'It [the Society] was at first whimsical', he informed a startled William Meyler, a Bath bookseller, 'became afterwards ridiculous, and is now detestable.'[63] Instead he attended the rational political debates hosted by the Caradogion Society, an English-speaking debating society which met on Saturday evenings at the Bull in Walbrook and in which, according to Iolo, 'very curious ebulitions of Welsh blood may be observed'.[64]

No one exuded such ebullience with more passion than Iolo himself. Ever since he had returned to London in the springtime of the French Revolution he had been itching to establish a regular 'tribunal' or Gorsedd which would actively promote the cultural and democratic cause on behalf of the despised Welsh. According to his masterplan, bardic assemblies would be convened at the equinoxes and solstices within a circle of stones, the Circle of the Covenant (*Cylch Cynghrair*). The Presiding or Ruling Bard (*Prifardd*), who exercised all the bardic functions, would stand by the presidial stone (*Maen Gorsedd*) surrounded by fully accredited, barefoot and bare-headed bards. The bardic order was to be divided into three: the True Bards (*Beirdd Braint*) would wear light blue robes, the emblem of peace, the Druidic Bards (*Derwyddon*) white robes, the emblem of purity and truth, and the Ovatian Bards (*Ofyddion*) green robes, the symbol of learning. Each order was judged to be equal in rank and honour. No bard was to bear a naked weapon or engage in contention, and it was expected that each member of the Gorsedd would be a herald of peace. Iolo served notice of his intention of holding the first Gorsedd on Primrose Hill – the finest vantage point in London for a sun worshipper – at the summer solstice of 1792. True to his word, just before sunrise on 21 June he led a hand-

---

[62] Graham Thomas, 'Gwallter Mechain ac Eisteddfod Corwen, 1789', *NLWJ*, XX, no. 4 (1978), 408; Geraint H. Jenkins, *Cadw Tŷ mewn Cwmwl Tystion: Ysgrifau Hanesyddol ar Grefydd a Diwylliant* (Llandysul, 1990), pp. 235–7; idem, 'An Uneasy Relationship: Gwallter Mechain and Iolo Morganwg', *MC*, 97 (2009), 73–99.
[63] *CIM*, I, p. 447, Iolo Morganwg to William Meyler, [?1792].
[64] NLW 21400C, no. 27. For the background to the Caradogion Society, see *HHSC*, pp. 128–9.

ful of his Caradogion colleagues to the top of Primrose Hill where, using small stones or pebbles, he made a circle and conducted a druidical court or moot 'in the eye of the sun and in the face of light'. Little is known of this inaugural session of the 'Gorsedd of the Bards of the Isle of Britain' and it was probably a fairly low-key affair. But Iolo went on to hold at least three other assemblies at the same venue in 1792–3 which won much greater recognition, but without catching the imagination of the public.[65] Only later, well into the Victorian period, did the Gorsedd become a truly Welsh national institution.

Iolo himself was the centrepiece of the ceremonies and mummeries associated with the Gorsedd.[66] Convinced that his doctrines derived from divine revelation and that the Muse had singled him out to be 'Bard of Britain's Isle', he did not lack self-confidence. No longer a 'groveling Worm', he oozed authority as an authentic Welsh bard: 'Of Liberty possess'd, I felt my self a Man.'[67] Indeed, he felt uniquely equipped to convey to the Welsh that new liberties and glories were at hand, and that it had fallen upon him to deploy the ancient bardic tradition of Wales to proclaim 'the Truth against the World' ('Y Gwir yn erbyn y Byd'). Others who had delved in such matters – Rowlands, Borlase, Macpherson, Pinkerton and other 'shallow-brained' romancers – were simply 'Moon-rakers' or truffle-hunters who never looked to the skies for inspiration but raked about in vain at the bottom of silt-laden ponds. But he, the genuine article, had walked 'the paths of nature' and had mastered the truly patriarchal theology which underpinned the bardic and druidic mysteries which had prevailed two thousand years ago and which had been smoothly assimilated by Christianity.[68] This polity had stoutly resisted the 'torrent of superstition' generated by 'the Pope and his imps of Priests, Monks &c.'[69] and had also held fast to 'an Invincible Spirit of Liberty', a spirit which Edward I – 'Long-Shanked Edward' – had vainly sought to extinguish by ordering the massacre of the Welsh bards, a deed which meant that his name was held 'in that detestation that is justly due to an astonishing majority of the kings that this world has, to its cost and sorrow, [known]'.[70] But a new chapter had now opened in the history of humankind:

---

[65] *HGB*, pp. 22–3; Geraint Bowen, *Golwg ar Orsedd y Beirdd* (Caerdydd, 1992), chapter 1.
[66] For some of his writings on the bardic institution, see NLW 13097B, pp. 239–63, 267–76; NLW 13121B, pp. 303–9; *CIM*, I, pp. 524–6, Iolo Morganwg to the *Gentleman's Magazine*, 22 September 1792. See also Geraint Bowen, 'Gorsedd y Beirdd – From Primrose Hill 1792 to Aberystwyth 1992', *THSC* (1992), 115–39; Dillwyn Miles, *The Secret of the Bards of the Isle of Britain* (Llandybïe, 1992) and, most convincing of all, Cathryn A. Charnell-White, *Bardic Circles: National, Regional and Personal Identity in the Bardic Vision of Iolo Morganwg* (Cardiff, 2007).
[67] NLW 13097B, pp. 296, 298, 303–4, 310–11.
[68] Ibid., pp. 283–314.
[69] NLW 13089E, pp. 422, 452.
[70] NLW 13097B, pp. 288, 434, 448, 450–1.

> New time appears! Thou glorious West
> How hails the World thy rising sun!
> O! Truth! in rays of Glory dress'd,
> Thy deathless reign is now begun.[71]

In his writings and in the odes which he sonorously recited at Gorseddau, Iolo projected himself as the 'Bard of Liberty', as the purveyor of ancient and modern liberties.

In expounding the doctrine of Welsh druido-bardism, he had no qualms about incorporating Christian and Hindu notions in showing how the transmigration of souls brought humans into a state of liberty.[72] The lowest starting-point for every created being was *annwn*, from which the soul embarked on a journey through several modes of existence until it reached the highest point, a state of permanent happiness from which it could never fall. Since God is determined to bring every being to this state of felicity, the likes of Iolo were duty-bound to cooperate with the Deity in combating evil and promoting the general good:

> The Creator brings all his works to trial and test at the point of Liberty. Liberty can never exist but in a point between two motives that counteract each other with equal force and influence; and man subjects himself to the one or the other in proportion to his antecedent attachments to good or evil at a time when he was under no powerful influence, which is the only time when comparative reasoning can possibly take place.[73]

God's benevolent servants were charged with the task of acting as 'warm advocate[s] of Rationality and Liberty'[74] and promoting honesty, truth, wisdom, justice and peace. Iolo and his fellow bards thus saw themselves as heralds of peace. In all assemblies held at the solstices and equinoxes, the spirit of peace was to prevail. No bard was permitted to bear a naked weapon or adopt a warlike stance, for the 'Goddess Liberty', the world's eternal friend, urged them to suffer pain rather than inflict harm on others:

> Peace, dove-eyed Peace, with sunny smile,
> High lifts her wand in Britain's Isle,
> Hell's horrid gorge receives the despot Pride.
> The *Bardic song* shall now resound,

---

[71] Ibid., p. 301; Williams: *PLP*, II, p. 212.
[72] For an illuminating discussion on this theme, see Hutton, *Blood and Mistletoe*, pp. 156–7.
[73] NLW 13097B, p. 303. See also William Owen, *The Heroic Elegies and Other Pieces of Llywarç Hen* (London, 1792 [1793]), p. xxix; Williams: *PLP*, II, pp. 239–48.
[74] NLW 13097B, p. 288.

> Trill through these *templed hills* around;
> Come, Sons of Truth! your paths are clear!
> In robes of light, in heav'nly forms appear,
> For Justice wears the crown, reigns now th'eternal guide.[75]

In these ways, the Gorsedd acquired a reputation as an outlet for enlightened sociability, radical idealism and republican sentiments. Iolo took pride in being the orchestrator of an institution which exhibited 'a noble spirit of Liberality, genuine morality, and Liberty'.[76] Its concern with pressing public issues, its bewildering dependence on arcane and esoteric knowledge, and its fondness for Jacobin emblems and traitorous rhetoric meant that the Gorsedd was seen as a potentially subversive enclave. Iolo did nothing to quell such rumours. His exposition of bardic lore, as Mary-Ann Constantine has detected, contained 'echoes of the ceremonious . . . language of the new French State',[77] and his colleagues long cherished his declamation of a fiery ode dedicated to Rhita Gawr, a legendary figure who, when he stamped his foot, caused the earth, skies and stars to tremble, and who, having slayed many tyrannical kings, fashioned a robe made from their beards. 'I am determined to follow his example', he cried, 'and hope to be soon furnished with an excellent warm great Coat.'[78] He composed or adapted triads which voiced his moral vision and egalitarian sentiments within Gorsedd circles[79] and, in this 'golden age of mystification',[80] when Rosicrucian freemasonry and the Illuminati of Bavaria produced a bewildering set of revelations which provoked confusion and alarm, it is not surprising that conspiracy theories flourished. John Walters, who famously described the Gorsedd as 'a made Dish',[81] in which masonry loomed large, was one of many who found its procedures remarkably similar to the exclusivity and secrecy of masonic lodges. Iolo vigorously refuted such charges, insisting that his beloved assemblies were, without exception, held at a conspicuous site in full public gaze.[82] But political loyalists seized every opportunity to blacken the name of Iolo's bardic society.

---

[75] Williams: *PLP*, II, pp. 214–15.
[76] NLW 13121B, p. 306; Owen, *The Heroic Elegies and Other Pieces of Llywarç Hen*, p. xxiv.
[77] Williams: *PLP*, II, pp. 220–1; Mary-Ann Constantine, 'Ossian in Wales and Brittany' in Howard Gaskill (ed.), *The Reception of Ossian in Europe* (London, 2004), p. 80. See also *Bardic Circles*, pp. 21–4.
[78] NLW 13094E, p. 144; NLW 13122B, pp. 320–2; NLW 13144A, p. 258; NLW 13158A, pp. 217–20; NLW 21323B, p. 41; NLW 21398E, no. 29a.
[79] Williams: *PLP*, II, pp. 217–56; *MAW*, III, pp. 190–6, 199–318; Rachel Bromwich, *Trioedd Ynys Prydein: The Triads of the Island of Britain* (3rd edn., Cardiff, 2006).
[80] J. M. Roberts, *The Mythology of the Secret Societies* (London, 1972), p. 90; Margaret C. Jacob, *Living the Enlightenment: Freemasonry and Politics in Eighteenth-Century Europe* (Oxford, 1991), pp. 3–22.
[81] Cardiff 3.104, vol. 6, letter no. 3, John Walters to Edward Davies, 3 May 1793; G. J. Williams, 'Gorsedd y Beirdd a'r Seiri Rhyddion', *LlC*, 7, nos. 3 and 4 (1963), 213–16.
[82] NLW 13100B, p. 182.

In many ways it is remarkable that Iolo was able to maintain this momentum. Dogged by bouts of asthma, headaches and delirium, he pined for his wife and 'four little babes' (his fourth child, Elizabeth, had been born on 5 May 1790). Slumming in a cold garret close to where Chatterton had earlier died in mysterious circumstances, he bemoaned his lot in this fount of miseries.[83] At one stage in autumn 1792 he contemplated suicide. Blood-letting, purgings, and even a course of electrotherapy in Soho had brought him little relief, and he confessed that only copious supplies of laudanum had saved him from 'the jaws of death'.[84] Somehow he found a new will to live and, following a spirited public declamation at the Gorsedd held on 22 September,[85] he began to challenge the hordes of demons which filled his head and tormented him. Already familiar with high Enlightenment debates on commerce, luxury and inequality, as well as with issues regarding constitutional reform, he began writing essays which expressed his moral distaste for unfettered wealth, commerce and luxury.[86] Written in an earthy, pungent style, calculated to demonstrate his independence as a simple but honest Welsh journeyman, his drafts bristled with passion and anger, so much so that at times he had to rein himself in: 'I must suffer myself to cool a little!'[87] Iolo seldom wrote without getting worked up, and his 'Letters on Universal Legislation', as he called this critique, is no exception.

As a man of feeling, an active citizen, and one who had himself suffered the indignities of poverty, debt and imprisonment, Iolo was aware that the politics of consumption were beginning to demand attention. The concept of consumption was increasingly viewed as a motor which drove the economy and enriched the wealth of nations. A wide range of fashionable and luxurious consumer goods had become available in towns and cities and encouraged heavy spending. Equally, the advance of technology – the introduction of spinning jennies, carding engines and the flying shuttle – was transforming the means of production. The question was how far unfettered consumption and the proliferation of mechanical contrivances were dehumanizing processes

---

[83] *CIM*, I, pp. 467–8, 471, 489–90, 507–8, 515–16, 527–8, Iolo Morganwg to Margaret (Peggy) Williams, 4 February 1792, 11 February 1792, 5 May 1792, 20 July 1792, 9 August 1792, 27 October 1792.
[84] NLW 23187E, no. 9. See also Geraint Phillips, 'Math o Wallgofrwydd: Iolo Morganwg, Opiwm a Thomas Chatterton', *NLWJ*, XXIX, no. 4 (1996), 391–410.
[85] *HGB*, p. 26.
[86] NLW 21323B; NLW 21395E; NLW 21396E.
[87] NLW 21395E, p. 4.

which favoured the rich at the expense of the poor.[88] Iolo had no doubts. His own livelihood was of course threatened by the burgeoning consumer culture and the factory system, but his fierce criticisms arose largely from his acute sense of right and wrong, especially on matters relating to social division and exclusion.

Broadly speaking, Iolo's argument ran as follows. From the Creation one of the principal foundation stones of the rights of man had been equal rights to the possession of land. Nature and providence had intended that each man be given a subsistence and a claim to the necessaries of life. But 'Wealthful Ambition' and 'Ambitious Wealth', practised by 'the Monopolizing Merchant, Slave-possessing Planter, land-Engrossing Farmer, all-grasping Manufacturer, Blood-sucking Usurer, or common Purse-proud Master', had robbed common people of their inheritance.[89] Owners of 'immoderate wealth' fed on inequality and reduced thousands of innocent people to a state of abject poverty. Commerce – 'the God of Gods' – undermined the common good by permitting manufacturers to turn working people into 'a species of automata', passing their days in poverty and ignorance as 'Bloodsucking machines' took hold. Wading 'deep in blood', commerce exercised 'horrid barbarities' in the gold and silver mines of Peru and Mexico, enriched the cowskin hero in the sugar plantations of the Caribbean, and propped up the thrones of kings: 'Oh! Commerce, thou Great Thief of the World. Thou that, a Canibal, feedest on human blood, quenchest thy thirst in the tears of Widows, of Orphans, of Wretches of all descriptions.'[90]

The eldest daughter of 'King Commerce' was Fashion, whom Iolo instinctively coupled with extravagance, frivolity and waste. All around him in London, Bristol, Bath and other urban centres with which he was familiar, there were clothes, textiles, furnishings, decorative goods and ornamental metalware which encouraged over-indulgence and gratuitous spending. Luxuries stimulated inequality and enabled 'fools of fashion' – preening courtiers, strutting bucks, debauchees and strumpets – to flaunt themselves in courts, parks

---

[88] For the background, see John Brewer and Roy Porter (eds.), *Consumption and the World of Goods* (London, 1993); Maxine Berg, *The Age of Manufactures 1700–1820: Industry, Innovation and Work in Britain* (new rev. edn., London, 1994); idem and Helen Clifford (eds.), *Consumers and Luxury: Consumer Culture in Europe 1650–1850* (Manchester, 1999); Martin Daunton and Matthew Hilton (eds.), *The Politics of Consumption: Material Culture and Citizenship in Europe and America* (Oxford, 2001); Maxine Berg, *Luxury and Pleasure in Eighteenth-Century Britain* (Oxford, 2005). For the response of Romantics to imperialism, colonialism and commercialism, see Tim Fulford and Peter J. Kitson (eds.), *Romanticism and Colonialism: Writing and Empire, 1780–1830* (Cambridge, 1998), Saree Makdisi, *Romantic Imperialism: Universal Empire and the Culture of Modernity* (Cambridge, 1998) and James Chandler and Maureen N. McLane (eds.), *The Cambridge Companion to British Romantic Poetry* (Cambridge, 2008).

[89] NLW 21323B, pp. 1, 9, 16, 19–20.

[90] Ibid., pp. 21–40; NLW 21395E, p. 4.

and gardens in order to impress the multitude and 'throw dust in the eyes of Reason and good sense'.[91] The more Iolo reflected on the prodigious size of London, its rampant commercialism and 'Belching Luxury', the more he indulged in anti-metropolitan rhetoric. London was like 'a monstrous and foul Cancer, corroding Britain to the heart', a parasitic city which robbed its hinterland, the provinces and the Celtic countries of people and resources. In Wales the prevalence of great landowners and monopolist farmers had depopulated the countryside and forced people to migrate to the capital where they were contaminated with 'enormous vices' which reduced many of them to abject poverty.[92] A devolutionist by instinct, he believed in prohibiting the development of great cities, in diffusing trade and commerce, and in breaking the Oxbridge monopoly on higher education. He also warned the Americans not to found a 'Great Babylonian' city in Washington lest it wither into a den of iniquity and disgrace the name of its founder.[93]

Here was a man thirsting for change and convinced that better days were fast approaching: 'Man begins now to learn the Language of Nature, of Reason, of Truth, of Humanity. O! for a Song in the divine Language, to the tune of an Angel's Harp, to celebrate the glorious Revolutions of France and America.'[94] He strongly believed that common people, so unforgivably derided by Burke as the 'swinish multitude', would shortly be roused 'like a sleeping Lion awaked by the tread of a Monkey': 'Eyes, Ears, in short all the mental senses of man are opening.'[95] Paine's great work was the subject of popular conversation and, as rulers remained deaf to the desires of the people, 'danger, tumult, insurrection, Revolution, are breeding very fast in Britain'.[96] The principal enemies of the third estate were usurping kings, aristocrats and landowners who, by oppression, tyranny, commerce and war, had appropriated the lands, wealth and rights of the people and caused such depredation and suffering that the world had become 'one horrid Scene of Blood'.[97] Since God was the only rightful sovereign, the ideal form of government was one which obeyed and practised the 'grand principles' of Christianity – justice, liberty, peace and truth. By contrast, earthly monarchs were bound to be tyrannical because their ambitions were governed by wealth, war, luxury, commerce, inequality and the suppression of the natural rights of man. Warmongering kings, feeding like ravens, kites, hawks, eagles and vultures on human remains on battlefields, had no interest in settling differences peacefully and to the satisfaction of

---

[91] NLW 21323B, pp. 41–50.
[92] Ibid., p. 51.
[93] Ibid., pp. 58–9.
[94] NLW 21395E, p. 7.
[95] NLW 21323B, pp. 8–9.
[96] Ibid., p. 13.
[97] NLW 21395E, p. 16.

all parties, while editors of newspapers like *The Times* nourished their ambitions with paeans to war and slaughter. Iolo mocked the latter in ironic vein:

> Last Friday on the Plains of Champaign the Most Magnanimous Duke of Brunswick gave a truly magnificent Dinner to his Royal Friends, Cousins, and Allies, The Bears of Berne and Russia, The Austrian Vulture and the Spanish Condor. The British Lion was invited, but did not attend. The first Course consisted of one hundred thousand Frenchmen, who having asserted that their Lives and properties were their own, and persisting in this their Wicked Error, were first excommunicated by the Pope, and then according to the well known Imperial Laws in such case made and provided, Slaughtered. We are not able at present to give further particulars, only that after the most delicious wines, the whole company regaled themselves plentifully with the Tears of Widows, Orphans, etc. and every heart was glad.[98]

A community devoted to war and bereft of religious principles left people vulnerable to infidelity – 'the greatest bane of society' – and the kind of priestcraft which turned religion into a matter of trade and profit. True toleration, peace and goodwill were based on individual conscience, civil duty and morality. 'None can be tollerated', he declared, 'who will not tollerate.'[99] Iolo dreamed of a society in which humankind, impelled by the spirit of Christian benevolence, established communities of people dedicated to peace, compassion and toleration.

As far as individual states, including Britain, were concerned, there was no doubt in his mind by this stage that the republican model was the ideal polity. The absolute sovereignty of the people was the corner-stone of his programme: 'This Will of the People is the True and Lawful Sovereign . . . The People once, the People forever.'[100] Yet, unlike the London Corresponding Society, Iolo did not champion the cause of universal manhood suffrage, let alone universal suffrage. He believed that voters should be drawn from among those he judged to be 'active citizens', namely married men, widowers and unmarried persons who had given eminent public service to the state. Although he conceded that radical feminists like Catherine Macaulay and Mary Wollstonecraft and others would have 'figured to greater Advantage in the House of Lords than half the wooden headed peers in the kingdom', he could not bring himself to plead the rights of women except in so far as their voice was implied in the joint suffrage of husband and wife.[101] He did not believe that bachelors and spinsters had a stake in the future of society and

---

[98] Ibid., p. 18.
[99] Ibid., pp. 24–5.
[100] Ibid., pp. 20, 29; NLW 21323B, p. 61.
[101] Ibid., pp. 60–6; NLW 21395E, pp. 30–9; NLW 21396E, no. 10.

thus, together with criminals and idiots, they were 'passive citizens' outside the pale of the constitution. Although the latter would have no power to cast votes or make laws, they still possessed natural rights and could apply for redress of grievances and the amendment of unjust laws: 'The voice of Truth, Reason, Wisdom, Justice and Benevolence shall be heard and respected from all quarters, from every individual Citizen whether passive or active.'[102] On two days in the year – 21 March and 21 September (days which corresponded with Iolo's Gorseddau) – vernal and autumnal conventions would be held in which the people would assemble in their respective provinces and those who were eligible would cast their vote by ballot.

Legislative power was to be vested in a Senate whose membership consisted of three delegates from each province, elected for three years annually on a rotation basis in order to ensure that it retained experienced delegates as well as absorbing new blood. The Senate would sit for at least two or three hours a day and its powers should never be suspended to accommodate a general election. It should sit in perpetuity, constantly renewing its membership, thereby ridding the land of those disorderly parliamentary elections which disfigured the political process. Two-thirds of the total membership would constitute a quorum and the body as a whole would represent the collective will and wisdom of the nation.[103] Besides the Senate there would be a National Council made up of the most experienced and able judges whose task would be to subject bills to rigorous scrutiny on three separate occasions before ratification by Senate. The Council would have no power to enact laws, but it would elect a head of state to be known as President. No longer, Iolo rejoiced, would there be 'such Villains as Henry the Eighth, knaves as Louis the Sixteenth, or Fools as many as we know'.[104]

Living in a city which was the fulcrum of British imperial expansion and commercial activity, Iolo was well placed to meditate on the widening gulf between rich and poor, the extent to which people were driven by commercial greed, carnal appetites and bibulous excess, and how libertarian politics suffered at the hands of tyrants who thrived on militarism and war, and heaped indignities on poor, defenceless people at home and abroad. His indignant response, expressed in these passionate political essays, reflected in part his own personal tragedy but was mainly provoked by the very real possibility that the time was ripe for Britain to emulate America and France by pinning its faith on republican government based on the sovereignty of the people. Iolo's debt to the writings of Price, Paine and others is plain, but he was never a slavish imitator of other models, and his essays, enlivened by irony, parody

---

[102] NLW 21395E, p. 36.
[103] NLW 21396E, nos. 8–9.
[104] Ibid., no. 10; NLW 21395E, p. 35.

and bristling anger, possess enormous imaginative verve as well as impressive political acumen. As always, he oversimplified and exaggerated, but of his moral courage there is no doubt, and he was clearly thrilled to be living through a time of unprecedented political, social and cultural change.

By this stage, in spite of growing evidence of a government clamp-down on free speech, Iolo was becoming increasingly politically active. He had some command of French and books relating to France were on his shelves.[105] He frequented lectures, meetings and dinners organized by Francophile societies like the London Revolution Society and the Society for Constitutional Information, proposed spirited toasts to the French republic, and rendered 'Ça Ira' and the new marching song, the 'Marseillaise', with gusto.[106] 'Liberty' songs appealed to him and he courted attention by flirting with the London Corresponding Society which, from its inception in January 1792, had appealed to working-class mechanics, artisans and tradesmen by espousing the right of every citizen to participate in politics and universal manhood suffrage.[107] Congratulatory addresses were dispatched by the SCI and LCS to the French National Convention in late 1792 and Iolo used his links with David Williams and Tom Paine to swell his list of subscribers by winning the approval of the Girondist movement. Among them was Jacques-Pierre Brissot, leader of the Girondins, a former police spy and hack writer who, heavily influenced by David Williams's *Letters on Political Liberty* (1782), became an ardent republican and a crusader for universal freedom.[108] Brissot was probably instrumental in bringing the Welsh philosopher to Paris to act as an unofficial adviser to the committee which had been set up to draft the new French constitution. Tom Paine was also among Brissot's closest friends and might well have wheedled a subscription from him for Iolo either in London or during his time in Paris. Ironically, however, by the time *Poems, Lyric and Pastoral* had appeared, Brissot had fallen foul of Robespierre and been guillotined in October 1793. Another

---

[105] NLW 21410E, no. 36.
[106] Albert Goodwin, *The Friends of Liberty: The English Democratic Movement in the Age of the French Revolution* (London, 1979), p. 217.
[107] Henry Collins, 'The London Corresponding Society' in John Saville (ed.), *Democracy and the Labour Movement* (London, 1954), pp. 103–34; Mary Thale (ed.), *Selections from the Papers of the London Corresponding Society 1792–1799* (Cambridge, 1983); Michael T. Davis (ed.), *London Corresponding Society, 1792–1799* (6 vols., London, 2002); idem, 'The Mob Club? The London Corresponding Society and the Politics of Civility in the 1790s' in idem and Paul A. Pickering (eds.), *Unrespectable Radicals? Popular Politics in the Age of Reform* (Aldershot, 2008), pp. 21–40.
[108] Williams: *PLP*, I, p. xxvi; Dybikowski, 'David Williams (1738–1816) and Jacques-Pierre Brissot: Their Correspondence', *NLWJ*, XXV, no. 1 (1987), 71–97; ibid., no. 2 (1987), 167–90. According to Dybikowski, Brissot was Williams's 'most significant friend'. Dybikowski, *On Burning Ground: An Examination of the Ideas, Projects and Life of David Williams*, p. 194; Foner, *Tom Paine and Revolutionary America*, p. 235.

Girondin in Paris who supported Iolo's anthology of poems was 'Citizen' Henri Jansen, a translator and editor from The Hague who became a successful publisher in Paris during the Directory.[109] To have the support of those who were unleashing the revolutionary potential of the press in France delighted Iolo, as did the news that Paine, who had fled to Paris, had been made an honorary French citizen. Iolo's ardent Francophilia, however, horrified his wife, and when she learned that he had publicly declaimed pro-Gallic and pro-Paine propaganda in his 'Ode on the Mythology of the Ancient British Bards' she accused him of aligning himself with those 'likely to be the cause of drenching theyr cuntery with blood' and being 'more warme then wise forever, all ways runing from one extreme to the other'. 'For God sake', she cried angrily, 'have nothing to say to them [i. e. Jacobins] leste you should repente to late.'[110] But the call of 'Liberty' was ringing loudly in his ears. When Prince Talleyrand embarked on a charm offensive in London in the winter of 1792–3, Iolo was captivated by his 'dangerous glamour' and the enthusiasm with which he exclaimed the words '*Ah! la Liberté!*'[111]

But the French dimension of the radical movement was also its Achilles heel since it was easy for loyalists to brand the likes of Iolo as 'Jacobins' and 'Levellers'. The forces of reaction were advancing. In May 1792 a royal proclamation had warned against uttering or publishing seditious words and, by September, the Association for the Preservation of Liberty and Property against Republicans and Levellers, spearheaded by a London magistrate John Reeves, had been established.[112] On 21 January Louis XVI was executed and within ten days the French Convention had declared war on Britain. The political climate had changed and those who had publicly supported French liberty were harried and maltreated by 'Church and King' mobs. 'All is bustle now in this vast metropolis', wrote William Richards, Welsh Baptist minister at Lynn, 'It is evidently the war of Kings, Peers, Priests, civil and religious Corporations, and privileged orders, against Freedom and the Rights of Man.'[113] Loyalists

---

[109] Carla Hesse, *Publishing and Cultural Politics in Revolutionary Paris, 1789–1810* (Berkeley, Calif., 1991), pp. 192–3.

[110] *CIM*, I, pp. 542–3, Margaret (Peggy) Williams to Iolo Morganwg, 1 January 1793.

[111] Simon Schama, *Citizens: A Chronicle of the French Revolution* (London, 1989), p. 680; *RAEW*, p. 48. Iolo told his biographer Waring that he had met Talleyrand at David Williams's home, but we know that the latter complained that Talleyrand did not 'do me the honour of calling at my house'. Jones, *David Williams: The Anvil and the Hammer*, p. 119. In old age, Iolo's memory was fallible and he must have encountered Talleyrand elsewhere in London.

[112] Eugene Charlton Black, *The Association: British Extraparliamentary Political Organization, 1769–1793* (Cambridge, Mass., 1963), chapter 7; David Eastwood, 'John Reeves and the Contested Idea of the British Constitution', *British Journal for Eighteenth Century Studies*, 16 (1993), 197–212.

[113] John Oddy (ed.), *The Writings of the Radical Welsh Baptist Minister William Richards (1749–1818)* (Lewiston, NY, 2008), p. 208.

preyed on the fear of the masses by depicting France as an ungovernable nation racked by mob rule. Iolo, of course, was strongly anti-war and just as hostile to the infamous atrocities committed in France in the name of liberty. But by early April rumours were spreading in the Vale of his affiliations with Jacobins, of an alleged visit to France, and of treasonable correspondence between him and the French Convention. When his wife alerted him to these accusations, he scoffed at them: 'For God's sake do not talk any more such nonsense . . . I only laugh at these things.'[114]

Almost immediately, however, his world fell apart when news arrived of the death of his beloved three-year-old daughter Elizabeth. His soul ravaged with grief, he hastened homeward and insisted on exhuming the body so that he could see his 'dear little dead Lizzy' for the last time.[115] Inconsolable over the summer, he could not bring himself to return to the 'hell, commonly called London'[116] until late September. But he continued his tireless fight against kingcraft and priestcraft by supplying the London Welsh with Welsh triads ('There are three men who wish to live on the property of others: a king, a priest and a thief'), an annotated version of his 'Ode, on converting a sword into a pruning hook' in which he chastised 'despot kings' and 'modern cut th[roats] of kingly brood', and a thunderous assault on the Church of England: 'What does it do? What has it ever done since it was called a church (or rather nicknamed thus) towards spreading knowledge of the truth? Not a jot!'('Beth y mae hi yn ei wneuthur? Beth a wnaeth hi erioed er pan a'i galwyd yn eglwys (neu'n hyttrach a'i llysenwyd felly) tuag at dannu gwybodaeth o'r gwirionedd? Dim yn y byd!')[117]

But however often Iolo vilified London and Londoners, he still loved to be at the centre of things. As Roy Porter pointed out, the capital possessed 'a special demotic energy, which many affected to hate but in reality found a drug'.[118] Iolo had no intention of abandoning his ambition of publishing his long-delayed anthology of English poems. There were drafts to complete, revisions to be made, proofs to be read, and more unsuspecting subscribers to ambush. Pursuing an erratic course among diverse groups of political radicals, he moved into the orbit of Rational Dissent with increasing enthusiasm. Liberal-minded Dissenters in London played a key role in the campaign against

---

[114] *CIM*, I, p. 559, Iolo Morganwg to Margaret (Peggy) Williams, 6 April 1793.
[115] NLW 21387E, no. 26; NLW 21285E, no. 818a; *CIM*, I, p. 559, Iolo Morganwg to Margaret (Peggy) Williams, 8 April 1793.
[116] Ibid., I, p. 600, Iolo Morganwg to Margaret (Peggy) Williams, 20 September 1793.
[117] Ibid., pp. 571–4, Iolo Morganwg to William Owen Pughe, 18 June 1793; ibid., pp. 585–9, 589–93 (trans.), Iolo Morganwg to the publisher of *Cylch-grawn Cynmraeg: neu Drysorfa Gwybodaeth*, 27 July 1793. See also Geraint H. Jenkins, *Iolo Morganwg y Gweriniaethwr* (Aberystwyth, 2010).
[118] Roy Porter, *London: A Social History* (London, 1994), p. 182.

the Test and Corporation Acts and in encouraging free speech and enquiry. Iolo's unorthodox mind was influenced by David Hartley's *Observations on Man, his Frame, his Duty, and his Expectations* (1749), not least because the Hartleian notion that actions are governed by experience and association helped to underpin his commitment to disinterested benevolence.[119] He also admired Joseph Priestley for his wide-ranging experimentalism and bravery. According to Elijah Waring, when Priestley was driven out of Birmingham by a furious 'Church and King' mob in 1791 and took up co-pastorship of the Gravel Pit Meeting House in Hackney, Iolo became 'a partial, though not an implicit disciple' of his.[120] His debt to Priestley is apparent in his emphasis on the deterministic philosophical notion of necessarianism, moral virtue and benevolent behaviour. He claimed that Priestley had been influential in securing his election to the London Philosophical Society and that he was present when Priestley set sail for America in 1794, a poignant moment which he marked with a farewell poem.[121] At some point Iolo began worshipping at Essex Street chapel, the mother-church of Unitarians in London where non-trinitarians like Theophilus Lindsey, Andrew Kippis, Thomas Belsham and John Disney nourished heterodox tendencies, social justice and liberal politics.[122] Rational Dissenters adopted a variety of doctrinal positions and it was difficult for Iolo, who always appeared to be a bundle of inconsistencies, to maintain a firm stance during the fraught and dangerous 1790s. Waring reckoned that 'he was so much a being *sui generis*, that he had his own peculiar modifications of almost every opinion, speculative or conventional'.[123] For instance, he found no difficulty in reconciling his belief in metempsychosis with necessarianism, and believed that both were optimistic doctrines which encouraged people to undertake acts of benevolence and promote human happiness. A man of such

---

[119] Richard C. Allen, *David Hartley on Human Nature* (Albany, NY, 1999). For points of contact on this issue between Blake and Iolo, see Jon Mee, '"Images of Truth New Born": Iolo, William Blake and the Literary Radicalism of the 1790s' in *Rattleskull Genius*, pp. 181–2. See also Evan Radcliffe, 'Revolutionary Writing, Moral Philosophy, and Universal Benevolence in the Eighteenth Century', *Journal of the History of Ideas*, 54, no. 2 (1993), 221–40.

[120] *RAEW*, p. 134; Isabel Rivers and David L. Wykes (eds.), *Joseph Priestley, Scientist, Philosopher, and Theologian* (Oxford, 2008). For the background to Rational Dissent, see Knud Haakonssen (ed.), *Enlightenment and Religion: Rational Dissent in Eighteenth-Century Britain* (Cambridge, 1996).

[121] *CIM*, II, p. 15, Iolo Morganwg to Theophilus Lindsey, 10 February 1797; *RAEW*, p. 134; NLW 21392F, no. 24^v.

[122] The principal authority on the Unitarian chapel in Essex Street is Grayson M. Ditchfield. See his edition of the correspondence of Theophilus Lindsey. Grayson M. Ditchfield (ed.), *The Letters of Theophilus Lindsey (1723–1808). Volume I: 1747–1788* (Woodbridge, 2007). In April 1822 Iolo described himself as the 'oldest Unitarian in Wales and, I believe, the only one now living of Mr Lindsey's first congregation in Essex Street'. *CIM*, III, p. 620, Iolo Morganwg to [?John Christie], 29 April 1822.

[123] *RAEW*, p. 34.

strong intelligence was bound to attract the attention of literary-minded Dissenters, and Iolo was happy that 'so many literary friends . . . call on me to take an evening [c]up of tea'.[124]

A key figure in his life was Joseph Johnson, a Unitarian bookseller at St Paul's Churchyard who knew every radical writer of note and who prided himself on being known as 'Honest Joe'.[125] Johnson was editor of the *Analytical Review*, the most influential radical monthly of the 1790s, and Iolo almost certainly conversed and argued with his clients and associates, who included Price, Priestley, Blake, Godwin and Wollstonecraft. The crossfertilization of ideas which occurred among this radical literati made the experience all the more enjoyable for Iolo. John Aikin, physician, writer and a forthright Dissenter, read some of his work in manuscript and introduced him to his sister Anna Letitia Barbauld, a poet, essayist and critic whose commitment to the notion of a benevolent deity and its implications for ethical behaviour made a profound impression on Iolo.[126] Both gladly subscribed to his anthology of poems, and probably introduced him to abolitionists in anti-slavery quarters and the anti-war lobby known as 'Friends of Peace'.[127] These included unorthodox Cambridge graduates who had sat at the feet of Robert Robinson, a pugnacious Baptist, at Cambridge.[128] Two of them caught Iolo's eye. Gilbert Wakefield, a biblical scholar and a waspish pamphleteer, was an unusually courageous crusader against war and slavery. Iolo wept profusely when he died of typhus in 1801 and recalled him as being as 'fearless as a Lion . . . [and] the warmly benevolent friend of Peace'.[129] The other, George Dyer, was a compassionate, book-reading

---

[124] *CIM*, I, p. 613, Iolo Morganwg to Margaret (Peggy) Williams, 30 October 1793.
[125] Helen Braithwaite, *Romanticism, Publishing and Dissent: Joseph Johnson and the Cause of Liberty* (Basingstoke, 2003). See also Brian Rigby, 'Radical Spectators of the Revolution: The Case of the *Analytical Review*' in Ceri Crossley and Ian Small (eds.), *The French Revolution and British Culture* (Oxford, 1989), pp. 63–83.
[126] *CIM*, I, pp. 614–15, John Aikin to Iolo Morganwg, [?November 1793]; Daniel E. White, 'The "Joineriana": Anna Barbauld, the Aikin Family Circle, and the Dissenting Public Sphere', *Eighteenth-Century Studies*, 32, no. 4 (1999), 511–33; Anne Janowitz, 'Amiable and Radical Sociability: Anna Barbauld's "Free Familiar Conversation"' in Gillian Russell and Clara Tuite (eds.), *Romantic Sociability: Social Networks and Literary Culture in Britain, 1770–1840* (Cambridge, 2002), pp. 62–81; William McCarthy, *Anna Letitia Barbauld: Voice of the Enlightenment* (Baltimore, Md., 2008). In one of his letters to Johnson, Iolo wished to be remembered to 'literary friends that frequent your shop, Dyer, Disney, Aikin, Mr & Mrs Barbauld, G. & W. Morgan & all others'. *CIM*, I, p. 772, Iolo Morganwg to [Joseph Johnson], [?September 1795].
[127] J. E. Cookson, *The Friends of Peace: Anti-War Liberalism in England, 1793–1815* (Cambridge, 1982).
[128] George Dyer, *Memoirs of the Life and Writings of Robert Robinson* (London, 1796); David Turley, *The Culture of English Antislavery, 1780–1860* (London, 1991), p. 163.
[129] NLW 21408E, no. 10. See also ibid., nos. 8–9. For Wakefield, see *ODNB*.

Unitarian whose eccentricity and disorderly ways matched those of Iolo.[130] Dyer's moving works, *Complaints of the Poor People of England* (1793) and *A Dissertation on the Theory and Practice of Benevolence* (1795) left their mark on the Welshman and the two men often discussed the travails of the times over cups of tea.

By moving in these circles Iolo became enmeshed in the anti-slave trade and anti-war campaigns in London. He regularly frequented warehouses, counting-houses, shops and bookstores where traders, ship-owners, speculators and abolitionists assembled, and interrogated culprits about the morality of wrenching healthy young men from their families in Africa, herding them like animals on to slave ships, and setting them to work as slaves in harshly administered sugar plantations in the Caribbean. A man of sensibility like Iolo, who was increasingly sympathetic to the downtrodden victims of society, deplored the fact that many of the blessings which Christians took for granted were bought 'with the misery of others'.[131] His heart bled as he contemplated the fate of Spanish slaves in the mountains of Peru and African slaves in the West Indies, whose tears and blood make up 'a considerable part of the sugar which is so sweet to us, but very bitter to them'.[132] Denouncing 'Cowskin heroes, alias negro drivers', he refused to disgrace his list of subscribers with the names of those 'who villainously abet the slave trade',[133] abstained from using Caribbean sugar, and broke off relations with his slave-owning brothers in Jamaica.[134] He familiarized himself with abolitionist literature, especially the heart-rending poems of Cowper, Samwell and Southey,[135] and publicly voiced

---

[130] *CIM*, I, pp. 630, 631, George Dyer to Iolo Morganwg, [?1794]. For Dyer, see 'George Dyer', *Emmanuel College Magazine*, XV (1905–6), 194–213, Nicholas Roe, 'Radical George: Dyer in the 1790s', *Charles Lamb Bulletin*, 49 (1985), 17–26, and *ODNB*.

[131] *CIM*, I, p. 630, Iolo Morganwg to Margaret (Peggy) Williams, [?1794].

[132] Ibid., p. 629.

[133] NLW 21400C, no. 23; *CIM*, I, p. 384, Iolo Morganwg to William Bulgin ('Jacobus Placo'), [?June 1791]. His animadversions on slave-trading and the 'Idiotic Dullness' of Bristolians provoked a scabrous response from the bookseller Bulgin, who threatened to clap Iolo's nose 'in the Bastile of my Fingers'. NLW 13089E, p. 176. See also Mary-Ann Constantine, *'Combustible Matter': Iolo Morganwg and the Bristol Volcano* (Aberystwyth, 2003).

[134] NLW 21387E, no. 8. For the background, see Andrew Davies, '"Uncontaminated with Human Gore"? Iolo Morganwg, Slavery and the Jamaican Inheritance' in *Rattleskull Genius*, pp. 293–313. Iolo believed that his brothers had become 'as hard-hearted as the devil'. *CIM*, I, p. 602, Iolo Morganwg to Margaret (Peggy) Williams, 20 September 1793.

[135] For Iolo and Cowper, see *RAEW*, pp. 42–4, and NLW 21401E, no. 19, in which Iolo describes Cowper as 'our incomparably sweet Bard of Humanity'. For Samwell's support for Iolo against William Bulgin, see *CIM*, I, pp. 401–3, David Samwell (Dafydd Ddu Feddyg) to Iolo Morganwg, 11 August 1791. Samwell's 'unusually subtle' poem 'The Negro Boy' was published in the 'Anonymous' category in James G. Basker (ed.), *Amazing Grace: An Anthology of Poems about Slavery, 1660–1810* (London, 2002), pp. 565–6. I'm grateful to Dr E. Wyn James for pointing out this error to me. Herbert G. Wright, 'The Relations of the Welsh Bard Iolo Morganwg with Dr Johnson, Cowper and Southey', *Review of English Studies*, VIII, no. 30 (1932), 129–38. For Southey's anti-slave trade poems, see Lynda Pratt (ed.), *Robert Southey: Poetical Works 1793–1810. Volume 5: Selected Shorter Poems, c.1793–1810* (London, 2004), pp. 48–54.

his admiration for 'Great' Wilberforce for exposing 'BRITAIN's foul disgrace' and for continuing to condemn the slaving lobby even as his motions against the slave trade were rejected one by one in Parliament.[136]

As we have seen, Iolo had also long believed that war was incompatible with the teachings of Christianity. He joined activists like Anna Letitia Barbauld, William Frend and Gilbert Wakefield in arousing public consciousness against war. He admired Barbauld's *Sins of the Government, Sins of the Nation* (1793), and Wakefield's equally trenchant *Spirit of Christianity* (1794) and also the satirical anti-war publications of the fiery pamphleteer William Fox in which 'he laid the Scourge with a powerful arm on the brawny shoulders of kings, statesmen and all Other Abettors of War'.[137] He was also impressed by the willingness of Quakers to wave the banner of peace publicly. He attended Quaker meetings in London and read Quaker tracts by Robert Barclay, John Bell and Hugh Turford which had run to several editions during the course of the eighteenth century.[138] His blunt manner, prodigious tea-drinking and use of homeopathic medicines were also consonant with the lifestyle of members of the Society of Friends and he was known to visit their burial grounds.[139] Iolo firmly believed that William Penn's Holy Experiment in seventeenth-century Philadelphia was 'a sublime example to all the Kings and Senates of the Earth'.[140] He filled reams of paper with anti-war songs and tirades against the 'ferocious warlike disposition' of the British.[141] Vowing never to dip his hands in blood, he insisted that war should never be mentioned except with 'that horror and detestation that its infernality requires'.[142] He strongly believed that an authentic Welsh bard was duty-bound to celebrate those who beat swords into ploughshares and spears into pruning hooks. It is one of the ironies of Iolo's life that a man who was such a vociferous critic of violence and war would often fly into a rage at the slightest provocation.

Early in January 1794, much to the relief of Iolo and his long-suffering wife, *Poems, Lyric and Pastoral* was published. Containing 101 poems, fairly evenly distributed in two volumes, and supported by as many as 676 subscribers, some of whom had ordered six or twelve sets, the work represented poems written over a period of two decades. He was proud of his achievement and personally delivered signed copies to the British Museum and Dr Williams's Library. During the protracted and vexatious process of bringing them into the

---

[136] Williams: *PLP*, II, pp. 209–10; *RAEW*, p. 61.
[137] NLW 13141A, pp. 365–9.
[138] Ibid., pp. 155–8.
[139] *RAEW*, pp. 22–4.
[140] NLW 21401E, no. 15; Williams: *PLP*, II, pp. 49–69.
[141] NLW 21401E, no. 26; NLW 21392A, no. 22ᵛ; NLW 21396E, no. 27; Williams: *PLP*, II, pp. 132, 136–44.
[142] NLW 13089E, p. 288.

public domain,¹⁴³ however, the politically-minded Iolo had often been urged to draw in his horns. He deeply regretted having shown his work to Christopher Anstey, the elderly Bath poet, who had taken it upon himself to edit poems and make 'interventions' which enraged Iolo.¹⁴⁴ Patrons like Mary Nicholl of Remenham, aware of his indomitable spirit, had urged him to make compromises which would promote sales of his book. Against his better judgement, Iolo was persuaded by Nicholl to write a suitably ingratiating letter to the Prince of Wales, seeking his imprimatur. As someone who loathed having to beg for favours, this was a task which Iolo abhorred. He knew full well that the son of George III was a controversial figure. A playboy and a spendthrift, the Prince of Wales pursued whores and duchesses with equal relish, and ran up enormous debts by spending lavishly on furnishing his sumptuous home at Carlton House.¹⁴⁵ Yet this pampered brat was known to be a generous and discerning patron of authors and artists, and Iolo was acutely aware that his hopes of gaining literary fame in the metropolis would be enhanced by securing the blessing of the future king on his publication. He would also have been aware that his friend David Williams had not only addressed his celebrated *Letters to a Young Prince* (1790) to the Prince of Wales but had also adorned the book with an engraved portrait of him.

Iolo soon regretted indulging in this 'bit of vanity'¹⁴⁶ and was distraught when royal permission was received, largely through the good offices of the Revd Frederick William Blomberg who, ironically, was widely thought to be the natural son of George III.¹⁴⁷ This meant that Iolo, heavily prompted by Mary Nicholl, was expected to compose a letter of fulsome thanks. He spent several weeks agonizing over the precise wording of different drafts. Determined not to produce a version reeking of 'the incense of flattery',¹⁴⁸ he depicted himself as an inoffensive, humble journeyman who had a wife and four young children to support and whose principal aim was to make an honest living as the last of the ancient Welsh bards. But he floundered as he reflected on the wild behaviour of the royal whoremonger. In one draft he mocked the

---

¹⁴³ See Mary-Ann Constantine, '"This Wildernessed Business of Publication": The Making of *Poems Lyric and Pastoral* (1794)' in *Rattleskull Genius*, pp. 123–45. Iolo's own copy in the National Library of Wales (Wb 904–5) contains handwritten corrections and insertions ready for a second edition which never materialized.
¹⁴⁴ *CIM*, I, pp. 375–6, Iolo Morganwg to John Walters, 24 February 1791; ibid., II, p. 50, Iolo Morganwg to Mary Barker, 26 March [1798]; Williams: *PLP*, I, pp. xvii–xviii.
¹⁴⁵ For the Prince of Wales's self-indulgent career, see Christopher Hibbert, *George IV* (Harmondsworth, 1976) and Saul David, *Prince of Pleasure: The Prince of Wales and the Making of the Regency* (London, 1998).
¹⁴⁶ *CIM*, I, p. 490, Iolo Morganwg to Margaret (Peggy) Williams, 5 May 1792.
¹⁴⁷ Ibid., I, pp. 490–1, Mary Nicholl to Iolo Morganwg, 31 May [?1792]; Arthur Aspinall (ed.), *The Correspondence of George, Prince of Wales, 1770–1812* (8 vols., London, 1963–71), VI, pp. 278, 543.
¹⁴⁸ *CIM*, I, p. 492, Iolo Morganwg to George, Prince of Wales, [?June 1792].

Prince as 'Mr Nobody or . . . Mr All-body, sans soul'.[149] Some kind of letter expressing his gratitude, perhaps the one he labelled 'Best Copy', must have been sent in due course, though Iolo once more regretted his involvement with such a rascal when he learned that the Prince had dismissed the Whig Lord Erskine as his attorney following his eloquent defence of Tom Paine against a charge of seditious libel.[150] Eventually, Iolo's blushes were spared when John Aikin advised him to include a short prefatory dedication, rather than an adulatory epistle, to the Prince which ran as follows: 'These volumes are, by permission, and with the respect of gratitude, dedicated to His Royal Highness George Prince of Wales, by his most humble servant, Edward Williams.'[151]

In a self-pitying, twelve-page preface, written 'with an *Ancient Briton's warm pride*',[152] Iolo maintained that his ambitions had always been thwarted by hardship, misfortune and malice. He was bitterly resentful at being roughly treated by envious enemies and wrote even more plainly about weathercock friends and hostile attorneys in unpublished drafts.[153] As for the poems, those contained in the first volume were characterized by an appreciation of landscape, rural nostalgia, local pride and a strong sense of moral sensibility. Many poems in the second volume, however, were hard-edged, pungent pieces, appreciably more controversial than anything found in the first two hundred pages. Three of his hard-hitting odes – on the muse, the mythology of the bards, and on converting swords into pruning hooks – were given their first airing in print, heavily buttressed by forthright annotations which he later described as 'king-flogging notes'.[154] In a song entitled 'God save the King' he dubbed the anthem 'that old *War Song of British Savages*' and in a note on 'The Horrors of War' he condemned 'our still *unchristianized* RULERS, and their *minions*'.[155] Nor was the established church spared: thanks to 'the scourge of offended *Priestcraft*', clerics enslaved the souls of their flocks and made 'execrable' attempts 'to force the *English language* on the *Welsh*'.[156] As we have seen, Iolo was already an advocate of republican principles, but he knew that injudicious writing could lead to prosecution, imprisonment or exile. Still, it is a matter for regret that he chose to omit this striking passage from his volume:

---

[149] Ibid., I, p. 494, Iolo Morganwg to George, Prince of Wales, [?June 1792].
[150] Ibid., I, pp. 539–40, Iolo Morganwg to George, Prince of Wales, [?1793]; John Hostettler, *Thomas Erskine and Trial by Jury* (Chichester, 1996), pp. 91–2.
[151] *CIM*, I, pp. 614–15, John Aikin to Iolo Morganwg, [?November 1793]; Williams: *PLP*, I, p. [v].
[152] Ibid., p. xix.
[153] NLW 21387E, no. 9.
[154] *CIM*, I, p. 648, Iolo Morganwg to John Walters, 21 January 1794.
[155] Williams: *PLP*, II, pp. 132, 143. See also NLW 21392F, no. 6.
[156] Williams: *PLP*, II, pp. 55, 56.

> Must my Politics be mentioned? Then to be in this as in every thing else sincere and honest. I am in my principles moderately republican. I believe that in a good Government, the power of making Laws, and of controlling every other part of the legislature, should be vested in the people, as it is in the British House of Commons. I care not whether the supreme magistrate be hereditary or elective, provided he be properly limited by Laws and have no will of his own independent of what the law has. I care not to what titles any one is born, but to the power none can be born. Power can never be the birthright of any, no more than wisdom or folly, merely from the circumstance of the parents have been possessed of these things. I wish for a reformation in our British Constitution, but rather than see my Country drenched with the blood of a revolution let me be for life chained to the oar. How long must it remain the disgrace of human reason, of high civilization, etc. that a reformation in Gov! cannot without bloodshed take place? As long doubtless as any will find it in their Interest to keep the people in Ignorance, in undue subjection. As long as Kings and others are brought up to the infernal trade of war; and of course under the necessity of extorting from their subjects the wealth required to enable them to force or seduce a dreadful number of thousands of unoffended and unoffending people to cut each other's throats while the real delinquents escape.[157]

In retrospect, he admitted that his annotations could have been bolder: 'Too general, no particular application. Tis too late to repent, or alter for the better.'[158] Yet he hoped that his book would make 'some noise', even though he was 'not Tom Paine yet'.[159] He fully expected his *Poems* to be minutely examined by the Attorney General, Sir Archibald MacDonald, and that '*Bearmongers*' like John Reeves would soon be on his tail.[160] So it proved.

The truth is that the politically forthright poems and notes published in *Poems* were the tip of the iceberg. Over many months Iolo had been assembling a portfolio of 'seditious' material and seems to have delighted in sailing close to the wind. 'Kingcraft' and 'Priestcraft' were his main targets. As John Barrell has eloquently shown, a diverse range of pamphlets, poems and songs invited readers to imagine the death of the king and what the consequences might be.[161] Iolo needed no second bidding. No Welsh republican of the day was more assiduous in undermining the dignity and honour of George III and the monarchy in general. He derived great satisfaction from composing scurrilous (but unsent) letters to the king in which he substituted pronouns of address with the Quaker style of 'thee' and 'thou'.[162] Anyone who was 'a vile worm

---

[157] NLW 21387E, no. 11.
[158] *CIM*, I, p. 649, Iolo Morganwg to John Walters, 21 January 1794.
[159] Ibid.
[160] Williams: *PLP*, I, p. xi.
[161] John Barrell, *Imagining the King's Death: Figurative Treason, Fantasies of Regicide 1793–1796* (Oxford, 2000), p. 114.
[162] NLW 21396E, no. 11.

of the earth' could not expect to be addressed as 'His Majesty'. Nor could he respect a king who shamelessly dispatched innocent young men to slay thousands of enemies 'on a grand imperial scale' on distant battlefields. A man of blood, George III was currently waging 'the most bloody war that Europe, perhaps the World, has hitherto known'.[163] 'God Save the King' was a 'vile murdering bloodthirsty song' which encouraged monarchs to commit butchery: 'What in low life we call murder, is in the language of Royalty called War.'[164] One of his cleverest essays, at least in its satirical edge, is his account of 'Demophobia', a disorder known as the king's evil but which, in Iolo's imagination, turned out to be a species of canine madness engendered by 'a German Whelp' for which the only cure was to dispatch the diseased dog and all his 'mangy mongrels' to the distant shores of Botany Bay.[165] Such language could easily be construed by the authorities as treason and Iolo must have known that, by expressing extreme anti-monarchical views, he was likely to be prosecuted and locked up.

The established church was another of his targets. In his eyes 'Priestcraft' was inimical to truth, reason and justice. Archbishops and bishops were 'ministers of Antichristianity', while clergymen were 'a gang of scoundrels'.[166] He loathed the pomp, ceremony and humbug of the state church, its devotion to the 'blood-built pallades of Kings'[167] and its delight in robbing parishioners of tithes and dues. He believed that the time was ripe to abandon the 'school of priestcraft' and to establish priestless societies which would encourage Bible-reading and promote morality, goodness and truth among the lower classes who, from the days of Christ to those of Tom Paine, had shown themselves to be friends of humankind.[168] As for the Anglican church:

> Do you think Sir that I am or ever will be of this Religion? No Sir. I will remain a convert to the religion of that place, tho it be hell it self, where there are no Babylonian Kings, no antichrist priests, no Graces of Canterby (holinesses of Rome may be admitted for without holiness no one shall see the Lord), no right revd father in God of human manufacture, no Grace bestowed, given, or conferred by a blasphemous earthly worm of a monarch, not even by Emperor of America, but surely the place where these are not to be found can never be hell. It is that place where S.t John tells us all are kings and priests – i.e. all are equal in the divine love and estimation. Of course this place may with strictest propriety be called the Land

---

[163] Ibid.
[164] NLW 21401E, nos. 1, 19, 20. See also in similar vein NLW 13094E, pp. 182, 186, 191; NLW 13130A, p. 260; NLW 21392F, no. 6; NLW 21401E, nos. 21–6.
[165] NLW 21433E, no. 4.
[166] NLW 13094E, pp. 182, 186, 191; NLW 21396E, no. 20.
[167] NLW 13123B, p. 158.
[168] Ibid., pp. 161–4; NLW 21396E, no. 25; Williams: *PLP*, I, pp. 104–8.

of Levelling – and as thus described by an inspired writer, it must [be] a heaven indeed. What a heaven where I shall no longer be trodden by Kings, Priests etc.[169]

This, too, was combustible stuff which could easily provoke the authorities to bring him before the courts.

So, too, could his anti-war stance. Iolo believed that the prosecution of the war with France and the unprecedented military activity of the 1790s were caused by 'Kingcraft' and 'Priestcraft'. The hellishness of war turned his stomach and he added epithets such as 'diabolical', 'infernal' and 'rascally' to words such as 'great' and 'glorious' used in British war songs and anthems.[170] He planned to publish a pamphlet entitled 'War incompatible with the Spirit of Christianity' and composed a flurry of anti-war songs like 'Bella! horrida Bella' and 'Invocation to Peace', in which he condemned the 'blood trade' which had become the sport of royalty and ecclesiastics.[171] To a paranoid government, such outspoken, disloyal language was likely to pollute the popular mind and give comfort to the enemy. But Iolo believed that, as a genuine British bard, he had a duty to assure the public that Truth was awakening and that the cause of Peace and Justice would soon 'blaze out in full radiance of day'.[172]

Certainly in Welsh, and possibly in wider, circles, Iolo had thus gained a reputation as a political gadfly, an agitator, a crypto-Jacobin and a Leveller who had adopted the French revolutionary form of address ('Citizens') and phraseology. He became used to being branded with 'opprobious' names, and he also knew that it would be wise to conceal or remove any papers which might be construed as incriminating.[173] It is a fair guess that he mischievously played cat-and-mouse with spies and snoopers, probably flummoxing them by using Welsh when challenged,[174] but even he could not have imagined that one of his friends among the London Welsh was laying snares for him. Sometime in May 1794 he was interrogated by William Pitt, Lord Grenville and Henry Dundas. Whereas Dundas was characteristically brusque and ill-tempered, Pitt was courteous and gentlemanly, especially when it transpired that, apart from a few libertarian songs, no incriminating evidence had been found in Iolo's papers. The prime minister showed him to the door and bade him take his papers with him. True to nature, Iolo bridled and told Pitt that since his papers had been seized without his consent they should be returned to him at his

---

[169] NLW 21396E, no. 11.
[170] NLW 21401E, no. 17.
[171] NLW 21400C, no. 38; NLW 21392A, nos. 22, 24.
[172] Ibid., no. 22ᵛ.
[173] *CIM*, I, pp. 672–3, Iolo Morganwg to Margaret (Peggy) Williams, 28 May 1794.
[174] He confessed that on one occasion when he was faced by a 'king-ridden mob' of loyalists in London he 'jabber'd Welsh, squeaked out "Church *sans* King", in as broken a manner as I could, and passed for a Dutchman with all but a Welshman or two, who laughed at me'. *CIM*, I, p. 676, Iolo Morganwg to Hugh Jones, 4 June 1794.

house.¹⁷⁵ The prime minister bowed to his wishes. As we saw in his earlier contretemps with Samuel Johnson, Iolo liked to give the impression that he always had the last word, and he may well have embroidered the account of his parting shot to Pitt. But his mood darkened when he discovered afterwards that he had been betrayed by Edward Jones, the so-called 'King's Bard', a loyalist from Merioneth who had taken umbrage when Iolo had dubbed him a shameless plagiarist and had also chastised him for singing 'God Save the King' at a meeting of the Gorsedd at the winter solstice of 1793.¹⁷⁶ Thereafter he castigated Jones at every opportunity and sought to undermine his credibility as a musician, an editor and an honest man. 'The Blunderhead harpist', he cried, 'may have some wit at his finger's ends. He may also, for ought I know have a trifle at the lower extremities of his carcase, but at the upper he certainly has not a single atom.'¹⁷⁷

But once Iolo's *Poems* were circulated and news of his appearance before the Privy Council was made known, some of his old patrons abandoned him. Mary Nicholl, who had drummed up many subscribers for the supposedly artless Welsh labouring poet, bitterly reproached him for promoting republican principles in his anthology and soliciting her support under false pretences. Writing to him in the third person, she declared that on no account would she admit any Jacobins under her roof.¹⁷⁸ Iolo's response to 'the Billingsgate bitch',¹⁷⁹ as he privately dubbed her, was characteristically intemperate. Signing himself 'Edward Williams, A Leveller', he informed her that the days of 'antiquited idolatry of kings, of nobles, of pomposity, imaginary greatness, &c.' were numbered and that common people were determined to ensure that sound principles of government prevailed.¹⁸⁰

It is highly unlikely that Iolo was involved in any way in clandestine plotting or underground insurrectionary politics. Yet he thrived on his reputation as a Welsh firebrand and instinctively shunned 'that infernal Goddess Prudence'.¹⁸¹ In a strange way, he behaved as if he craved martyrdom. He exposed himself to serious risks by running the gauntlet of 'Church and King' mobs, a deed which he celebrated in imitation of Horace:

---

175 Ibid., I, pp. 632–3, David Pugh to Iolo Morganwg [?1794]; *RAEW*, pp. 104–5.
176 David Pugh, a Welsh-born alderman in London, had informed Iolo of Jones's betrayal. For the plagiary issue, see NLW 13121B, pp. 445–8, and Tecwyn Ellis, *Edward Jones, Bardd y Brenin, 1752–1824* (Caerdydd, 1957), pp. 27, 32–3. An account of the Gorsedd in December 1792 is in *The Times*, 1 January 1793. David Samwell also warned Iolo against Jones: 'Iorwerth, despise that foolish harper, / He's little better than a sharper.' *CIM*, I, p. 634, David Samwell (Dafydd Ddu Feddyg) to Iolo Morganwg [?1794].
177 NLW 13144A, p. 276; NLW 13130A, p. 221. See also Iolo's amusing reference to 'Yorick Humstrum's Hobby-horsisms', NLW 13142A, p. 309.
178 *CIM*, I, p. 669, Mary Nicholl to Iolo Morganwg, 19 May [?1794].
179 Ibid., I, p. 693, Iolo Morganwg to Margaret (Peggy) Williams, 13 September 1794.
180 Ibid., I, p. 670, Iolo Morganwg to Mary Nicholl, [?20 May 1794].
181 NLW 21387E, no. 9.

> As late I walk'd out with my Soul in a flame
> Up-kindled by songs to sweet Liberty's name
> A gang of Informers came plump in my way,
> I cried room for Tom Paine! and all scamper'd away.[182]

On another occasion he was less fortunate. He stumbled across a mob of asinine bully-boys marching through the streets, beating drums and blowing trumpets:

> God save the King was the bawl, and to every one that passed by in silence they cried God save the King you republican son of a bitch, God save the King and damn the Jacobins – by way of change, they now and then roared out Church and King! Church and King, and damnation to the Presbyterians . . . now down on your marrow bone, damn your eyes and say 'God save the King'.[183]

When he foolishly (or bravely) refused to comply, he was saved from a severe beating by a gentleman who whisked him away to his house. The experience reminded him of tyrannical Babylonian monarchs whose servants bundled the ancestors of 'the Priestleys, the Paines and the Welsh Bards of those days' into the fiery furnace.[184] As contemptible war songs rang out in streets, taverns and brothels, Iolo vowed that if John Reeves and his raving mob went to heaven he would find his own way to hell.[185]

As he courted retribution and possible martyrdom, Iolo familiarized himself with the deliberations of the Scottish conventions held in Edinburgh between 1792 and 1794 and the show trials which led to the transportation for sedition of five Scottish 'martyrs' to the penal colonies in Botany Bay.[186] He was especially attracted to the Unitarian minister Fyshe Palmer – 'Palmer I give thee a tear',[187] he once wrote – to whom he sent a copy of his *Poems* and received a movingly appreciative reply from faraway Sydney.[188] Iolo read and pondered over printed broadsides which condemned so-called 'British Patriots' who threatened peaceful citizens and destroyed their properties.[189] Determined never to worship the beast, he stood up for the right of freedom of speech:

---

[182] NLW 21401E, no. 34.
[183] NLW 21396E, no. 12. See also NLW 21401E, no. 15.
[184] NLW 21396E, no. 12.
[185] Ibid., no. 11.
[186] Frank Clune, *The Scottish Martyrs: Their Trials and Transportation to Botany Bay* (Sydney, 1969); Bob Harris, *The Scottish People and the French Revolution* (London, 2008), chapter 3; Gordon Pentland, 'Patriotism, Universalism and the Scottish Conventions, 1792–1794', *History*, 89, no. 295 (2004), 340–60.
[187] NLW 21396E, no. 12.
[188] *CIM*, I, p. 775, Thomas Fyshe Palmer to Iolo Morganwg, 12 September 1795.
[189] NLW 21401E, no. 36.

I will not shrink from it. There is very warm blood in my heart, and every drop of it solemnly dedicated to the cause of Truth. Furnish Smithfield once more with a stake and faggot if you please. I will not flinch nor recede an inch from it, but walk, and that hastingly, to it, with a Song of triumph on my tongue.[190]

Stubbornly refusing to succumb to political pressure or heed the plaintive cries of his wife, Iolo consorted with kindred radicals of lowly background and avidly read their publications. The Northumbrian antiquary Joseph Ritson was a man after Iolo's heart. Following a visit to France in 1791, he returned a staunch republican who addressed his friends as 'Citizens' and dated his letters according to the French revolutionary calendar.[191] Iolo knew him, corresponded with him on antiquarian, literary and musical matters, and shared his passion for French libertarians.[192] He also cherished the publications of Thomas Spence, a tiny, querulous Geordie whose eccentric manners and stubborn disposition matched those of Iolo. On four occasions in the 1790s Spence was dragged from his bookshop by Bow Street runners and indicted for publishing radical material. That Spence's twelve-year-old son was arrested for selling the broadside *The Rights of Man*, in verse, made a deep impression on Iolo and, although he did not share Spence's enthusiasm for appropriating private land, he applauded much of what he read in *Pig's Meat*, Spence's penny weekly, notably the animus against the slave trade and the uncompromising view of kings and aristocrats.[193] Iolo also associated with the radical activist and publisher of Paine's works, Daniel Isaac Eaton, whose *Politics for the People* ran to sixty numbers between 1793 and 1795, and from whom Iolo bought pamphlets, broadsides and handbills which were marked by scabrous wit.[194] Likewise, Iolo took to William Fox, a fiery pamphleteer who collaborated with the bookseller Martha Gurney in publishing sixteen political tracts on radical issues between 1791 and 1794.[195]

---

[190] NLW 21396E, no. 12.
[191] Bertrand H. Bronson, *Joseph Ritson: Scholar-at-Arms* (2 vols., Berkeley, Calif., 1938), I, pp. 143, 150, 154.
[192] Joseph Frank (ed.), *The Letters of Joseph Ritson, Esq.* (2 vols., London, 1833), II, pp. 82, 221–2; Mary-Ann Constantine, 'Chasing Fragments: Iolo, Ritson and Robin Hood' in Sally Harper and Wyn Thomas (eds.), *Cynheiliaid y Gân / Bearers of Song: Essays in Honour of Phyllis Kinney and Meredydd Evans* (Cardiff, 2007), pp. 51–7.
[193] P. Mary Ashraf, *The Life and Times of Thomas Spence* (Newcastle upon Tyne, 1983); Peter Linebaugh and Marcus Rediker, *The Many-Headed Hydra: Sailors, Slaves, Commoners, and the Hidden History of the Revolutionary Atlantic* (London, 2000), pp. 293–5; NLW 13136A, pp. 35, 41–2; NLW 21401E, no. 30.
[194] Daniel L. McCue, Jr., 'The Pamphleteer Pitt's Government Couldn't Silence', *Eighteenth-Century Life*, 5 (1978–9), 38–49; *CIM*, I, p. 773, Iolo Morganwg to [Joseph Johnson], [?September 1795]; ibid., I, p. 788, Iolo Morganwg to [?], 11 November 1795.
[195] NLW 13120B, pp. 365, 368; Timothy Whelan, 'William Fox, Martha Gurney, and Radical Discourse of the 1790's', *Eighteenth-Century Studies*, 42, no. 3 (2009), 397–411.

Consonant with the spirit of Tom Paine, Thomas Spence's *Pig's Meat* and Daniel Isaac Eaton's *Hog Wash* were rejoinders on behalf of common people to Burke's derisive comments about the 'swinish multitude'. Iolo was captivated by this material and took upon himself the task of being the mouthpiece of 'the poor Swinish multitude of Britain', those who had been deprived by bloodthirsty tyrants, kings, peers, placemen, sycophants, packed juries and churchmen of their 'due portion of Grains', but who now understood that, while ignorance was the mother of slavery, knowledge was the weapon that would 'break the galling chain' and bring them liberty.[196] During 1794 a spate of mock playbills, composed by plebeian writers, subjected leading political figures to withering ridicule.[197] No stranger to satirical songs, lampoons and burlesques, Iolo joined in the anti-Pitt campaign as the self-styled 'Mad Welsh Bard'.[198] Readers were forewarned of 'Dissertations on Duck-milking, with curious examples from Pady O Burke, Archi Macblunder, etc. By Wicked Welsh Bard' to be printed at the Sign of the Golden Leek in Liberty Square, London.[199] 'A Push at the Pillars of Priestcraft, By Sampson Sans-culotte-Citizen, with notes by Citizen Equality', dedicated to the notorious common hangman 'Sir' John Ketch, expressed the hope that His Majesty would 'honour thee with his custom, enabling and authorising thee [to] exalt highly the King's head before thy shop'.[200] Some of his more irreverent advertisements not only sported a sharp class dimension but also a strongly Welsh identity which made them different from the anti-royal satires usually found on the streets of London:

> Royal antiquities or anecdotes of Kingism and Kingcraft. By Morgan ap Howel, ap Shenkin, ap Griffith, ap Llewelyn, ap Taffid, ap Owen ap Harry, ap Gronw, ap Tudor, ap Einion, ap Rhys, ap Owen Glendower, of the uninterrupted line of Cadwalader King of Wales and England and Scotland, and Ireland, and the Plains of Shinar, and the Tower of Babel, Antiquary to the Swinish Multitude, and let the people say

---

[196] NLW 13121B, p. 448; NLW 21396E, no. 5; NLW 21401E, no. 1.

[197] John Barrell, *'Exhibition Extraordinary!!': Radical Broadsides of the mid 1790s* (Nottingham, 2001), p. xi. See also Iain McCalman, *Radical Underworld: Prophets, Revolutionaries and Pornographers in London, 1795–1840* (Cambridge, 1988); David Worrall, *The Politics of Romantic Theatricality, 1787–1832* (Basingstoke, 2007).

[198] See Iolo's annotated drafts by 'a Mad Welsh Bard . . . one of the Swinish Multitude' in NLW 21401E, no. 1.

[199] NLW 21392F, no. 92^v.

[200] NLW 21400C, nos. 28, 28a–b. John or Jack Ketch was the sadistic hangman in the reign of Charles II whose bungling executions were a byword and whose name was invoked whenever certain individuals were thought to deserve to be dispatched from this life in as grisly a manner as possible. Brian Bailey, *Hangmen of England: A History of Execution from Jack Ketch to Albert Pierrepoint* (London, 1989), pp. 8–11. Punch and Judy shows attracted large crowds at popular venues and drew raucous applause when Jack Ketch himself was hanged. Peter Linebaugh, *The London Hanged: Crime and Civil Society in the Eighteenth Century* (2nd edn., London, 2003), pp. 402–4.

Amen. Wales, Printed by Perkin Pritchard, Benjamin Bearhard, Stephen Strikehard, Harry Hithard, and sold at the sign of the Leek and Lousetrap by the Hands etc. etc., where may be had a new and improved Edition of the Lousiad, a new Poem entitled the Royal Lousehead, sold also at the Guilotine and ease [?] of Liberty, Cromwell street St James Park, London.[201]

This humorous work, alive with political resonances – the loyalism of the Welsh in north Wales, the brutalities of 'Church and King' mobs, the new and radicalized version of Pope's *Dunciad*, and the Cromwellian and sans-culotte connotations – was couched in the satirical and ironical tones which Iolo had mastered and was aimed at a popular audience.

By the early summer of 1794, however, the government was convinced that leaders of the London Corresponding Society were on the brink of calling a general convention on the French model.[202] Twelve of them were locked up and eventually it was decided to begin proceedings against Thomas Hardy, Horne Tooke and John Thelwall.[203] In the meantime Iolo assured his despairing wife that he had taken the precaution of sending his inflammatory writings to a friend in Bristol, and that he was keeping his head down and avoiding the snares which his enemies laid for him and all attempts to brand him as a subversive.[204] Yet he felt compelled to keep watch on the three leaders in the Tower of London and to monitor events during the run-up to the 'Treason Trials'. Horne Tooke had subscribed to his *Poems*, possibly as a result of the intervention of the actuary William Morgan, nephew of Richard Price. Morgan was a leading member of the Revolution Society and it is conceivable that Iolo joined leading radicals, including Paine, Tooke and Earl Stanhope, who gathered at Morgan's handsome home at Stamford Hill, to discuss the political climate and sing seditious songs.[205] As his later correspondence reveals, Iolo also came to know John Thelwall, whose lectures in Soho had caused a sensation.[206]

---

[201] NLW 21400C, no. 32. See also Iolo's 'To the Prince of the Powers in the Air . . . by his most sacred majestys most redoubted and Democrat Antagonist, and Republican opponent, E. Williams', ibid., no. 30. See Marcus Wood, *Radical Satire and Print Culture 1790–1822* (Oxford, 1994).

[202] For the mood of the times, see David Worrall, *Radical Culture: Discourse, Resistance and Surveillance, 1790–1820* (Hemel Hempstead, 1992); John Barrell, *The Spirit of Despotism: Invasions of Privacy in the 1790s* (Oxford, 2006).

[203] Alan Wharam, *The Treason Trials, 1794* (Leicester, 1992); John Barrell and Jon Mee (eds.), *Trials for Treason and Sedition, 1792–1794* (8 vols., London, 2006–7).

[204] *CIM*, I, pp. 686–9, 691–3, Iolo Morganwg to Margaret (Peggy) Williams, 27 August and 13 September 1794.

[205] J. Ann Hone, *For the Cause of Truth: Radicalism in London 1796–1821* (Oxford, 1982), pp. 22–3; Christina and David Bewley, *Gentleman Radical: A Life of John Horne Tooke 1736–1812* (London, 1998), pp. 74, 139–40.

[206] Steve Poole (ed.), *John Thelwall: Radical Romantic and Acquitted Felon* (London, 2009); Robert Lamb and Corinna Wagner (eds.), *Selected Political Writings of John Thelwall* (4 vols., London, 2009). For Thelwall's Welsh connections, see Walford Davies, *Presences that Disturb*, chapter 5.

Iolo's marginal notes show that 'Citizen' Thelwall's 'libel of the Bantum Cock', which compared George III to a cock on a farmyard dunghill and which was published by Daniel Isaac Eaton, was familiar to him, as was his habit of turning up for lectures in a cudgel-proof hat.[207]

When proceedings against Hardy, Tooke and Thelwall began at the Old Bailey, Iolo was present on the public benches, at least on certain days, and prided himself on being 'an eye and an ear witness' to William Pitt's shameful fit of amnesia at Tooke's trial.[208] Even though the case for the prosecution was embarrassingly flimsy, without the brilliant eloquence of the defending barristers Thomas Erskine and Vicary Gibbs, the three libertarians might well have been convicted of high treason. To widespread joy, however, the three were acquitted in turn and medals bearing their profiles were struck. Iolo's own profile in radical circles had never been higher and, although the level of political surveillance had become even more acute, he appeared to revel in exposing himself to risks. He might not have drawn attention to himself by tramping the streets in a red nightcap as William Blake did or by cropping his hair in Thelwall-like mode, but he wore his Jacobinism on his sleeve in supporting the struggle for freedom of debate. Much to the dismay of his wife, he refused to deny his radical self or return home. 'Dear Ned', she wrote, 'do not suffer your aspireing spirit and violent pationess to ruing you and yours . . . For God's sake return to your children.'[209] But Iolo, thriving in the world of political and religious controversy, made his excuses and stayed.

As he moved in free-thinking circles Iolo became aware of the rising tide of infidelity[210] and it is a measure of the esteem in which he was held that he was considered sufficiently well-informed to be invited by rational and secular advocates of religious and political liberty to think through and argue about thorny questions. Damian Walford Davies has revealed that, on 2 January 1795, Iolo was invited to tea at George Dyer's home with William Godwin, Richard Porson, Thomas Holcroft, Benjamin Staley and John Thelwall, where he was almost certainly forthright in his condemnation of thoroughgoing atheism. The cut and thrust of debate resumed the following evening at Cleve House, the home of the geologist and writer Thomas Northmore, where the guests at dinner were 'Bard' Williams, Godwin, Gilbert Wakefield, John Disney,

---

[207] NLW 21396E, no. 24.
[208] *CIM*, I, p. 661, Iolo Morganwg to Margaret (Peggy) Williams, 19 February 1794 [1795]. Much to Iolo's glee, satirists ensured that Pitt 'would not be allowed to forget what he could not remember'. Barrell, *Imagining the King's Death*, p. 375.
[209] *CIM*, I, pp. 713–14, Margaret (Peggy) Williams to Iolo Morganwg, 10 December 1794.
[210] Martin Priestman, *Romantic Atheism: Poetry and Freethought, 1780–1830* (Cambridge, 1999). Iolo contrasted 'the divine lights of Christianity' with 'noxious blasts of scepticism'. NLW 21387E, no. 7.

Brand Hollis and Thomas Walker and where there was much 'talk of God'.[211] Excessive prudence was foreign to Iolo and it is easy to imagine him at least holding his own in such distinguished company, even though he was deeply hurt by Godwin's insulting behaviour towards him.

Iolo was particularly exercised at this stage by the influence of Tom Paine's *Age of Reason*, a best-selling work published in two parts in 1794–5. Paine claimed that the Christian faith was a fraudulent set of doctrines based on mystery, miracle and prophecy rather than on rational thought. Couched in unambiguous language, the work argued that the Bible owed nothing to revelation and that organized Christianity fed the greedy ambitions of monarchs, warmongers and priests. Iolo was deeply offended by Paine's critique and was moved to defend 'the sublimely beautiful column of Christianity that has for ages been thrown down by Priests and Tyrants' in a short and unfinished essay.[212] In his inimitable way he decried Paine's credentials. He pitied his old friend's 'poor brain', maintained that his 'old Great Grandmother' was a more profound philosopher, and derided his 'curiously whimsical kind of mill-wheel-and-cog-work'. In Iolo's eyes, 'Citizen Paine' had become a 'second Iscariot', a villainous, duplicitous knave.[213]

But even in this culture of surveillance, treason trials, witch-hunts, physical intimidation and anti-Christian literature, there were moments for Iolo to savour. At the Crown and Anchor Tavern on 4 February, over nine hundred people paid 7s. 6d. for the privilege of attending a dinner to celebrate the acquittals of Hardy, Thelwall and Tooke and in honour of Erskine and Gibbs. George Dyer sang a song of praise, as did a euphoric Iolo, rounding off his *Trial by Jury, The Grand Palladium of British Liberty* with a flourish:

> Boast, Britain, thy Juries! thy glory! thy plan!
> > They treat the stern Tyrant with scorn.
> O! bid them descend, the best Guardians of man,
> > To millions of ages unborn!
> Far and wide as the light, of true Freedom the soul,
> > Be thy blest Institution proclaim'd;
> With Erskine, with Gibbs, on Eternity's roll,
> > In the language of glory be named.[214]

The song was duly printed and circulated among his supporters, and its content also noted by prying loyalist eyes. 'A general alarm prevails', Iolo told his

---

[211] Damian Walford Davies, '"At Defiance": Iolo, Godwin, Coleridge, Wordsworth' in *Rattleskull Genius*, p. 154.
[212] NLW 21396E, no. 33.
[213] NLW 21392F, no. 9; NLW 21396E, nos. 18–22, 34–5; NLW 21400C, no. 11.
[214] NLW 13221E, no. 1; NLW 21401E, nos. 32, 32a; NLW 21334B, pp. 27–8; NLW 21335A, pp. 15–16; Edward Williams, *Trial by Jury, the Grand Palladium of British Liberty* (London, 1795).

increasingly frantic wife,[215] but he still courted attention by styling himself 'Bard of Liberty' and visiting dissidents like William Winterbotham in Newgate prison.[216] Convinced that he was living through a period of 'terror', he took refuge in Christian revelation and especially biblical prophecies. Although scornful of William Owen Pughe's obsession with Joanna Southcott, he was deeply interested in the apocalyptic aspects of radicalism. Just as had occurred in the mid-seventeenth century, the turmoil of the 1790s produced an outpouring of eschatology.[217] Prophets great and small ransacked the Scriptures and became embroiled in the millennial expectations of the times. Iolo read about the doctrines of the Moravians, Sandemanians and Swedenborgians, subjected anonymous pamphlets like *Antichrist in the French Convention* (1795) to critical scrutiny, and came to believe that monarchical tyranny (represented by the first Beast) and ecclesiastical tyranny (represented by the second Beast) would destroy themselves by the end of 1796 and usher in a 'happy day' of justice and peace.[218] These were clearly times of hope and expectation. True to character, Iolo dipped his toe into perilous waters by taking up the cause of Richard Brothers, a discharged naval lieutenant who had entered the limelight in the summer of 1794 by claiming to be the Prince of the Hebrews and the Nephew of the Almighty. He addressed prophetic letters to the King, Queen and government foretelling events which had never been revealed to any other person on earth. His most striking message was the imminent dethronement of George III, whom he fully expected to succeed. Astonishingly, the Sanskrit scholar Nathaniel Halhed (whose works were known to Iolo) endorsed his prophecies, prompting the authorities to take Brothers seriously and view him as a Jacobin agent. On 4 March Brothers was arrested and brought before the Privy Council, but the political case against him was so unconvincing that it was thought more appropriate to commit him to a lunatic asylum.[219]

William Leathart, historian of the London-Welsh societies, shrewdly described Iolo as 'a man of really good heart; a love of justice ever prompted him in all his dealings'.[220] In this case, as in many others, he felt compelled to intervene on behalf of the hapless Brothers. He knew Brothers and had had first-hand experience of his accounts of conversations with angels who had

---

[215] *CIM*, I, p. 727, Iolo Morganwg to Margaret (Peggy) Williams, 12 February 1795.
[216] *RAEW*, pp. 47–8.
[217] Clarke Garrett, *Respectable Folly: Millenarians and the French Revolution in France and England* (Baltimore, Md., 1975).
[218] NLW 13136A, pp. 165–83; NLW 21396E, nos. 1, 30; NLW 21400C, no. 33.
[219] Cecil Roth, *The Nephew of the Almighty* (London, 1933); Garrett, *Respectable Folly*, pp. 177–207; Jon Mee, *Dangerous Enthusiasm: William Blake and the Culture of Radicalism in the 1790s* (Oxford, 1992), pp. 28–34; Barrell, *Imagining the King's Death*, chapter 15.
[220] William D. Leathart, *The Origin and Progress of the Gwyneddigion Society* (London, 1831), p. 68n.

also revealed themselves to him in person. But Iolo realized that Brothers had been deceived by two French ventriloquists (one of whom may have been the printer George Riebeau) bent on using him as a tool of the French Republic.[221] Iolo forwarded this evidence to Pitt and was summoned to Downing Street in mid-March where, following a long conversation, Pitt complimented Iolo 'on the sagacity of his discovery'. Brothers remained under lock and key in the madhouse, oblivious to the enormous public interest in the affair, leaving Iolo to believe that he had at least done something on behalf of (as Waring uncharitably put it) 'the poor crazy Pretender to the throne of Judea'.[222]

Still determined to stay in the limelight, Iolo once more turned his attention to the Prince of Wales. When the Prince married the odious Princess Caroline of Brunswick on 8 April 1795, Iolo personally delivered an epithalamium – made up of ten anodyne verses (composed through gritted teeth) to celebrate the event.[223] In a public expression of class identity, he wore the distinctive clothes (including a new apron of white leather) and the insignia and tools of the stonemason when he visited Carlton House. Cash-strapped, he hoped for a handsome reward for his pains. But, having been led to believe that he would receive fifty guineas, he was mortified to receive two measly guineas.[224] Thereafter he always spoke of the Prince of Wales with chilly contempt: 'ill usage from the world', he informed his wife, 'is grown very familiar to me.'[225]

In spite of the enormous loyalist upsurge and the repressive authority of the state, however, at no stage did Iolo's commitment to the radical cause waver. Others took fright, recanted or faded away, but Iolo stood firm. For instance, at 8 p.m. on 20 May 1795 'citizens and sansculottes' George Dyer and Iolo arrived at William Owen Pughe's house to drink tea, eat bread and butter and 'to talk of politics, republicanism, Jacobinisms, Carmagnolism, sansculololisms, and a number of other wicked and trayterous isms against the peace of the lords, kingism and parsonism, their crowns and dignities'.[226] But his days in London were coming to an end. The authorities were clamping down severely on those who spoke out of turn. Moreover, Iolo's father had just died, part of his house had fallen down and his children were starving.[227] Even the selfish, wilful Iolo could no longer ignore his wife's pleas and in early June he began his march homewards, still wearing his republicanism as a badge of pride:

---

[221] *CIM*, I, p. 743, John Carthew to Iolo Morganwg, 11 March 1795; ibid., I, pp. 756–7, Iolo Morganwg to [Hannah More], [?May 1795]; *RAEW*, pp. 81–6.
[222] Ibid., pp. 85–6.
[223] *CIM*, I, pp. 746–7, Iolo Morganwg to George, Prince of Wales, [6 April 1795].
[224] *RAEW*, p. 114; *CIM*, I, p. 758, Iolo Morganwg to Margaret (Peggy) Williams, 2 May 1795.
[225] Ibid., p. 759.
[226] Ibid., I, p. 760, Iolo Morganwg to William Owen Pughe, 20 May 1795.
[227] Ibid., I, p. 750, Margaret (Peggy) Williams to Iolo Morganwg, 28 April 1795; ibid., I, p. 758, Iolo Morganwg to Margaret (Peggy) Williams, 2 May 1795.

I am still an honest Republican. I am whatever the foul Slanderous mouths of the believers in the Gospel according to St. Burke (which seems to be the creed of Church-and-Kingism) may be pleased to call me. Democrate, Leveler, Jacobin, San[s]culotte, or any thing that may be manufactured from the cream that swims on the surface of their malevolence, or from the black dregs at [the] bottom. I glory in all these titles. In my long avowed principles I will live, in them and for them I will die.[228]

---

[228] NLW 21392F, no. 9.

5

'[He] is now a seller of seditious Books and will be planting Treason wherever he goes'

As Iolo made his way home on foot, belatedly delivering sets of his *Poems* to some subscribers en route, he took bed and lodgings in Bristol for several nights. Although he greatly admired the city's fine architecture, he was rather less impressed by the 'Idiotic Dullness'[1] of its citizens. His animus against them dated from his earlier altercation with William Bulgin, an abrasive champion of the slave trade, and his disgust on witnessing the manner in which Bristolians had celebrated the rejection of Wilberforce's anti-slavery bill in 1791 by ringing the bells of St Mary Redcliffe Church, firing cannon on Brandon Hill and lighting up the sky with a bonfire and a fireworks display.[2] As he marched along the spacious quay, interrogating traders, ship-owners, speculators and mariners as they scurried in and out of shops, counting houses and sugar refineries, he seethed with rage at the evils of slavery. He almost certainly paid a shilling on the evening of 16 June for the privilege of joining an audience composed of Dissenters, abolitionists and consumers to hear Samuel Taylor Coleridge's famous address on the slave trade at the Assembly coffee house on the Quay.[3] Iolo was well aware that the injustices and excesses of the slave trade were a humanitarian issue, but even he must have sat up sharply on being reminded by Coleridge that sugar, tea, coffee and chocolate contained the blood of human slaves. Significantly, too, he lodged with Owen Rees, the eldest son of Josiah Rees of Gelli-gron, the Arian minister at Gellionnen. A trained bookseller, Rees had a flourishing bookshop in Wine Street and was also a partner in the Longman publishing business. Doubtless Iolo sought his views on the advisability of

---

[1] NLW 13089E, p. 176.
[2] *RAEW*, p. 61; Kenneth Morgan, *Bristol and the Atlantic Trade in the Eighteenth Century* (Cambridge, 1993), p. 151; Madge Dresser, *Slavery Obscured: The Social History of the Slave Trade in an English Provincial Port* (London, 2001), p. 163.
[3] Lewis Patton and Peter Mann (eds.), *The Collected Works of Samuel Taylor Coleridge: Lectures 1795 On Politics and Religion* (London, 1971), pp. 235–51; Mary-Ann Constantine, 'Iolo Morganwg, Coleridge, and the Bristol Lectures, 1795', *Notes and Queries*, new series, 52, no. 1 (March 2005), 42–4.

setting himself up as a shopkeeper and bookseller.[4] Printers, booksellers and bookbinders were sprouting up in most market towns in south Wales in response to an enormous surge in demand for both Welsh and English printed literature,[5] and since Iolo could not be sure of finding regular work as a stonemason he needed some gainful employment which would also allow him to promote the radical cause.

From the time of his return to Glamorgan in June 1795 to the founding of the Unitarian Society of South Wales in 1802, Iolo never abandoned his reputation for bloody-minded independence or his concern for the 'poor distress'd and shamefully oppressed humanity'.[6] The gloomy outlook for political radicalism did not deter him and he was amused to learn that prim ladies in his native patch were in the habit of referring to him as 'a terrible Jacobin'.[7] The inhabitants of Cowbridge had not forgotten his past misdemeanours or the questionable activities which had made him a potentially dangerous political activist. They would soon discover that, although the Flemingston stonemason was now forty-eight, his passions had not cooled and he was still prepared to play with fire. Unlike many celebrated, but lily-livered, radicals in England who recanted and retreated from the political arena, Iolo stood firm. Using the 'bloodless weapons of Truth, of Reason, of the Christian Religion',[8] he was determined never to succumb to the forces of reaction. Indeed, on returning to Glamorgan he seems to have gained a new lease of life.

In September 1795 the Jacobin firebrand set up a shop in what is now 14 High Street, Cowbridge,[9] a prime location for a seller of goods and a purveyor of ideas. Late eighteenth-century Cowbridge was a flourishing 'county' town, much frequented by gentry, professional people and farmers. Its hotels, inns and taverns were thriving and were the focus for societies like the Cowbridge Book Society and the Glamorganshire Agricultural Society. The Royal Mail Coach, which ran from London to Pembrokeshire, offered a daily service along the turnpike route, while post office facilities were made available at 50 High Street from 1796 onwards.[10] For £8 per annum Iolo

---

[4] *CIM*, I, p. 762, Iolo Morganwg to Margaret (Peggy) Williams, 14 June 1795; NLW 11138D, ff. 15ʳ–16ʳ, 38ʳ, 39ʳ; *The Cambrian*, 16 September 1837; *DWB* s. v. Josiah Rees.

[5] Eiluned Rees, 'Developments in the Book Trade in Eighteenth-Century Wales', *The Library*, 5th series, 24 (1969), 33–43.

[6] NLW 21396E, no. 27.

[7] *CIM*, II, p. 51, Iolo Morganwg to Mary Barker, 26 March [1798].

[8] NLW 21319A, p. 1.

[9] Ibid., pp. 5–6; *Cowbridge: Buildings and People. Sources and References* (Cowbridge, 2000) s. v. 14 High Street. A memorial tablet was unveiled here on the centenary of the death of Iolo on 18 December 1826. See Hywel Gethin Rhys, *'A Wayward Cymric Genius': Celebrating the Centenary of the Death of Iolo Morganwg* (Aberystwyth, 2007).

[10] I'm grateful to Mr Brian Ll. James for allowing me to read his unpublished paper on 'Iolo Morganwg and Cowbridge'. See also Jeff Alden (ed.), *Old Inns and Alehouses of Cowbridge* (Cowbridge, 2003).

rented the property at 14 High Street from Isaac Skynner, a hatmaker and leader of the Wesleyan Methodist congregation in the town.[11] As far as we know, this was the first fair trade shop in Wales. Presumably using funds from the sale of his *Poems*, Iolo bought most of his groceries and beverages – teas, chocolate, cocoa, figs, currants, raisins, cinnamon, nutmeg, cloves, pepper, ginger and mustard – from Tucketts and Fletcher in Bath Street, Bristol,[12] and made no bones about his opposition to the slave trade by openly advertising East Indian sugar 'uncontaminated with human gore'.[13] In a jocular (but yet deadly serious) handbill, he emphasized that only free-labour goods were for sale:

> At Cowbridge the name of Ned Williams appears,
> A shop-keeping Bard, having choicest of wares,
> To those that have money, be this understood,
> Ring the bell at his door, he sells ev'ry thing good.
>
> He is a Jack of all trades, many labours he plies,
> Hopes that above want he can honestly rise,
> Fair dealing he loves, is no vender of trash,
> Come and see what you want, and exchange it for cash.
>
> Of Teas the most fragrant assortments are seen,
> Here's black and all blacks, here's the finest of green;
> Your favours, ye fair, let your Bard thus invoke,
> Here's chocolate, coffee, with Fry's patent coke.
>
> Here are currants and raisins, delicious french plumbs,
> The Christian free sugar from East India comes.
> And brought from where Truth is not yet in the bud,
> Rank Church-and-King sweets for the lovers of blood.
>
> Here to furnish high flavours are all sorts of spice
> Of Liberty's growth, fine American Rice.
> All that makes a good pudding, or well-season'd pye,
> May be found at this shop do but take them and try.[14]

Even though he knew that the pro-slavery lobby in Cowbridge and neighbouring Cardiff, let alone Bristol, was strong, Iolo felt duty-bound to champion the lot of black African slaves by boycotting sugar, rum and tobacco which

---

[11] *CIM*, II, pp. 7–11, Iolo Morganwg to Isaac Skynner, 4 February 1797; A. H. Williams (ed.), *John Wesley in Wales 1739–1790* (Cardiff, 1971), p. 107, n. 1.
[12] NLW 13138A, pp. 268–9; NLW 21410E, nos. 28–9.
[13] *RAEW*, p. 108.
[14] NLW 21410E, no. 29a.

stemmed from 'that most horrid traffick in human blood'.[15] He gave short shrift to customers who maintained that slaves in the Caribbean lived better lives than they had ever done in Africa and that if Britain were to renounce or lose its colonies in the West Indies the beneficiaries would be France or America, its principal rivals in this lucrative trade. To Iolo, plucking innocent young blacks from their 'Kingless Freedom' in Africa and dehumanizing them in 'slavery's hateful toils on foreign plains' was a monstrous injustice.[16] He felt a moral obligation to awaken public opinion, to urge the apathetic and the prejudiced to boycott tainted Caribbean goods, and to sign petitions against the evils of inhuman bondage. He sensed that popular opinion was beginning to change, even though the prolonged war with France and revolts by slaves in the West Indies had provoked a right-wing backlash. Articles in newspapers and pamphlets, Welsh-language ballads, Thomas Clarkson's fiery orations and Josiah Wedgwood's extraordinary design, depicting a kneeling slave and the motto 'Am I not a man and a brother?', were gaining wider currency and were pricking consciences.[17] Wilberforce's annual anti-slave trade motions in the House of Commons, though defeated in turn, kept the issue alive. One can easily imagine Iolo bombarding his customers with graphic accounts of how the traffic of humans had created in the Caribbean 'a landscape of blood, garlanded with gibbeted bodies and severed heads of the executed'.[18] Nor did he spare his siblings during these tirades. His three slave-owning brothers in Jamaica were not only sustaining the iniquitous slave trade but also causing him deep offence by decrying in their letters 'the diabolical and infomose politicks of the French Convention', vilifying the Maroons who had risen in revolt at Trelawny, and soiling their hands still further by helping to build a statue in Spanish Town to commemorate the victory of George Bridges Rodney – one of Iolo's *bêtes noires* – over the French at the battle of the Saints in 1782.[19] Those of his customers who were brave enough to reject the abolitionist cause were treated – very loudly – to a passionate denunciation of a Britain in which 'Justice never sway'd':

> Britain beware! 'tis at thy guilty land
> The storms all point, at thy commercial strand,
> At thy vile Senate, at its arm of pow'r,

---

[15] NLW 21387E, p. 8^{r-v}.

[16] NLW 21392F, no. 29.

[17] See Gwynne E. Owen, 'Welsh Anti-Slavery Sentiments, 1795–1865: A Survey of Public Opinion' (unpublished University of Wales MA thesis, 1964) and John Pinfold, *The Slave Trade Debate* (Oxford, 2007). For the background, see also Adam Hochschild, *Bury the Chains: The British Struggle to Abolish Slavery* (London, 2005).

[18] Chris Evans, *Slave Wales: The Welsh and Atlantic Slavery, 1660–1850* (Cardiff, 2010), p. 69.

[19] *CIM*, I, pp. 776–8, John Williams to Iolo Morganwg, 27 September 1795; ibid., II, pp. 152–3, Miles Williams to Iolo Morganwg, 11 November 1798.

> At him whose av'rice would whole worlds devour.
> Rouse up thy Conscience, and in time repent.
> Ere from above th' avenging plagues are sent,
> And on thy guiltful head their gather'd powr's are spent.[20]

Since Isaac Skynner had retained an outbuilding on the premises for his hat-making business, Iolo also sold hats and caps. His serious commitment to the ideal of liberty did not prevent him from enjoying the surprise on the faces of customers, especially spies, as they encountered his range of headware:

> Here are hats of all sorts, good as ever were seen,
> One guinea, one shilling, all prices between,
> And fearless of spies and th' Informer's fell traps,
> He'll soon become dealer in Liberty caps.[21]

On All Fools' Day (1 April), which Iolo liked to celebrate with his inimitable brand of pranks, jokes and satirical songs, he was true to his word. He could offer 'a Sansculotte's Cap' that would fit all heads, 'a Cowskin hero's cap' for infamous slavers, and 'A Cap of Liberty, worn by an ancient Briton, with a leek stuck in it' for every warm-blooded patriot. His collection of wigs included a 'fullbottom's Grizzle' for a parson, a wig with two tails 'full of impudence' for a barrister and a 'scratch wig' for a country curate.[22] To this mixed bag of wares, he added walking sticks, umbrellas, fish-hooks and tackle, razors, shaving boxes, scissors and perfume.[23] By flaunting his political prejudices, Iolo simply made what was already an insecure career even more perilous.

His convivial, but controversial, den in High Street was also looked upon with suspicion by loyalists because it became a honey-pot for radical activists and book-buyers. Iolo bought supplies of writing paper, pencils, slates, ink-stands, pens, crayons, wafers, sealing wax, letter cases and catalogues from book-shops in London, Bristol and Swansea, and stocked his shelves with almanacs, Bibles, prayer books, psalters, dictionaries, grammars, spelling-books, magazines like the *European Magazine*, the *Gentleman's Magazine*, the *Critical Review* and

---

[20] NLW 21392F, no. 28; T. C. Evans, *Gwaith Iolo Morganwg* (Llanuwchllyn, 1913), pp. 53–60; E. Wyn James, 'Caethwasanaeth a'r Beirdd, 1790–1840', *Taliesin*, 119 (2003), 37–60; idem, 'Welsh Ballads and American Slavery', *WJRH*, 2 (2007), 59–86. Iolo owned a copy of the first anti-slave trade publication in Welsh, *Achwynion Dynion Duon, mewn Caethiwed Truenus yn Ynysoedd y Suwgr* ([1791]), NLW 21405E. See also Geraint H. Jenkins, 'Iolo Morganwg a Chaethwasiaeth' in Tegwyn Jones and Huw Walters (eds.), *Cawr i'w Genedl: Cyfrol i Gyfarch yr Athro Hywel Teifi Edwards* (Llandysul, 2008), pp. 59–85.
[21] NLW 21410E, no. 29a.
[22] NLW 13130A, pp. 222–3.
[23] NLW 21410E, no. 30.

the highly radical *Cambridge Intelligencer*.[24] More tellingly, he stocked and pressed on his customers works by Richard Price, Tom Paine, John Aikin, Joseph Priestley, John Milton, Gilbert Wakefield and Voltaire.[25] Sailing close to the wind, he advertised 'A book about Bony party', Peter Pindar's 'book about the lice in the Kings head – a damn good thing', and 'a book about Oliver Cromwell'.[26] He corresponded with John Reed of Bristol, who implied in one of his letters to Iolo that Hannah More's *Village Politics* was best ignored since it 'smell[ed] strongly of royalty'; in another, Reed poked fun at 'our immaculate Pitt'.[27] Iolo had plans to set up a circulating library in the town which would offer subscribers a selection of presumably incendiary books 'superior to the trash' usually found in such libraries.[28] He made no attempt at all to disguise his political sympathies:

> Th' abettor of slav'ry, the Church-and-King Turk.
> Here may be supplied with the quibbler of Burke.
> Cowper's king-flogging Talk, how delightful the strain!
> And for lovers of Truth, Rights of Man by Tom Paine.[29]

Penurious parsons were allowed credit for just a fortnight, whereas radical friends were enjoined to 'pay as soon as you can'.[30]

In his shop Iolo lived up to his reputation as 'Whimsical Ned'.[31] He confessed to being 'rattleskulled' ('tafodrydd') and 'wilful' ('penrhydd'), and those who shared his radical views were regaled with biting satires about the follies and foibles of George III.[32] He liked to quote the satirist Peter Pindar: 'I murmur not at Kings, if good for aught / I only quarrel when they're good for naught'.[33] Songs against 'bold flogging parsons' and the 'great and glorious drinkers' of Cowbridge were often followed by elegies (or dirges as he called them) to departed local villains, including pettifogging attorneys, surly sextons

---

[24] *CIM*, I, pp. 787–90, Iolo Morganwg to [?], 11 November 1795; ibid., I, pp. 801–3, Samuel and John Reed to Iolo Morganwg, 13 January, 20 January, 3 February 1796.
[25] NLW 21407C, nos. 1, 2, 5, 6, 8; NLW 21414E, nos. 17, 17a.
[26] NLW 13146A, pp. 128–31.
[27] *CIM*, I, p. 810, John Reed to Iolo Morganwg, 30 March 1796; ibid., I, p. 840, John Reed to Iolo Morganwg, 29 November 1796.
[28] NLW 13089E, pp. 142–3; NLW 21407C, no. 12; *CIM*, I, pp. 795–6, Iolo Morganwg to the Clergy of Cowbridge [?1796].
[29] NLW 21410E, no. 29a.
[30] Ibid.
[31] NLW 21335B, p. 35.
[32] NLW 21415E, no. 27; NLW 13136A, p. 152; NLW 21429E, nos. 5, 9; NLW 21431E, no. 8.
[33] NLW 13103B, p. 300; *CIM*, I, pp. 523–4, John Wolcot [Peter Pindar] to Iolo Morganwg, 6 September 1792. See also Howard D. Weinbrot, *Eighteenth-Century Satire: Essays on Text and Context from Dryden to Peter Pindar* (Cambridge, 1988).

and boneheaded surgeons at whose burials drunken parsons would intone at appropriate junctures 'Ale to ale, Tipple to tipple, Drink to drink'.[34] John Rosser, the parish clerk and sexton, was singled out by Iolo as being a suitable subject for a premature epitaph:

> Here lies interr'd upon his back,
> The carcase of old surly Jack,
> *Fe dyngwys lawer yn ei fyw*
> *Myn crog, myn Cythraul, a myn Duw.*
> [He swore many times in his life
> By the cross, by the devil, and by God.]
> With many a curse and many a damn,
> *Da gwyddai'r Diawl ag yntau pam,*
> [He and the Devil knew full well why,]
> But now he struts, a blustering blade
> *Le mae'r Iaith honno'n iaith y wlâd!*
> [Where that language is the language of the land!][35]

David Jenkin, a bibulous Cowbridge carpenter, also found himself a target for Iolo's satire even though he was still in the land of the living:

> Here lies deceas'd a guzzling beast
> Who burst his paunch by drinking.
> A wenching blade – a Rake by Trade
> His name was Davy Jenkin.
> He down his guts whole pipes and butts
> So speedily would pour
> That Cowbridge ale grew never stale
> Had never time to sour.[36]

Always capable of self-mockery, Iolo depicted himself as 'a very wicked Welsh Bard' and, in an uncharacteristically clumsy piece of doggerel, as 'a consumed San[s]culotte' into whose guts democracy had been crammed and whose ambition was to slaughter clergymen, slit the king's throat, and turn towns like Cowbridge into hotbeds of republicanism.[37] For those who longed for his demise, he composed mock epitaphs ('Here lies the dust of needy Ned'), some of which bore witness to his political obsessions.

Iolo was so outspoken that he invited close surveillance and retribution. It was widely rumoured that his premises was a branch of the London Corresponding

---

[34] NLW 21424E, no. 5; NLW 21335B, pp. 36–7; NLW 21328A, pp. 243–5.
[35] NLW 13146A, p. 371.
[36] NLW 21424E, no. 16.
[37] Ibid., no. 6a; ibid., no. 2.

Society,[38] and his friends, anxious for his future, urged him to hide at least some of his lights under a bushel. William Owen Pughe was astonished by his temerity: 'you sell the *Rights of Man* and other seditious books; you open your shop on the fast day; you court persecution'.[39] George Dyer, who had gone into his shell, warned him against throwing himself 'in to the way of people who can do you harm',[40] but Iolo derived great satisfaction from giving local informers a run for their money. Aware that his next-door neighbour Robert Rich and a stranger called Curtis were spying on him, he placed in the shop window a book labelled 'The Rights of Man'. Curtis spotted it, paid five shillings for it, and planned to use it in evidence against Iolo as a subverter of the realm. 'This shall go to Billy Pitt', he cried triumphantly. But on opening the volume he discovered that he had been sold a Bible. When he demanded his money back, Iolo flatly refused: 'I am no cheat – you will find in that book the best and dearest RIGHTS OF MAN.'[41] Everything suggests that he revelled in his reputation as an agitator and a turner-of-the-world-upside-down.

During his first few months as a shopkeeper, Iolo was confident that his venture would not only help to form opinion on controversial political issues but would also bring him the financial security he craved. He even refused a lucrative offer from Evan Williams, the London bookseller, to edit a new periodical, the *Cambrian Register*.[42] Yet he was barely scratching a living during 1796 and John Reed urged him to abandon 'tag rag & bobtail' at Cowbridge for the more affluent and liberally-minded inhabitants of Swansea. In December of that year John Bedford, a brickmaker at Cefncribwr, advised him to transfer his business to a more central and progressive town like Bridgend, and Iolo himself bemoaned the 'scanty gains of my trade' in a long letter to William Pitt.[43] Early in the new year he entered into a war of words with his landlord Isaac Skynner. According to Iolo, his landlord had deliberately run down his hat-manufacturing business and left the premises uninhabitable, claiming that the tenant was responsible for carrying out repairs to the doors and window frames

---

[38] NLW 21319A, p. 7.
[39] *CIM*, II, p. 4, William Owen Pughe to Iolo Morganwg, 1 January 1797.
[40] Ibid., II, p. 6, George Dyer to Iolo Morganwg, [?February] 1797. For Dyer's retreat from radical politics, see Nicholas Roe, 'Radical George: Dyer in the 1790s', *Charles Lamb Bulletin*, 49 (1985), 17–26.
[41] *RAEW*, pp. 108–9; John W. Warter (ed.), *Southey's Common-place Book. Fourth Series* (London, 1850), p. 364. For some of those who suffered from state repression and loyalist pressures in the 1790s, see Kenneth R. Johnston, 'Whose History? My Place or Yours? Republican Assumptions and Romantic Traditions' in Damian Walford Davies (ed.), *Romanticism, History, Historicism: Essays on an Orthodoxy* (Abingdon, 2009), pp. 79–102.
[42] *CIM*, I, pp. 782–3, 784–5, Evan Williams to Iolo Morganwg, 11–12 October, 20 October 1795.
[43] Ibid., I, p. 811, John Reed to Iolo Morganwg, 30 March 1796; ibid., I, p. 844, Iolo Morganwg to William Pitt, 16 December 1796; ibid., I, pp. 841–2, John Bedford to Iolo Morganwg, 10 December 1796.

abutting on his shop and to the leaking roof. Iolo was not the sort of person to allow himself to be deceived or bullied by a Wesleyan Methodist, but his veiled threats probably made things worse for him.[44] In May 1797 Skynner ordered the local solicitor Francis Taynton to distrain Iolo's goods and chattels, valued at eighteen guineas, in lieu of unpaid rent, and in September Iolo was ordered to surrender the key of the property to Taynton.[45] Another of his business enterprises had collapsed and his debts were mounting. Once more he was forced to fall back on his skills as a stonemason.

His failure as a shopkeeper was also at least partly attributable to his inability to concentrate on the job in hand. Too many other temptations, or 'hobby-horses' as he called them, claimed his attention, especially those which could provide a supplementary income. One such opening caught his eye in the summer of 1796. Three years earlier the government had established a Board of Agriculture which, with the aid of an annual grant of £3,000, set itself the demanding task of preparing a national survey of agriculture on a county basis.[46] Its president, Sir John Sinclair, author of the highly regarded 21-volume series *The Statistical Account of Scotland* (1790–7), was a public-spirited promoter of improvement who had a reputation for getting things done.[47] No one envied his task in a period of war, inflation, harvest failures and general political upheaval, but Sinclair had good friends in high places and, although he lacked practical experience of farming, he was steeped in the political economy. As far as Wales was concerned, the Board was eager to appoint a suitably qualified person to undertake a survey of the agricultural and domestic economy of north and south Wales, on the basis of which appropriate recommendations would be made in order to raise standards of farming. The prospects were far from good. Hitherto the Board had been bitterly disappointed in the quality of reports and Arthur Young, its diligent secretary, believed that some county surveyors hardly knew the right side of a plough. Iolo himself described John Fox's preface to his 1796 survey of Glamorgan as 'a glaring imposition on the public and on the Board of Agriculture he visited, or rather intruded on'.[48] He was convinced he could do better and, having seen an advertisement published by the Royal Bath and West Agricultural Society seeking a suitably qualified person to conduct a survey of the agricultural condition of south Wales, he set his heart on winning the commission.

---

[44] Ibid., II, pp. 7–11, Iolo Morganwg to Isaac Skynner, 4 February 1797.
[45] NLW 21410E, no. 36; *CIM*, II, p. 39, Francis Taynton to Iolo Morganwg, 17 September 1797.
[46] Rosalind Mitchison, 'The Old Board of Agriculture (1793–1822)', *EHR*, LXXIV (1958), 41–69.
[47] Idem, *Agricultural Sir John: The Life of Sir John Sinclair of Ulbster 1754–1835* (London, 1962).
[48] NLW 21413E, no. 50.

Iolo was clearly excited by the prospect and no one could deny that he had several important qualifications. He was deeply interested in the landscape, geology and agriculture of his native county and was eager to play a prominent part in the drive for socio-economic improvement. He knew every species of bird, flower and plant in his locality and his powers of observation were second to none. Since he was a tireless walker, familiar with the highways and byways of south Wales, and thoroughly bilingual, he believed that he was well equipped to interrogate farmers and labourers and to compile a comprehensive, well-written report and make suitable recommendations which would raise agricultural standards. On the other hand, his mixed fortunes as a farmer during the 1780s and his penchant for advocating weird and wonderful ideas about where and when to grow tea, rice and sugar maple in south Wales were likely to count against him. Moreover, he had spent a year behind bars and was widely thought to be an unusual and probably subversive figure. His chances were slim.

Using William Matthews, secretary of the Royal Bath and West Agricultural Society, as an honest broker, Iolo lobbied tirelessly as he eyed the coveted prize. His great rival for the post was Walter Davies (Gwallter Mechain), who was curate of Meifod in Montgomeryshire at the time and also one of Iolo's correspondents. Aware of Sir John Sinclair's expertise as a statistician, Davies projected himself as a meticulous counter of heads and as a practical husbandman. His statistical account of the parish of Llanymynech had been published in 1795 and, unlike Iolo, he was adept at currying favour.[49] In order to improve his prospects, Iolo shut his shop for the best part of a fortnight in June 1796 and embarked on a tour of Glamorgan, and especially Carmarthenshire, with a view to collecting preliminary data about farming practices and the domestic economy in general. Even though he could not expect any remuneration or expenses for this expedition, Iolo was convinced that the experience would stand him in good stead and that William Matthews would use his report to the best advantage. In short, his survey was to serve as a sprat to catch a mackerel.

In his report Iolo wrote illuminatingly, and often amusingly, about the behaviour of farmers, especially their marked reluctance to abandon age old and unproductive agricultural methods and to embrace innovatory ways of fertilizing the land, rotating crops and improving the quality of animals. Since he was a Glamorgan man through and through, he was especially critical of the lack of enterprise and faint-hearted lethargy of farmers in Carmarthenshire, many of whom were presumably resentful at being preached to by a

---

[49] NLW 1732F; Walter Davies, 'A Statistical Account of the Parish of Llanymyneich in Montgomeryshire', *Cambrian Register*, I (1796), 265–83; Geraint H. Jenkins, 'An Uneasy Relationship: Gwallter Mechain and Iolo Morganwg', *MC*, 97 (2009), 73–99.

Jacobin bard whose record as a farmer and businessman was far from impressive.[50] His account was also marred by his tendency to gallop off on some of his pet hobby-horses or, as he put it, to 'fall into eccentricities'.[51] 'I digress too much', he confessed en route, 'but it is my wicked way and I cannot help it.'[52] Whenever he saw instances of philistinism, injustice or crass stupidity, he simply had to speak his mind, and some of his political diatribes were bound to raise the hackles of members of the Board of Agriculture. Appalled as he was by the atrocities of the slave trade, Iolo condemned the Bishop of St David's as he passed his palace at Abergwili ('this grovelingly great place') for his endorsement of such inhuman behaviour: 'O! that I could consign this Parish, Bishop and all, for a while, to the slave traders! I had almost said, to the D[evi]l.'[53] Likewise, by condemning the inhumanities perpetrated by bloodthirsty kings, Iolo was hardly likely to endear himself to the nobles and landowners who sat on the Board of Agriculture:

> I thank God that I am no King, no lover of Kings, no Slave of a King. And the only war that I wish may occur in this world, in any world whatever, is that of the Christian prophecy, the battle of Armageddon, wherein all the murderous (vulgo warring) Kings of the world shall be slain, wherein all the abettors of such Kings, killers with the sword, shall be killed with the sword.[54]

William Matthews's initial doubts about Iolo's recklessness had been amply confirmed and he despaired of ever persuading him to put pen to paper 'without aiming a shaft at tyrants and priests'.[55] Having failed to prove that he was capable of writing a dispassionate report, Iolo's application was rejected. His reputation for speaking out of turn was well known in London and the records of the Board reveal that it had no intention of affording him the opportunity to flaunt his prejudices and 'disseminate republican doctrines in Glamorganshire'.[56] Sir John Sinclair subsequently offered the commission to the topographical writer Richard Fenton, who declined, and so the post went to Walter Davies, a much safer pair of hands than the tempestuous Glamorgan bard. Iolo was incensed and William Owen Pughe did not help matters by teasing him for not being 'pliant enough to tell a few smooth lies' to the Board

---

[50] NLW 13115B; Muriel Bowen Evans, 'Sir Gaeriaid: Some Comments on Carmarthenshire and its People by Iolo Morganwg', *CA*, XXIV (1988), 33–55.
[51] NLW 13115B, p. 44.
[52] Ibid., p. 51.
[53] Ibid., pp. 57–8, 85–7, 361–3.
[54] NLW 13156A, p. 341.
[55] *CIM*, I, p. 834, William Matthews to Iolo Morganwg, 6 October 1796.
[56] Mitchison, 'The Old Board of Agriculture', 51.

of Agriculture.[57] Davies's initial task was to survey the counties of north Wales and he set about it with such brisk zeal that Sinclair engaged him to cover the counties of south Wales as well. At this point Owen Jones (Owain Myfyr), who was evidently aware of Iolo's straitened circumstances and his sulky response to being overlooked by the Board of Agriculture, strongly advised Davies to employ Iolo as his assistant.[58] Iolo agreed to lend a hand, probably because he had no wish to see a Powysian misrepresent the state of agriculture in his beloved Glamorgan. In the event, however, he proved to be an elusive ally and one who had no qualms about making controversial statements in his reports about the iniquities of war, violence and slavery. When Davies came to publish his *General View of the Agriculture and Domestic Economy of South Wales* in 1815 he readily acknowledged his debt to the researches of Iolo,[59] but eliminated from the text all mention of scoundrels, villains and devils as well as gratuitous comments like the following:

> A Welshman who has attended to the real state of civilization in Wales cannot otherwise than rejoice at the appearance of new dissenting meeting houses, and of late they have been numerous. There is much more knowledge, and much more morality among the Dissenters in Wales than amongst those who call themselves of the established Church. Of this Church there are doubtless many good Christians, but under the same Church and King Banner with these rank all the Blackguards, all the scoundrels, all the greatest villains of every description, none of which are to be found in a state of membership amongst Dissenters of any denomination however absurd in their tenets some of them (chiefly the Calvinists) may be.[60]

Few could match Iolo in expressing pent-up exasperation and both Davies and the Board were probably right in remaining profoundly suspicious of his motives.

In some ways, his failure as a shopkeeper was a blessing in disguise since he was now free to renew his sense of independence as a peripatetic stonemason, to make greater use of his stout pairs of walking boots, and to fulfil some of his creative literary ambitions. He became a familiar figure on the highways of south Wales and was often to be seen observing local features, writing and sketching in fields and on cliffs and mountains. Dressed in a blue jacket, worsted trousers and a tall beaver hat, and with a knapsack, stuffed with books,

---

[57] *CIM*, II, p. 22, William Owen Pughe to Iolo Morganwg, 15 June 1797.
[58] Geraint Phillips, 'Bywyd a Chysylltiadau Llenyddol Owain Myfyr (Owen Jones), 1741–1814' (unpublished University of Wales Ph.D. thesis, 2006), pp. 238–9.
[59] Walter Davies, *General View of the Agriculture and Domestic Economy of South Wales* (2 vols., London, 1815). See also David Ceri Jones, '"Mere Humbug": Iolo Morganwg and the Board of Agriculture', *THSC*, 10 (2004), 76–97.
[60] NLW 1760A, 6/14–15.

manuscripts, notepads, pencils and a clean shirt, on his back, he strode briskly with a staff in one hand and a book in the other. 'Here comes Old Iolo!' was a popular cry as he marched along and he was often the victim of 'malevolent ridicule'.[61] Wherever he went, fingers were pointed at him as people wondered whether a man of fifty who refused (for humanitarian reasons) to ride a horse was a harmless crank or a dangerous subversive. As he walked through Carmarthen in June 1796 he noticed that one Richard Watkins looked on him with an evil eye as he passed his house: 'I am surely a spy, but he wonders why I should notice him as he is no republican.'[62] Depending on his mood, he would often accost other travellers and, in the case of slavers, merchants, stewards, constables and Calvinistic Methodists, greet them with a volley of imprecations. Indeed, he seized every opportunity on his travels to rail against practically everyone who perpetrated the injustices which prevailed in late Georgian Wales.

By tramping so widely on foot, and composing copious letters when it suited him, Iolo managed to establish a network of like-minded radicals, small groups of intelligent, active and belligerent individuals who campaigned for religious toleration, political reform and peace. In so doing, such minority groups distanced themselves from society. But influence is never simply a matter of numbers and, as the Flemingston piper called the tune, his followers and associates appeared, at least in the eyes of the authorities, to be much more numerous and threatening than they actually were. Whilst Iolo believed that the truth of the Christian revelation was fully attested in the prophecies and miracles of the Scriptures, he reckoned that Unitarianism offered a convincing blend of rational theology and social justice. The Arians and Unitarians with whom he mixed campaigned enthusiastically for universal tolerance and constitutional change. They revelled in the new political vocabulary generated by the Atlantic revolutions and raised their glasses heartily to the 'Rights of Man'.

Several of the major intellectual influences on him, however, had either died or would shortly pass away. The spiky freethinker John Bradford had died in 1785 and the erudite lexicographer John Walters, the Anglican minister whom Iolo tried very hard to mythologize as a Unitarian sympathizer, died in 1797.[63] Then, a year later, Edward Evan(s), Iolo's druidic colleague from Aberdare and allegedly the only other party to the bardic secrets of Glamorgan, was (in William Owen Pughe's apt phrase) taken to 'the circle of bliss' ('cylç y

---

[61] NLW 21426E, no. 3.
[62] NLW 13115B, p. 89.
[63] In NLW 13123B, p. 27, Iolo wrote: 'M\\\\r. Walters, once a Unitarian'.

gwynvyd').⁶⁴ Further north, in the rural parish of Llangadfan, Montgomeryshire, the redoubtable William Jones, a small farmer who resembled his great hero Voltaire and was described by his rector as 'a rank Republican [and] a Leveller', was a man after Iolo's heart.⁶⁵ Iolo corresponded with him, welcomed him into his bardic circle in London, and shared his low opinion of deferential Welsh bards from Gwynedd.⁶⁶ But this courageous, stubborn Voltairean heretic died in November 1795, thereby leaving the field open to his disciple, the priggish loyalist Walter Davies, to dampen radical enthusiasm.

Such losses impoverished Iolo's life, but he drew comfort and inspiration from his contacts with heterodox friends and colleagues in London. Although the philosopher David Williams had every reason to regret the day he 'unwittingly stumbled' on such an unreliable and ungrateful correspondent as Iolo,⁶⁷ he remained an influential contact, not least because subventions from the Royal Literary Fund, which he had founded, helped to keep Iolo alive and active. Iolo also kept in touch with leading lights at the Essex Street chapel, especially Theophilus Lindsey, the founding father of Unitarianism in England, in whom he confided his 'warm hopes that I shall live to see a glorious Unitarian church in Wales, emerging out of that wilderness into which we have been driven by the fury of the great dragon'.⁶⁸ He was pleased to receive a message from his friend, the disorderly and eccentric George Dyer, praising him for 'play[ing] off the rights of man so well' and forwarding the good wishes of prominent Rational Dissenters like Northmore, Toulmin and Wakefield.⁶⁹ In spite of his many foibles, William Owen Pughe was still admired by Iolo and he kept him informed of the latest developments among dissident and heterodox thinkers in London. He was also glad to assist Pughe's brother, John Owen, a courageous publisher and bookseller in London who had been financially ruined for 'a libel on our happy constitution', in finding a house and some land in St Athan.⁷⁰

But Iolo also turned to people in his own locality who were attracted to antitrinitarianism and the excitement of political change. His old friend Wiliam Dafydd, a weaver from Aber-cwm-y-fuwch in the Vale of Ogmore, was

---

⁶⁴ *CIM*, II, p. 101, William Owen Pughe to Iolo Morganwg, 4 September 1798. Evan(s) died on 21 June 1798. NLW 13159A, pp. 142–4; NLW 21398E, no. 1; R. T. Jenkins, 'Bardd a'i Gefndir', *THSC* (1946–7), 97–149.
⁶⁵ NLW 1806E, p. 786, William Jones to Walter Davies (Gwallter Mechain), 18 October 1793; NLW 21401E, no. 14b.
⁶⁶ See Geraint H. Jenkins, '"A Rank Republican [and] a Leveller": William Jones, Llangadfan', *WHR*, 17, no. 3 (1995), 365–86.
⁶⁷ *CIM*, I, p. 795, David Williams to Iolo Morganwg, 29 December 1795.
⁶⁸ Ibid., II, p. 12, Iolo Morganwg to Theophilus Lindsey, 10 February 1797.
⁶⁹ Ibid., II, p. 6, George Dyer to Iolo Morganwg, [? February] 1797.
⁷⁰ Ibid., II, pp. 22–3, William Owen Pughe to Iolo Morganwg, 15 June 1797; Glenda Carr, *William Owen Pughe* (Caerdydd, 1983), pp. 59–60.

rejuvenated as Gwilym Glyn Ogwr in bardic and radical circles by the mid-nineties.[71] In Cowbridge itself Iolo had become a kind of guru to his namesake Edward Williams, better known as Iolo ab Iorwerth Gwilym or Iolo Fardd Glas.[72] One of the political young, he idolized his mentor and hung on every word that came from 'his lips uncorrupted, brave and upright' ('Ddiwiair enau ddewr yniawn').[73] Just as interesting and committed was Rees Evans (brother of the more famous Thomas Evans alias Tomos Glyn Cothi), who ran a woollen factory in Tonyrefail and was described by Iolo as 'a very intelligent Unitarian, and excellent character'.[74] These self-educated and articulate Welsh speakers, and other versatile artisans and craftsmen like them, shared Iolo's taste for theological debate, biting satire and republican rhetoric. The younger turks particularly enjoyed provoking him during their jousts and skirmishes. On one occasion, as he walked from Flemingston to St Hilary, Iolo became extremely irate as Rees Evans deliberately raised his hackles by likening Priestley's necessarianism to the Calvinist doctrine of election. Thwacking his staff on the ground, Iolo thundered: 'There is as much difference between them as there is between Heaven and Hell. One begins in all evil and ends in all pain; the other begins in all wisdom and goodness, and ends in complete bliss.' ('Y mae cymaint o wahaniaeth rhyngddynt ag y sydd rhwng Nefoedd ac Uffern. Mae un yn dechreu yn mhob drwg ac yn terfynu yn mhob poen; a'r llall yn dechreu yn mhob doethineb a daioni, ac yn terfynu yn mhob gwynfyd'.)[75] Such exchanges sometimes spilled over into satirical charades and pieces of burlesque in which church ceremonies were mocked by this irreverent coterie. At Llandyfodwg church towards the end of March 1798 they cocked a snook at trinitarianism:

Ni a gawsom yr anrhydedd o gael agoriad y lle sangctaidd ir diben o gael gweled harddwch â chywrcinwaith y lle, ond ni doedd yn bressennol ond Rys Evans a William Davis y gwaetrydd, ac un dieithr imfi, a minne [Iolo Fardd Glas]. Ac ymmlhith petheu ereill, ni a gawsom yr happusrwydd o glywed pregeth â chrêdo y drindod wladaidd o'r gadair ymmadrodd gan y Parchedig Rys ap Evan Cethinog, a ninneu oll ar ein glinieu yn dywedyd Amen, a melus yr oedfau ydoedd.

---

[71] Williams: *IM*, pp. 125–6.
[72] *HGB*, pp. 33, 36, 39, 52, 113, 116–17, 127, 131, 135–6, 167; E. G. Millward, 'Merthyr Tudful: Tref y Brodyr Rhagorol' in Hywel Teifi Edwards (ed.), *Merthyr a Thaf* (Llandysul, 2001), p. 51.
[73] *CIM*, I, pp. 790–1, 791–2 (trans.), Edward Williams (Iolo ab Iorwerth Gwilym) to Iolo Morganwg, 20 November [?1795].
[74] Ibid., II, p. 1, Iolo Morganwg to [?Theophilus Lindsey] [?1797]; Morien and Thomas Morgan, *Hanes Tonyrefail* (Caerdydd, 1899), pp. 36, 50–2, 60–4, 66.
[75] *Yr Ymofynydd*, IV, no. 51 (1851), 243.

(We were honoured to received the key to the holy place so that we could see the beauty and the skilful construction of the building, but no one was present save Rees Evans and the red-faced Wiliam Dafydd, and another who was a stranger to me, and myself [Iolo Fardd Glas]. And among other things, we had the happiness of hearing the sermon and the creed of the rustic trinity from the pulpit by the Reverend Rhys ab Evan, Cethinog, each one of us on our knees saying Amen, and it was a pleasant service.)[76]

Yet, as even an irremediable local patriot like Iolo would have admitted, the fountain-head of anti-trinitarianism lay in south-west Wales, in the notorious 'Black Spot' in north Carmarthenshire and south Cardiganshire where Calvinists did all in their power to discredit and demonize Rational Dissenters. Carmarthen was one of the fastest-growing towns in Wales, and its printing presses, Dissenting academy, grammar school, book societies and masonic lodges had produced a highly literate and politicized society. Within 'the smouldering hinterland of *sans-culotte* Carmarthen'[77] and especially around Llwynrhydowen, the newly rebuilt mother church of the anti-trinitarians, there emerged, in Iolo's words, 'people most intelligent of any in Wales'.[78] The quality of their pastors put the established church to shame. David Lloyd (Dafydd Llwyd) of Brynllefrith, an extraordinary polyglot and preacher, attracted up to three hundred people to his services at Llwynrhydowen,[79] while David Davis, the portly Arian head of the Castellhywel academy, ensured that his devoted pupils were taught in a tolerant environment and also given a liberal dose of his spellbinding sermons.[80] Such men were so well versed in religion and politics that few were prepared to challenge them publicly. One notable exception was Samuel Horsley, bishop of St David's (1788–93), an overbearing prelate who, according to Iolo, waged a rather nasty vendetta against anti-trinitarians by crying 'mad dog' and assembling 'a huge host of unitarian hunters'.[81] Iolo despised 'high Parson Horsely'[82] and was delighted when David Jones, a native of Llandovery who adopted the pen name 'The Welsh Freeholder', became a prickly thorn in the ample flesh of the bishop, to whom he addressed five

---

[76] *CIM*, II, pp. 66, 67 (trans.), Edward Williams to Iolo Morganwg, 26 March 1798.
[77] Gwyn A. Williams, *The Welsh in their History* (London, 1982), p. 61.
[78] NLW 13156A, p. 179.
[79] D. Elwyn Davies, *'They Thought for Themselves': A Brief Look at the Story of Unitarianism and the Liberal Tradition in Wales and Beyond its Borders* (Llandysul, 1982), pp. 34–5.
[80] Idem, *Cewri'r Ffydd: Bywgraffiadur y Mudiad Undodaidd yng Nghymru* (Cymdeithas Undodaidd Deheudir Cymru, 1999), pp. 47–53.
[81] NLW 13145A, p. 343; F. C. Mather, *High Church Prophet: Bishop Samuel Horsley (1733–1806) and the Caroline Tradition in the later Georgian Church* (Oxford, 1992), p. 166.
[82] NLW 13112B, p. 318. Iolo's friend Gilbert Wakefield described Horsley as 'a *prelatical Hercules*'. J. T. Rutt and Arnold Wainewright (eds.), *Memoirs of the Life of Gilbert Wakefield* (2 vols., London, 1804), I, p. 325.

hard-hitting pamphlets in the early 1790s in which he depicted him as an enemy to free inquiry and civil rights. A former disciple of Richard Price, Jones succeeded Priestley at the New Meeting House, Birmingham, in 1792 and, as we shall see, when he subsequently became a barrister Iolo was glad to call on his practical support in defence of a colleague.[83]

During the closing decades of the eighteenth century a steady stream of gifted young ministers, most of whom had been trained at the Carmarthen academy or at Castellhywel, left south-west Wales to serve Unitarian congregations in places like Alcester, Birmingham, Coventry, Evesham and Walsall.[84] The 'Black Spot' also produced several plebeian Jacobins, mostly of artisan/craftsman stock, who travelled and read widely as they scraped a living. One of the most intriguing was Thomas Evans, a breeches-maker from Carmarthen who is most often referred to in library catalogues as 'Thomas Evans Bromsgrove'. Iolo delighted in the company of this stubborn, mottled figure and found him a lively correspondent. Evans had close links with Unitarians in the Midlands like William Huddy, Presbyterian minister at Bromsgrove, and David Evans, a former student at Swansea and Carmarthen academies who became a Unitarian minister at Wirksworth, Preston, and then at Bromsgrove from 1794 to 1798.[85] In his letters to Iolo he gaily traduced chinless wonders like William Wentworth, 2nd Earl Fitzwilliam, and Willoughby Bertie, 4th Earl of Abingdon. 'Should you not', he invited Iolo, 'like to have their heads under the grate and the poker in your hand to poke the fire upon them?'[86] Profoundly disenchanted but unbowed by government repression, he urged Iolo and his fellow republicans to hold firm in 'the spirit of truth and liberty'[87] and to join him in singing 'Brittons born free':

> Brittons born free, how envi'd are wee
> Because of our liberties dear,
> Wee may laugh drink and sing, but say no^t. of the King,
> And then wee have nothing to fear, my brave boys
> And then we have nothing to fear.

---

[83] *DWB* s. v. David Jones (1765–1816).
[84] George Eyre Evans, *Midland Churches: A History of the Congregations on the Roll of the Midland Christian Union* (Dudley, 1899), pp. 12–13, 57, 125, 127, 165.
[85] *Monthly Review*, new series, II (1828), 419; George Eyre Evans, *Record of the Provincial Assembly of Lancashire and Cheshire* (Manchester, 1896), p. 153.
[86] *CIM*, I, p. 836, Thomas Evans to Iolo Morganwg, 9 October 1796.
[87] Ibid., I, p. 832, Thomas Evans to Iolo Morganwg, 20 September [?1796].

> We too have a right, to convene and unite
> If we'll not exceed forty nine,
> And there we may think, give a nod and a wink,
> But take care how we utter our minds, my brave boys
> But take care how we utter our minds.[88]

People in Cowbridge would have happily thrown Evans to the wolves, especially since he disgraced himself by fathering an illegitimate child in the parish.[89]

Another roguish Thomas Evans also loomed large in Iolo's life from the mid-1790s onwards. A short, stubby man, fond of his pipe and mead, this Evans was known in Carmarthenshire as 'Twm Penpistyll', within poetic circles as 'Tomos Glyn Cothi', and among radicals as 'Priestley bach' (little Priestley).[90] Iolo came to know him in 1795 and visited him at his cottage at Penpistyll, near Brechfa, on several occasions, including during his journey through the county in June 1796. Seventeen years younger than Iolo, Evans was a travelling weaver who sold his wares at fairs and markets in south Wales and the West Country. His liberally-minded father had marched him to Alltyblaca meeting house to listen to David Davis's powerful sermons and had also plied him with several treatises by Priestley.[91] Not surprisingly, therefore, Evans was the first to disseminate Priestleyan doctrines in the Welsh language. He even christened one of his sons Joseph Priestley Evans. On 11 September 1794 he was ordained Unitarian minister at Gwernogau in Carmarthenshire and, with the financial support of Theophilus Lindsey and other affluent anti-trinitarians in London, he built the Cwm Cothi meeting house at Brechfa to which Iolo affixed a specially carved and inscribed tablet in 1796 to mark the founding of the first Unitarian congregation in Wales.[92]

Iolo and Thomas Evans were two of a kind: rough-and-ready, impulsive to the point of recklessness, forthright in their opinions, and fearless in the face of loyalists. The Lindseys, however, did not know what to make of the Brechfa weaver. Theophilus Lindsey wearied of his 'extraordinary front' and

---

[88] NLW 21398E, no. 3. The song, which is included in Iolo's papers, is in Evans's hand, though it is possible that Iolo composed it.

[89] The child, christened Mary, was the daughter of Ann Sweeting and was baptized on 1 August 1796. Iolo acted on Evans's behalf in this 'sad affair' by negotiating maintenance costs with Ann Sweeting's father. Glamorgan Archives, Llanblethian PR; *CIM*, I, pp. 831–2, Thomas Evans to Iolo Morganwg, 20 September [?1796].

[90] *Gardd Aberdâr, yn cynwys y Cyfansoddiadau Buddugol yn Eisteddfod y Carw Coch, Aberdar, Awst 29, 1853* (Caerfyrddin, 1854), p. 109; Geraint Dyfnallt Owen, *Thomas Evans (Tomos Glyn Cothi)* ([Abertawe], 1963).

[91] John Gwili Jenkins, *Hanfod Duw a Pherson Crist* (Liverpool, 1931), pp. 310–11.

[92] NLW 13103B, p. 300; *CIM*, II, p. 1, Iolo Morganwg to [?Theophilus Lindsey] [?1797].

importunities, while his wife Hannah deplored his 'high conceit of himself'.[93] Nor was a monoglot English bishop like Horsley happy to see a self-educated weaver peddling the Welsh-language equivalents of 'Unitarianism' (Undodiaeth) and 'Unitarians' (Undodiaid) under his watch.[94] As for Calvinistic Methodists, their local luminaries did all in their power to discredit and demonize this outspoken rustic. But Evans was more than ready to challenge those whom he believed to be enemies of truth and freedom. In 1795 he launched *The Miscellaneous Repository: Neu, Y Drysorfa Gymmysgedig*, a quarterly magazine which, despite its innocent-sounding title, was much spikier than its better-known predecessor, Morgan John Rhys's *Cylch-grawn Cynmraeg: neu Drysorfa Gwybodaeth*. Preoccupied with the plight of African slaves, political martyrs and anti-war protesters, Evans laced his texts with denunciations of 'oppressors thirsting for blood, plundering the world, and spreading desolation throughout countries' ('treiswyr sydd yn sychedu am waed, yn anhreithio'r byd, ac yn gwasgaru anghyfannedd-dra dros y gwledydd').[95] An implacable enemy of fast days, he urged dissidents to use such occasions to pray for the speedy downfall of tyrants: 'Cast down headlong within a minute all the world's oppressors; Oh! Almighty God, scatter those who gorge themselves on human blood' ('Yn bendramwnwgl bwr i lawr, / Holl dreiswyr byd mewn munud awr; / O! gwasgar Hollalluog Dad, / Y rhai sy'n pesgi ar ddynol-waed').[96]

Iolo immediately took to this kindred spirit and, whenever possible, trekked to Brechfa to raise a glass with him to the radical cause. They discussed and argued about the ideas of Godwin, Milton, Paine and Spence, selected striking passages from Benjamin Flower's issues of the *Cambridge Intelligencer*, and exchanged examples of the homespun epigrams of Ben Franklin.[97] Their conversation was often studded with unkind references to 'the Truly Dishonourable William Pitt', whom they regarded as a butcher and a traitor whose eventual fate would be to plunge headlong into the 'Bottomless Pitt'.[98] They transcribed each other's poems and squibs, and declaimed popular liberty songs like *Ça Ira* and the *Marseillaise*. Evans was most probably the composer of the Welsh translation of the *Marseillaise* which appeared in *Y Geirgrawn* in May 1796[99] and, not to be outdone, Iolo penned an English translation with a suitably rousing refrain:

> To the field ye brave!
> Our full resolution shall be

[93] Dr Williams's Library 12.57, nos. 12, 33.
[94] See *GPC* s.v. Undodiaeth, Undodiaid.
[95] *The Miscellaneous Repository: Neu, Y Drysorfa Gymmysgedig* (1795), 14–16.
[96] Ibid., 17.
[97] See the miscellaneous political material in 'Y Gell Gymysg' (NLW 6238A).
[98] NLW 6238A, p. 282; NLW 3281D, p. 35; NLW 21399E, no. 20.
[99] *Y Geirgrawn: neu Drysorfa Gwybodaeth*, May 1796, 127–8.

> Advance! advance! We will go one and all
> To die or live free.[100]

Letting off steam in this way in the fastness of Carmarthenshire or on isolated hilltops in Glamorgan brought them some satisfaction and helped to stiffen their moral courage.

Martin Fitzpatrick has described the 'Black Spot' as 'an almost unique example of an enduring rural Enlightenment',[101] but even the thriving heterodox academies in the south-west were unable to produce sufficient numbers of ministers and converts to repudiate Calvinism and the notion of 'twice-born' salvation. Bishops and clergymen might have been 'ministers of Antichristianity'[102] in Iolo's eyes and Calvinistic Methodists fanatical leapers who charmed 'the silly crowd',[103] but by refusing to make windows into people's souls or fixing their eyes upon heaven, anti-trinitarians were bound to appeal only to a tiny religious minority. The potential for a much larger, and more radical, constituency lay to the south-east where, along the northern rim of the valleys of Glamorgan and Monmouthshire demographic changes and large-scale ironworking were wreaking a momentous transformation in the economy. During the 1790s the iron industry entered an era of unprecedented expansion, largely as a result of the demands of war. New blast furnaces and forges dotted the landscape around Merthyr Tydfil as ironmasters from outside Wales invested substantially in the lucrative iron industry and trade.[104] As we have seen, Iolo was acutely aware that this transformation was occurring in communities that sported a rich inheritance of creative dissidence which stretched back to Cromwellian times. He often referred to the rootedness of the inhabitants of the upland parishes of Glamorgan in the culture of Dissent and contrasted this with the values which fired the new industrial Titans. Robust groups of Arminians, Arians and Unitarians were emerging at Cefn-coedycymer and Ynys-gau. These thoughtful, book-reading farmers, tradesmen, craftsmen and industrial workers championed the works of Tom Paine and, by developing a taste for astronomy, mathematics, philosophy and theology, formed a nucleus for the Cyfarthfa Philosophical Society founded in

---

[100] NLW 21401E, no. 29.
[101] Martin Fitzpatrick, 'Enlightenment' in Iain McCalman (ed.), *An Oxford Companion to the Romantic Age: British Culture 1776–1832* (Oxford, 1999), p. 303.
[102] NLW 13094E, p. 182. See also NLW 13160A, p. 365; NLW 13162A, p. 319.
[103] NLW 13170B, pp. 184–6.
[104] Trevor Boyns, Dennis Thomas and Colin Baber, 'The Iron, Steel and Tinplate Industries, 1750–1914' in *GCH V*, pp. 107–9; Chris Evans, *'The Labyrinth of Flames': Work and Social Conflict in Early Industrial Merthyr Tydfil* (Cardiff, 1993).

1807.[105] By instinct and precept, Iolo's sympathies lay with them and he made it his business to support growing bands of worshippers who were strongly in favour of the radical cause.

Iolo was not an enemy to economic progress – he once claimed that there was 'something benignly favourable to human happiness in Industry'[106] – but he was acutely aware that the 'Iron Kings' of the Glamorgan *Blaenau*, where the druids and bards of yore had been held in high repute for their just dealings, were not only perpetrators of cruelty and violence in their own forges and furnaces but were also benefiting enormously from the labours of enslaved men and women in the Caribbean. By the mid-1790s Cyfarthfa was the largest ironworks in Britain and its owner, the forthright Yorkshireman Richard Crawshay, was obsessively preoccupied with making money and enhancing his family's fortunes. The ego of 'Moloch the Iron King',[107] as he was known, was even greater than that of Iolo, and he despised everyone who refused to bow and scrape in his presence. Iolo developed an undying hatred for him as his efforts to nurture libertarianism were scotched by the tyrannical ironmaster. Convinced that an 'evil Spirit prevails strongly amongst our Dissenters from the Damnable Doctrines of D^r. Priestley & Payne which wants a Gentle Checque',[108] Crawshay urged judges to bestir themselves in dealing with rebellious 'uncivilis'd Welch Workmen'[109] and encouraged loyal churchmen to cultivate the habit of having nails hammered into their boots to form the initials TP, thereby enabling them to trample the infidel underfoot as they marched to work. Small wonder that Iolo dubbed Merthyr 'the devil's hand' ('Llaw'r Dia[w]l').[110]

Crawshay despised Iolo's inquisitiveness and his liberal politics. Word had swiftly reached him of the stonemason's republican principles and he warned Sir John Sinclair against offering him any commission on behalf of the Board of Agriculture. The 'Cowbridge Poet', he told Sinclair in December 1796, 'is a broken Fellow Char'd by various Acts of Insolvency - and is now a seller of seditious Books and will be planting Treason wherever he goes'.[111] Well aware of Crawshay's low opinion of him, Iolo continued to torment the ironmaster by inviting him to fund his passage to America where, in the light of his skills as a stone- and marblemason and his grasp of architecture, arithmetic, book-

---

[105] Tom Lewis, *The History of the Hen Dŷ Cwrdd, Cefn Coed y Cymmer* (Llandysul, [1947]), p. 138; Glanmor Williams, 'The Earliest Non-conformists in Merthyr Tydfil', *MH*, I (1976), 84–95.
[106] NLW 21323B, p. 57.
[107] Evans, *'The Labyrinth of Flames'*, p. 121.
[108] Gwent Record Office (Cwmbrân), D2. 162, f. 130, Richard Crawshay to George Hardinge, 16 October 1792.
[109] Chris Evans, *The Letterbook of Richard Crawshay 1788–1797* (Cardiff, 1990), p. 139.
[110] *CIM*, II, p. 265, Iolo Morganwg to William Owen Pughe, 8 February 1800.
[111] Evans, *The Letterbook of Richard Crawshay*, p. 160.

keeping, geometry and mensuration, he would be an ideal person to superintend the work of gangs of masons at ironworks he was rumoured to be about to establish in the Land of the Free.[112] Crawshay's scribbled reply was curtly negative and he and his fellow ironmasters must have longed to see this turbulent Unitarian and Jacobin, who liked to vilify William Pitt and condemn Nelson as 'the murdering giant and the great pirate' ('Cawrlofrudd a'r Morleidr Mawr'), placed behind bars.[113] The animosity was mutual. Iolo privately castigated Crawshay as 'an old iron shopkeeper [who] by purchasing from thieves and by such means amassed an infamous fortune reigns as a king'.[114] Iolo's son Taliesin ruefully noted some time later that failing to cringe before the Crawshays was 'a sin unto death in their eyes'.[115] Nevertheless, Iolo had the good fortune to outlive his sworn enemy and to witness an appreciable growth in anti-trinitarianism in and around Merthyr during the early nineteenth century.

His prospects of setting up durable cells in north Wales were much bleaker. Since he was permanently short of money he had few opportunities to judge how far political radicalism had penetrated that region. But when Owain Myfyr funded an expedition by Iolo to Gwynedd in search of manuscript material that would enrich the proposed *Myvyrian Archaiology of Wales*, he set off on one of his 'rambles' in the summer of 1799. Although he was plagued by chronic migraine and sciatica, he appears to have behaved impeccably even when his equanimity was severely tested by John Williams, a mentally unstable schoolmaster at Llanrwst who was as fond of decrying Painites as he was of tippling. Convinced that the 'little republican Bard' was propagating 'democratical stuff', Williams yearned for the opportunity to cast him 'into the Menai for his Quixotick principles'.[116] To his credit, Iolo held his temper and made no derisive public comments about the famous 374-page *cywydd* to the trinity published by David Richards (Dafydd Ionawr) or about the loyalist poet and schoolmaster David Thomas (Dafydd Ddu Eryri) whom he referred to privately as 'the Snowdon Drunkard'.[117] On his travels, he kept a wary eye open for 'the tallons and fangs of Methodism'.[118] Having heard the Methodist preacher Edward Jones ('Ginnico Jones') of Llansannan 'bawling away' in the pulpit and demonizing all Painites, including John Jones (Jac Glan-y-gors),

---

[112] *CIM*, II, pp. 298–300, Iolo Morganwg to Richard Crawshay, 20 June 1800.
[113] Ibid., II, pp. 300–1, Richard Crawshay to Iolo Morganwg, [30] June 1800; NLW 13134A, p. 219.
[114] NLW 13174A, p. 26ᵛ.
[115] *CIM*, III, pp. 715–16, Taliesin Williams to Iolo Morganwg, 28 October 1824.
[116] Ibid., II, p. 202, Iolo Morganwg to Owen Jones (Owain Myfyr), 22 July 1799; Phillips, 'Bywyd a Chysylltiadau Llenyddol Owain Myfyr', p. 206.
[117] David Richards (Dafydd Ionawr), *Cywydd y Drindod* ([Wrexham], 1793); NLW 13138A, p. 61.
[118] *CIM*, II, p. 197, Iolo Morganwg to William Owen Pughe, 10 July 1799.

author of two Welsh paraphrases of Paine's *Rights of Man*, in a private letter to Owain Myfyr he conjured up a sentence which pulsates with irony: 'As in Glan y Gors all die, so in Ginnico Jones shall all be made alive.'[119] Iolo felt little sense of fellowship with the 'Deudneudwyr' and came away believing that, like the tireless loyalist *cywyddwr* David Richards, they wanted 'nothing to do with the French Revolution, nor British Politics'.[120]

Many of those, from far and near, whom Iolo admired and counted among his most loyal colleagues and friends gave their sympathetic support to the totemic pageant which had become associated with his name since its inception in 1792. Early in 1795 Iolo publicly voiced his intention of enacting a Gorsedd ceremony annually at Bryn Owain (the Stalling Down), near Cowbridge.[121] In the event, he held druidic moots more frequently than that and at more than one location. Using his own Welsh-language nomenclature for the solstices (Alban Eilir: 21 March; Alban Hefin: 21 June; Alban Elfed: 21 September; Alban Arthen: 21 December), between 1795 and 1798 he held two per annum, initially at Bryn Owain and then at Mynydd y Garth (Garth Mountain) in Pentyrch, at Mynydd y Fforest (Forest Mountain), above Ystradowen some two miles north of Cowbridge, and at Glynogwr, Llandyfodwg. During his sojourn in Gwynedd in 1799 Iolo also held a Gorsedd at Bryn Dinorwig, Llanddeiniolen, and had he been able to afford to travel more freely he might well have conducted similar 'tribunals' outside his native county.[122] Although his chosen venues were not as striking as Primrose Hill, they offered the natural scenery, impressive vistas and relative seclusion congenial to Druids, bards and democrats. Yet, these were public ceremonies. Iolo still insisted that the procedures be conducted 'in the face of the sun and eye of the light' and culminate with the rousing injunction 'Y Gwir yn erbyn y Byd' (The Truth against the World).

As was the case in London, the numbers involved in these mummeries were small and the bards were probably personally invited by Iolo. By this stage he was in the process of completing and, as was his wont, titivating 'The History of the Ancient British Bards or Druids', an exposition of the bardic institution and its association with theology, philosophy, morality and literary criticism.[123] His Gorseddau, now held exclusively in Welsh, were designed not only to sustain the historical and literary memory of his people but also to take their place as a progressive outlet for radical idealism and more representative

---

[119] Ibid., II, p. 203, Iolo Morganwg to Owen Jones (Owain Myfyr), 22 July 1799.
[120] Richards, *Cywydd y Drindod*, sig. A4ʳ.
[121] *HGB*, p. 35.
[122] NLW 13104B, p. 207; NLW 13123B, pp. 42–5; NLW 13128A, pp. 407–11; NLW 13144A, pp. 7–16.
[123] See NLW 13091E, p. 326; NLW 13097B, pp. 239–63; NLW 13121B, pp. 303–9. For this theme in general, see *Bardic Circles*, esp. pp. 158–250.

forms of government. Among the 'singular' doctrines of the bards were the rights of man, liberty and peace, and as the climate of discussion became more intense Iolo's fund of cultural wisdom inevitably acquired a sense of political modernity. He and his accredited disciples sang on themes such as religious liberty, moral principles, and the dawn of knowledge and peace.[124] The names of George III and William Pitt were regularly taken in vain as tyrants and warmongers were condemned. Iolo's voice was never more shrill than when he sang 'Breiniau Dyn' (Rights of Man) – declaimed in the same metre as 'God Save the King' – at Bryn Owain in the fraught year of 1798:

> Rhyddid y sydd yn awr
> Fel llew rhuadwy mawr,
>   Pob tir a'i clyw;
> A'r gwir sydd ar ei daith,
> Dros yr holl ddaear faith,
> Yn seinio peraidd iaith
>   I ddynol ryw.

(Liberty now / It's like a great roaring lion / heard in every land; / And truth is on the march / Through the whole world / Declaiming sweet words / To humankind.)[125]

Venomous tirades were launched against wicked kings and gluttonous clerics, and it was at this point that magistrates decided that these tribunals were crypto-republican agencies whose primary aim was to facilitate a French invasion. Undeterred, Iolo went elsewhere to raise the political temperature. At Bryn Dinorwig in autumn 1799 he tested the mental and physical powers of concentration of the bards of Gwynedd by reciting his eighteen-stanza poem 'Cywydd Gorymbil am Heddwch' ('An Earnest Plea for Peace') with mounting passion.[126] Four days before Christmas 1799 he was expected to attend what Thomas Evans called an 'eisteddfod' at Penpistyll but, to the chagrin of the host, he failed to turn up to support a handful of poets who sang lustily on themes such as religious liberty, the bloody reign of George III, the so-called 'justice' of William Pitt, and the flames of hell.[127] But he still believed that the Gorsedd, perhaps as a surrogate for some kind of national convention or parliament, could play a significant role in democratizing and uplifting society.

---

[124] NLW 13097B, p. 253; NLW 13104B, p. 207; NLW 13123B, pp. 42–5; NLW 13141A, pp. 17–19, 23–9, 35–6.
[125] NLW 13148A, pp. 286–92, 297–300; E. G. Millward (ed.), *Blodeugerdd Barddas o Gerddi Rhydd y Ddeunawfed Ganrif* (Cyhoeddiadau Barddas, 1991), pp. 242–5.
[126] NLW 13134A, pp. 33–48.
[127] NLW 13157A, p. 205; *CIM*, II, p. 261, Thomas Evans (Tomos Glyn Cothi) to Iolo Morganwg, 17 January 1800.

Much of this activity — selling radical literature, orchestrating radical networks, conducting open-air druidic moots — was nevertheless undertaken in the shadow of persecution or under the threat of persecution. Ever since his return to the Vale of Glamorgan, Iolo had been a marked man. His past sins had not been forgotten and his republican rhetoric, proclaimed at a time of severe economic crisis and social disaffection, meant that the authorities believed that he was actively encouraging and assisting the enemy. In retrospect we can appreciate that he represented a tiny minority and was hardly a major security risk. But ever since the outbreak of war in 1793 Wales had been deluged by loyalist propaganda in the form of sermons, addresses, broadsides, prints and songs which warned against treasonable activity and sang the praises of king, church and country. Loyalist associations multiplied appreciably from 1792 onwards as civic leaders awoke to the potential threat of Painism.[128] In 1792 Cardiff Corporation funded a public ceremony in which a fully-dressed effigy of Tom Paine was hanged and burnt by the borough's hangman, thereby giving rise to the popular refrain 'They laughed and burnt poor Tommy Paine / In seventeen-ninety-two'.[129] A flinty anti-Paine diatribe, 'Cân Twm Paen', by Dafydd Ddu Eryri, was widely circulated,[130] as were Welsh versions of Hannah More's *Village Politics*, a riposte to Tom Paine's work. The Welsh eisteddfod, revived by the Gwyneddigion in 1789 as a means of encouraging political reform, was engulfed by a swelling tide of loyalism and Francophobia. Among 'true Britons' the spirit of loyalism was alive and well.

Yet, the government and the propertied classes were terrified by the possibility of a bloody insurrection, a reprise of the horrors of the September massacres and the Terror on British soil. Poor harvests, food riots and anti-war protests made 1795 a particularly turbulent year. Troops and militiamen were on the march as cries of 'No war, no Pitt, Cheap Bread' multiplied and riots and disturbances broke out in ports and towns.[131] As he and his government lurched from crisis to crisis, Pitt instituted an array of public order measures. Habeas corpus was suspended from May 1794 to July 1795 in a bid to curtail the depredations of so-called 'Jacobins' and 'Levellers'. But the threat of public disorder continued to grow. Towards the end of June 1795 around 100,000 people assembled in London to call for lower grain prices, political

---

[128] Mark Philp, 'Vulgar Conservatism, 1792–3', *EHR*, CX, no. 435 (1995), 42–69; Hywel M. Davies, 'Loyalism in Wales, 1792–1793', *WHR*, 20, no. 4 (2001), 657–716.

[129] J. H. Matthews (ed.), *Cardiff Records* (6 vols., Cardiff, 1898–1911), II, pp. 311–12. See also NLW, Bute L46/30.

[130] David Thomas (Dafydd Ddu Eryri), *Corph y Gaingc, neu Ddifyrwch Teuluaidd* (Dolgelley, 1810), pp. 196–204.

[131] David J. V. Jones, *Before Rebecca: Popular Protests in Wales 1793–1835* (London, 1973); David W. Howell, *The Rural Poor in Eighteenth-Century Wales* (Cardiff, 2000); Sharon Howard, 'Riotous Community: Crowds, Politics and Society in Wales, c.1700–1840', *WHR*, 20, no. 4 (2001), 656–86.

reform and peace. Doubtless Iolo, who was by this stage deeply worried about the consequences of the costs of the war and the alarming increase in the National Debt, would have been present had he still been living in the capital. By October the public mood had worsened and, when the king's carriage was hooted and mobbed by furious crowds brandishing tiny loaves in black crêpe on sticks, Pitt responded by passing the 'Gagging Acts'. These prohibited, on the pain of a charge of treason, the incitement to express hatred of the king or his government or the constitution, either orally or in writing, and restricted public meetings to fewer than fifty persons unless a magistrate was prepared to give permission to exceed that number well in advance. Both bills became law in December 1795. The aim was clearly to curtail personal liberties and silence the reform movement. To Iolo, however, William Pitt was an engine of destruction. He had opposed parliamentary reform, provoked an unnecessary war with France, encouraged loyalist mobs to persecute radicals, committed perjury at the Treason Trials, and introduced a raft of repressive measures that curtailed basic freedoms. Iolo was convinced that he was living through an 'Age of Terror' and at the end of a turbulent year he wrote to Pitt on 16 December 1796 protesting furiously against the high price of grain and soaring levels of taxation on daily necessities, especially his favourite beverage, tea. He also remonstrated with Pitt for his bellicosity: 'How is it, sir, that Christian powers are much more at war with each other, and always have been, than the Mahometan or any other governments? Why is there more infernality in countries professing the religion of the Prince of Peace than else-where?'[132] The prime minister did not respond. Undeterred, Iolo maintained that, by instituting a reign of terror, the true Jacobins were Pitt, Dundas and their vile understrappers.[133]

In a carbon copy of events in the mid-seventeenth century, the turmoil of the mid-1790s produced a striking outpouring of eschatology. Prophets great and small discovered in the Scriptures, notably in the Book of Daniel and in Revelations, prophecies which threw significant light on the politico-religious events of the times and also pointed to the Second Coming of Christ.[134] Iolo's reading of Sir William Jones's *Institutes of Hindu Law* (1796) convinced him that scriptural testimonies clearly foretold the day when tyrannical monarchies

---

[132] *CIM*, I, pp. 846–7, Iolo Morganwg to William Pitt, 16 December 1796. Iolo transcribed from newspapers extracts regarding poor people who froze to death in December 1796 and January 1797. NLW 13104B, pp. 199–200.
[133] *CIM*, II, p. 61, Iolo Morganwg to Mary Barker, 26 March [1798].
[134] Clarke Garrett, *Respectable Folly: Millenarians and the French Revolution in France and England* (Baltimore, Md., 1975); Hywel M. Davies, 'Morgan John Rhys and James Bicheno: Anti-Christ and the French Revolution in England and Wales', *BBCS*, XXIX, part 1 (1980), 111–27.

would be cast down in favour of truth, justice and benevolence.[135] In a short critique of an anonymous pamphlet, *Antichrist in the French Convention* (1795), he identified a trinity of anti-Christian forces within society – civil tyranny, ecclesiastical tyranny and infidelity – which, he believed, would destroy themselves and usher in a theocratic polity in which peace would prevail.[136]

Given his propensity for speaking out of turn, often in public, and advertising his radical agenda, it is extraordinary that Iolo escaped arrest and prosecution. In several parts of Wales small farmers, artisans and labourers who voiced republican sentiments, vilified the king and complained bitterly about socio-economic burdens were brought before the courts. John Ellis, a yeoman farmer from Llanbryn-mair, was so incensed by the oppressive rich that he called for a new government, to be instituted by bloody means if required.[137] John Griffith, a Neath labourer, declared that he could fashion a better king than George III from alder wood,[138] and it was widely known that many of the lower orders despised the 'German Butcher' who 'delighted in blood'.[139] As Iolo's papers amply reveal, he was even more outspoken than these transgressors in his sentiments about the 'Bottomless Pitt' and about what William Owen Pughe called his 'kingophobia and other demon matters'.[140] In southeast England, especially London, some of his radical friends and others of Welsh stock were harshly punished for writing or publishing seditious libels. In 1797 John Gale Jones, a radical apothecary and a fiery public speaker in the Thelwall mould whose oratory left a deep impression on the Welsh Chartist leader John Frost, was convicted of seditious libel, though he was later released upon appeal.[141] The bookseller Thomas Williams was less fortunate. Found guilty of publishing and selling a cheap edition of Paine's *Age of Reason*, he was sentenced to a year's hard labour in Cold Bath Fields prison and saddled with a £1,000 bond for life.[142] Gilbert Wakefield, Iolo's great friend, was charged with seditious libel in January 1798 – he had condemned Pitt as a warmonger and an enemy of the poor – and was sentenced to two years in Dorchester gaol and a fine of £500.[143]

---

[135] *CIM*, II, pp. 161–2, Iolo Morganwg to William Owen Pughe, 20 December 1798.
[136] NLW 13136A, pp. 165–83. See also NLW 13159A, pp. 290–302.
[137] NLW, Wales 4/196/1.
[138] NLW, Wales 4/630/5.
[139] Hilary M. Thomas (ed.), *The Diaries of John Bird of Cardiff: Clerk to the first Marquess of Bute 1790–1803* (Cardiff, 1987), pp. 132–4.
[140] *CIM*, II, p. 189, William Owen Pughe to Iolo Morganwg, 14 June 1799.
[141] David Williams, *John Frost: A Study in Chartism* (Cardiff, 1939), p. 13; E. P. Thompson, *The Making of the English Working Class* (Harmondsworth, 1968), pp. 154, 159, 162, 171, 181, 197.
[142] J. Ann Hone, *For the Cause of Truth: Radicalism in London 1796–1821* (Oxford, 1982), pp. 223–4; David Nash, *Blasphemy in Modern Britain* (Aldershot, 1999), pp. 77–8.
[143] *RAEW*, p. 50. For Wakefield, see Rutt and Wainewright (eds.), *Memoirs of the Life of Gilbert Wakefield*. Iolo admired him as a 'fearless, but not virulent, assertor of what I believe to be Truth'. NLW 21408E, no. 10.

Iolo might well have suffered a similar fate had he ventured into print during these years. In general, courts were more likely to impose severe punishments on those who wrote or published seditious libels than on those who uttered seditious expressions or kept their traitorous views private.[144] Prosecutions were the exception rather than the rule and Iolo was an elusive quarry for those magistrates, informers and whistle-blowers whom he castigated as 'a loathsom swarm of the vilest bloodsucking insects that ever dishonoured the Creation'.[145] But fear of persecution and imprisonment can play on the mind and Iolo was wise enough to dispatch his most inflammatory writings to trusted friends.[146] A descendant of the Truman family of Pantlliwydd claimed that when Iolo's liberties were seriously curtailed he 'needed to escape there periodically, and carry away as much as he could clear [?] on his shoulders'.[147]

By 1797–8, however, it became even more difficult for him and his family to sleep soundly at night. Radical societies and individuals were subjected to much higher levels of surveillance and invasions of privacy. Further draconian legislation was introduced when the French invasion in Pembrokeshire in 1797, the Irish uprising in 1798, and mutinies in the British fleets at Spithead and the Nore concentrated the minds of John Bulls and anti-Jacobins. The Traitorous Correspondence Act, first passed in 1793, was extended in 1798 to include correspondence with Holland, habeas corpus was suspended between April 1798 and March 1801, and the infamous Combination Laws of 1799 and 1800 proved to be a major impediment to individual liberties and trade union activity. For someone like Iolo who habitually sailed close to the wind, these savage reprisals were deeply troubling. Not surprisingly, the widespread mood of bitterness and despair prompted several erstwhile radicals to recant or contract out of the reformist cause.

In a Welsh context and far beyond, the so-called 'French invasion' in February 1797 proved to be a major milestone. A thrill of horror spread throughout Britain when news arrived that General William Tate, an American renegade, and some 1,400 blackguards who made up the infamous Légion Noire, had arrived in four warships on 22 February 1797, laid anchor at Carreg Gwastad Point near Fishguard, and landed on Welsh soil the following day. Contrary to

---

[144] Clive Emsley, 'An Aspect of Pitt's "Terror": Prosecutions for Sedition during the 1790s', *Social History*, 6, no. 2 (1981), 155–84; idem, 'Repression, Terror and the Rule of Law during the decade of the French Revolution', *EHR*, C (1985), 801–25; Steve Poole, 'Pitt's Terror Reconsidered: Jacobinism and the Law in two South-Western Counties, 1791–1803', *Southern History*, 17 (1995), 65–88.

[145] NLW 13112B, p. 367. In NLW 21373D, p. 7, he described informers as 'state lights made of base stuff who, when they've burnt themselves down to the snuff, stink and are thrown away – and fair enough'.

[146] *CIM*, II, p. 86, Iolo Morganwg to William Owen Pughe, 12 May 1798.

[147] Cardiff Central Library 3.1.

their expectations, the French were greeted as demons rather than liberators and were so roughly treated by zealous Protestant males and redoubtable Amazonian women, including the legendary Jemima Nicholas, that they surrendered meekly three days later. As future re-enactments by schoolchildren have emphasized, the bizarre event had all the hallmarks of a comic opera.[148] Iolo made light of the affair, as his amusing account to William Owen Pughe reveals:

> Breeches, peticoats, shirts, shifts, blankets, sheets (for some received the news in bed) have been most wofully defiled in south Wales lately on hearing that a thimble-full of French men landed on our coast. I hope that you will have the goodness to compassionate our unfortunate wash-women. Our dragooners sent us some compan[ies] of dragoons after the old women of Pembrokeshire had secured the damned republicans, as it seems we are requested to call them. Are there no lamp-irons in Downing Street? I fear that the hemp crops of the last season failed. We must allow that the French are before hand with us in the most useful arts and sciences – witness their invention and use of the guillotine.[149]

But to loyalists the invasion was a horrifying example of the vulnerability of the Welsh coastline and of the strong likelihood that Dissenters were plotting with the enemy to undermine the state. A local Baptist and a Congregationalist were immediately singled out and sent to trial for allegedly assisting Tate's banditti: Thomas John was a yeoman farmer from Summerton in the parish of Little Newcastle and Samuel Griffith, also a farmer, came from Poyntz Castle, near Solva, in the parish of Brawdy. The prosecution case, however, depended almost entirely on the flaky testimony of French prisoners of war and it soon became clear that their evidence was insufficient to hang a dog let alone two alleged traitors. Much to the dismay of John Lloyd, chief justice of the Carmarthen circuit of the Courts of the Great Sessions, who had hoped to lock up the prisoners for a very long time, the Crown case collapsed ignominiously. According to William Richards of Lynn, who championed the cause of the Pembrokeshire 'martyrs' and anathematized 'five monsters' ('pum anghenfil') from among the local Tory gentry for bribing witnesses and fuelling sentiments against Dissent, the gratuitous comments of the judge about Welsh 'sectaries',

---

[148] David Salmon, *The Descent of the French on Pembrokeshire* (Carmarthen, 1930); E. H. Stuart Jones, *The Last Invasion of Britain* (Cardiff, 1950); John Kinross, *Fishguard Fiasco: An Account of the Last Invasion of Britain* (Tenby, 1974); J. E. Thomas, *Britain's Last Invasion: Fishguard 1797* (Stroud, 2007).

[149] *CIM*, II, p. 19, Iolo Morganwg to William Owen Pughe, 7 March 1797.

as he dubbed them, were redolent of slurs heard in the days of the infamous George Jeffreys.[150]

Iolo kept a watchful eye on these events from afar and was particularly interested to note that mounting alarm following the French landing had led to the formation of several volunteer corps in different parts of Wales. Volunteer companies of infantry or cavalry were expected to support the local militia in protecting the honour of the king and defending the realm against external enemies.[151] A good many males joined the volunteers in order to avoid the more onerous and dangerous militia duty. As part-time soldiers, there was inevitably a rag, tag and bobtail element among them, and the Fishguard Fencibles, for instance, were so poorly trained that they did not exactly cover themselves with glory when confronted by French marauders in February 1797.[152] But in their uniforms volunteers were a glorious sight to loyalists and their sartorial elegance was matched by their patriotic zeal. War patriotism was strong in Glamorgan and no corps was prouder than the Cowbridge Volunteer Infantry who, founded and assembled by Captain John Beavan in March 1797 and dressed in low crowned caps, red coats and white breeches, and armed with muskets and pikes, sported a standard bearing the motto 'Ein Duw, Ein Gwlad, Ein Brenin' (Our God, our country, our king).[153] Charged with the task of defending the coastal waters where Napoleon's forces were likely to land, they periodically indulged in flurries of urgent activity, including musket practice, and joined forces with local magistrates in keeping Iolo under close surveillance and disrupting his Gorseddau. Iolo felt dangerously beleaguered as the forces of law and order watched his every move. Convinced that 'the Devil is both God and Great King at Cowbridge',[154] he was forced to wind up the Gorseddau he had held on local hilltops and suffer the scorn of correspondents who mocked his 'senseless pantomime' and

---

[150] [William Richards], *Cwyn y Cystuddiedig* (Caerfyrddin, 1798), *passim*; R. T. Jenkins, 'William Richards o Lynn', *TCHBC* (1930), 17–68.

[151] J. R. Western, 'The Volunteer Movement as an Anti-Revolutionary Force, 1793–1801', *EHR*, LXXI (1956), 603–14; R. Paul Evans, 'The Flintshire Loyalist Association and the Local Holywell Volunteers', *FHSJ*, 33 (1992), 55–68; Nicholas Rogers, 'The Sea Fencibles, Loyalism and the Reach of the State' in Mark Philp (ed.), *Resisting Napoleon: The British Response to the Threat of Invasion, 1797–1815* (Aldershot, 2006), pp. 41–59; Kevin B. Linch, '"A Citizen and not a Soldier": The British Volunteer Movement and the War against Napoleon' in Alan Forrest, Karen Hagemann and Jane Rendall (eds.), *Soldiers, Citizens and Civilians: Experiences and Perceptions of the Revolutionary and Napoleonic Wars, 1790–1820* (Basingstoke, 2009), pp. 205–21; Ffion Mair Jones, '"A'r Ffeiffs a'r Drums yn roario": Y Baledwyr Cymraeg, y Milisia a'r Gwirfoddolwyr', *Canu Gwerin*, 34 (2011), 19–42.

[152] Kinross, *Fishguard Fiasco*, pp. 53–5.

[153] Bryn Owen, *The History of the Welsh Militia and Volunteer Corps 1757–1908. Volume 3, Glamorgan. Part 2, Volunteers and Local Militia, 1796–1816; Yeomanry Cavalry, 1808–1831* (Wrexham, 1994), pp. 24–5.

[154] NLW 21414E, no. 17.

'Charlatanic efforts' to beckon Napoleon 'and bring him over the British channel to the top of Garth'.[155]

Then, out of the blue, Iolo composed a 'Song for the Glamorgan Volunteers' (by whom, of course, he meant 'the Cowbridge Volunteers'), in which, so mythology has it, he renounced his anti-war stance and defended the constitution.[156] From the 1920s onwards, Welsh historians, following in the footsteps of David Davies and J. J. Evans,[157] have maintained that this patriotic song proves that Iolo had succumbed to Pitt's well-oiled machinery of coercion and abandoned the republican cause. It is worth bearing in mind that similar accusations were levelled against Robert Burns who, a year before his death in 1796, not only composed a praise-poem to the Royal Dumfries Volunteers but also drilled and marched with them in a blue coat, red cape, cockaded hat, white vest and trousers.[158] This public display of loyalty has been used to argue that Burns the radical had recanted but, as Liam McIlvanney has persuasively shown, the Royal Dumfries Volunteers were not a clutch of fanatical church-and-king supporters. Far from it. Many political radicals staffed its ranks and revelled in its 'true civic humanist style' and independent status. Moreover, the song's central theme of legitimate resistance to putative French invaders was not inconsistent with Burns's radical politics and his fierce opposition to any so-called 'liberation' wrought by a foreign army.[159] Likewise, Iolo's 'Song for the Glamorgan Volunteers', to be sung to the tune 'Batchelors All', was a celebration of brave local 'Britons' who, unlike those 'Devils incarnate . . . Infernals of the deepest black' that served the government in the armed forces, had answered 'Liberty's call' by volunteering to take up arms to defend their loved ones, their homes and their beloved shire against the enemy. Their courage was not motivated by a desire to defend privilege or the institutions of state, but by an overwhelming urge to emulate those ancient heroes – Caratacus, Ifor Bach and Morgan ap Hywel – who had resolutely stood up against usurpers and 'atrocious villains' whilst defending their national rights and ancient laws.[160] Defending the sacred liberties of Glamorgan through repelling invaders by land and sea was deemed by Iolo to be thoroughly admirable:

---

[155] *Cambrian Register*, II (1799), 465.
[156] NLW 13089E, pp. 258–61; NLW 13116B, pp. 292–9; NLW 21392F, nos. 35–8.
[157] David Davies, *The Influence of the French Revolution on Welsh Life and Literature* (Carmarthen, 1926); J. J. Evans, *Dylanwad y Chwyldro Ffrengig ar Lenyddiaeth Cymru* (Lerpwl, 1928).
[158] Robert Crawford, *The Bard: Robert Burns, A Biography* (London, 2009), pp. 382–6.
[159] Liam McIlvanney, *Burns the Radical: Poetry and Politics in Late Eighteenth-Century Scotland* (East Linton, 2002), pp. 235–40.
[160] NLW 13089E, pp. 258–61.

> One and all!
> One and all!
> At our dear Country's call,
> Vanquish all foes that would Britain enthral.[161]

Once this goal had been achieved, Iolo insisted that all military action should cease immediately and that citizens should be reminded that 'the laws and reasons of peace we derive from Heaven; those of War, only from Hell'.[162] Iolo the local patriot, the ardent republican and anti-war zealot remained passionately hostile to political loyalism and the orthodox mainstream, and this controversial poem was probably written in order to deflect mounting hostility towards him as a potential insurgent. 'My life is given up', he doggedly declared, 'is devoted to the Great cause.'[163]

Yet, there were signs by this stage that he had softened his stance somewhat since 1792. In a fascinating letter, dated 26 March 1798, to Mary Barker,[164] a novelist and a confidante of his friend Robert Southey, he continued to support steadfastly the principle of the sovereignty and independence of an elected senatorial House of Commons. But, even though he conceded that the monarchical model was 'little more than a lifele[ss] piece of mechanism', he was more ambivalent about the status of whoever sat on the throne – 'I care not whether the king be hereditary or elective, or which the title given him be King, Emperor, President, Lord Protector, or whatever else the caprices of mankind may stumble upon in the dark'[165] – and readier to entertain the notion of having a hereditary second house peopled by experienced men of probity. But there are grounds for believing that Iolo's revised blueprint had been tailored to quell the suspicions of Miss Barker (whom he did not know personally) and others who were convinced that he was a turner-of-the-world-upside-down. True, his proverbial 'wild warmth' was less apparent in this letter and he was clearly more concerned about the effects of the spilling of innocent blood in wars and exposing the evils of the slave trade than in discussing the niceties of the constitution. But he was also anxious to convince Miss Barker that, even though his Welsh blood was 'up on some occasions', he was not hatching 'some dark plot'.[166] With a family to support in troubled times, he could not afford to be bundled off to prison on some trumped-up

---

[161] Ibid., p. 259.
[162] Ibid., p. 258.
[163] NLW 13112B, p. 367.
[164] *CIM*, II, pp. 47–66, Iolo Morganwg to Mary Barker, 26 March [1798].
[165] Ibid., p. 52.
[166] Ibid., pp. 56, 65.

charge. Better to play it cool with a stranger who, by her own admission, loathed Jacobins.

Yet, as he had earlier pointed out to William Pitt, only a fool in Whitehall would underestimate the depth of anger that simmered in local communities among upright citizens who remained 'sullenly silent' only because it was unsafe for them to vent their feelings publicly.[167] Iolo continued to fulminate in private against the warmongering of George III. At a time when the king was portrayed as an avuncular, cultural icon,[168] Iolo depicted him as a bloodthirsty demon whose reign of blood had led to the most horrifying 'deathful carnage' around the globe.[169] Sickened by the sheer scale of bloodshed and destruction during the French wars – a conflict which may have wiped out five million people[170] – he liberally sprinkled his king-flogging notes with descriptions of the 'blood trade' and denunciations of George 'the Butcher'.[171] 'The compassion of George the Miser – to destroy and burn wherever he goes' ('Trugaredd Sior y Crinwas – lladd a llosgi'r ffor[dd] y cerddo'), he told William Owen Pughe in 1801.[172] Two years later the same recipient was assured that 'the bloodthirsty Crinwas' ('y Crinwas gwaedgar') was a man 'given to destruction and devastation, his sword is unsheathed against every justice, every truth, and every peace' ('Gwr wr[th] ddifrawd ac anrhaith, noeth yw ei gledd ef yn erbyn pob cyfiawnder, pob gwirionedd, a phob tangnef[edd]').[173] In moments of darkest gloom, he flirted with the idea of seeking asylum in America, but there was so much still to do, not least in promoting Rational Dissent.

In an open letter, entitled 'The Divine Unity Asserted',[174] Iolo complained that Methodist societies in Glamorgan habitually depicted him as an infidel, a Jacobin, a republican and a democrat. Of these labels, he was 'not ashamed of being thought a Democrat or republican'. Nor was he in any way reluctant to be dubbed a Unitarian. But he did resent what he believed to be a concerted campaign by Calvinistic Methodists to suppress 'infant Societies of Unitarians'. Indeed, among the themes which he promised to include in his proposed memoirs was 'Methodism and its Rancours'.[175] Iolo despised the unthinking zeal of Methodist evangelists, their unswerving commitment to predestinarianism, and their opposition to rational thought. Much to his dismay, the strongly

---

[167] Ibid., I, p. 848, Iolo Morganwg to William Pitt, 16 December 1796.
[168] Marilyn Morris, *The British Monarchy and the French Revolution* (Yale, 1998), p. 2.
[169] NLW 21333B, p. 67.
[170] David A. Bell, *The First Total War: Napoleon's Europe and the Birth of Modern Warfare* (London, 2007), p. 7. See also J. E. Cookson, *The British Armed Nation 1793–1815* (Oxford, 1997).
[171] For just some examples, see NLW 13094E, pp. 182, 186, 191; NLW 13130A, p. 260; NLW 13159A, p. 308; NLW 21401E, nos. 18, 19, 21, 22.
[172] *CIM*, II, p. 367, Iolo Morganwg to William Owen Pughe, 15 February 1801.
[173] Ibid., II, p. 524, Iolo Morganwg to William Owen Pughe, 1 August 1803.
[174] NLW 21396E, no. 3.
[175] NLW 21387E, no. 3.

evangelical ministry of David Jones at Llan-gan had turned the parish into the Vale's equivalent of Bala or Llangeitho, the twin epicentres of Calvinistic Methodism in north and mid-Wales. With characteristic hyperbole, Iolo believed that this 'greatest pest of all true religion' was threatening to make south Wales as Methodistical as hell and that he was being publicly vilified for referring to them as the offspring of 'that bloodthirsty Bigot, Jack Calvin' and for raucously singing 'A Jumper's Hymn', with its wickedly suggestive refrain 'and a jumping we will go'.[176] As the content of Thomas Jones's *Gair yn ei Amser* (1798) bears out, evangelical fundamentalism and political conservatism went hand in hand in Wales, and Thomas Charles, the principal spokesman of Calvinistic Methodism, avoided the 'empty noise' of politics like the plague.[177]

A particularly unedifying battle between orthodox and heterodox forces occurred in the parish of Aber-thin, near Cowbridge, where Peter Williams, the powerful preacher and Bible commentator, had been expelled from the Calvinistic Methodist movement in 1791 for preaching Sabellianism, a heretical, anti-trinitarian doctrine.[178] Badly affected by this setback, Williams died of heart failure five years later, leaving many distraught sympathizers at Aber-thin. But when David Davies, an uncompromising trinitarian from Rhayader, was appointed Independent minister at Aber-thin he seized every opportunity to blacken the name of 'Priestleyans' and expel by force those who refused to toe the orthodox Calvinist line.[179] An alliance of church-and-king clergymen and Methodists urged Davies to 'preach up Trinitarianism with might and main', only for the anti-trinitarians, who constituted a majority, to give him due warning that his contract would not be extended. In high dudgeon, Davies and his supporters abused them in his sermon the following Sunday, and one of his henchmen cried out from the gallery: 'We will tear them to pieces.' Iolo, who was present, was horrified and immediately sought the advice of Theophilus Lindsey regarding how best to withstand such 'virulent church-and-kingists'.[180]

In the 'Black Spot', too, anti-trinitarians were under severe pressure. In 1800 Thomas Evans (Tomos Glyn Cothi) complained to John Disney that

---

[176] *CIM*, II, p. 13, Iolo Morganwg to Theophilus Lindsey, 10 February 1797; ibid., II, p. 197, Iolo Morganwg to William Owen Pughe, 10 July 1799; NLW 21335B, pp. 23–5; NLW 13170B, pp. 184–6; NLW 21328A, pp. 89, 196–7; NLW 21330E, p. 48; NLW 21424E, no. 1.

[177] D. E. Jenkins, *The Life of the Rev. Thomas Charles BA of Bala* (3 vols., Denbigh, 1908), II, p. 95.

[178] Gomer M. Roberts, *Bywyd a Gwaith Peter Williams* (Caerdydd, 1943), pp. 93–136.

[179] 'Jones o Langan, a'i Amserau', *Y Traethodydd*, VI (1850), 145–6; G. J. Williams, 'Sabeliaid Aberthin', *Y Cofiadur*, 25 (1955), 23–8; Gomer M. Roberts, *Emynwyr Bethesda'r Fro* (Llandysul, 1967), pp. 24–8; W. Rhys Nicholas, *Thomas William Bethesda'r Fro* (Abertawe, 1994), pp. 13–17; E. Wyn James, 'Thomas William: Bardd ac Emynydd Bethesda'r Fro', *LlC*, 27 (2004), 113–39.

[180] *CIM*, II, pp. 12–17, Iolo Morganwg to Theophilus Lindsey, 10 February 1797.

Unitarianism 'meets with violent opposition' from clerics and Dissenters.[181] David Peter, senior tutor at the Presbyterian academy in Carmarthen, broke with tradition by refusing to admit young Unitarian students, and the appointment in February 1801 of George Murray to the see of St David's ushered in a successor in the mould of the intolerant Horsley. There were fears that Irish agents were fomenting sedition and strife in south-west Wales and the turbulent corn riots of 1800–1 meant that magistrates and militia were kept on full alert.

In March 1801 Iolo received a desperate plea for help from Thomas Evans (Tomos Glyn Cothi) who had been summonsed to appear before the Court of the Great Sessions to face a charge of having sung a seditious version of the Carmagnole at a particularly boozy and raucous bid-ale (*cwrw bach*) at Brechfa.[182] According to the plaintiff George Thomas, a shoemaker who had been expelled from Evans's congregation and who bore a grudge against him, Evans and two others – a husbandman and a victualler – had sung the following inflammatory verse:

> And when upon the British shore
> The thundering guns of France shall roar,
> Vile George shall trembling stand
> Or fly his native land,
> With terror and appal,
> Dance Carmagnol, Dance Carmagnol.[183]

As we have seen, Evans was no stranger to satirical and seditious declamations, though it is by no means clear why he should have sung in English during an overwhelmingly Welsh-language occasion. George Thomas may have been an agent provocateur as well as a bearer of grudges, and local magistrates were itching to single out a prominent dissident for exemplary punishment. 'My innocency is my shield',[184] cried Evans, but he was clearly in serious trouble from the moment Thomas filed charges against him. Deeply moved by his friend's poignant letter, Iolo immediately downed tools and set off for Brechfa, doubtless cursing the injustices of life as he bustled westwards. He lost no time in interviewing witnesses and drawing up a petition. Over the

---

[181] Aneirin Lewis, 'Tomos Glyn Cothi a'r Dr John Disney', *LlC*, 6, nos. 3–4 (1961), 220.
[182] *CIM*, II, pp. 371, 372 (trans.), Thomas Evans (Tomos Glyn Cothi) to Iolo Morganwg, 21 March 1801. For a full account of this trial and its implications, see Geraint H. Jenkins, '"A Very Horrid Affair": Sedition and Unitarianism in the Age of Revolutions' in R. R. Davies and Geraint H. Jenkins (eds.), *From Medieval to Modern Wales: Historical Essays in Honour of Kenneth O. Morgan and Ralph A. Griffiths* (Cardiff, 2004), pp. 175–96.
[183] NLW, Wales 4/753/1–3. Evans had earlier written a poem urging the Welsh to repel the French invaders in February 1797. NLW 13144A, p. 175.
[184] *CIM*, II, p. 371, Thomas Evans (Tomos Glyn Cothi) to Iolo Morganwg, 21 March 1801.

decade he had become familiar with the workings of the law not only by observing the plight of the labouring poor and those who found themselves in foundling hospitals, asylums, hospitals and prisons but also by keeping abreast of legal proceedings and appointments to courts and offices. A regular frequenter of courts of law, he made a point of observing the behaviour (and prejudices) of judges, solicitors and juries, and recording what he believed to be outrageously partial sentences. Since witnesses for the defence at Brechfa had little or no English, it fell to Iolo to assemble and prepare written evidence. He also enlisted the help of John Prior Estlin, Unitarian minister at Lewin's Mead, Bristol, who then apprised barristers in London of the circumstances of Thomas Evans's alleged transgression and the testimony of witnesses.[185]

On 17 August 1801 the case came before George Hardinge, chief justice of the Brecknock circuit of the Courts of the Great Sessions and a notorious scourge of trouble-makers. A dapper old Etonian and Cambridge graduate, Hardinge was the grandson of a chief justice, formerly solicitor-general to Queen Charlotte, and Conservative MP for Old Sarum. A poet and a writer, he was unquestionably a cultured man. Sir William Jones addressed a sonnet to him, he discussed literature with Horace Walpole, and his *Nugae Antiquae et Novae* (1782) was a distinctive contribution to authenticity debates surrounding the works of Chatterton. Byron once referred to him as 'the waggish Welsh Judge'.[186] Ironically, Iolo knew him quite well. Whilst in Cardiff prison, he had petitioned Hardinge for redress and, through various means, had later conveyed to him his bardo-druidic vision and his views on patriarchal government. The learned judge duly bought six sets of Iolo's *Poems, Lyric and Pastoral* in 1794 and, by the time of Thomas Evans's trial, he had become deeply interested in Celticism and the Celtic languages.[187] Indeed, the fact that Hardinge regarded William Owen Pughe, Iolo's ally, as 'a very ingenious and clever man',[188] and Edward 'Celtic' Davies, Iolo's sworn enemy, as a serious scholar worthy of patronage,[189] lent an air of piquancy to the trial at Carmarthen.

Of far greater importance was the fact that Hardinge was an avowed enemy of Dissenters, Jacobins and rioters. Both in his highly political addresses and previous verdicts he had already served notice of his determination to silence friends of the French Revolution. He believed that he was duty-bound to

---

[185] Ibid., II, pp. 382–3, John Prior Estlin to Iolo Morganwg, 23 September 1801.
[186] *Gentleman's Magazine*, LXXXVI (1816), 469–70; John Nichols (ed.), *The Miscellaneous Works, in Prose and Verse, of George Hardinge* (3 vols., London, 1818); *ODNB* s.v. George Hardinge.
[187] Williams: *PLP*, I, p. xxix; Cardiff Central Library 3.79, 3.91; NLW 145C, pp. 247–347.
[188] Cardiff Central Library 3.79, p. 173.
[189] Frank R. Lewis, 'Edward Davies, 1756–1831', *TRS*, XXXIX (1969), 8–23; Moira Dearnley, '"Mad Ned" and the "Smatter-Dasher": Iolo Morganwg and Edward "Celtic" Davies' in *Rattleskull Genius*, pp. 426–42.

guard against anarchy and rebellion, and the 'brutal passions' of incendiaries and rioters.[190] Working closely with local magistrates, he was reminded of Iolo's reputation as a Jacobin and also of his former links with John Thelwall who, since 1797, had leased a farm at Llys-wen, on the banks of the Wye and, though dubbing himself 'the Recluse', was still in contact with dissidents.[191] Thelwall invited Iolo to visit him, promising him a bed, a rasher of bacon, ale and 'such other homely accomodations as suit a poet, a philosopher & a democrat',[192] and local people were so convinced that he was plotting treason that one of them attacked him with a pick-axe.[193] The ironmaster Samuel Homfray was certain that the food riot which broke out in Merthyr on 23 September 1800 had been fomented by the likes of Thelwall, who had secretly 'influenced the Minds of the lower Class of People'.[194] Homfray and Crawshay made their feelings known to Hardinge, who assured them of his implacable commitment to guarding against the threat of public disorder by punishing the enemy within. Four months before Thomas Evans was brought before him, Hardinge had presided over the court in which three young men from Merthyr were sentenced to death for stealing sums of money during the riotous assembly at Merthyr in September 1800. In his address to the Grand Jury, Hardinge emphasized that by robbing innocent citizens at a time of war and dearth the defendants had committed an act of rebellion and trampled on Christ's cross. 'The duty of insurrection', he intoned frostily, 'is . . . fit only for the monsters and fiends who have acted upon it, and are a disgrace, as well as the pestilence of the world.'[195]

Not surprisingly, when Hardinge summed up the case and addressed the Grand Jury at the Guildhall, Carmarthen, on 17 August 1801, the Unitarians among the assembled throng were deeply apprehensive. The trial had not gone well. The defence counsel, probably inadvertently misled by Iolo, had failed to realize that only three of Evans's twenty witnesses had actually been present at the bid-ale and, as Hardinge's impatient and testy manner deepened the gloom, the case for the prosecution was strengthened appreciably as George Thomas and his allies stuck to their guns. Throughout the proceedings Iolo scowled ferociously at the prosecuting counsel and scribbled copious notes. How he must have winced when Hardinge, in his concluding address, described

---

[190] NLW, Bute L48/57iiij.
[191] John Thelwall, *Poems, Chiefly Written in Retirement 1801* (Oxford, 1989), pp. xxxvi, 153–4, 154–5, 157–9; Penelope J. Corfield, 'Rhetoric, Radical Politics and Rainfall: John Thelwall in Breconshire, 1797–1800', *Brycheiniog*, XL (2009), 17–36.
[192] *CIM*, II, p. 83, John Thelwall to Iolo Morganwg, 10 May 1798.
[193] Damian Walford Davies, *Presences that Disturb: Models of Romantic Identity in the Literature and Culture of the 1790s* (Cardiff, 2002), pp. 208–9.
[194] Penelope J. Corfield and Chris Evans, 'John Thelwall in Wales: New Documentary Evidence', *BIHR*, LIX, no. 140 (1986), 237–8.
[195] NLW, Bute L48/57ii.

George III as the 'most innocent and the best man, the best character, in the kingdom'. By contrast, he gratuitously lamented the growth of Dissent in Wales, and claimed that the defendant was clearly a man 'of a very bad and dangerous disposition'.[196] Amid widespread consternation, he sentenced Evans to two years in prison, to be pilloried annually in public, and to be bound over to keep the peace for seven years. Downcast Unitarians watched in stunned silence as their minister was frogmarched to Carmarthen prison. Since Evans had a wife and a houseful of children to support, an appeal for financial support was launched by Charles Lloyd of Coedlannau Fawr, a Unitarian minister and farmer, to which the likes of Estlin and Lindsey responded generously.[197] To Iolo's great pleasure, David Jones, 'The Welsh Freeholder', also agreed to deploy his skills as a barrister in preparing an appeal to the Crown.[198] Understandably angry and embittered, Thomas Evans was eventually persuaded to throw himself on the mercy of the king by protesting his loyalty to the realm, but his sentiments made no impression on the Home Secretary and he served a full sentence in what he described as 'the house of bondage'.[199] In the wake of this 'very horrid affair',[200] Iolo wrote to Hardinge to assure him that he would remain true to his principles as a Unitarian Christian and continue to campaign for 'more equity, more justice, more benevolence'.[201]

The trial and its outcome convinced Iolo that the time was ripe for Unitarians in Wales to organize themselves more efficiently. He no longer wished to suffer the embarrassment of having to go cap in hand to colleagues in Bristol and London whenever legal aid or funds to publish Welsh books were required. As soon as Thomas Evans was bustled off to prison he convened a meeting of Unitarians in Carmarthen and prevailed on fourteen signatories to support his aim of establishing a society which would help anti-trinitarians in Wales to stand up for themselves, face the enemy, and prepare for the day when Unitarian worship was legalized.[202] With the help of Josiah Rees, Iolo worked hard to lay the administrative foundations and at Gellionnen on 8 October 1802 the Unitarian Society of South Wales was formally established.[203] Its secretary David Davis, son of the eponymous tutor, preacher and

---

[196] NLW 21373D, no. 8.
[197] Ibid., no. 10.
[198] *CIM*, II, p. 402, John Prior Estlin to Iolo Morganwg, 2 January 1802. For Iolo's account of the trial and subsequent petitioning, see NLW 21373D, no. 6, pp. 1–22.
[199] National Archives, HO 47/27, pp. 297–301; *CIM*, II, p. 557, Thomas Evans (Tomos Glyn Cothi) to Iolo Morganwg, 25 October 1803.
[200] Ibid., II, p. 381, Iolo Morganwg to Owen Jones (Owain Myfyr), 21 August 1801.
[201] Ibid., II, p. 459, Iolo Morganwg to [George Hardinge], [?1803].
[202] NLW 13152A, p. 350.
[203] Cardiff Central Library 2.1020; NLW 13145A, pp. 159–74, 278–98; Edward Williams, *Rheolau a Threfniadau Cymdeithas Dwyfundodiaid yn Neheubarth Cymru* (Llundain, 1803); *CIM*, II, p. 440, Iolo Morganwg to William Owen Pughe, 25 October 1802.

poet from Castellhywel, who had settled as a Unitarian minister in Neath and opened a classical and commercial school on the Parade, tickled Iolo's vanity by referring to him as 'our father'.[204] Basking in the adulation, Iolo dubbed himself 'Bard to the Theo-Unitarian Society of South-Wales' and began mobilizing his connections on its behalf.[205]

It bears repeating that there are no grounds for believing that Iolo had discarded the radicalism of his London days or mislaid his passion for contrariness. Unlike more celebrated people like Coleridge, Dyer, Southey and Wordsworth, he refused to turn away from radical politics or hang up his cudgels. Amid a wealth of combustible writing, one piece of evidence – a private diary by Iolo describing his journey from London via the Midlands to his home in Glamorgan in the summer of 1802[206] – makes for a compelling read since it proves beyond any reasonable doubt that he had remained true to his republican sympathies. This unpublished manuscript shows Iolo giving free rein to his feelings, prejudices and convictions, and also offers an illuminating commentary on what Elijah Waring called his 'alliance to the *genus irritabile*'.[207] This self-styled 'Citizen of the World' set off from London on 29 May. As he shook the dust of the metropolis off his boots, he amused himself by imagining how best to embellish the fast day scheduled for 1 June. Eager to do a good turn for humanity, he concluded that something on the lines of a 'Grand Illumination' would enliven the gloomy occasion and provide the great unwashed with heart-warming entertainment. He proposed that 300 ropes be suspended from the roof of St Paul's Cathedral, each with a noose attached to accommodate the neck of deserving rascals like kings, nobles and parsons. A lamp would be tied to every rascal's hand so that a gallery of moving lights would light up the skies as these unlamented victims experienced the agonizing convulsion of death. In full flounce he then wandered into Oxford, where an array of colleges 'manufactured' clergymen of 'heavy stupidity' before packing them off to do their worst in Welsh livings. As he plodded on, many examples of the baneful effects of 'priestcraft' caught his eye, prompting him to compose a new triad: 'Parsonism, Kingism, and Devilism, the three grand curses of the world'. The *saeva indignatio* which was his trademark was nowhere more evident than when he witnessed grotesque examples of inhumanity in the industrialized parts of the Midlands. Some of these reminded him of the sufferings he had endured at the hands of 'the toad eaters, the Journey-men

---

[204] *CIM*, II, p. 724, David Davis to Iolo Morganwg, 26 October 1805.
[205] NLW 13145A, p. 450; Geraint H. Jenkins, '"Dyro Dduw dy Nawdd": Iolo Morganwg a'r Mudiad Undodaidd' in idem (ed.), *Cof Cenedl XX: Ysgrifau ar Hanes Cymru* (Llandysul, 2005), pp. 65–100.
[206] NLW 13174A.
[207] *RAEW*, p. 14.

scoundrels (I had almost said Journey-men Kings)' and other 'superlatively depraved souls'. Gazing at the walls of Shrewsbury prison, he sorrowfully contemplated the plight of 'poor Thomas Spence', whose bravery he had long admired and who was now languishing behind its bars for having called for the destruction of private property:

> Shame? Shame? What is Shame? Who feels it? Who amongst Kings? Who amongst those who live by licking up the spittle of Kings? Who? I ask again, Who?

Having crossed the border into mid-Wales and feeling utterly exhausted, he dreamt one night of his *bête noire*, George III. Vividly, he saw an old butcher wearing a tarnished gold crown. On hearing a voice from the bottomless pit urging him to devour copious amounts of blood, the royal butcher commanded tens of thousands of soldiers to slaughter innocent men and women in the name of Beelzebub. Countless widows and orphans wept, tore their hair, rent their garments, and cursed the butcher so loudly that God intervened by bringing him before the judgement seat where, amid universal rejoicing, he received his just deserts. In private jottings such as these, Iolo expressed his opinions with passionate intensity.[208]

In his waking hours and dreams, therefore, Iolo continued to support the democratic (and, by implication, seditious) cause in his own distinctive, slightly quirky, way. At fifty-five, there was still a good deal of life left in this doughty crusader and his acolytes evidently worshipped him. 'Perish kings and emperors', cried David Davis of Neath, 'but let the Bard of Liberty live.'[209]

---

[208] NLW 13174A, pp. 2^r, 3^r, 21^r, 25^v, 35^v, 40^r, 72^r, 74^v.
[209] *CIM*, II, p. 466, David Davis to Iolo Morganwg, 12 February 1803.

6

'I have as much Cimbric patriotism as any man living'

By closing down Iolo's politically radical channels of expression – his shop in Cowbridge and his Gorseddau on local mountain tops – the authorities probably believed that they had successfully sidelined if not silenced this troublemaker. But Ned Williams, the self-styled 'very wicked' Welsh bard,[1] had no intention of yielding to what he called 'the Terrorism of M.ʳ Pitt'.[2] His maverick spirit and ego meant that he would always be at odds with mainstream opinion. Revelling in his individuality and his reputation for subversive activity, following his return to Wales in 1795 he also left his stamp by deliberately rebelling against traditional historical and literary conventions. The past mattered a good deal to Iolo and by assembling, transcribing and 'manufacturing' great swathes of bardic and antiquarian material, he constructed for his people a version of their history which was designed to underpin their sense of national identity. He recognized the importance of salvaging original sources and of tweaking them where necessary in order to express the aspirations of the present as well as the preoccupations of the past. As he wrestled with notions of nationhood and its component parts, Iolo came to believe that his subversive impact could be just as great by becoming a remembrancer and a nation builder. As a writer, he was convinced that he had a responsibility to follow the truth wherever it led him and to vent 'the wisdom of the nation of the Cymry [the Welsh], and the memorial of the privileges and usages of the nation of the Cymry'.[3]

While D. O. Thomas was right to point out that the political and religious liberty which Iolo extolled was couched in universal terms, he was mistaken in arguing that there was no specifically Welsh aspect to his political thought.[4] Anyone familiar with Iolo's archive will have been left in no doubt that one of his principal motives in conflating history and forgery was to bolster the

---

[1] NLW 21424E, no. 6a.
[2] NLW 13159A, p. 201.
[3] John Williams Ab Ithel, *Barddas; Or, A Collection of Original Documents, Illustrative of the Theology, Wisdom, and Usages of the Bardo-Druidic System of the Isle of Britain. Volume I* (Llandovery, 1862), pp. 399, 401.
[4] D. O. Thomas, *Ymateb i Chwyldro / Response to Revolution* (Caerdydd / Cardiff, 1989), p. 81.

indigenous culture of Wales by identifying those different strands which stimulated national sentiment and awareness. At a time when 'the national question' was rarely asked in Wales, Iolo exulted in the illustrious past of 'Cenedl y Cymmry'[5] (the Welsh nation) and sought to rescue it from older Whiggish versions in which it skulked on the margins of history. Proud of his *'Ancient Briton's warm pride*'[6] and of his self-anointed role as the sole surviving member of the ancient Welsh bards, he became increasingly dogmatic and egotistical as the 1790s unfolded. The number of uncompleted drafts he produced of his proposed autobiography, or 'My Own Life' as he often called it, reflected his desire to shape his own persona for posterity. 'I Iolo Morganwg' ('Myfi Iolo Morganwg') figured so prominently in his manuscripts and public declarations that his enemies tired of listening to him. David Thomas (Dafydd Ddu Eryri) was outraged by his egotisms: 'Mi Iolo Morganwg. Mi Iolo Morganwg. I. M. I. M. so on – ad infinitum.'[7] Keenly aware of his standing as 'Pontifex Maximus' within Welsh druidic circles, Iolo viewed such criticisms with disdain. 'You are talking of what you don't understand – of what none but a Welshman, and a British Bard can possibly understand' was his testy response to Elijah Waring's queries.[8]

When some of Iolo's bardo-druidic writings had earlier fallen into 'the tallons of Will Pitt',[9] he had been reassured by the fact that the prime minister and other members of the Privy Council could make neither head nor tail of the material. On his return to Glamorgan, therefore, he seized the opportunity to disguise his political radicalism and nationalist agenda as antiquarian dogma. Writing a new and rather grander narrative of the history of Wales was a field in which Iolo could challenge discredited versions of the past and the political consensus. Being an 'ancient Briton' instinctively made him hostile to 'the Incense of flattery' and liable to be 'warm in the cause of liberty', a trait which he believed was integral to the Welsh character.[10] 'I have as much Cimbric patriotism as any man living',[11] he informed William Owen Pughe, and those who knew him best were perfectly aware that his idea of nationhood had a strong politico-cultural dimension and that he was convinced that providence had vouchsafed future glory for the Welsh.[12]

[5] NLW 13121B, p. 271.
[6] Williams: *PLP*, I, p. xix. See also NLW 21392F, no. 68; NLW 21395E, p. 2.
[7] NLW 13116B, p. 265; NLW 13140A, p. vii; BL Add. 15029, f. 137^r, David Thomas (Dafydd Ddu Eryri) to Owen Jones (Owain Myfyr), 13 August 1804.
[8] *RAEW*, pp. 33, 53.
[9] NLW 13093E, p. 157.
[10] NLW 21392F, no. 90; NLW 21323B, p. 1.
[11] *CIM*, II, p. 668, Iolo Morganwg to William Owen Pughe, 28 April 1805.
[12] Iolo intimated to Owain Myfyr that 'the Welsh nation and language, like the Jews, are by providence reserved for future glory'. Ibid., II, p. 244, Iolo Morganwg to Owen Jones (Owain Myfyr), 27 November 1799. See also Montserrat Guibernau and John Hutchinson (eds.), *History and National Destiny: Ethnosymbolism and its Critics* (Oxford, 2004).

In order to assess Iolo's contribution as a nation builder we need first to contextualize his work. Although Wales was by no means a cultural backwater, unlike Scotland it could not boast a reputation as a land of learning. Iolo was painfully conscious of his nation's infrastructural deficit. It had no institutions of statehood or sovereignty. Following the Acts of Union (1536–43), the dictum 'England *and* Wales' had reflected the latter's status as a subordinate entity. The formation of a unitary state in 1707, when the Union Jack became the principal emblem of British identity, again confirmed Wales's subaltern standing. It was not represented on the Union Jack and not until 1 March 1960 did the red dragon, on a green and white backcloth, become the official flag of Wales.[13]

In some ways, the absence of the trappings of statehood were less important than the lack of public spheres in which those who did not toe the official line were able to discuss questions relating to political liberty and national identity, and to communicate with a wider public. Even though Swansea had already emerged as a Copperopolis of global significance and Merthyr as the greatest iron-making town in the world, the 1801 census revealed that only a dozen Welsh towns could boast a population in excess of 2,000. Without a national metropolis like Dublin or Edinburgh, Wales could not nurture a robust sense of civic consciousness and pride. It could not boast public monuments, commemorative plaques or *lieux de mémoire* which bore witness to the illustrious deeds of its sons. Critically, too, there were no universities or a national library, no historical institutes or central archives. Although Iolo was often scathing about the 'vain academical spinners of Theories' at Oxford and Cambridge,[14] he knew that institutions of higher learning were key factors in promoting rigorous thought and establishing scholarly principles. To have had one or more in Wales would have helped to tell the nation's story and protect its identity. As things stood, the nation's finest products, including academy-trained Dissenters like Richard Price and David Williams, were obliged to cultivate their minds and advance their careers in London. Could a nation-to-be recover or construct its identity without a civic base, a seat of higher learning, an anthem to sing, a flag to unfurl and statues to honour its past heroes?

Just as depressing from Iolo's point of view was the extent to which cultural politicization had robbed the Welsh of their history. He was familiar with Humphrey Llwyd's *Cronica Walliae* as well as David Powel's *The History of Wales* (1584), and the amended and emended versions published by William Wynne in 1697 and Thomas Evans in 1774, the gist of which was that after the Edwardian conquest in 1282–3 everything done in Wales which was worthy

---

[13] See Nick Groom, *The Union Jack: The Story of the British Flag* (London, 2006), p. 293.
[14] NLW 13089E, p. 172. See also NLW 13120B, p. 192, and NLW 13097B, pp. 285–6.

of memory was 'to be redde in the Englishe Cronicle'.[15] Thereafter, the 'blessed Effect' of the Acts of Union enabled Wales to become a stable, progressive Protestant society, a transformation which had proved wholly and mutually beneficial.[16] Political union had brought about rich economic, spiritual and cultural rewards for the Welsh. It was evident, therefore, that the likes of Llywelyn ap Gruffudd and Owain Glyndŵr, who were depicted as brave but deluded rebels, had done their people a disservice not only by resisting homogenizing forces but also by opposing the will of providence. Mercifully, however, by Hanoverian times the history of Wales had been subsumed into that of its powerful neighbour: 'the history of both nations, as well as the people is united'.[17] A purple passage in William Warrington's *The History of Wales* (1786) neatly sums up the way in which Wales had become a victim of the Whig interpretation of history:

> It was, indeed, an interesting spectacle, and might justly have excited indignation and pity, to have seen an ancient and gallant nation falling the victims of private ambition, or sinking under the weight of a superior power. But such emotions, which were then due to that injured people, have lost, at this period, their poignancy and force. A new train of ideas arise, when we see that the change is beneficial to the vanquished: when we see a wild and precarious liberty succeeded by a freedom, secured by equal and fixed laws: when we see manners hostile and barbarous, and a spirit of rapine and cruelty, softened down into the arts of peace, and the milder habits of civilized life: when we see this Remnant of the ancient Britons, uniting in interests, and mingling in friendship with the English, and enjoying with them the same Constitutional Liberties; the purity of which, we trust, will continue uncorrupted as long as this Empire shall be numbered among the nations of the earth.[18]

As we shall see, Iolo, who knew something about history, would tell a very different story from the imperial narrative presented by English historians.

Just as important for the well-being of the nation, so Iolo believed, was enlightened and benevolent leadership by the ruling class. Here, too, the

---

[15] Humphrey Llwyd, *Cronica Walliae*, ed. Ieuan M. Williams (Cardiff, 2002), p. 224.

[16] David Powel, *The History of Wales* (London, 1774), p. 326. See also NLW 13160A, p. 1; NLW 13161A, p. 221.

[17] Powel, *The History of Wales*, p. 329. In *A Postscript to the Origin of Language and Nations* (London, [1768]), p. 16, Rowland Jones, memorably described by Iolo as 'of insane notoriety' (NLW 13150A, p. 144), maintained that the peoples of England and Wales had been incorporated 'both by nature and policy, as one people'.

[18] William Warrington, *The History of Wales* (London, 1786), pp. 556–7. For the wider context, see Herbert Butterfield, *The Whig Interpretation of History* (London, 1931), and the Welsh context, Geraint H. Jenkins, 'Historical Writing in the Eighteenth Century' in Branwen Jarvis (ed.), *A Guide to Welsh Literature c. 1700–1800* (Cardiff, 2000), pp. 23–44, and idem, 'Clio and Wales: Welsh Remembrancers and Historical Writing, 1751–2001', *THSC*, new series, 8 (2002), 119–36.

portents were ominous. As the long eighteenth century unfolded, a privileged ring of landowners had come to dominate Welsh society. This landed elite of absentee English and Scottish magnates, often referred to as 'Leviathans' or 'petty princes', had emerged at the expense of the native home-keeping Welsh gentry who had fallen victim to biological failures, crippling mortgages and improvidence.[19] Old patriarchs had been replaced by new parasites. Many commentators bemoaned the fate of the traditional custodians of the Welsh countryside since their demise broke down communities and jeopardized the future of Welsh-language culture. Iolo was no friend of the rich. 'I have long had good reason', he wrote, 'for considering the British nobility . . . the most abominable Monsters of depravity under the sun.'[20] Never one to doff his hat to the 'great unresiding Proprietors' who scoffed at the plebeian culture of the Welsh and who preferred to consort with 'pimps, panders, Whores, and Toad eaters',[21] Iolo reserved his sympathy for those who fell foul of their stewards and agents. Time and again he castigated the gentry for 'brow-beating and trampling upon inferiors' and vilifying Welsh speakers.[22] 'Go out away! Get ye off'[23] was their surly response to itinerant bards who sought patronage and Iolo himself had first-hand experience of their 'unfeeling cruelty'.[24] He also deplored the avarice of swaggering industrial Titans like the Crawshays, whose massive iron-making centres were not only obliterating familiar landmarks in his beloved *Blaenau* but also unleashing engines of destruction in a world bedevilled by war and slavery.

Even communities close to his home were suffering from the ruinous effects of absentee landowners and monopolists. Ruined farmhouses and cottages in the parishes of St Athan, Flemingston, Boverton and Llantwit Major bore lamentable witness to 'the Robespierian sword'[25] which had robbed families of their livelihood and forced many of them to seek a better life in the New World. He vented his feelings to the prime minister in no uncertain terms:

> There are no more little farmers. Farms are all now monopolized, are in the possession of some one great farmer whose illiberality of mind, whose unprincipled soul, whose hardened conscience, callous to every humane and even honest feeling, has

---

[19] The best work on this theme is Philip Jenkins, *The Making of a Ruling Class: The Glamorgan Gentry 1640–1790* (Cambridge, 1983). For broader trends, see Geraint H. Jenkins, 'Wales in the Eighteenth Century' in H. T. Dickinson (ed.), *A Companion to Eighteenth-Century Britain* (Oxford, 2002), pp. 392–402.
[20] NLW 13174A, p. 4ᵛ.
[21] Ibid., p. 77ʳ; NLW 21319A, p. 38.
[22] NLW 13121B, p. 471.
[23] A. Cynfael Lake (ed.), *Blodeugerdd Barddas o Ganu Caeth y Ddeunawfed Ganrif* (Cyhoeddiadau Barddas, 1993), p. xv.
[24] *CIM*, I, p. 754, Iolo Morganwg to [Hannah More], [?May, 1795].
[25] NLW 13152A, pp. 233–4; NLW 13114B, pp. 52–3; NLW 21323B, p. 52.

enabled some, in conjunction with a prudence that has nothing in view but money at any rate, to grow rich.[26]

Could over-taxed and exploited plebeians rely on a ruling class which was so far removed from their lives and customs to respect the old bardic order and preserve the memory of the Island of Britain? The answer, at least to Iolo, was self-evident and it made him all the more determined to march 'boldly into the *byd niwliawg* [misty world] of mythology'.[27] If the supposedly 'natural' rulers of society were unfit for purpose, Iolo would do their work for them.

Iolo's animadversions against the ruling elite in Wales also reflected his deepening Anglophobia. Over the years his personal contacts and extensive reading had bred within him a 'mortal hatred of the Saxons'.[28] He was deeply wounded by the popular depiction of the Welsh as England's poor and despised relations. Satirical prints, cartoons and chapbooks portrayed 'Poor Taff' as a penurious, mendacious ne'er-do-well, chomping leeks and swilling glutinous ale, tending goats or donkeys, strumming harps, and communicating in a tongue which resembled 'the Gobling of Geese, or Turkeys' or 'the ravishing sounds of a cat-call'.[29] Iolo had a long memory and he brooded over the abuse and slights he had suffered at the hands of the English: the subterfuges and racist comments of Kentish stonemasons; the arrogance of Johnson, who had automatically believed that a provincial upstart like Iolo had nothing important to say; the fury of malevolent church-and-king mobs towards a republican Welshman; being frozen out of dinner-table conversation by the plain-spoken William Godwin; the cold and hostile demeanour of English nobles when he had sought subscriptions from them for his poems; and the contempt in which he was held by hard-hearted English ironmasters like Richard Crawshay. All these perceived wrongs still aroused intense emotions in Iolo and, as we shall see, his national self-awareness often expressed itself as a defensive hostility to the 'other', a stance which was further enhanced by his obsession with ancient conflicts and grievances in the history of Wales.

---

[26] *CIM*, I, pp. 842–3, Iolo Morganwg to William Pitt, 16 December 1796.
[27] Ibid., II, p. 403, William Owen Pughe to Iolo Morganwg, 8 January 1802.
[28] NLW 13108B, p. 97.
[29] Ned Ward, *A Trip to North-Wales* (London, 1701), p. 3; Joseph Hucks, *A Pedestrian Tour through North Wales, in a Series of Letters* (London, 1795), p. 135; Michael Duffy, *The Englishman and the Foreigner* (Cambridge, 1986), p. 18; Peter Lord, *Words with Pictures: Welsh Images and Images of Wales in the Popular Press, 1640–1860* (Aberystwyth, 1995), pp. 68–72; Paul Langford, *Englishness Identified: Manners and Character 1650–1850* (Oxford, 2000), p. 198.

Over the past three decades, the issue of national identity has proved to be a lively and hotly disputed subject among historians and social scientists.[30] To the likes of Gellner, Hobsbawm and Breuilly, the notion of 'the nation' is a modern concept dating from the post-Enlightenment and post-French Revolution period. Nations, nationality, nationalism were the product of modern, industrialized societies.[31] Other authors like Benedict Anderson have viewed nations as 'imagined communities', constructed and identified by internal or external perceptions.[32] Then there is the work of the sociologist Anthony D. Smith, who has highlighted authentic ethnocentric ideologies within the nations of Europe over *la longue durée* and the overwhelming desire among intellectuals to revive or invent ceremonies, customs and symbols which would enable infant nations or nations-to-be to survive and prosper.[33] Smith's interpretation of the importance of 'historical ethno-symbolism' clearly has relevance for Iolo's mission, as does his emphasis on the manner in which nation builders set about mobilizing collective cultural communities. Iolo fits particularly neatly into the category of those who adopted 'a twofold strategy of furnishing "maps" of the community, its history, its destiny and its place among the nations, and of providing "moralities" for the regenerated community, ones that could inspire present generations to emulate the public virtues deemed to express the national character'.[34]

The idea of the nation was very much in vogue by the 1790s and Herderian notions of the cultural nation had a peculiar resonance in a country like Wales which, though it lacked independent statehood, could boast a common ethnicity as well as a distinctive language and literature. In the late seventeenth century the Welsh almanacker Thomas Jones had expressed fears that the Welsh were close to being '*blotted . . . out of the Books of Records*',[35] but within a century cultural patriots like Iolo were responding to Herder's invitation to

---

[30] For useful introductions, see Montserrat Guibernau and John Hutchinson (eds.), *Understanding Nationalism* (Cambridge, 2001); John Breuilly, 'Historians and the Nation' in Peter Burke (ed.), *History and Historians in the Twentieth Century* (Oxford, 2002), pp. 55–87; and Timothy Baycroft and Mark Hewitson (eds.), *What is a Nation? Europe 1789–1914* (Oxford, 2006).

[31] Ernest Gellner, *Nations and Nationalism* (Oxford, 1983); Eric Hobsbawm, *Nations and Nationalism since 1780* (Cambridge, 1990); John Breuilly, *Nationalism and the State* (2nd edn., Manchester, 1993).

[32] Benedict Anderson, *Imagined Communities: Reflections on the Origin and Spread of Nationalism* (rev. edn., London, 1991).

[33] See, in particular, Anthony D. Smith, *The Ethnic Origins of Nations* (Oxford, 1986); idem, *National Identity* (Harmondsworth, 1991); idem, *Nationalism and Modernism* (London, 1998). See also Colin Kidd, *British Identities before Nationalism: Ethnicity and Nationhood in the Atlantic World, 1600–1800* (Cambridge, 1999).

[34] Smith, *National Identity*, p. 65.

[35] Thomas Jones, *The British Language in its Lustre* (London, 1688), sig. A3ʳ.

small nations to write their names 'in the book of mankind'.[36] The flowering of cultural activity among growing numbers of middling sorts was a striking feature of Welsh life. Greater activity and liveliness in the fields of printing and publishing, visual culture, architecture and music-making, as well as far-reaching changes in spiritual life, had made the Welsh more collectively aware of themselves than had been the case since the later middle ages.[37] Although the United Kingdom of Great Britain and Ireland was instituted on 1 January 1801, the British state operated more as a multi-national entity than as a powerful hegemonic state. The diverse and plural identities accommodated by the state offered a window of opportunity to members of a non-dominant ethnic community to revive, reconstruct and invent the past.[38] In the wake of the death of Evan Evans in 1788 and of William Jones, Llangadfan, in 1795, Iolo emerged as the most strident cultural nationalist in Wales. No one knew better than the Bard of Liberty of how his Welsh predecessors had defended their national heritage and, to their great cost, even withstood the mighty Edward I in their bid to oppose imperialism and cultural displacement.

The weight of tradition bore down heavily on Iolo. The ancient British bards had been 'Sons of Truth and Liberty',[39] but now that his plans of holding regular Gorseddau in Wales had been thwarted he was under great pressure to reveal to the world the glorious literary tradition of the Welsh in long-promised works like 'Cyfrinach Beirdd Ynys Prydain' and 'The History of the British Bards'. Dogged by ill health, too easily diverted by other projects, and always prone to draft, redraft and constantly revise different versions, he could never bring himself to complete his cherished assignments. Then, in 1799, came a golden opportunity to redeem himself. Ever since the days of Moses Williams, Edward Lhuyd's most gifted disciple in the early eighteenth century, Welsh scholars had dreamed of publishing a comprehensive collection of Welsh manuscripts. The Morris brothers (whose contribution Iolo was at pains to underplay) and Evan Evans had drawn attention to many rare literary

[36] Robin Okey, 'Wales and Eastern Europe: Small Nations in Comparison' in T. M. Charles-Edwards and R. J. W. Evans (eds.), *Wales and the Wider World: Welsh History in an International Context* (Donington, 2010), p. 187. For a stimulating analysis of the growth of national awareness and modern statehood in Central Europe, see R. J. W. Evans, *Austria, Hungary, and the Habsburgs: Essays on Central Europe, c. 1683–1867* (Oxford, 2006).

[37] Prys Morgan, *The Eighteenth Century Renaissance* (Llandybïe, 1981); idem, 'From a Death to a View: The Hunt for the Welsh Past in the Romantic Period' in Eric Hobsbawm and Terence Ranger (eds.), *The Invention of Tradition* (new edn., Cambridge, 1992), pp. 43–100; Sam Smiles, *The Image of Antiquity: Ancient Britain and the Romantic Imagination* (London, 1994); Geraint H. Jenkins, 'The Cultural Uses of the Welsh Language 1660–1800' in idem (ed.), *The Welsh Language before the Industrial Revolution* (Cardiff, 1997), pp. 369–406; Peter Lord, *The Visual Culture of Wales: Imaging the Nation* (Cardiff, 2000).

[38] Laurence Brockliss and David Eastwood (eds.), *A Union of Multiple Identities: The British Isles, c. 1750–c. 1850* (Manchester, 1997), p. 195.

[39] Williams: *PLP*, II, p. 223.

items, and Iolo himself had beavered away diligently in the British Museum during his sojourn in London. Joep Leerssen has maintained that 'a primal urge in the cultivation of culture is that of *inventory* and *salvage*',[40] but until the foundation of the Society for the Publication of Welsh Manuscripts in 1837 it was left to individual scholars and wealthy patrons to bring important texts into the public domain. The correspondence of the London Welsh, notably that of William Owen Pughe and Owen Jones (Owain Myfyr), as well as Iolo's papers, show very clearly that they were deeply concerned about the vulnerability of Welsh manuscripts stored in private libraries in Wales. Iolo bemoaned the fact that landowners had lost the '*Amor patriae*'[41] which had animated their predecessors and when William Owen Pughe visited the Hengwrt library he was shocked to find the collection 'all in confusion and mouldy'.[42] Something needed to be done.

Such palpable neglect prompted Owain Myfyr to set in motion a scheme to publish a standard compendium of ancient Welsh manuscripts. The initial, perhaps optimistic, aim was to publish a series of volumes, perhaps two per annum, but in the event only three volumes saw the light of day. Volumes one and two appeared in swift succession in June 1801, but the third volume was delayed until 1807, largely because the finances of Owain Myfyr, who had bankrolled the project to the tune of £5,000, had become seriously depleted. The original aim, suggested by Paul Panton, was to entitle the compendium 'The Welsh Archaiology', and only reluctantly did the modest furrier allow his colleagues to recognize his largesse by christening it *The Myvyrian Archaiology of Wales*.[43] This was the most significant, and certainly the largest, publication relating to Welsh culture since Edward Lhuyd's *Archaeologia Britannica* in 1707. Each volume was given a separate title: *Barddoniaeth, sev Gwaith Cynveirdd a Gogynveirdd Cymru* [Poetry, i.e. The Work of the Early Poets and the Fairly Early Poets of Wales] (1801); *Hanesion Cenedyl y Cymry* [The Histories of the Welsh Nation] (1801); and *Doethineb Cenedyl y Cymry* [The Wisdom of the Welsh Nation] (1807). In total the trilogy comprised 1,891 pages. Whatever its flaws might have been, this was an epic landmark publication.

When Owain Myfyr initially sought the cooperation of owners of manuscripts in Wales, the likes of Thomas Johnes of Hafod and Paul Panton of Plas

---

[40] Joep Leerssen, 'Nationalism and the Cultivation of Culture', *Nations and Nationalism*, 12, part 4 (2006), 570.
[41] *MAW*, I, p. [ix].
[42] Glenda Carr, *William Owen Pughe* (Caerdydd, 1983), p. 110.
[43] G. J. Williams, 'Hanes Cyhoeddi'r "Myvyrian Archaiology"', *JWBS*, X, no. 1 (1966), 2–12; Mary-Ann Constantine, 'Welsh Literary History and the Making of "The Myvyrian Archaiology of Wales"' in Dirk Van Hulle and Joep Leerssen (eds.), *Editing the Nation's Memory: Textual Scholarship and Nation-Building in Nineteenth-Century Europe* (Amsterdam, 2008), pp. 109–28.

Gwyn readily agreed to loan their volumes. But there was mounting evidence that many collections had already been lost or scattered like chaff in the wind. Some had been deliberately burnt or allowed to fall into the clutches of rats and mice, and many owners, like the Vaughans of Hengwrt, had gained a reputation for hoarding priceless literary treasures and, as Iolo put it, 'then hiding them for ever'.[44] But the main priority was to find a suitable person to visit private libraries in Wales, unearth relevant material, and either borrow or transcribe it. Given Iolo's deep knowledge of manuscript sources and his general erudition, he was clearly the best-equipped candidate. Privately, however, Owain Myfyr must have nursed some misgivings. Iolo's hot temper, his involvement in political strife, and his dilatoriness were not likely to endear him to landowners and churchmen in north Wales. Even at his most optimistic, Myfyr could hardly have expected Iolo both to behave himself and to succeed in his mission. As far as Iolo was concerned, so long as his benefactor stumped up enough money to cover his food and lodgings, he was prepared to venture north on foot for several months. Although there was a jaunty spring in his step when he set off in May 1799, his excursion was not without its alarms.[45] As he trudged through seven counties, he braved bouts of torrential rain, chronic migraines, violent colds and sciatica. At Llanelltud in Merioneth, he nearly died from asphyxiation by sleeping next to a limekiln.[46]

It soon dawned on him that several hosts had been forewarned of his political sympathies and, to his credit, he did his utmost to choose his words carefully and keep his temper in check. Thomas Johnes of Hafod, who had got wind of Iolo's 'kingophobia and other demon matters',[47] warily greeted the stonemason, but once the two men began discussing the manuscript tradition in Wales and beyond the landowner's *froideur* swiftly dissolved. Anecdotal evidence suggests that Johnes was so concerned about Iolo's chronic asthma and inability to sleep in a horizontal position that he arranged for a carpenter on his estate to fashion for his guest a wooden chair which could also serve as a desk for his work as a transcriber.[48] Ironically, the loss of many critically important Welsh manuscripts during the disastrous fire which later occurred at Hafod in 1807 enabled Iolo to produce bogus transcriptions of material allegedly lost in the flames. Having convinced Johnes that his mission was purely cultural, Iolo plodded northwards where apprehensive loyalists awaited him. Anxious to

---

[44] NLW 13112B, p. 318. Iolo had no qualms about describing the celebrated Robert Vaughan of Hengwrt as a 'ridiculously bungling Antiquary' whose writings displayed 'wonderful ignorance'. NLW 13151A, p. 103; NLW 21295B, p. 1.

[45] This epic tale is recounted in Geraint Phillips, 'Forgery and Patronage: Iolo Morganwg and Owain Myfyr' in *Rattleskull Genius*, pp. 415–19.

[46] NLW 13128A, pp. 450–1.

[47] *CIM*, II, p. 189, William Owen Pughe to Iolo Morganwg, 14 June 1799.

[48] *Literary and Historical Legacy*, pp. 20–1.

locate and wheedle manuscripts from stubborn clerics and Calvinistic Methodists, Iolo was on his best behaviour and even managed to persuade 'the wild old Welsh playwright' Thomas Edwards (Twm o'r Nant) to part with some of his valuable manuscripts so that he could copy them to his heart's content.[49] In fact, Iolo's legendary stamina stood him in good stead during this journey. He used his time as profitably as possible, spending up to twenty hours a day unravelling parchment rolls and transcribing material in private homes or taverns in places like Bangor, Beaumaris and Plas Gwyn. Exhausted, he claimed to have 'almost written myself blind'[50] and was clinically depressed by the time he returned to his wife and family in late summer.

Iolo's excursion had not been an unqualified success. He had been refused access to the critically important collections at Hengwrt, Gloddaith and Wynnstay and, equally seriously, he had infuriated Owain Myfyr by delaying the release of his transcripts and stubbornly refusing to bring them with him to London. The man whom Iolo had previously hailed as a latter-day Ifor Hael (Ivor the Generous)[51] was now plied with a host of excuses – ill health, the demands of his trade as a mason, unreliable and mendacious carriers – for failing to fulfil his remit.[52] As a result, the third volume of *The Myvyrian Archaiology of Wales* did not appear until 1807, by which time Iolo had fallen out acrimoniously and irrevocably with Owain Myfyr, claiming that the latter had reneged on a promise to award him an annual pension of £50 for life to fund his research and publications. He had also abandoned William Owen Pughe to his Southcottian delusions. Never again would they meet to patch things up. Even in old age Iolo still remembered his old benefactor Owain Myfyr as 'that most artful of all scoundrels',[53] but even though a true version of the events will probably never be known we can be pretty sure that Iolo was far from blameless. In his handling of his fellow editors he was clever, manipulative and ruthless, never more so than in the process of supplying them with bogus material.

The publication of *The Myvyrian Archaiology of Wales* caused a considerable stir. Although Wales could boast a strong tradition of preserving, transcribing and borrowing Welsh manuscripts, little of the material had been made

---

[49] *CIM*, II, p. 196, Iolo Morganwg to William Owen Pughe, 10 July 1799.
[50] Ibid., II, p. 233, Iolo Morganwg to Owen Jones (Owain Myfyr), 23 October 1799.
[51] Ibid., II, p. 106, Iolo Morganwg to William Owen Pughe, 29 September 1798. He also described Owain Myfyr as 'a man without parallel in the world' ('dyn heb ei gyffelyb yn y byd').
[52] Ibid., II, pp. 329–35, Iolo Morganwg to Owen Jones (Owain Myfyr), 6 October 1800; ibid., II, pp. 551–7, Iolo Morganwg to William Owen Pughe, 11 October 1803.
[53] Ibid., III, p. 520, Iolo Morganwg to Evan Williams, 12 May 1819.

available in print.[54] But now, by 1807, the Welsh public could take pride in a three-volume building block designed to bolster their national pride. What they did not know was that the sorcerer from Flemingston had cast his spell once more by indulging his passion for imaginative re-creation. We need always to bear in mind that practising counterfactual fraud in the Romantic period was not considered intellectually demeaning in any way. Conflating history and forgery in order to prop up national cultures was common and, as far as Iolo was concerned, the forging of usable history in the interests of his own nation was a perfectly legitimate pursuit.[55] The fabricated chronicles, tales, triads and proverbs which he inveigled into volumes two and three of *The Myvyrian Archaiology* were simply the tip of the iceberg. From the time of his return to Wales in 1795 he had spent every available hour of leisure time building up an archive of historical and literary material, rescuing hidden treasures, and also exercising his extraordinary gift for imitating the prose, style and diction of medieval documents. As the years unfolded, the floor space in his tiny cottage virtually disappeared as mounds of books, transcripts and papers tottered precariously around him.

Although early twentieth-century scholars, led by a raging Sir John Morris-Jones, were quick to assign or at least impute the crudest motives to Iolo's fabrications and to depict him as a fiendish figure, recent writers have taken a more generous and appreciative view of the way in which gifted forgers in the eighteenth century reinvented the past by blurring the boundaries between demonstrable fact and inspired fiction. From Psalmanazar's Formosan hoax at the dawn of the century to William Henry Ireland's Shakespearean fraud at its end, debates over literary and historical deception lay at the heart of eighteenth-century culture.[56] Iolo referred to his own times as 'the present age of forgery'[57] and he was thoroughly familiar with the controversies and dust-ups which blew up around Chatterton, Ireland and Macpherson. He believed that the creative literary artist who brooded over conflicting or incomplete evidence had every

---

[54] Catherine McKenna, 'Aspects of Tradition Formation in Eighteenth-Century Wales' in Joseph F. Nagy (ed.), *Memory and the Modern in Celtic Literatures. CSANA Yearbook 5* (Dublin, 2006), pp. 37–60.

[55] Roy Porter and Mikuláš Teich (eds.), *Romanticism in National Context* (Cambridge, 1988), p. 5.

[56] In this swiftly burgeoning and sometimes bewildering field of study, the following works are especially valuable: Ian Haywood, *Faking It: Art and the Politics of Forgery* (Brighton, 1987); Anthony Grafton, *Forgers and Critics: Creativity and Duplicity in Western Scholarship* (London, 1990); Paul Baines, *The House of Forgery in Eighteenth-Century Britain* (Aldershot, 1999); Nick Groom, *The Forger's Shadow: How Forgery Changed the Course of Literature* (London, 2002); Margaret Russett, *Fictions and Fakes: Forging Romantic Authenticity, 1760–1845* (Cambridge, 2006); Jack Lynch, *Deception and Detection in Eighteenth-Century Britain* (Aldershot, 2008). On Iolo himself, the outstanding works are Gwyneth Lewis, 'Eighteenth-Century Literary Forgeries, with Special Reference to the Work of Iolo Morganwg' (unpublished University of Oxford D.Phil. thesis, 1991) and *Truth against the World*.

[57] NLW 13104B, p. 124.

right to condense sharply different eras either by ellipsis or by inserting new information, and also to add a touch of spice and excitement to the sheer drudgery of transcription and composition by secretly and subversively insinuating his own voice into the story of the past. Truth, of course, whether against or in opposition to the world (as Iolo put it), is an elusive and sometimes illusive concept, and 'Quid est veritas?' was a question he asked many times as he tinkered with, and redrafted, texts.[58] Even though he often conceded that 'facts are stubborn things',[59] he did not exclude the possibility that the remembered past might well be a piece of fiction.

As is the case with most literary forgers, Iolo's motives were manifold. Making money was emphatically not one of them. He despised riches and was reconciled to living out his life in poverty. The cheques he received from Owain Myfyr and the subventions which arrived periodically from the Royal Literary Fund did no more than keep the wolf from the door. He prided himself on his skills as a forger. Having escaped detection for fathering his own beautiful poems on Dafydd ap Gwilym, he was emboldened to embark on a new wave of forging activity. Caroline Franklin believes that he took 'an amoral Brechtian delight in subverting the "superstructure" of orthodox scholarship'.[60] He certainly liked to flirt with the danger of discovery – he sent several hints of his mischief-making to an unsuspecting Owain Myfyr – and he derived considerable pleasure from hoodwinking the so-called literary 'establishment' in London. He chortled loudly when his *bête noire* Edward Jones published in *The Bardic Museum* (1802) a spurious manuscript which he had forwarded to him,[61] and there were doubtless cases of what Jack Lynch calls 'motiveless malignity'.[62] As Mary-Ann Constantine has shrewdly observed: 'it is disconcertingly hard to know whether . . . Iolo is . . . winking at us across two hundred years'.[63] At times, too, the pleasures and torments of opium played their part. As Iolo's respiratory ailments worsened, he consumed laudanum in larger doses. While this alleviated the pain, it also probably stimulated his creative powers

---

[58] For some examples, see NLW 13088B, pp. 60–1; NLW 13115B, p. 317; NLW 13144A, pp. 427–9; NLW 13159A, p. 86. For conjectural history as practised by admirers of Montesquieu, see Mark Salber Phillips, *Society and Sentiment: Genres of Historical Writing in Britain, 1740–1820* (Princeton, NJ, 2000), chapter 7.

[59] NLW 13138A, p. 90; NLW 21400C, no. 46; *CIM*, II, p. 626, Iolo Morganwg to [Hugh] Maurice, 11 September 1804.

[60] Caroline Franklin, 'The Welsh American Dream: Iolo Morganwg, Robert Southey and the Madoc Legend' in Gerard Carruthers and Alan Rawes (eds.), *English Romanticism and the Celtic World* (Cambridge, 2003), p. 72.

[61] *CIM*, II, p. 415, Iolo Morganwg to Edward Jones (Bardd y Brenin), 24 May 1802. The saga behind Iolo's 'most glorious laugh' at his enemy's credulity is told in *Truth against the World*, chapter 13.

[62] Lynch, *Deception and Detection in Eighteenth-Century Britain*, p. 169.

[63] *Truth against the World*, p. 203.

and his capacity for self-delusion.[64] Amid the clutter and confusion of having such 'a vast heap of crude papers'[65] in his home, it is not surprising that he sometimes found it impossible to distinguish between authentic and bogus texts. Renan would later claim that committing historical errors was an integral part of nation-building.[66] Iolo would surely have agreed.

There are very good reasons, therefore, for arguing that Iolo's principal motive in intervening in the past, tweaking data, counterfeiting material and investing it with a moral and political dimension was to promote national self-understanding. If Scotland could boost its own national culture with fictitious poetry, spurious genealogies and fabricated histories, then Wales, with its superior literary inheritance, deserved an even grander narrative. In doing so, Iolo introduced a new genre of writing in Wales. He subverted received wisdom, radicalized the understanding of the past, and staked his claim as the nation's principal remembrancer.[67] Although still defiantly a Glamorgan man, his chief loyalty was to his nation and he believed that it fell to him to ensure that the depiction of the past met the needs of the present. On St David's Day 1806 he informed William Owen Pughe that serving the national cause was his primary consideration: 'It is for Wales, for the Welsh nation, for the Welsh language and literature to [atten]d which, I have sacrificed all the comforts of life.'[68] The Bard of Liberty had become a national remembrancer.

Iolo was profoundly dissatisfied and sharply critical of just about all the historical works he read. While he always relished the intellectual challenge posed by Enlightenment thinkers like Diderot, Rousseau and Voltaire, he deplored the slipshod and flawed work of British historians who refused to veer away from the well-worn paths of historical writing. For several reasons, he found

---

[64] Iolo seems to have become increasingly disabled by his asthmatic complaint after 1800 and his addiction to opium, though it may have eroded his critical faculties, may also have helped him to see the past in stimulating ways. See Alethea Hayter, *Opium and the Romantic Imagination* (rev. edn., Wellingborough, 1988) and Louise Foxcroft, *The Making of Addiction: The 'Use and Abuse' of Opium in Nineteenth-Century Britain* (Aldershot, 2007).

[65] *CIM*, II, p. 469, Iolo Morganwg to William Owen Pughe, 15 February 1803. See also his despairing comments in ibid., II, p. 493, Iolo Morganwg to William Owen Pughe, 7 June 1803.

[66] Hobsbawm, *Nations and Nationalism since 1780*, p. 12.

[67] It is regrettable that neither Iolo nor Wales figure in the otherwise admirable series of volumes, based on a research programme funded by the European Science Foundation, entitled 'Representations of the Past: The Writing of National Histories in 19th and 20th Century Europe'. See in particular, Stefan Berger (ed.), *Writing the Nation: A Global Perspective* (Basingstoke, 2007); Stefan Berger, Linas Eriksonas and Andrew Mycock (eds.), *Narrating the Nation: Representations in History, Media and the Arts* (Oxford, 2008) and Stefan Berger and Chris Lorenz (eds.), *The Contested Nation: Ethnicity, Class, Religion and Gender in National Histories* (Basingstoke, 2008).

[68] *CIM*, II, pp. 764–5, Iolo Morganwg to William Owen Pughe, 1 March 1806.

old-style Whiggish writing colourless and defective.⁶⁹ It lacked passion and drama. It privileged the wealthy and the powerful. Worse still, it subsumed Wales in an Anglocentric narrative. Iolo found Gibbon's work overly secular and unheroic, and much as he admired Hume's writings he was sharply critical of his sceptical reasoning. He recognized the learning and distinction of these writers, but reckoned that for the most part they cast 'false lights on some things, and impervious darkness on others'.⁷⁰

Iolo took no delight either in the writings of Welsh historians. 'The Taffyland Historians', he wrote wearily, 'have hitherto been sad Dogs for the most part.'⁷¹ He especially deplored the influence of the 'ridiculously fabulous history'⁷² written by Geoffrey of Monmouth. Welsh versions of *Historia Regum Britanniae* still constituted a significant element in the historical identity of the Welsh in the eighteenth century. The Trojan origins of the Welsh figured prominently in influential works like *Drych y Prif Oesoedd* (1716; 1740)⁷³ and some of the other associated themes discussed by its author Theophilus Evans were vigorously debated by members of the Walters family, though Iolo was far from convinced by the lucubrations of 'The Florus of Cambria'.⁷⁴ The myth of Brutus, sedulously fostered by so many Welsh writers, was unappealing to Iolo since it presumed English supremacy following the division of Britain among the sons of Brutus. Moreover, the bloody chronicles of Saxon and Norman kings and princes held little interest for him. This explains his vitriolic denunciations of the work of Lewis Morris, whom he believed to have set too great a store on the fabulous lies of Norman chronicles. 'The whole labours of his life', he informed William Owen Pughe, 'were employed in feeble attempts to prop up a monstrous lie.'⁷⁵

More serious still, in Iolo's view, was the fact that Welsh historians, for whatever reason, had not based their interpretations on the evidence found in Welsh manuscripts, and had been content to use a limited number of biased sources and to repeat the words of their predecessors. In a revealing piece of

---

⁶⁹ Benedikt Stuchtey, 'Literature, Liberty and Life of the Nation: British Historiography from Macaulay to Trevelyan' in Stefan Berger, Mark Donovan and Kevin Passmore (eds.), *Writing National Histories: Western Europe since 1800* (London, 1999), pp. 30–46. For different historiographical trends in Scotland, see Colin Kidd, *Subverting Scotland's Past: Scottish Whig Historians and the Creation of an Anglo-British Identity, 1689–c.1830* (Cambridge, 1993).
⁷⁰ NLW 13103B, pp. 277–8.
⁷¹ NLW 13118B, p. 135.
⁷² *CIM*, II, p. 636, Iolo Morganwg to William Owen Pughe, 9 November 1804. See also his condemnation of Geoffrey of Monmouth's 'Idle Trojan Dreams' in NLW 13115B, p. 144, and his 'monstrous fables' in NLW 13106B, p. 133.
⁷³ Geraint H. Jenkins, *Theophilus Evans (1693–1767): Y Dyn, ei Deulu, a'i Oes* (Adran Gwasanaethau Diwylliannol Dyfed, 1993), pp. 37–40.
⁷⁴ NLW 6515B, pp. 17, 21. For extracts (translated into English) from parts of *Drych y Prif Oesoedd* in Iolo's hand, see NLW 13091E, p. 307.
⁷⁵ *CIM*, II, p. 510, Iolo Morganwg to William Owen Pughe, 23 June 1803.

marginalia, entitled 'On Historians of Wales', he insisted that the most popular and seemingly reliable 'national' histories were deeply flawed and incomplete:

> . . . what knowledge of ancient traditionary and even written Welsh history find we in Warrington, even in Dr Powel's *History of Wales*, wherein we find little besides a translation of Caradoc Llangarfan? What find we in Charles Edwards' *Hanes y Ffydd, Hanes y Byd a'r Amseroedd, Oes Lyfr* and even in *Drych y Prif Oesoedd*? Their authors, tho' writing in the Welsh language, were absolutely ignorant of our written records, which they ou[gh]t to have consulted by all means.[76]

To some extent, his criticisms were valid, though it should be borne in mind that previous scholars had been denied access to many of the manuscripts which Iolo had found and transcribed in the late eighteenth century. Nor should we forget that his aim of constructing a new and more assertive narrative necessarily entailed rejecting conventional accounts of the past.

His own personal prejudices also prompted him to tarnish the reputation of writers whom he believed to be ignorant or impertinent scoundrels. Writers from north Wales were judged to be especially culpable in this respect. David Powel in particular had done the nation a disservice by referring to the 'immorigerous *Welch*' and by pointing out 'those unnatural Differences' which had separated the Welsh from the English.[77] Who, on witnessing the 'puny' monuments on the landscape of Anglesey, could give any credence to Henry Rowlands's argument in *Mona Antiqua Restaurata* (1732; 1766) that the island had once been the headquarters of druidism in Britain? Iolo simply could not believe that any serious scholar would rely on such a 'confused Mass of violations of history, audacious assertion, groundless conjecture, superstitious tradition, false etymology, and a shameful ignorance of the ancient MSS, and even the Language of Wales'.[78] Rowlands's work was doubtless defective on many counts, but Iolo's damning judgement was at least in part prompted by his desire to associate the words 'Druidic' and 'patriarchal' in the public mind with his native Glamorgan. Iolo's hostility towards Anglicanism also predisposed him to deprecate, even defame, those writers whose version of the past reflected their enthusiasm for the established church and who, as it happens, were also deeply suspicious of 'the frauds and the tricks of Ned Williams'.[79] Although

---

[76] Quoted in *'The Bard is a Very Singular Character'*, p. 318. For a list of Iolo's books on Welsh history, see NLW 13136A, pp. 141–55.
[77] Powel, *The History of Wales*, pp. 318, 326.
[78] NLW 13130A, p. 292. See also NLW 13089E, p. 434, and NLW 13097B, pp. 285–6.
[79] Cardiff 3. 104, letter no. 17, Theophilus Jones to Edward Davies, [?] June 1807. The Anglican clergyman Edward Davies was an especially flinty critic of Iolo's system. Moira Dearnley, '"Mad Ned" and the "Smatter-Dasher": Iolo Morganwg and Edward 'Celtic' Davies' in *Rattleskull Genius*, pp. 425–42.

A History of Brecknockshire (1807) by the lawyer Theophilus Jones (a grandson of Theophilus Evans) was, and still is, regarded as a valuable county history, Iolo found it seriously defective: amid the 'low irony, vulgar witticisms, coxcombical sarcasms, and ignorance' he failed to discover more than 'a few shrivel'd grains of historical truth'.[80] Another buffoon in Iolo's eyes was David Peter, head of the Dissenting academy at Carmarthen, whose animus against young Unitarian students caused Iolo to liken his history of religion in Wales from the earliest times to 'a mad-Moll's pitcher' composed of 'beef, broth, meal, beer, wool, an old pair of shoes, a piece of soap, a paper of pins, shoe-blacking and in general whatever any one might give her'.[81] Apart from Sharon Turner and Peter Roberts, there were not many writers who escaped Iolo's onslaughts at the turn of the eighteenth century and his abrasiveness must have been as tiresome to his enemies as it was amusing to his dwindling number of friends. He genuinely believed that books on Welsh history were fit only to be hurled at a bookseller's head (preferably Evan Williams of the Strand)[82] and that heaping sarcasm on their authors was the best way of discrediting their views on the past.[83] Since their volumes were incomplete, defective or untrustworthy, it was time to replace the work of 'our Jack-a-lanthorne Historians'[84] with a more challenging and inspiring narrative.

As we have seen, Iolo's preferred historical narrative involved imagining and constructing memories, myths and traditions. But it was also designed to be that much stronger for having a set of public virtues or moralities to guide it. The striking galaxy of fictional or semi-fictional heroes who populated the Welsh past possessed different values from the English who, in recounting the history of great men in public life or the armed forces, had always idolized 'the *Arts of war*'.[85] By contrast, the Welsh historian, mindful of the way in which the ancient Welsh had pinned their faith on benevolent maxims like 'The Truth against the World', 'God and all goodness' and 'Heart joined to heart', was better placed to highlight sentiments which encouraged human empathy and moral rectitude.[86] He was expected to 'inform, illuminate and improve

---

[80] NLW 13136A, pp. 96–7. For a similar diatribe, see NLW 21419E, no. 51, and *CIM*, III, p. 231, Iolo Morganwg to David Davis, 15 January [1814].
[81] *CIM*, III, p. 246, Iolo Morganwg to Thomas Rees, 25 February 1814.
[82] Ibid., III, p. 151, Iolo Morganwg to Thomas Rees, 3 May 1813.
[83] Iolo wrote as follows to Thomas Rees: 'I cannot help using the language of sarcasm when I am obliged to mention the stuff that has been written on Welsh history.' *CIM*, III, p. 151, Iolo Morganwg to Thomas Rees, 3 May 1813.
[84] NLW 13089E, p. 449. He claimed that they were 'partial to every thing but *Truth*'. Williams: *PLP*, I, p. xviii.
[85] NLW 21392F, no. 2.
[86] NLW 21369A, p. 21^{r-v}.

the mind'[87] by concentrating on ethical behaviour which cultivated peace and civilization and by fulminating against those whose bellicose behaviour had brought shame and disgrace to the nation:

> I wish all the nations in the world would suffer the histories of their Kings and their wars, their established religion and all other infernalities to sink into the deepest oblivion, and to keep memorials only of what arts of peace and civilization thus have appeared amongst them. This is the first step, in my opinion, that should be taken towards reforming or rather civilizing mankind. If war must on some occasions, or for some purposes be unavoidably mentioned let it be always with that horror and detestation that its infernality requires. If Kings must be remembered, let it be as the Michaels and Gabriels of Belzebub, as the firebrands kindled in hell that in all ages have set the world on fire.[88]

In Iolo's eyes, history was not meant to be a dispassionate affair. It was a vehicle for strong passions, moral lessons and universal truths. This was especially the case as far as Welsh civilization was concerned, for there were practical benefits and wisdom to be gained from studying the people's social regulations, habits of living, bardic and religious institutions, and moral tastes. In the national mythology which he created, the Welsh were portrayed as a peace-loving people who were instinctively humane and democratic, hostile to warmongers, Catholic zealots and martyr-burning bigots, and committed to the cause of justice and truth. Any histories which, for whatever reason, excluded these traits were no better than 'a series of old wives tales, idle chat about nothing at all of any real use'.[89] In short, a self-respecting chronicler of the past should possess a profound sense of right and wrong and be prepared to serve the cause of humanity. Iolo certainly did and he had no qualms about constructing a past designed to meet contemporary political needs as he saw them.

While some critics, both then and afterwards, mocked Iolo's interpretation of the past as being tarnished by radical politics, others maintained that it was as much a story about Glamorgan as it was about Wales. He retained a life-long affection for, and loyalty to, his home turf. Regional loyalties were still extremely strong in his day and in all his writings, not simply in his vision of the past, Iolo was determined to cast Glamorgan in a superior light to all other Welsh shires. His readiness to champion and defend its reputation was often reflected in his recital of its supposed superior virtues and his hostility towards

---

[87] *CIM*, II, p. 147, Iolo Morganwg to David Thomas, 20 October 1798. See also ibid., II, p. 653, Iolo Morganwg to William Owen Pughe, 14 February 1805.
[88] NLW 13089E, p. 288.
[89] NLW 13088B, pp. 75–6; NLW 13089E, p. 287; NLW 13121B, pp. 303–6; NLW 13143A, pp. 297–300; *CIM*, II, p. 147, Iolo Morganwg to David Thomas, 20 October 1798.

everything associated with the 'barbarous' culture of north Wales.[90] Whereas Glamorgan was the throbbing pulse of the new progressive Wales, 'Deudneudwyr' inhabited an outlandish province far from centres of learning and political radicalism:

> Myned i Sir Gaer, myned i wlad bell,
> Myned i Sir Benfro, myned ni wyddys i ble,
> Myned i Sir Aberteifi, myned i maes o'r Byd,
> Myned i Wynedd, myned i Ddiawl.[91]

> (Going to Carmarthenshire, going to a distant country,
> Going to Pembrokeshire, going to an unknown place,
> Going to Cardiganshire, going out of the world,
> Going to Gwynedd, going to the Devil.)

More serious, and more subversive, than such gibes was the manner in which he placed Glamorgan at the heart of the Welsh literary tradition. As he mythologized the past, he drew heavily on Glamorgan examples and wove into his tapestry a rich array of fictitious and semi-fictitious writers as well as authentic figures whose association with Glamorgan was tenuous to say the least. He elevated the Silurian dialect above all others and condemned northerners for 'arrogating to themselves all philological excellence'[92] and subjecting the literary heritage of Glamorgan to contempt. John Williams of Llanrwst, for instance, had infuriated him by asking: 'Do you think that your systems in Southwales are as perfect as ours?'[93] Unflinchingly, Iolo insisted that the 'Dwarfish System' imposed by Dafydd ab Edmwnd at the Carmarthen eisteddfod c. 1453 was a discredited construct far inferior to the Glamorgan metrical system practised by authentic poets in south Wales.[94] He was determined not to be outflanked or bullied by former colleagues in north Wales or London, but in so doing he ran the risk of compromising his efforts to nurture a Welsh national identity and a deeper sense of integration. Although Wales remained the primary focus in his exposition of the past, the intrusive presence of Glamorgan still coloured the whole enterprise.[95]

---

[90] Cathryn Charnell-White, *Barbarism and Bardism: North Wales versus South Wales in the Bardic Vision of Iolo Morganwg* (Aberystwyth, 2004).
[91] NLW 13146A, p. 37.
[92] NLW 13130A, p. 180.
[93] *CIM*, II, p. 742, Iolo Morganwg to William Owen Pughe, 12 January 1806.
[94] NLW 13130A, pp. 188–99. He also described the Carmarthen eisteddfod as 'that mountain which brought forth a mouse'. *CIM*, II, p. 213, Iolo Morganwg to William Owen Pughe, 13 August 1799.
[95] *Bardic Circles*, chapter 4.

Some might argue that the originality of Iolo's insights were blunted by all these preoccupations, but those of a sunnier disposition might well conclude that his prejudices made his vision all the more vivid and readable. By the time of the completion of *The Myvyrian Archaiology of Wales* in 1807 he had acquired a reputation as a remembrancer who was 'profound and sagacious in every thing curious relating to the customs, manners, and history, of his native principality'.[96] Moreover, his extraordinary depth of learning and range of interests meant that he was well placed to embark on another large-scale enterprise. Egged on by his admirers, he seriously contemplated writing a new history of Wales in six volumes, an enterprise of some 2,400 pages composed of texts as well as commentary on the known (and as yet unknown) history of the nation from the earliest times onwards.[97] Even as late as 1819 he was still assuring Anglican clerics that, with adequate assistance, this was a feasible task.[98] But although Iolo assembled a mass of material and wrote drafts of his plans and proposals of his publication, he never fulfilled his ambition of bringing the work to a triumphant conclusion. His proverbial dilatoriness, the disorderly nature of his archive, the sheer size of the task and his impoverished personal circumstances dogged his progress at every turn. Such handicaps rankled with him and often triggered explosions of rage.

Iolo's many unpublished writings on history, though riddled with imprecision and contradictions as well as imaginative speculations, offered a very different perspective on the past from that of previous writers. Broadly speaking, his version ran as follows. Since he was no believer in the Gomerian mythology, he did not stipulate the date of the Creation or dwell too long on the time-frame for pre-history. The Almighty, whose voice reverberated like 'ten thousand thunders', had declared his existence even as the world co-instantaneously acquired life.[99] His 'shout of joy' was that of 'the most exquisite melody' that could possibly exist.[100] This sweet sound was accompanied by the appearance of three rays of light which radiated from the deity and represented the unity of the creation. On this basis, Iolo devised the symbol /|\ , known as the *nod cyfrin* (mystic sign) which embodied the virtues of truth, love and justice.[101] Menu, the first man, conveyed to his son, the legendary hero Einigan Gawr (Einigan the Giant), an account of the creation and taught him how to

---

[96] Benjamin H. Malkin, *The Scenery, Antiquities, and Biography, of South Wales* (2nd edn., 2 vols., London, 1807), I, p. 195.
[97] NLW 21392F, nos. 1–2; NLW 21400C, no. 15; *RAEW*, pp. 181–5.
[98] *A Prospectus of Collections for a New History of Wales in Six Volumes* (Carmarthen, 1819). He had also planned to publish in 1807 'Ancient Historical Documents, relating to Wales and the Welsh Nation'. NLW 21375A, pp. 7ᵛ–8ʳ.
[99] NLW 13112B, p. 293; NLW 13121B, p. 439.
[100] NLW 13107B, p. 2; NLW 13093E, p. 167.
[101] NLW 13093E, p 167; Dillwyn Miles, *The Secret of the Bards of the Isle of Britain* (Llandybïe, 1992), p. 63.

pronounce the sounds embodied in the three first letters enunciated by the deity. This formed the basis of the idea of expressing different sounds and names by means of an alphabet which Einigan imparted to his children and which was then passed down to the tribe known as the 'Cimmeri' or the 'Kymmry' (whose variants as a national appellative were well known to Iolo),[102] who were located in Deffrobani or 'Gwlad yr Haf' (Land of Summer) and who, having wandered aimlessly for five hundred years, became the earliest people to settle in Britain, probably c.1500 BC.[103] In answering the question 'where did the Welsh come from?', Iolo therefore dismissed the 'glaring lies' of Geoffrey of Monmouth,[104] scoffed at the supposed Gomerian origins of his people as 'a wild conjecture',[105] and introduced a new pantheon of heroes on to the historical stage whose cast of mind and socio-political ideals resembled his own.

Iolo exulted in belonging to a people who could claim to be the authentic proprietors of Britain and who at one stage possessed their own rights and liberties. The principal patriarch of the nation was Hu Gadarn (Huw the Mighty) who, via Deffrobani, had come from Constantinople to lead the Welsh to the Isle of Britain. Widely reckoned to possess attributes and powers unknown to man, he introduced the arts of agriculture and husbandry, renounced violence, and actively promoted strict-metre poetry in Welsh.[106] Another pillar of the 'Political (national) Community'[107] of Britain was Prydain ab Aedd Mawr, after whom the island became known. A virtuous, intelligent leader, much loved by his people, he imposed a wise and benevolent government upon the island of Britain and became the first national lawgiver.[108] The third key figure was Dyfnwal Moelmud whose prowess as a codifier of laws had been noticed by Geoffrey of Monmouth and Robert Vaughan of Hengwrt, and whose assiduous work in the formulation of Welsh law prepared the way for his illustrious successor Hywel Dda.[109] Iolo was especially interested in the latter, not least because of his own experience of how the law, formulated and practised by arbitrary, oppressive kings and nobles, robbed innocent people of their liberties. He was keenly aware of how the rights of the 'free-born Briton'

---

[102] NLW 13128A, pp. 45–6, 181–4, 247–51; NLW 13129A, pp. 105–15, 121–2.
[103] *RAEW*, p. 188.
[104] Williams: *PLP*, II, p. 3.
[105] Ibid., II, p. 8.
[106] NLW 13088B, p. 89; NLW 13108B, p. 7; NLW 13130A, pp. 353–8; NLW 13152A, p. 57; William Owen Pughe, *Hu Gadarn, Cywydd o 111 Caniad* (Llundain, 1822).
[107] NLW 13088B, p. 88; NLW 13101B, p. 149.
[108] *MAW*, II, p. 37; Rachel Bromwich, 'Trioedd Ynys Prydain: The *Myvyrian* "Third Series"', *THSC* (1968), 322.
[109] Morfydd E. Owen, 'Royal Propaganda: Stories from the Law-Texts' in T. M. Charles-Edwards, Morfydd E. Owen and Paul Russell (eds.), *The Welsh King and his Court* (Cardiff, 2000), pp. 229–32.

had been defended in ancient times, of the value of *rhaith gwlad* (the oath of the country), and of how despotism, misrule and violence had, by Hanoverian times, enabled monarchs, judges and juries to persecute libertarians.[110] As this characteristically witty passage shows, historical and etymological knowledge could throw light on the iniquities of the present:

> It is not very clear what the Welsh Bard means by K[ing]s. It may possibly be Knaves. The word in the original Welsh is Brenin, which anciently signified K[in]g, synonymous to Knave. In its modern acceptation it signifies any Officer that executes the Law, from the Monarch up to the Hangman. This may be wrong, tho' it does not yet appear to be so, for the Welsh Bards and their language are very barbarous things. I asked the old Celtic Rhymer what he meant by the word Brenin. Why said he, I mean a Journey-man K[ing], that is a Bumbailiff, Hangman, Informer, Attorney General, or, in short, a place-man of any description whatever: – what an ignorant old fellow! That he is so in the extreme will appear from the following particular: I asked him what he meant by the Welsh term Rheithwyr-anudon. Why, said he, I mean a Pack'd Jury or which is the same thing a special Jury. Now having myself some knowledge of the language, I am able to assure the reader that Rheithwyr-anudon signifies literally Foresworne Juries – so let every loyal Englishman say 'From Welsh Bards, Good Lord deliver us'.[111]

In the days of Dyfnwal Moelmud, however, benevolent laws had been reduced into a constitution by which the whole island was governed by an elected king, hereditary princes, elders of families and experienced, wise men.[112] In Iolo's scheme of things, therefore, the three major heroes and pillars of the Welsh nation had been Hu Gadarn, Prydain ab Aedd Mawr and Dyfnwal Moelmud. Brutus was conspicuous by his absence.

In matters relating to the coming of Christianity, too, Iolo was just as forthright. He rejected the claim made by Bishop Richard Davies in his preface to the first Welsh translation of the New Testament in 1567 that the Christian faith in its 'uncorrupted' form had been brought to Britain by Joseph of Arimathea.[113] To Iolo, this 'monkish legend' had been misguidedly utilized by English historians and too easily swallowed by the Welsh. All the reliable evidence suggested that the 'sun of righteousness' ('haul cyfiawnder') had dawned upon Wales when Brân Fendigaid (Brân the Blessed) – a sacred patriarch who happened to be a Glamorgan man and whose memory had been erased by historians such as Humphrey Llwyd and David Powel – converted to Christianity during his incarceration in Rome with his illustrious and brave son

---

[110] NLW 13088B, p. 59; NLW 13109B, pp. 1–61; NLW 13143A, p. 296.
[111] NLW 21401E, no. 11.
[112] NLW 13088B, p. 88.
[113] Glanmor Williams, *Reformation Views of Church History* (London, 1970), pp. 39, 44, 63–4.

Caratacus.[114] On his release, Brân returned to Wales, bringing with him the pure, unsullied Christian faith which captured the imagination of his compatriots. Thereafter the Christian flame was kept alive by small groups of believers, many of whom drew inspiration from the high moral and devotional standards set by the Welsh saints. Iolo was particularly impressed by St Illtud, a learned and attractive personality who transformed the monastery of Llantwit Major into a renowned centre of piety and intellectual liveliness. Illtud was an abstemious man who used to bathe in ice-cold waters and subsist on one meal a day which, as Iolo mischievously observed, 'did not continue for the whole day as it is with some of our modern Parsons'.[115] Past and present came together in the church at Llantwit which boasted several important early Christian stones, one of which – Samson's Pillar-cross – he claimed to have unearthed himself.[116] Although Iolo was deeply sceptical of the supernatural powers attributed to the early saints, he readily acknowledged the spiritual example set by holy men, notably David, Illtud, Padarn and Teilo.

Iolo believed that the work of these extraordinary men had helped to create a sense of belonging to a nation called Wales. But even greater honour was conferred on the nation by the civilized and benevolent habits of its bards, notably Tydain, the father of poetic genius, who had encouraged his people to expand the number of characters in the bardic alphabet and to develop the practice of inscribing or cutting letters on wood.[117] The part played by fictitious or semi-fictitious early bards, especially Plennydd, Alawn and Gwron, in formulating and sustaining the bardic system was hard to exaggerate, and Iolo himself strongly believed that the moral precepts of Welsh bardistry was 'the glory of our ancient literature, a single sentence of which is worth a thousand volumes of such history as that of the infernally bloodthirsty princes of Wales at some periods, or of wars at any period'.[118] Ancient bards and their descendants had thus formed a peace-loving priesthood whose Christian mission was to civilize mankind, thereby conferring honour upon the nation. In a purple passage published in the introduction to the first volume of *The Myvyrian Archaiology of Wales*, Iolo insisted that these men of letters had composed 'beautiful poetry', cast 'new and great lights on history' and revealed the capacity of the Welsh language to reach 'depths that are almost unfathomable to other languages'.[119]

---

[114] NLW 13116B, p. 298; NLW 13119B, pp. 270–2; NLW 13120B, pp. 40–1; NLW 13141A, pp. 26, 30–4; *MAW*, II, p. 61.
[115] NLW 13158A, pp. 152–3.
[116] *CIM*, II, pp. 32–6, Iolo Morganwg to Sir Richard Colt Hoare, 18 August 1797; Richard Suggett, 'Iolo Morganwg: Stonecutter, Builder, and Antiquary' in *Rattleskull Genius*, p. 222.
[117] *MAW*, II, p. 67; *RAEW*, pp. 189–91.
[118] *CIM*, II, p. 653, Iolo Morganwg to William Owen Pughe, 14 February 1805.
[119] *MAW*, I, pp. xvi–xix.

In all his writings Iolo set great store by the Welsh language and its literature, so much so that, as the three-volume *Myvyrian Archaiology* took shape, he assured Owain Myfyr that he was bringing into the public domain 'the greatest curiosities that exist in Europe, perhaps in the whole world'.[120] Iolo's many discourses on his native tongue strongly reflected Herder's view on 'der Genius der Sprache' and he unquestionably regarded it as the cornerstone of nationhood. Although, like Herder, he was less interested in the origin of languages than their evolution, he rejoiced in the purported status of Welsh as the oldest living and literary language in Europe.[121] Iolo knew perfectly well that language and languages had become a burning political issue by his day and that the genius and perhaps even the soul of a nation could be measured by the attributes and status of its native tongue. Painfully aware that the English language was increasingly being considered 'a national treasure' by the literati,[122] he was determined to promote public consciousness of the assets of Welsh. Indeed, he devoted an extraordinary amount of time and energy to preparing essays which maintained that, in antiquity, purity and copiousness, Welsh eclipsed its European rivals:

> . . . during the Middle, or, as they are called, dark ages, I do not find that the Welsh literature was any thing inferior to that of most of our continental neighbours. Thro' all those ages we wrote in our own native language, our own vernaculum, which no other Nation in Europe but ourselves did. We thus not only preserved our language, but absolutely improved without altering it. We cultivated, fix'd its idiom, extended its bounds and its powers by forming legitimate terms and phrase[s] from our own native roots. For all the purpose of the progressive and extending views of the human mind, the process is still going on, slowly indeed, but it crawls on.[123]

Deliberately politicizing the subject, Iolo subverted the traditional image of England as 'civilized' and Wales as 'barbarous' by depicting the Welsh peasantry as a far more literate, moral and humane people than their English counterparts who were still wedded to 'savage rudeness' and barbarity.[124] The Welsh

---

[120] *CIM*, II, p. 289, Iolo Morganwg to Owen Jones (Owain Myfyr), 17 June 1800.
[121] Hans Aarsleff, *The Study of Language in England, 1780–1860* (new edn., London, 1983), p. 148; Caryl Davies, *Adfeilion Babel: Agweddau ar Syniadaeth Ieithyddol y Ddeunawfed Ganrif* (Caerdydd, 2000), pp. 237–9.
[122] Jon Mee, 'Language' in Iain McCalman (ed.), *An Oxford Companion to the Romantic Age: British Culture 1776–1832* (Oxford, 1999), p. 369.
[123] NLW 13120B, p. 181. See also NLW 13098B, pp. 1–78, 177–228; NLW 13121B, pp. 423–30; NLW 13123B, pp. 27–9.
[124] NLW 13089E, p. 324; NLW 13118B, pp. 98–9; NLW 13121B, p. 474; Margaret Mary Rubel, *Savage and Barbarian: Historical Attitudes in the Criticism of Homer and Ossian in Britain, 1760–1800* (Oxford, 1978).

had benefited enormously from having been a province of the Roman empire and subsequently had not been tainted by the consumerism and inequalities which characterized wealthy elites in England. In short, the Welsh excelled their nearest neighbours in self-cultivation, moral taste and common decency. Whereas the English language and its literature had been used to encourage 'the sordid acquisition of wealth' and to trample on the poor and hold them in 'the thraldom of ignorance', the Welsh language had been employed to improve the minds and morals of the Welsh and enable them to pursue truth and knowledge.[125] As the self-appointed representative of the swinish multitude as well as the most authentic druido-bard, Iolo was evidently projecting the present on to the past at a time when libertarians were using new forms of expression. As he ruminated over the unlovely effects of English expansionism and brutishness, he would often return to those values which he cherished:

> The object of True Civilization is to patronize and enforce true morality, Rational Religion, truly beneficient Arts and Sciences, and that Equality which Genuine and properly restrained Liberty demands, to distribute justice, to secure competency to every member of the Community, and to curb with an invincible Bridle the arrogancies and Tyranies of Power, Rank, Title, and illgotten Wealth that at present enslave every part of the world, the whole race of mankind.[126]

All the while, too, Iolo stimulated the imagination by combining fact and fiction, producing vivid narratives and embarking on inspired imaginary leaps. He felt obliged to peddle tales about semi-fictional poets and lyricists like Geraint Fardd Glas, Rhys Goch ap Rhicert and the remarkable Ieuan Fawr ap y Diwlith, an orphan allegedly born on Twmpath Diwlith at Margam, and who reputedly became a wise fount of inspiration for Glamorgan bards. To these shadowy figures he added the names of highly respected icons of the Welsh literary tradition – Taliesin, Aneirin, Myrddin, Llywarch Hen and Catwg Ddoeth – and passed them off either as Glamorgan men or as people who were associated with the kingdom of Siluria.[127] In one striking tale he maintained that the celebrated poet Dafydd ap Gwilym had been born under a hedge in Glamorgan.[128] He also expanded and distorted people's vision of their history by continually concocting bogus material. In preparing documents for *The Myvyrian Archaiology of Wales*, for instance, he realized that 'Brut y Tywysogyon' (The Chronicle of the Princes) contained very little of the history of Glamorgan. He thus surreptitiously recast it and, under the

---

[125] NLW 13121B, pp. 471–2.
[126] NLW 13088E, p. 76.
[127] *Bardic Circles*, chapter 5.
[128] NLW 13139A, pp. 77–80.

name 'Brut Aberpergwm' (Gwentian Chronicle), tailored it to what he believed to be the politico-cultural needs of his county.[129] Iolo spun a seductive web in producing this material and since medieval writers were, as he put it, prone to 'curtail, to amplify, to interpolate, and to alter',[130] he saw no good reason not to follow suit, especially since his additions were designed to celebrate the glories of the past. To inform, to edify, and to entertain were all part of his remit as a nation-building poet and writer.

Even more audacious was the way in which he pressed aphoristic material into service. He often referred to the 'diarheboldeb'[131] (proverbialness) of the Welsh and their age-old fondness for proverbs, maxims, sayings and especially triads. He attributed some of these to wise old owls (several of whom were probably fictitious or semi-fictitious) whom he called 'yr hen ŵr o Regoes' (the old man from Regoes) and 'yr hen Saffin' (old Saffin),[132] but most reflected his own fertile imagination and political agenda. This was especially true of triads. Having previously been transmitted orally, *Trioedd Ynys Prydain* (the Triads of the Isle of Britain) were first transcribed in the mid-thirteenth century and had come to be seen as epitomizing 'the collective wisdom and knowledge bequeathed by the remote past'.[133] Their survival in later times owed a good deal to the assiduous labours of antiquaries like Robert Vaughan, John Jones of Gellilyfdy and Moses Williams. By dint of its terseness, the triad was a valuable mnemonic device, especially in sustaining a substantial corpus of oral lore.[134] Many of them carry inescapable echoes of Rousseau's idea of a social contract as a core pillar of society. No one was more aware than Iolo of the triad's potential for imparting information, cultivating wisdom and inculcating truth. Bardic schools had successfully used the triad as a mnemonic aid and from the early 1790s Iolo had been composing triads which reflected his own views about liberty and justice as well as his growing understanding of human nature. By the time he had been enlisted by Owain Myfyr to contribute to *The Myvyrian Archaiology of Wales* he had coined dozens of them and, having been betrayed (as he put it) by his benefactor, he proceeded to

---

[129] *MAW*, II, pp. 468–582; NLW 13113B, pp. 1–74; G. J. Williams, 'Brut Aberpergwm: A Version of the Chronicle of the Princes' in Stewart Williams (ed.), *Glamorgan Historian, 4* (Cowbridge, 1967), pp. 205–20.

[130] *CIM*, II, p. 333, Iolo Morganwg to Owen Jones (Owain Myfyr), 6 October 1800.

[131] NLW 13102B, p. 26.

[132] Ibid., pp. 27–8.

[133] Rachel Bromwich, *'Trioedd Ynys Prydain' in Welsh Literature and Scholarship* (Cardiff, 1969), p. 6. See also the standard work by eadem (ed.), *Trioedd Ynys Prydein: The Triads of the Island of Britain* (3rd edn., Cardiff, 2006).

[134] NLW 13091E, p. 293; NLW 13141A, pp. 138–9; Williams, *Barddas*, I, p. 107; Morfydd E. Owen, *Y Meddwl Obsesiynol: Traddodiad y Triawd Cyffredinol yn y Gymraeg a'r Myvyrian Archaiology of Wales* (Aberystwyth, 2007).

take revenge by composing many more bogus triads and allowing the unsuspecting Owain Myfyr to publish them in the third volume. Iolo knowingly manipulated and exploited the Welsh triads for political ends. His overriding concern was to foster a genuine national consciousness in which some of the ancient glories of Wales would be its dominant motifs. In his home-made booklets of triads, as well as in *The Myvyrian Archaiology of Wales*, he tampered with existing triads, embellished them with his own politicized view, and composed new ones which redounded to the credit of what he consistently called 'the Nation of Cymmry'.[135] Large numbers of them were ethical triads of 'e[x]quisite sentiment',[136] though 'Whimsical Ned' was also not loath to pen coarse and lewd examples designed to 'shock modern hypocritically-delicate ears'.[137]

In many triads Iolo allowed his growing sense of Anglophobia to take wing. A vengeful man, he had axes to grind with the English and the triad gave him the opportunity to express pretty strident views. He depicted them as boastful, bellicose, mendacious and treacherous in a rancorous battery of aphorisms, of which the following are representative:

Tri pheth goreu pa leiaf o honynt yng Nghymry, Tlodi, Pechod, a Sais.[138]
(Three things the less of them the better in Wales, Poverty, Sin, and an Englishman.)

Tri pheth y sy'n ymborth ar waed, Chwannen, Rhyfelwr cyflog, a Sais.[139]
(Three things which feed on blood, a Flea, a Mercenary, and an Englishman.)

Tri pheth nid oes daw arnynt, clap y felin, Bwmbwr y môr, a chelwydd Sais.[140]
(Three things which never cease, the clack of the mill, the roar of the sea, and the lies of an Englishman.)

These forthright sentiments reflected his own experience of suffering personal slights and insults but also arose from his knowledge of instances of deceit and malevolence by the English in past times. It pained Iolo to read of how the Welsh had been dispossessed by 'bloody-speared intruders' and 'lawless and tyrannical' monarchs who had committed Welsh princes to war, subverted

---

[135] See NLW 13089E, p. 443; NLW 13121B, p. 271; NLW 13101B, p. 149; NLW 13120B, p. 157; NLW 21361B, p. 1.
[136] NLW 13089E, p. 443.
[137] *CIM*, II, p. 691. Iolo Morganwg to Owen Jones (Owain Myfyr), 30 July 1805.
[138] NLW 13124B, p. 306.
[139] Ibid.
[140] Ibid., p. 311.

the ancient patriarchal government, and wrought the most calamitous depredations.[141] Small wonder that he believed that hell was filled to the rafters with kings, priests and thieves. To patriotic dissidents like Iolo, Hanoverian monarchs were known as 'plant Alis, a phlant Alis y Biswail' ('the Brood of Beast-excrement Alis')[142] and it is perhaps as well that Owain Myfyr and William Owen Pughe chose not to publish some of Iolo's most pungent triads. The latter had covered his tracks so well that his co-editors had no inkling that many of the triads were either bogus or heavily embellished. When William Probert came to translate them into English he was so impressed by the courage and steadfastness of the 'free-born Cambrians' that, to him, the triads seemed to 'breathe a spirit of freedom that would not disgrace the polish of the nineteenth century'.[143]

Yet there is abundant evidence that Iolo's brand of cultural nationalism was not simply fuelled by socio-cultural injustices, political displacement and anti-English prejudices. Preserving and nourishing a robust sense of national consciousness was better achieved by enhancing his countrymen's sense of pride in their cultural inheritance. Time and again he reminded them that they, as the oldest occupants of Britain, had once been the undisputed masters of an undivided island.[144] Even though acts of treachery and external incursions had robbed them of their inheritance, all hope of recovering territories had not been lost forever. As long as the bards and other remembrancers kept alive the memory of the nation through triads and verse, there was every reason to believe that the Welsh would redeem themselves. 'Triodd y Cymro' (the Triads of the Welshman) and others of the same ilk clearly set out the required duties:

> Tri pheth y dylai Gymro eu car o flaen dim:
> Cenedl y Cymry, Moesau'r Cymry, ac Iaith y Cymry.[145]
> (Three things a Welshman should love above all else:
> the Welsh nation, the morals of the Welsh, and the Welsh language.)

> Tri pheth a ddylai Gymro farw yn eu plaid:
> ei wlad, ei air da, a'r Gwirionedd ba bynnag y bo.[146]
> (Three things a Welshman should die for:
> his country, his good name, and the Truth wherever it may be.)

---

[141] NLW 21361B, pp. 2, 22.
[142] NLW 13101B, p. 171. See also *CIM*, II, p. 315, Iolo Morganwg to Owen Jones (Owain Myfyr), 26 July 1800.
[143] William Probert (trans.), *The Ancient Laws of Cambria* (London, 1823), p. [1].
[144] See Iolo's 'A Short Review of the Present State of Welsh Manuscripts' in *MAW*, II, pp. ix–xxi.
[145] NLW 13124B, p. 301.
[146] Ibid.

Either in oral or written form, Iolo reckoned that triads were a more valuable mirror to the national past than the 'wretched cuckoo song stuff'[147] peddled by loyalist poets in north Wales.

As Iolo well knew, most of the authentic triads were written down from the thirteenth century onwards, by which time successive military conquests had robbed the Welsh of their ancient freedoms. In his view, the glory years were over and the true bards were hard pressed to defend their national heritage. He railed against the bellicosity of Welsh medieval princes and the 'wild martial sentiments'[148] of the times. In particular he deplored the barbaric behaviour of the princes of Aberffraw and Mathrafal: 'what castrating of brothers, uncles, cousins! What putting out of their eyes! What murdering of such relatives, giving their bodies to the dogs!'[149] No murder was more treacherous than the assassination of 'our last Natural Prince', Llywelyn ap Gruffudd, not least because the subjugation of Gwynedd by 'Edward Longshanks' had broken the spirit of the people and planted within them an 'ignoble species of loyalty' towards the Crown.[150] Iolo also made no bones about his contempt for the 'atrocious principles'[151] on which the medieval church was based. He feared that a compilation of the lies and forgeries of the Church of Rome would prove to be a task too arduous even for a hundred men, 'even should all of them live to the age of old Methuselah'.[152] Popes, abbots and priests were enemies of the truth, famous for their 'shameless swindling' and 'infamous pardoning of murders'.[153] During these 'long, dark and fiery ages'[154] blood was spilled with impunity and it was incomprehensible to him that Iolo Goch, Owain Glyndŵr's bard, should have broken ranks by calling on Sir Roger Mortimer to crush the rebellious Irish by force: 'Pei'r Diawl ai cant ni allasai ganu yn fwy gwaedgar, yn fwy lladdgar, yn fwy rhyfelgar, nag yn fwy anrheithgar' ('If the Devil had sung it he could not have sung more bloodthirstily, more murderously, more belligerently, nor more rapaciously').[155] Even those Catholics who did not thirst for blood became targets for Iolo's ire. Monasticism was 'clogged with loads of Superstition, false philosophy, fabulous History, and vice-producing maxims of morality'.[156] An arch-enemy

---

[147] NLW 21375A, p. 45ᵛ.
[148] NLW 13106B, p. 75.
[149] NLW 13108B, p. 98; NLW 13113B, pp. 101–88.
[150] NLW 13116B, p. 296; NLW 13128A, pp. 484–5.
[151] *CIM*, II, p. 133, Iolo Morganwg to David Thomas, 20 October 1798.
[152] NLW 13116B, p. 299; NLW 21430E, no. 6.
[153] NLW 13116B, p. 163. See also NLW 13153A, p. 173.
[154] NLW 13103B, p. 107; NLW 13097B, p. 288.
[155] BL Add. 14970, f. 68ᵛ. Quoted in David Johnston, 'Iolo Goch and the English: Welsh Poetry and Politics in the Fourteenth Century', *CMCS*, 12 (1986), 89 and n. 77.
[156] NLW 21375A, p. 14ᵛ.

of celibates, he inveighed against cloistered monks whose isolation rendered them as 'useless in the world as it was possible for any one to conceive'.[157]

Fortunately, so Iolo believed, genuine bards had held firm during these dangerous times. In spite of his genocidal edict, Edward I had failed to massacre all of them, and the bravest had continued to resist the machinations of the 'vicegerential God of Rome', flout 'Romish superstitions' and preach liberty and peace.[158] Through their poetry they chronicled the glorious history of the Welsh, mourned departed heroes, including Owain Glyndŵr, 'the greatest of the greats' ('y mwyaf o'n mawrion')[159] and ensured that the bardic tradition was the most reliable guardian of truth.[160]

One of the most interesting features of Iolo's grand version of the Welsh past was his view of the Acts of Union of 1536–43. Unlike previous historians he was convinced that it had not been enacted or implemented in the best interests of the Welsh. Determined not to allow received wisdom about the benefits of political and administrative assimilation to pass unchallenged, he became the first historian to declare publicly that union had been seriously damaging to Welsh culture because the notorious 'language clause' of 1536 had deliberately discriminated against the Welsh language.[161] Cynically, but probably rightly, believing that 'Gov.^t can always engage the superior classes in its designs',[162] he argued that the Welsh gentry had colluded with the Tudor government in seeking to snuff out all languages in Britain except one:

> . . . it was not safe or politic to suffer the Welsh language to live; the use of it was discouraged, and all that could decently, and with saving-appearances, be done, was attempted, to suppress and annihilate it.[163]

Romantics like Iolo were acutely aware of the significance of territorial divisions, linguistic frontiers or corridors which struggled for definition,[164] and he castigated the Tudors for arbitrarily depositing Welsh-speaking parishes on

---

[157] NLW 13112B, p. 142.
[158] NLW 13089E, pp. 439–40.
[159] NLW 13106B, pp. 69–70.
[160] NLW 13097B, p. 239.
[161] Geraint H. Jenkins, '"Taphy-land Historians" and the Union of England and Wales 1536–2007', *Journal of Irish and Scottish Studies*, 1, no. 2 (2008), 1–27.
[162] NLW 13089E, p. 264. He also maintained: 'How little are the Welsh Nation or Welsh Literature indebted to the superior Classes of their Country.' Ibid.
[163] *MAW*, I, pp. [ix]–x. See also his forthright comments in drafts of the preface to the first volume of *The Myvyrian Archaiology*. NLW 13089E, pp. 264–73; NLW 13104B, pp. 119–29; NLW 13112B, pp. 11–36.
[164] Claire Lamont and Michael Rossington (eds.), *Romanticism's Debatable Lands* (Basingstoke, 2007).

the wrong side of the border with England.[165] Even though he recognized that the translation of the scriptures into Welsh had brought countless blessings, in post-Elizabethan times Welsh landowners had treated the native culture with flagrant disregard and successive governments had sought to 'uncivilize, to brutalize'[166] the Welsh by promoting the use of the English language in civil and church life. He was also of course not unaware of the fact that 'the great change in our political condition'[167] had made the Welsh disturbingly inactive in the field of radical politics and ill-informed about their nationhood. With a touch of irony, he enquired: 'Is not Wales conspicuously the least turbulent part of the British Dominions at this very day?'[168]

The nationalism which Iolo espoused, though it also possessed a radical cutting edge, was cultural in both origin and content. Aware that so many of the elements which made the Welsh a distinctive people were 'hastening daily into the land of oblivion', he was eager to ensure that those components were rescued and 'fixed in the national memory'.[169] This could only be done effectively by establishing nation-building institutions which would underpin, preserve and foster the ethnic identity of the Welsh, their language, literature, history and popular traditions:

> Strong traits of National character derive their existence from the peculiar Genius and Influence of National Institutions that in their tendencies guard and perpetuate in a peculiar manner certain dispositions of humanity and annihilate, or at least greatly suppress, others.[170]

With this in mind, he identified the pressing need for a national library, a learned academy, a college, and a bardic powerhouse made up of the Gorsedd and the eisteddfod.

The case for establishing a central repository to preserve and protect records relating to Wales had been made as early as the mid-seventeenth century. In 1641 Richard Lloyd of Esclus in Denbighshire, Attorney General for north Wales, had called for an institution to which legal records could be sent. More than a century later, two of the most active Morris brothers – Lewis and Richard – had highlighted the need to safeguard the literary and historical material which they had assembled and deposited in the Welsh School in

---

[165] Geraint H. Jenkins, Richard Suggett and Eryn M. White, 'The Welsh Language in Early Modern Wales' in Jenkins (ed.), *The Welsh Language before the Industrial Revolution*, pp. 56–7.
[166] NLW 13118B, p. 98.
[167] *MAW*, I, p. vi.
[168] NLW 13097B, p. 293. According to Jim Smyth, the Welsh 'scored handsomely for innocuousness'. Jim Smyth, *The Making of the United Kingdom, 1660–1800* (Harlow, 2001), p. 156.
[169] *CIM*, II, p. 277, Iolo Morganwg to Owen Jones (Owain Myfyr), 15 April 1800; NLW 13121B, p. 309.
[170] NLW 13097B, p. 293.

London.[171] But Iolo could lay claim to being the first to make an overriding case for setting up a truly national library in Wales (presumably in Glamorgan) to house the precious literary treasures which had been lovingly transcribed and transmitted down the centuries and which constituted 'the living memory of the people'.[172] In an undated scribbled note found on the dorse of a publication relating to the state lottery, he wrote: 'National Library, when founded in Wales [I] will give my MSS to it with an injunction that permission be given in the library to copy any thing, but not out of it.'[173]

Iolo valued his unpublished transcripts and documents beyond all price and vowed not to part with them until his death. He confessed that the task of transcribing with 'great care and fidelity' dozens of volumes relating to the history of Wales and Glamorgan had been 'the greatest and longest labour of my life'.[174] He also claimed that few private libraries had as many printed books as he had of manuscripts and in 1811 he informed the philosopher David Williams that his cottage was so heavily crammed with books and manuscripts that 'there is no room left for a single original idea to put forth its bud'.[175] Indeed, in his eightieth year he boasted that his collection was 'by far the greatest in number, and the most refined in Wales and in the whole of the Isle of Britain and in the whole world'.[176] Iolo was no stranger to hyperbole even in his dotage and he became used to fending off booksellers who urged him to publish his gems and not allow them to be 'food for cobweb & for rust'.[177] He learned a hard lesson late in life when he loaned some of his precious manuscripts to clerics associated with the Cambrian Society. To his dismay, the hoard was inadvertently mislaid and although he was hampered by severe rheumatism he set off on foot to south-west Wales 'with a resolution and perseverance worthy of an Argonaut'[178] to recover his treasures. The future of his collections preyed on his mind and he feared that his children would not be able to make effective use of them 'beyond that of privately amusing themselves, and of converting them into Hobby Horses . . . that will run with them wildly'.[179] In the event, however, his son Taliesin proved to be a dutiful curator, though after his death in 1847 it was more by accident than design

---

[171] David Jenkins, *A Refuge in Peace and War: The National Library of Wales to 1952* (Aberystwyth, 2002), pp. 2–3.
[172] Trevor Fishlock, *In This Place: The National Library of Wales* (Aberystwyth, 2007), p. 11.
[173] NLW 21426E, no. 1. See also *CIM*, II, pp. 610–11, Iolo Morganwg to Owen Jones (Owain Myfyr), 26 June 1804.
[174] NLW 21410E, no. 44.
[175] *CIM*, III, p. 45, Iolo Morganwg to David Williams, 8 January 1811.
[176] Ibid., III, p. 759, Iolo Morganwg to Taliesin Williams, 4 February 1826.
[177] Ibid., III, p. 32, Evan Williams to Iolo Morganwg, 19 September 1810.
[178] Ibid., III, p. 585, Iolo Morganwg to Taliesin Williams, 14 March 1821; *RAEW*, p. 125.
[179] NLW 21413E, no. 21.

that the Iolo archive eventually found its way, in two separate portions, to the National Library of Wales in Aberystwyth in the twentieth century.

In pursuing his ideals Iolo also realized that his formidable knowledge and eclectic interests would benefit from having an institution, dedicated to the preservation of language, folk culture and customs, which would provide a robust ethnocultural foundation for nationhood. Late in life, when he was seventy-three, he expressed his desire to set up a Welsh Corresponding Academy, modelled on the Académie des Inscriptions et Belles-Lettres, whose remit would be to bring together poets, historians, antiquaries, linguists and folklorists to cultivate the Welsh language, study history, music, folk tales, popular customs, agricultural practices and much else.[180] Having experienced the frustrations of working alone, he had come to appreciate the advantages of collaborative research and writing,[181] and to believe that a learned society devoted to the study of the arts and the humanities could stiffen pride in Welshness by bringing it to the attention of mainstream intellectual culture. Robert Southey and Sharon Turner were just two among many prominent authors who had implored him to preserve 'the stores of tradition' associated with the Welsh past which, in the imaginative climate of Romanticism, were likely to inspire national renewal.[182]

The Welsh language and its preservation were absolutely central to Iolo's vision of nationhood and his far-seeing plans for the Welsh Corresponding Academy revealed a heightened awareness of the merits of a spoken and written tongue which he believed to be 'nobly powerful and grandly beautiful'.[183] Nine of every ten persons living in Wales spoke Welsh in Iolo's day and their common linguistic inheritance meant that they had a clear sense of themselves as being Welsh.[184] Striking advances in literacy and book-reading had occurred during the latter half of the eighteenth century and Iolo himself penned glowing accounts of the development of the Welsh book trade. But he was also aware that urban and industrial developments, as well as the effects of puritan Dissent and evangelicalism, were a potentially powerful threat to the task of recovering and celebrating native culture and turning it into a profoundly national and perhaps subversive cause.

In this respect Iolo was interested in what Anthony Smith has referred to as 'vernacular mobilization'.[185] Over the course of the eighteenth century an

---

[180] *CIM*, III, p. 564, Iolo Morganwg to David Richards (Dewi Silin), 26 December 1820; NLW 13129A, pp. 114–15.
[181] *CIM*, II, pp. 143–6, Iolo Morganwg to David Thomas, 20 October 1798.
[182] *RAEW*, pp. 89–90.
[183] NLW 13129A, p. 109.
[184] Jenkins, Suggett and White, 'The Welsh Language in Early Modern Wales', pp. 45–62.
[185] Anthony Smith, 'The "Golden Age" and National Renewal' in Geoffrey Hosking and George Schöpflin (eds.), *Myths and Nationhood* (London, 1997), p. 56.

extraordinary amount of work had been undertaken in the fields of Welsh orthography and lexicography. Iolo himself had rubbed shoulders with Thomas Richards, John Walters and William Owen Pughe, and he shared their obsession with words and their meaning. It is worth noting that new Welsh words with politico-cultural significance were appearing: *gwladgarwch* (love of country), *cydraddoldeb* (equality) and *cenedligrwydd* (nationality) entered public discourse in 1776, 1797 and 1798 respectively.[186] By 1806 Iolo estimated that his personal collection of Welsh words numbered 'upwards of 25,000'[187] and some of the words which he coined – *brodorol* (native), *cyfundrefn* (system), *llenyddiaeth* (literature) and *ieitheg* (philology) – were pregnant with possibilities for a nation builder.[188] It also amused him to invite monoglot English speakers to pronounce tongue-twisters like *anghyflechtwynedigaetholion* and *gogyflechtywynedigaetholion*.[189] Since in his view current orthographical practices were blatantly flawed, he believed that the Welsh Academy could drive out the archaisms and barbarisms which were currently in vogue. His long-running feud with William Owen Pughe was partly provoked by the latter's bizarre ideas on word derivation and his execrable orthography which, much later, were reckoned by Sir John Morris-Jones to have been a colossal waste of time and effort.[190]

Iolo envisaged that the Welsh Academy would supervise the adoption and incorporation of words into the standard literary language. But it would also exercise control over the preservation of dialectal vocabulary, in which Iolo was especially interested. In jocular vein, he maintained that during his many itineraries through Wales he had made a habit of keeping 'all my ears open to every word and sound' of the provincial speech of 'Hwyntwyr' (South Walians) and 'Deudneudwyr' (North Walians), even to the extent of noting the peculiarities of 'Gwaedcwn Gwent' (Gwentian bloodhounds), 'Cŵn Edeirnion' (hounds of Edeirnion) and 'Moch Môn' (Anglesey swine) among many others.[191] He was the first to identify and classify four main Welsh dialects – Gwentian (Glamorgan, Monmouthshire and parts of Breconshire), Dimetian (the rest of south Wales), Powysian (mid-Wales) and Venedotian (north Wales)

---

[186] Geraint H. Jenkins, *Facts, Fantasy and Fiction: The Historical Vision of Iolo Morganwg* (Aberystwyth, 1997), p. 15.
[187] *CIM*, II, p. 743, Iolo Morganwg to William Owen Pughe, 12 January 1806.
[188] Prys Morgan, 'Dyro Olau ar dy Eiriau', *Taliesin*, 70 (1990), 38–45; idem, 'A Private Space: Autobiography and Individuality in Eighteenth- and Early Nineteenth-Century Wales' in R. R. Davies and Geraint H. Jenkins (eds.), *From Medieval to Modern Wales: Historical Essays in Honour of Kenneth O. Morgan and Ralph A. Griffiths* (Cardiff, 2004), pp. 171–3.
[189] Richard M. Crowe, 'Diddordebau Ieithyddol Iolo Morganwg' (unpublished University of Wales Ph.D. thesis, 1988), p. 199.
[190] Carr, *William Owen Pughe*, pp. 92–5. Iolo described Pughe's innovation as 'a new, capricious, and very cacophonous orthography'. NLW 21319A, p. 27.
[191] *CIM*, II, p. 693, Iolo Morganwg to William Owen Pughe, 15 August 1805.

– and he was so concerned about the future preservation and well-being of dialectal variations that he urged the Gwyneddigion Society to divert some of the prize money earmarked for annual eisteddfodau as sponsorship for a county-based campaign, to be undertaken over a six-year period, devoted to the collection of provincial dialects.[192] But his pleas fell on deaf ears among the 'becockneyed Welsh'[193] and their stubbornness convinced him that only a well-led, cohesive body like a Welsh academy could harness this venture effectively. Richard M. Crowe has described his plans as 'the first ever blueprint for collective corpus planning on behalf of the Welsh language'[194] and his labours in this field deserve attention. Of special importance was his interest in the radical potential to be found in the culture of common people, the vernacular of lower-class inhabitants with whom he was proud to be associated. Two of his acquaintances, Joseph Ritson and Thomas Spence, deliberately used the vulgar, unsophisticated and often subversive language of common people in order to register their disapproval of standard metropolitan English.[195] Likewise, in his collections of Welsh words, phrases and sayings, the liberty-loving stonemason included unsettling examples of the kind of plebeian language not used in mainstream scholarly circles but which could find a place in an academy designed to preserve the language of the people. Among them were:

Twlc y moch [pigsty], the prebend house at Llandaff
Lleng o foch [a legion of pigs], the prebends in their houses
Bardd y Brenin . . . an ass
Nyth y brain [a crow's nest] Rhydychen [Oxford]
Y Gwr o Dy'n y Dommen [the man from the dunghouse] Brenin [King].[196]

Iolo also expected the Welsh Academy to assemble and stockpile evidence of popular culture, work which reflected his great affection for rural life and customs, and subject it to thorough investigation. He believed that an infant nation needed to understand its communal past and to appreciate the rich array

---

[192] Ibid., II, p. 271, Iolo Morganwg to Owen Jones (Owain Myfyr), 10 April 1800; ibid., II, pp. 279–80, Iolo Morganwg to William Owen Pughe, 15 April 1800; Richard Crowe, 'Iolo Morganwg and the Dialects of Welsh' in *Rattleskull Genius*, pp. 315–31.
[193] *CIM*, II, p. 735, Iolo Morganwg to William Owen Pughe, 9 January 1806.
[194] Crowe, 'Iolo Morganwg and the Dialects of Welsh', p. 331.
[195] Olivia Smith, *The Politics of Language 1791–1819* (Oxford, 1986), p. 3; Marilyn Butler, 'Romanticism in England' in Porter and Teich (eds.), *Romanticism in National Context*, p. 47; Susan Manly, *Language, Custom and Nation in the 1790s* (Aldershot, 2007), chapter 2.
[196] NLW 13091E, pp. 97, 102–3. Iolo believed that whereas the English language was a vehicle for 'false principles and mere conceits', the Welsh language expressed 'real Truth and Nature'.

of ceremonies, customs and symbols which were part of the collective memory. The notion of the 'imagined community' – hard-working labourers, devout wives and innocent children dwelling in whitewashed cottages and living happy and independent lives – was worth preserving by a body which served as the guardian and transmitter of myths, symbols and legends.[197] Iolo was aware of the pan-European interest in plebeian culture and was particularly familiar with studies like John Brand's *Observations on Popular Antiquities* (1777) and Joseph Strutt's *Sports and Pastimes of the People of England* (1801). He was also interested in the supernatural – Elijah Waring was regaled with many tales of spectres, ghosts and fairies[198] – and he bought almanacs, broadsheets, broadsides, chapbooks and ballads by the dozen. Inspired perhaps by Robert Burns, from the mid-1790s he became preoccupied with national epics and national songs.[199] Although he had an unpleasantly raucous singing voice, he had a good ear for music and became the first serious collector of Welsh folk songs.[200] But rescuing and preserving material of this kind from 'that damnation with which they are threatened by Methodism',[201] as well as from the effects of rural depopulation and industrial and technological advances, were too onerous a challenge for an impoverished artisan. However much he enjoyed assembling data on festivals, folk songs, dances, pastimes, processions, sports and all other kinds of popular customs and festivities, Iolo knew that only collaborative research and archival work by a reputable academy could save a swiftly vanishing part of the nation's memory.

As is well known, Iolo's dreams of establishing a national library and a Welsh academy remained unfulfilled until the twentieth century. A Welsh college, however, arrived much sooner, though not perhaps with the kind of national-cum-radical mission that Iolo had envisaged. In 1828, two years after Iolo's death, St David's College, Lampeter – founded by Bishop Thomas Burgess, a sworn enemy of anti-trinitarians – became the first degree-awarding

---

[197] NLW 13123B, p. 203. For examples, noted by Iolo, of traditional customs and pastimes in Glamorgan, see NLW 13146A, pp. 208–9, 452. For cases of longevity, see NLW 13112B, p. 165; NLW 13116B, pp. 142–3; NLW 13152A, pp. 425–31, 435–9, 445, 453–4. For Iolo and the supposed 'suavity' of Glamorgan, see Williams: *IM*, pp. 35–72, and, for the general background, see Allan James, *Diwylliant Gwerin Morgannwg* (Llandysul, 2002).

[198] *RAEW*, chapter 5.

[199] NLW 13146A, p. 435; NLW 13221E, p. 93; *CIM*, II, pp. 452–5, Iolo Morganwg to William Owen Pughe, 19 December 1802; Daniel Huws, 'Iolo Morganwg and Traditional Music' in *Rattleskull Genius*, pp. 333–56.

[200] Daniel Huws, *Caneuon Llafar Gwlad ac Iolo a'i Fath* (Cymdeithas Alawon Gwerin Cymru, 1993); Mary-Ann Constantine, 'Chasing Fragments: Iolo, Ritson and Robin Hood' in Sally Harper and Wyn Thomas (eds.), *Cynheiliaid y Gân / Bearers of Song: Essays in Honour of Phyllis Kinney and Meredydd Evans* (Cardiff, 2007), pp. 53–8.

[201] Quoted in Lewis: *IM*, p. 60. Salutations, blessings and sayings were, according to Iolo, losing their currency as a result of the work of moralists: 'Puritanism began the work, and methodism finishd it of exploding these expressions as relics of popery'. NLW 21431E, p. 48.

institution in Wales. When the foundation-stone was laid six years earlier, Iolo, who bore no malice towards Burgess by that stage, praised his 'highly laudable exertion' in bringing higher education to Wales.[202] Yet, he could hardly have been satisfied. Wales had long been deprived of institutes of learning and lagged far behind its Celtic cousins. Dissenting academies were too small to meet demands for further education and, although they had nurtured the careers of some remarkably fine international philosophers, they catered for only a tiny proportion of the populace. As for the traditional universities in England, neither Oxford nor Cambridge saw it as part of their remit to serve the cause of learning in Wales. At the beginning of the eighteenth century Edward Lhuyd had referred to Oxford as 'the fountaine, from whence all the Learning of our Land flows',[203] but by Iolo's day widespread disaffection was expressed about its failure to provide avenues of advancement and high-quality tuition for Welsh-born students. Indeed, basing his judgement on the behaviour of university-trained clerics he had encountered, Iolo thought of it as a den of iniquity.[204] Less contentious was his belief, shared by many autodidacts, that the sterile curriculum of the traditional universities was deeply unsatisfactory. He thus made it a habit to avoid pedants who sheltered in cobwebbed cloisters.

We need not be surprised, therefore, that Iolo's ideal institute of higher learning was meant to provide a more challenging alternative by widening the syllabus, promoting supple intellectual inquiry, and opening minds to the politico-cultural aspirations of the young within the context of Romantic and enlightened thinking. By reading voraciously, Iolo had steeped himself in contemporary intellectual thought as well as in the lively political radicalism of the times, and he was thus eager to afford opportunities for the lower ranks of society to study subjects close to his heart. These might include the myth of origins, the roots of European civilization, imperialism and colonialism, the arts of peace, Celtomania and Indomania, as well as the Welsh bardic system, the growth of national sentiment and every other subject which ran counter to the philistinism of the age. Iolo had nothing but scorn for those who 'never look up to the skies where the original, whose reflections or shadow

---

[202] *CIM*, III, p. 671, Iolo Morganwg to Walter Davies (Gwallter Mechain), 23 September 1823. For the background, see Geraint H. Jenkins, 'Thomas Burgess, Iolo Morganwg and the Black Spot', *Ceredigion*, XV, no. 3 (2007), 13–36.
[203] NLW 309E, p. 134, Hugh Thomas to Edward Lhuyd, 9 July 1704.
[204] NLW 13174A, p. 2ᵛ. See also R. J. W. Evans, 'Wales and Oxford: Historical Aspects, National and International' in Charles-Edwards and Evans (eds.), *Wales and the Wider World*, pp. 118–38.

they endeavour to grasp at, appears in the light of self-evidence'.[205] In Iolo's national institution of learning one suspects that there would have been room even for provocative wishful thinking, make-believe, castle-building-in-the-air, and the kind of creative artistry which later made fools of accredited scholars in Victorian and Edwardian times.

Iolo did not regard Celticism very highly, partly because of his animus against Irish Catholicism and Scottish Presbyterianism, but mostly because, ironically, he had a low opinion of Macpherson's forgeries and misgivings about the quality of learning in seminaries in Gaelic fastnesses.[206] He preferred to draw inspiration from the Orient and from the works of Sir William Jones, whom he regarded as 'the greatest master of languages in the World'[207] as well as one of the most ardent political liberals and humane benefactors. Although Jones had died in 1794 his precepts lived on, and his capacity to make unexpected linguistic and literary comparisons and bring together different disciplines in innovatory ways appealed strongly to Iolo.[208] In particular, he perceived in Jones's work points of contact between empire-building and nation-building. Moreover, his correspondence with William Owen Pughe and his own private jottings clearly reveal that Jones and others had opened his eyes to the supposed affinities between Sanskrit, the mother of ancient tongues, and Welsh.[209] Iolo read in translation works on Hindu learning and philosophy and marvelled at the rich wisdom of Hindu culture. Indeed, he referred to the Hindus as 'our sister nation'.[210]

Increasingly after 1795 Iolo empathized with the civilizing virtues of Hindu culture and learned a good deal about the extent to which Indian and Asiatic nationalism had enhanced people's knowledge of their cultural heritage and embedded within them a profound distaste for colonialism and slavery. He

---

[205] NLW 13097B, p. 286. Iolo's phrasing was echoed by Lawrence Stone in his description of the imaginative historian as a parachutist who 'floats down from the clouds, surveying the whole panorama of the countryside, but from too great a height to see anything in detail very clearly'. Lawrence Stone, *The Past and the Present Revisited* (London, 1987), p. 8. See also Geraint H. Jenkins, '"The Taffy-land historians have hitherto been sad dogs for the most part": Iolo Morganwg the Historian', *Morgannwg*, LII (2008), 5–29

[206] He claimed that Macpherson should have been pilloried as 'a perjurer of intentional deceit'. NLW 13091E, p. 300. See Mary-Ann Constantine, 'Ossian in Wales and Brittany' in Howard Gaskill (ed.), *The Reception of Ossian in Europe* (London, 2004), pp. 67–90.

[207] NLW 13112B, p. 293. See also NLW 13158A, pp. 139–40.

[208] Michael J. Franklin, 'Sir William Jones, the Celtic Revival and the Oriental Renaissance' in Carruthers and Rawes (eds.), *English Romanticism and the Celtic World*, pp. 20–37; idem, 'The Colony Writes Back: Brutus, Britanus and the Advantages of an Oriental Ancestry' in Damian Walford Davies and Lynda Pratt (eds.), *Wales and the Romantic Imagination* (Cardiff, 2007), pp. 13–42. For the wider background, see Nigel Leask, *British Romantic Writers and the East: Anxieties of Empire* (Cambridge, 1992).

[209] *CIM*, II, pp. 291–7, Iolo Morganwg to William Owen Pughe, 17 June 1800.

[210] NLW 13129A, pp. 395–7; Davies, *Adfeilion Babel*, pp. 310–11; *CIM*, II, p. 295, Iolo Morganwg to William Owen Pughe, 17 June 1800.

yearned for the day when colleges would be established in the countries of Europe, including Wales, to study the ancient civilizations and languages, and to instil into gifted young people the inestimable benefits of benevolence, justice and peace as reflected in orientalist literature.[211] He was thrilled to hear of the Hindu College established in 1816 to educate the Calcutta elite about their rich cultural heritage, but feared that such a giant step would never be taken by warmongering nations closer to home:

> A College has lately been Instituted at Calcutta for the acquisition, and study of the Ancient Indias, and other Asiatic Languages; where will Such an establishment appear in Europe for the study of the Ancient Languages of Europe? Never! For money, and money only, is the great object of acquisition. Pluto the God of Riches is adored by one half of the Christian World (Blasphemously So nicknamed) and Mars the God of War by the other.[212]

Although Iolo graciously extended his good wishes to the founding fathers of the college at Lampeter when its foundation-stone was laid in 1822, there is no doubt that he had little faith in the readiness of an Anglican institution either to hearken to the wisdom of the Orient or serve as a major centre of national studies in Wales.

The national institution which was closest to Iolo's heart, however, was the Gorsedd of the Bards of the Isle of Britain. As we have seen, it had been founded in 1792, in the same year as the London Corresponding Society, and had been used by its founder as a political as well as a cultural tool. On his return to Glamorgan, however, and for the rest of his life, Iolo was determined to ensure that accredited druidic bards, whose ancestors after all had figured among the most ancient inhabitants of Britain, should be seen as playing a pivotal role in the development of the Welsh national tradition. Even when furious magistrates closed down his Gorseddau and placed him under constant surveillance he remained active and, once the Napoleonic Wars had ceased, he reconstituted his 'collegiate association of bards'[213] to suit his political and nationalist agenda. In sonorous didactic odes and colourful prose works he dilated on the bardic mythology and the manner in which the bardic tradition had survived through 'the winternight length of a dark age'[214] into the modern era and become the perfect forum for radical idealism and national aspiration. The ritual aspect, publicized at the solstices and equinoxes, was strengthened. Proclamation scrolls and colourful bardic gatherings within a more readily

---

[211] NLW 13121B, pp. 480–1; NLW 13159A, p. 149.
[212] NLW 13121B, p. 482.
[213] *CIM*, II, p. 606, Iolo Morganwg to Robert Macfarlan, 6 June 1804.
[214] NLW 13089E, p. 274.

identifiable Gorsedd circle, complete with a covenant stone and portal stones, provided the context for ceremonies in which qualified candidates were admitted, a sword unsheathed and sheathed, and recitations – on pressing national issues – declaimed in prose and song. Allegorical codes, symbols and maxims became part of the institution. *Peithynen* was the term he used for a four-sided billet or piece of wood which served as a writing surface on which words in the special bardic alphabet were inscribed and inserted in an upright wooden frame in order to allow each to be rotated.[215] The logo of the Gorsedd became the mystic sign (*nod cyfrin*), which represented the ineffable name of God and the attributes of love, justice and truth. A wealth of triads, too, were at hand in the third volume of *The Myvyrian Archaiology of Wales* to express integral components of Welsh nationality. Apart from the ritual aspects, the Gorsedd was expected to preserve and promote bardic learning according to the sciences of divinity, wisdom and courtesy, and to dedicate itself to the 'remembrance and preservation of every praiseworthy man and nation, and every event of the ages, and every natural wonder' ('a chôv a chadw ar bob moliannus ar wr a chenedyl; a phob dichwain amserau; a phob rhyveddawd anianawl').[216] It was duty-bound, too, to implement justice and the judgement of law, and to use its best offices to reform and improve the laws of the nation.

How far the symbolism and public ceremonial of the Gorsedd caught the public imagination during the early nineteenth century is impossible to tell. But its future was more or less assured when, in the most peculiar circumstances, it coupled itself with the provincial eisteddfodau. From around 1810 a small group of 'offeiriaid llengar' (literary parsons) set themselves the task of Cymricizing the established church and promoting things Welsh by hosting eisteddfodau under the banner of Cambrian Societies in the four ancient divisions of Wales.[217] These clergymen persuaded Bishop Thomas Burgess to host a public meeting in Carmarthen on 28 October 1818 in order to discuss how best to preserve the 'Antient British literature, poetical, historical, antiquarian, sacred and moral'.[218] Iolo was invited to this Anglican convention and the principal outcome of its deliberations was the first provincial eisteddfod, held at the Ivy Bush hotel, Carmarthen, on 8–10 July 1819, a so-called 'Cambrian Olympiad' which Burgess was determined to turn into an Anglican festival.[219] Burgess, who had made a poor fist of learning Welsh, had been led to believe that the old Welsh stonemason had drawn in his radical horns and was fit to

---

[215] NLW 13087E, pp. 15–25; NLW 13093E, pp. 155–74, 183–4.
[216] Williams, *Barddas*, I, pp. 399, 401.
[217] Bedwyr Lewis Jones, *Yr Hen Bersoniaid Llengar* ([Penarth], [1963]).
[218] NLW 1949E, unpaginated. See Geraint H. Jenkins, 'The Unitarian Firebrand, the Cambrian Society and the Eisteddfod' in *Rattleskull Genius*, pp. 269–92.
[219] NLW 1860B; *Carmarthen Journal*, 9 July 1819; *The Cambrian*, 17 July 1819; *Seren Gomer*, 28 July 1819, 229–35.

serve as an adjudicator and critic at the proceedings. Not for the first time in his life, however, the wily and unpredictable Iolo stole the show. To the delight of the assembled dignitaries, he delivered a rousing speech in which he celebrated the significance of the 'ancient and druidical learning' in the historic town of Carmarthen.[220] Thrilled by his oratory, the audience gave him a heartfelt standing ovation. Then, during the prize-winning ceremonies, Iolo took Burgess completely by surprise by pinning a white ribbon to his arm, thereby admitting him to the druidic fold. Although seething inwardly, Burgess kept his composure. On the final day, however, the Welsh Bard wrongfooted him once more by unexpectedly holding a Gorsedd ceremony in the hotel gardens. Dressed in his druidic finery, Iolo the officiating bard began initiating new bards, including Dissenters of a radical stamp, and celebrating the principles of liberty and rationalism. Burgess was incandescent and urged Iolo to dispense with the rituals and curtail such 'improprieties' at once.[221] But the damage – from the Anglican viewpoint – had already been done. Iolo had successfully hijacked the occasion and married off the Gorsedd of the Bards of the Isle of Britain to the eisteddfod movement. By the mid-Victorian period the Gorsedd and the eisteddfod had established themselves as integral components of Welsh national consciousness.

But how successfully did Iolo transmit his own precocious sense of nationhood and radical values to others in his own day? Those who knew the 'Welsh Bard' personally and hung on his every word were left in no doubt about the importance he attached to 'patriotism' and 'nationality'. Antiquaries like Sir Richard Colt Hoare and Richard Fenton visited him and were entranced by his desire to cultivate national pride by mythologizing the past. Benjamin Malkin, one of his greatest admirers, found him so compelling that he devoted a whole section of his two-volume survey of south Wales to his life story and ideals.[222] The well-regarded antiquary and archaeologist William Cunnington and the Hebrew scholar and orientalist Daniel Guildford Wait sought his advice on Welsh cultural matters, and printers and publishers urged him, as the 'only living chronicler of the Principality', to share his knowledge and secrets with the reading public.[223] The philosopher David Williams pestered him for literary and historical information, Justice George Hardinge looked to him for guidance on bardic affairs, and a posse of literary clerics, who shared his eagerness to cultivate a sense of nationality, resolved to bring the Welsh

---

[220] NLW 21430E, no. 15.
[221] Cardiff 3.82, Thomas Burgess to Edward Davies, 25 August 1819.
[222] Malkin, *The Scenery, Antiquities, and Biography, of South Wales*, I, pp. 195–204.
[223] *CIM*, II, pp. 628–9, William Cunnington to Iolo Morganwg, 21 September 1804; ibid., III, p. 125, Daniel Guildford Wait to Iolo Morganwg, 16 September 1812; ibid., II, pp. 872–6, Richard Rees to Iolo Morganwg, 22 August 1809.

language, its history and culture to the attention of English-speaking prelates in Wales and to incorporate in their own works Iolo's vision and sensibilities.[224]

In spite of his good intentions and inflated ambitions, however, Iolo's own forays into print were few. He was not bereft of publishing outlets – he knew Joseph Johnson and Evan Williams well – but he experienced the utmost difficulty in turning disconnected pieces of prose into a logical and readable text. He had learned from bitter experience that the financial rewards from publishing were not great and he was also apprehensive about the critical reception that works which appeared under his name might receive. Hypersensitive to criticism, he was prone, as William Owen Pughe observed, to aim 'at a perfection that is unattainable'.[225] Completing literary projects proved to be an enormous strain on his time and health and, deep down, he probably realized that his most cherished undertakings would never materialize. His history of Welsh bardism remained 'in a state of suspension' and *Cyfrinach Beirdd Ynys Prydain* did not emerge from the press until three years after his death.[226] Without Owain Myfyr's exertions on his behalf and periodic subventions from the Royal Literary Fund, Iolo floundered, and his reputation as a writer with radical and nationalist credentials was therefore largely based on his contribution to *The Myvyrian Archaiology of Wales*.

That Iolo was happier handling manuscripts than completing printed books cut across cultural trends at the time. He himself recognized that print was booming in Wales and that the extent of book-buying and book-reading was greater than ever before:

> We have more than a thousand printed books in the [Welsh] Language, probably near two thousand. We have ten presses at least in Wales employed in printing Welsh books, besides many that are printed in London. It has three or four periodical publications, or magazines, and is now equal if not superior to what English literature was in the Reigns of Elizabeth and James, everything considered . . . There can be no doubt but that the preservation and retention of the Welsh Language will be the greatest blessing of all others in Wales.[227]

---

[224] In response, Iolo often transferred bogus texts or exaggerated the significance of his material to correspondents. For example, David Williams was advised to include in his works 'short historical anecdotes of the arts of peace', while George Hardinge was enjoined to heed the 'very sublime mythological account given by our ancient bards . . . of the origin of human language'. *CIM*, II, pp. 525–6, Iolo Morganwg to [David] Williams, 6 August 1803; ibid., II, p. 601, Iolo Morganwg to George Hardinge, 29 May 1804.

[225] Ibid., II, p. 512, William Owen Pughe to Iolo Morganwg, 30 June 1803.

[226] Ibid., II, p. 66, Iolo Morganwg to Mary Barker, 26 March [1798]. For printed proposals for the publication of 'The History of the British Bards', see NLW 21400C, nos. 10, 10a–c. Iolo's manuscript copy of *Cyfrinach Beirdd Ynys Prydain* (1829) is in NLW 21320B–21321B. He had also hoped to incorporate an account of the bardic institute in a second edition of *Poems, Lyric and Pastoral*. NLW 21332B, p. iii.

[227] NLW 13121B, pp. 474–5. See also *MAW*, I, p. xv.

In his preface to *The Myvyrian Archaiology of Wales* he emphasized that a sense of nationality stimulated learning, book-reading and 'genuine civilization', and his heightened awareness of the significance of books in breeding a new generation of patriotic Welsh people must have aggravated his frustration over his inability to get his own voluminous material into a fit state for publication.[228]

Political repression also played its part in restricting his opportunities. Although Iolo could move around freely, he was closely watched by anti-Jacobins and often derided for his Welsh 'warmth'. But the London Welsh rallied to his cause. During his days in London, William Owen Pughe protected him by anonymously publishing in his edition of *The Heroic Elegies and Other Pieces of Llywarç Hen* Iolo's fantastical treatise on the descent of the bardic tradition in Wales from the ancient Druids onwards. In it he showed how bardism had become a potent institution, 'embracing all the leading principles which tend to spread liberty, peace and happiness amongst mankind'.[229] Pughe's *Cambrian Biography* (1803) popularized Iolo's ideas on the fabulous origins of the Welsh, as did journals like the *Cambrian Register* and the *Cambro-Briton*, and Iolo was delighted to detect his own thumb prints on two other significant works published in 1803. In his eyes, Peter Roberts's *Sketch of the Early History of the Cymry, or Ancient Britons* and Sharon Turner's *A Vindication of the Genuineness of the Ancient British Poems of Aneurin, Taliesin, Llywarch Hen, and Merdhin* not only vindicated his findings but were, as Pughe put it, portents of 'the dawn of a splendid day of Cymbrian lore, when Pinkerton and his disciples will be in the shades of oblivion'.[230] *The Myvyrian Archaiology of Wales* also worked its magic. In 1820–2 J. H. Parry published an English translation of the third series of triads,[231] and hard on its heels came William Probert's *The Ancient Laws of Cambria* (1823), which bore the heavy imprint of Iolo's preoccupation with the inspiring deeds and writings of Hu Gadarn, Prydain ab Aedd Mawr and Dyfnwal Moelmud.

Iolo's national vision also had an enormously influential after-life. Following his death in 1826 his son Taliesin dedicated his leisure hours to making sense of his chaotic literary legacy and bringing parts of it – most notably on

---

[228] *MAW*, I, p. [ix]. See also NLW 13112B, p. 11.

[229] William Owen, *The Heroic Elegies and Other Pieces of Llywarç Hen* (London, 1792 [1793]), p. xxiv. For an account of how bardic nationalism buttressed the national memory, see Katie Trumpener, *Bardic Nationalism: The Romantic Novel and the British Empire* (Princeton, NJ, 1997).

[230] *CIM*, II, p. 446, William Owen Pughe to Iolo Morganwg, 9 December 1802. The Scottish author John Pinkerton, known for his prejudice against the Welsh and his hostility towards 'Celtic nonsense', became one of Iolo's whipping boys. See his comments on Pinkerton as a Goth who 'loves to drink Celtic blood out of the skull of an enemy'. NLW 13097B, p. 287. See also NLW 13123B, pp. 38–9; NLW 21419E, nos. 6, 12; and *'The Bard is a Very Singular Character'*, pp. 90–5.

[231] The antiquary John Humffreys Parry, founder and editor of the *Cambro-Briton*, published the triads in his journal between 1820 and 1822.

cultural themes of national importance – into the public domain.[232] Works such as *Coelbren y Beirdd* (1840) and *Iolo Manuscripts* (1848) were designed not only to reflect Iolo's genius but also to show that the national literary heritage of the Welsh was still brimming with life and vigour. A second edition of *The Myvyrian Archaiology of Wales* – this time in one fat volume – was published in 1870, thereby giving Iolo's bogus triads as well as his pantheon of national heroes a new lease of life. Some decidedly unlikely scholars were hoodwinked. Karl Marx detected 'entirely communist' sentiments in the legal triads fathered on Dyfnwal Moelmud: 'Quite some lads, these Celts', he told Frederick Engels, 'But born dialecticians, everything being composed in triads.'[233] Iolo's vision was woven and rewoven into the fabric of cultural life in Victorian Wales as his own reputation attained mythological proportions. Renowned Celtic scholars like Rudolf Thurneysen and Sir John Morris-Jones found no reason to believe at this stage that they had been duped by bogus manuscripts or that Iolo's national vision based on bardism and the Gorsedd of the Bards was a piece of fiction.[234] Iolo had become a national celebrity.

No Welshman of his time had a worse reputation than Iolo for taking up unfashionable causes and uttering dangerous sentiments. Wherever seditious tongues wagged, he was to be found denigrating the king, praising French invaders, promoting Unitarian radicalism in druidic moots, and attacking tyranny and oppression. But he also drew attention to himself by seeking to stimulate a sense of Welsh national consciousness at the very time when Britishness was gaining ground.[235] He had no desire to promote the case for an independent political structure for Wales. Secessionism was not part of his brief. After all, the Welsh were the proud senior members of Ancient Britain. But his ideological journey had convinced him that 'a [Welsh] Nation now exists, and has from a very remote period existed',[236] that the history of that nation had been denied its rightful place, and that its 'true' story should be told. His nation was a cultural nation, a distinctive entity whose language, prose, poetry and history symbolized the ethnic unity of the people. By immersing himself in the past and by deploying his fertile imagination and vivid prose style, he engineered for the Welsh a usable history capable of inspiring a national revival. Moreover, he showed that an advanced sense of nationality could prosper only where there were national institutions to sustain the collective memory.

---

[232] Brynley F. Roberts, '"The Age of Restitution": Taliesin ab Iolo and the Reception of Iolo Morganwg' in *Rattleskull Genius*, pp. 473–4.
[233] Karl Marx and Frederick Engels, *Collected Works 1864–1868, Volume 42* (London, 1987), p. 549; idem, *Collected Works 1868–1870, Volume 43* (London, 1988), pp. 515–16.
[234] *Literary and Historical Legacy*, pp. 98–104.
[235] Linda Colley, *Britons: Forging the Nation 1707–1837* (rev. edn., London, 2009).
[236] NLW 13128A, p. 249.

Among the many examples in Iolo's writings of his precocious, often moving, sense of nationality and nationhood, none is more compelling than the following passage which he jotted down in pencil in his notebook as he approached his native land from England:

> To say that my Soul brightens up at a sight of my native Country will be termed nationality, prejudice, weakness, silliness, but why so? What is a man that does not love that Country that is most peculiarly his own, and in that, the spot that gave him birth? . . . [The] man who loves not his native home will never in a proper sense be a Citizen of the World.[237]

By openly engaging with the nation's past and urging his countrymen to stretch their imagination, this *citoyen du monde* became one of the founders of modern Welsh national consciousness.

---

[237] NLW 13174A, p. 35[r–v].

7

'I am what I am, and I most fervently thank God that I am what I am'

By the time of the foundation of the Unitarian Society of South Wales in 1802, Iolo was fifty-five and had completed two-thirds of his multifaceted and turbulent life. He could easily have been forgiven by his dwindling number of politically-radical friends had he decided to keep his head down and await more congenial times. But even during these dark days of war, persecution and bigotry, he continued to question and challenge prevailing norms, promote heterodox ideas and project himself as an active political figure. Indeed, he prided himself on being seen as one who was always ready to dispute with those who stood in the way of justice and fair play. He relished 'buckling on his armour for a tilting match'[1] with his opponents and reserved his deepest scorn not only for dyed-in-the-wool conservatives but also for those who had abandoned their republican convictions. He was scathing about the propensity of the Welsh in north Wales – led by that 'poor drunken fellow'[2] David Thomas (Dafydd Ddu Eryri) – to join 'the gangs of the establishment'[3] and he deliberately lost touch with members of the Gwyneddigion, including his patron Owen Jones (Owain Myfyr) and fellow savant William Owen Pughe, whose 'down-melted Milton'[4] in his Welsh version of *Paradise Lost* had made him a figure of fun in Iolo's eyes. Having once praised his former friend as 'Unrivald Southey',[5] he deplored the latter's abandonment of the radical agenda and his willingness to accept the poet laureateship in 1813: 'He is gone to the devil.'[6] Others who fell by the wayside were duly chastised and expelled from

---

[1] *RAEW*, p. 34. The Chartist Morgan Williams remembered him as 'an able disputant' who would 'wrestle and wrangle'. Morgan Williams, 'Notable Men of Wales: Iolo Morganwg (Edward Williams)', *The Red Dragon: The National Magazine of Wales*, II (1882), 102.
[2] *CIM*, II, p. 684, Iolo Morganwg to William Owen Pughe, 20 July 1805. About a month earlier Iolo had received a copy of a song by David Thomas (Dafydd Ddu Eryri) in which he had been depicted as being more wicked than Spinoza and Voltaire. Ibid. , II, pp. 672–5, Thomas Roberts to Iolo Morganwg, 25 June 1805.
[3] NLW 13128A, p. 485.
[4] *CIM*, III, p. 521, Iolo Morganwg to Evan Williams, 12 May 1819.
[5] NLW 13157A, p. 197.
[6] *CIM*, III, p. 195, Iolo Morganwg to Taliesin Williams, 12–15 October 1813.

his circle of friends and acquaintances. He made no apologies to Chief Justice George Hardinge for promoting Rational Dissent and the cause of liberty – 'I am what I am, and I most fervently thank God that I am what I am.'[7]

Iolo still derived inspiration from the politically-charged 1790s. As the nineteenth century dawned he began to copy radical poems and songs he had composed during the 'Reign of Terror' in order to refresh his memory and reinvigorate his commitment to the values implanted during 'the (alas) short reign of French Liberty'.[8] In 1803, for instance, he retranscribed and amended 'Carmen seculare, or the Jubilant Song', 'The Newgate Stanzas' and his celebration in verse of the acquittal of Hardy, Tooke and Thelwall following the Treason Trials.[9] Keeping the old flame burning was important to him, and he continued to keep a keen eye open for current political polemics, metaphysical disquisitions, shifts in public tastes and trends in booksellers' markets. Although less quixotic and less prone to fantasize about things, he was still bursting with energy and ideas. He peppered his correspondence with intriguing digressions into the fields of astronomy, science, engineering and geology, and he knew very well that he was living in an 'Age of Wonder'.[10] But since, as a Unitarian, he was still labouring under political and religious disabilities, he threw much of his energy into exposing the inequities of the parliamentary system, the handicaps imposed on anti-trinitarians, and the dehumanizing effects of slavery, militarism and war. He remained instinctively a 'man of feeling' and whenever he became engaged in intense political arguments he used to stand up belligerently to make his point. Elijah Waring, who admired his moral integrity on such occasions, recalled 'the raised arm and clenched hand – the kindled eye – the highly-pitched voice – and the emphatic foot, probationary of floor and joist'.[11]

In recalling the events of the 1790s Iolo simply could not let bygones be bygones. No one could persuade him that William Pitt was anything other than a monster who had spearheaded an intensive campaign against civil liberties. Pitt had ignored his written pleas for fairer taxes and had inflicted alarm and pain on his liberty-loving friends by prosecuting them in the courts and locking them up. His own business as a benevolent shopkeeper had been ruined and his attempts to popularize the Gorsedd of the Bards as a bastion of liberty had been thwarted. Moreover, untold horrors had been unleashed by the prosecution of war against France. It was a matter of great relief to Iolo, therefore, when news

---

[7] Ibid., II, p. 459, Iolo Morganwg to [George Hardinge], [?1803].
[8] NLW 21424E, no. 63 (d).
[9] NLW 21334B, pp. 12–28. Although he lightheartedly referred to his extraordinary range of transcripts as 'the relics of the mad' ('gwarged y gwallgof'), he could not bear to be parted from them.
[10] Richard Holmes, *The Age of Wonder* (London, 2008).
[11] *RAEW*, p. 129.

arrived that the prime minister had resigned on the issue of Catholic emancipation on 3 February 1801 after seventeen years at the helm.[12] 'So Wil Pwll Uffern [Will of hell's pit] is out at last', he chortled, as he reiterated his long-held belief that the powerless were never truly equal before the law: 'Cyfiawnder Wil Pwll Uffern – pob peth ond a fai ia[wn] [The justice of Will of hell's pit – everything save what is just]'.[13] Within three years, however, Pitt was back in Downing Street, though by this stage his health had deteriorated markedly and he died of gastric or duodenal ulceration on 22 January 1806. An avid tea-drinker like Iolo would no doubt have reminded the bibulous that the prime minister's addiction to alcohol had hastened his demise. He certainly did not share the sense of loss felt by the governing classes. Indeed, in a piece of marginalia, dripping with irony, he celebrated Pitt's belated arrival at the bottomless pit:

> Pandemonian Bulletin
>
> Jan 22ᵈ year of our Reign 5800. This day arrived at our Pallace our most illustrious friend and compeer William Pitt whose services to us in the world of human nature has been great beyond any thing ever hitherto known. He propagated and diffused our purest principles, with the greatest success, and especially so in the so much by us hated Christian part of that world which we now behold with rapture in flames lighted up by him, streaming which he has given to flow in a high deluge. But our great enemy above who has for so many ages been ruling us with his rod of Iron sent one of his assassins to despatch him in the moment of his enjoyment of the high career of glory, wherein he was proceeding with the greatest rapidity. All our Crowned friends in that world mournful[ly] join in the bitterest lamentation for the sudden departure of our own highly beloved and most illustrious friend. But we wish them not to dispair for phoenix-like out of his ashes will arise another and not one only but many William Pitts. In the mean time we are preparing for his reception in all the numberless of our extensive empire and orders have been issued for public rejoicing, and that on this solemn and grand occasion the most magnificent bonfires be lighted up. We have also prescribed the appropriate toast amongst others next to our own Royal person is to be given all the Kings of the Christian world, and may success attend them and their politics. Given at our Royal Pallace of Pandemonium the day and date above written
>
> By order of his Infernall Majesty
> Belzebub[14]

Right up until his death Iolo was so morally and socially engaged that he never lost his unfortunate tendency to rub people up the wrong way,

---

[12] William Hague, *William Pitt the Younger* (pbk. edn., London, 2005), p. 477.
[13] *CIM*, II, p. 367, Iolo Morganwg to William Owen Pughe, 15 February 1801.
[14] NLW 21286E, marginalia on letter no. 1056.

sometimes inadvertently. Following an innocent remark made in a tavern at Gelli-gaer on 28 June 1802, a furious innkeeper turned on him and cried: 'Dammo chwi, dilyn tinau'r offeiriaid yr ydych chwi. Ni chewch chwi un gwely yma na the na dim arall' (Damn you, you follow or attend the backsides of parsons (or clergymen). You shall have no bed here nor tea neither, nor any thing else).[15] He did not hesitate to remind petty thieves of their Christian obligations before prosecuting them for entering his garden and orchard and assaulting him when he attempted to defend his property,[16] and he had no qualms about vilifying those who had betrayed him by serving the cause of power or their own selfish interests.[17] Most people distrusted or feared him, while those who were aware of his straitened circumstances and ill health pitied him.

Although Iolo was sad to lose contact with old friends, his heart no longer ached for London and he seldom ventured further than Bristol. He now looked elsewhere for intellectual stimulation and ethical support from people he could trust and admire. Wherever political radicals – mostly Unitarians and Quakers – assembled in Glamorgan to debate burning issues became Iolo's natural habitat. Since he remained an active peripatetic stonemason into his seventies, he was well placed to observe the socio-economic effects of demographic change, vigorous industrial and commercial expansion, and urban developments in his native county.[18] The population of Glamorgan increased from 74,189 in 1801 to 107,263 in 1821 as major new work-places hummed with the kind of activity that attracted penurious rural migrants in droves.[19] Iolo's interest in geology and in what was often referred to as 'the spirit of improvement' meant that he was keenly aware of the potentially lucrative properties of iron, coal, lead, copper, manganese, calamine, freestone, millstone, alabaster and sandstone.[20] He was also impressed by the valuable contribution made by printing works, bookselling businesses and woollen factories to economic growth, and he continued to ply Walter Davies (Gwallter Mechain) with evidence of technological change and its effects on the pace and rhythm of people's lives.[21] He might have deplored the noise and the smoke, as well as the misuse of human

---

[15] NLW 21401E, no. 39.

[16] Glamorgan Archives, Q/S M14, pp. 49, 54, 97; NLW 21410E, nos. 55–64; *CIM*, III, pp. 186–7, Taliesin Williams to Iolo Morganwg, 3 October 1813.

[17] NLW 21400C, no. 48. His *bêtes noires* included Owen Jones (Owain Myfyr), William Owen Pughe, David Thomas (Dafydd Ddu Eryri), Thomas Evans (Tomos Glyn Cothi), David Peter, Edward Davies and David Saunders.

[18] Geraint H. Jenkins, 'The Urban Experiences of Iolo Morganwg', *WHR*, 22, no. 3 (2005), 463–98.

[19] Dot Jones, *Statistical Evidence relating to the Welsh Language 1801–1911 / Tystiolaeth Ystadegol yn ymwneud â'r Iaith Gymraeg 1801–1911* (Cardiff / Caerdydd, 1998), p. 17.

[20] NLW 13089E, p. 120; NLW 13114B, pp. 31–6; NLW 13115B, pp. 1–2.

[21] Walter Davies, *General View of the Agriculture and Domestic Economy of South Wales* (2 vols., London, 1815).

labour by the 'Iron Kings', but he understood the reasons behind the transformation of the landscape and was drawn towards forward-looking middling men who were resentful of the intimidating might of the landed elite and who expressed their social identity through good works, social programmes and the alleviation of poverty. They were also, it should be added, keenly interested in the book trade, in literature in general, and in greater tolerance within society.

It was logical therefore for Iolo to befriend and interact with such people. In the west of the county, Swansea and its environs were especially enticing. He had long been familiar with the town's burgeoning international reputation as an industrial and commercial centre, but he was increasingly impressed by the fact that there were improvers aplenty in the town who were ensuring that its social and recreational amenities outstripped all its urban rivals in Wales. The town's corporation invested heavily in the provision of assembly rooms, theatres and bathing houses, and the flourishing book trade and excellent library facilities certainly caught Iolo's eye.[22] Delighting in the publication in the town of *The Cambrian*, the first weekly English-language newspaper, in January 1804, he became one of its most avid readers.[23] Ten years later, in January 1814, Swansea became the home of *Seren Gomer*, the first weekly Welsh-language newspaper. Its Baptist editor Joseph Harris (Gomer) was no friend of anti-trinitarians and had vehemently denounced them in *Bwyall Crist*, published in 1804, but Iolo wished him well and urged him never to let his *Seren* (star) slide under a cloud of untruth ('Ceisiwch wilied rhag iddi lithro dan gwmmwl [anwiredd]').[24] Four years later Harris published Iolo's combustible *Vox Populi Vox Dei!* (1818) in which he vigorously decried all enemies to the integrity of the county's independent freeholders. Enlightenment men, drawn to Unitarianism as a result of its concern for the improvement of people's secular lot rather than the salvation of their souls in the hereafter, were extremely active. The cleric Walter Davies, who travelled extensively with Iolo in 1802, was struck by the great strides made by Dissent in the town: 'London itself has scarcely a religious congregation that is not here aped in miniature. A Mahometan Mosque is the only fabric wanted to complete the Swansea pantheon.'[25] Among

---

[22] D. Trevor Williams, *The Economic Development of Swansea and of the Swansea District to 1921* (Swansea, 1940); David Boorman, *The Brighton of Wales* (Swansea, 1986); Louise Miskell, 'The Making of a new "Welsh metropolis": Science, Leisure and Industry in early nineteenth-century Swansea', *History*, 88, no. 289 (2003), 32–52; eadem, *'Intelligent Town': An Urban History of Swansea, 1780–1855* (Cardiff, 2006), chapter 2.

[23] Glynden Trollope, *The Cambrian and General Advertiser for the Principality of Wales, 1804–1930* (Berkhamsted, 2003).

[24] *CIM*, III, pp. 206, 209 (trans.), Iolo Morganwg to David Jenkin, 15 November 1813. For Harris, see Glanmor Williams, 'Gomer: "Sylfaenydd ein Llenyddiaeth Gyfnodol"', *THSC* (1982), 111–38.

[25] NLW 1760B, p. 71.

those who were active founding members of the Unitarian Society of South Wales were Richard Aubrey (d. 1820), an old Swansea burgess who was 'universally esteemed by all who knew him',[26] his son Richard Aubrey (d. 1836), who served as a pastor in Manchester and Gloucester before becoming minister of the Presbyterian meeting house in Swansea in 1814, and his son-in-law John Rowlands who became treasurer and secretary of the Society.[27]

It is equally clear that Iolo was aware that new influences in the Swansea Valley were bringing life and vigour into small communities. He was especially taken by the benevolent instincts of Sir John Morris of Clasemont in housing copper-workers in a remarkable array of tenements and also by the achievement of John Morris I and the bridge-builder and engineer William Edwards in founding the new town of Morriston which, as Iolo observed, 'goes towards Swansea that walks out rapidly to meet it'.[28] Always impressed by public-spirited men who devoted time to promoting general improvement and the dissemination of culture, Iolo did his utmost to keep abreast of the age. He even had expectations and hopes for some traditionally isolated venues located on moorlands in the parish of Llan-giwg. The most promising of these was the meeting house at Gellionnen, above Pontardawe. Founded to serve the Independent cause in 1692,[29] it became a spearhead for Rational Dissent under the influence of Josiah Rees who became its minister in 1767 and in time turned its worshippers into Arians and then full-blown Unitarians. In 1801 the church was rebuilt and enlarged to meet the needs of the more radical congregation. Iolo thought very highly of Rees and it was at his home at Gelligron that the details of the constitution of the Unitarian Society of South Wales were hammered out in 1802. Rees gave the first sermon at the Society's first public assembly held at Cefncoedycymer on 26 June 1803. His death, aged fifty-nine, within a year was a major blow to Unitarianism in Glamorgan, but it inspired Iolo to keep the flame alive by enlisting the support of several of his sons.[30]

Josiah Rees had married twice and sired eleven children, three of whom were befriended by Iolo. Owen Rees served an apprenticeship as a bookseller in Bristol before moving to London where he became a partner in the

---

[26] *The Cambrian*, 4 November 1820.
[27] W. Tudor Jones, *The Rise and Progress of Religious Free Thought in Swansea* (Swansea, 1900), pp. 37, 39–41, 51–2.
[28] NLW 13115B, p. 100. For the background, see Stephen Hughes, *Copperopolis: Landscapes of the Early Industrial Period in Swansea* (Aberystwyth, 2000).
[29] John E. Morgan, *Hanes Pontardawe a'r Cylch* (Pontardawe, 1911), pp. 98–104; D. Elwyn Davies, *Capel Gellionnen 1692–1992* (s.l.: [Capel Gellionnen], 1992).
[30] W. J. Phillips, 'Iolo Morganwg and the Rees Family of Gelligron', *NLWJ*, XIV (1965–6), 227–36.

celebrated Longman publishing firm.[31] Richard Rees became an enterprising publisher in London and Plymouth,[32] but the most gifted son was Thomas Rees, who briefly served as minister at Gellionnen before following his brothers to London. Iolo was especially interested in him since he moved in Unitarian and philosophical circles in the metropolis and thus kept him informed of recent publications. He served as a trustee of the Dr Williams's foundation and also as secretary of the Unitarian Society. A very fine linguist and historian, Rees became the undisputed authority on the history of anti-trinitarianism in Europe and his *Racovian Catechism* (1818) was universally reckoned to be a stunning piece of work.[33] His fertile mind and deep learning made him one of Iolo's favourite correspondents, and he was also a valuable bridge between the stonemason and his former friends in London:

> Do you see Dr Aikin and his family, Mrs Barbauld, Dr Lindsay, Dr A[braham] Rees, Mr T[owill] Rutt, &c.? Why did I forget lazy George Dyer? If you do see them, and when you do, do me the favour of presenting my respects, with warm and grateful remembrance of the favours and kindnesses that I have experienced from them.[34]

Owen Rees had always been struck by the acuteness of Iolo's observations and his awesome capacity to become 'the wonder of every one who conversed with him' in London.[35] As the above quotation reveals, these included the very great Llanbryn-mair scholar Abraham Rees, an Arian in his religion and an expert in natural philosophy, mathematics, statistics, optics, geometry and Hebrew studies. Rees is one of the forgotten figures in Welsh intellectual history, but in his day the 'Reverend Doctor' was a formidably learned man. He was best known for his edition of *The New Cyclopaedia*, which appeared in 39 volumes, including six volumes of plates, between 1802 and 1819. This massive work of reference drew attention to many of the developments in industry, technology and mechanics which intrigued Iolo. In recognition of his learning and many-sidedness, Rees was made a fellow of the Royal Society, the Linnean Society, the American Philosophical Society and the Royal Society of Literature.[36] Expatriates like Rees were engaged in intense intellectual activity

---

[31] For Owen Rees, see *The Times*, 12 September 1837, and the entry for his brother Thomas in *ODNB*.

[32] For a family album kept by Richard Rees, Alltycham, see NLW 11138D and for his correspondence with Iolo, see *CIM*, II, pp. 579, 871–6; ibid., III, pp. 82–3.

[33] Davies, *Capel Gellionnen*, pp. 17–18; *DWB* s.v. Josiah Rees; *ODNB* s.v. Thomas Rees.

[34] *CIM*, III, p. 145, Iolo Morganwg to Thomas Rees, 12 March 1813.

[35] *RAEW*, p. 122.

[36] John Evans, 'Memoir of Abraham Rees, DD, FRS, FLS, etc.', *Christian Moderator*, 1, no. 1 (1826), 4–9; *DWB* s.v. Abraham Rees.

and Iolo never saw himself as out of place in their company or in corresponding with them.

In terms of population Neath was much smaller than Swansea, but it too was an attractive destination for Iolo. Thanks to an abundant supply of water, coal and timber, several metallurgical works and collieries had sprung up there and had caught the imagination of artists like Thomas Hornor.[37] Iolo himself was enchanted by the dramatic landscape of Neath and its environs, and it was an added bonus to encounter people of genuinely independent mind and forceful personality within the community. At the fore were Unitarians and Quakers. His first port of call was usually the Parade in Neath where David Davis, secretary of the Unitarian Society of South Wales, had opened a school in July 1800 in which he offered a liberal education to well-to-do pupils and introduced innovative teaching aids such as a machine for decomposing water and a hydrostatic apparatus.[38] Davis adored Iolo, looked forward to his visits, read and re-read his letters with renewed pleasure on each occasion, and arranged for him to attend fortnightly meetings frequented by his liberally-minded friends. These included William Davies of Cringell,[39] a classical scholar and historian, and Thomas Morgan, who served as minister at Blaen-gwrach for over thirty years and whose gravestone at Gellionnen, inscribed by Iolo, referred to his 'benevolence of heart, humility of mind, and purity of doctrine'.[40] Davis pleaded in vain with Iolo to settle in Neath, but was mollified when his son Taliesin was appointed assistant master at his school in 1813.[41] Parental responsibilities meant that Iolo was a regular visitor, though the manner in which he pampered and manipulated his beloved son often drew unfavourable comments.

Having long been an admirer of the Quakers' mode of living, their virtuous conduct and manner, and their unbending commitment to peace and harmony, Iolo relished the opportunity to ally himself with groups of Friends in Neath. During the 1790s affluent groups of manufacturers and merchants, whose faith in the inner light meant that they abhorred the bearing of arms

---

[37] D. Rhys Phillips, *The History of the Vale of Neath* (Swansea, 1925); Elis Jenkins (ed.), *Neath and District: A Symposium* (Neath, 1974); George Eaton, *A History of Neath from Earliest Times* (Swansea, 1987); Elis Jenkins, 'Artists in the Vale of Neath' in Stewart Williams (ed.), *Glamorgan Historian, 1* (Cowbridge, 1963), pp. 44–53. For Iolo's comments, see NLW 1760A, no. 14, pp. 11–12; ibid., no. 15, pp. 19–21.

[38] Thomas G. Davies, *Neath's Wicked World and Other Essays on the History of Neath and District* (West Glamorgan Archive Service, 2000), pp. 109–24.

[39] For his collection of manuscripts, see NLW 5209–15, 5231–4, 6598, 6606–15. See also D. Rhys Phillips, *A Forgotten Welsh Historian (William Davies, Cringell, Neath, 1756–1823)* (Swansea, 1916).

[40] D. Elwyn Davies, *Cewri'r Ffydd: Bywgraffiadur y Mudiad Undodaidd yng Nghymru* (Cymdeithas Undodaidd Deheudir Cymru, 1999), p. 36.

[41] *CIM*, III, p. 158, David Davis to Iolo Morganwg, 26 May 1813.

and military force in general, had moved into the area to develop iron-ore working and coal mining. The most prominent of them was the Price family from Cornwall. In 1799 Peter Price and his wife Anna (née Tregelles) settled at Cwm-y-felin, Neath Abbey, and in a remarkably short time turned its ancient ironworks into a flourishing concern. The most benevolent of men, Price used much of his wealth to relieve the poor, set up free schools and support missionary efforts.[42] His son Joseph Tregelles Price, who described himself to Iolo as 'a sober, well meaning Quaker'[43] and who doggedly refused to manufacture anything but implements of peace during the French wars, became managing director of the Neath Abbey ironworks in 1818. Four years earlier Elijah Waring, a native of Alton in Hampshire, had settled in Neath. He, too, was a Quaker, but is best known in Wales as the first biographer of Iolo. He married Deborah, Peter Price's third child, in August 1817 and swiftly made his mark in the locality by supporting liberty in church and state and by penning several intelligent articles on parliamentary reform in *The Cambrian* newspaper.[44] Peter Price's fourth child, Lydia, married Isaac Redwood, a Neath currier who, with his brother William, became extremely generous and supportive friends of Iolo during his final poverty stricken years.[45]

In many ways, however, the most intriguing figure among these earnest and 'parsonless'[46] Friends (as Iolo called them) was Evan Rees, the son of a Neath ironmonger and an active pacifist. In June 1816 Joseph Tregelles Price, in collaboration with William Allen, who owned suitable premises in London, was instrumental in founding the Society for the Promotion of Permanent and Universal Peace. Better known as the Peace Society, its aim was to abolish war.[47] Evan Rees became its first secretary and was also the moving spirit behind its house magazine, the *Herald of Peace*. In 1818 he published an English translation of Eugene Labaume's famous depiction of the military campaign in Russia in 1812. Entitled *Sketches of the Horrors of War*, it was a moving commentary on the futility of wars and their adverse effect on civilized values. Rees, who had lost an eye following a childhood accident, also suffered from a lung condition which led to his death, aged thirty, during a voyage to Australia in 1821.[48] Had he enjoyed better health and lived a longer life, he may well have become as well known a peace campaigner as his illustrious

---

[42] Phillips, *The History of the Vale of Neath*, pp. 288–91.
[43] *CIM*, III, p. 58, Joseph Tregelles Price to Iolo Morganwg, 25 February 1811.
[44] Glamorgan Archives, DD/SF; Phillips, *The History of the Vale of Neath*, pp. 441–2.
[45] Phillips, *The History of the Vale of Neath*, pp. 441, 445.
[46] *CIM*, III, p. 256, Iolo Morganwg to Taliesin Williams, [?22–23 March 1814].
[47] For the background, see Martin Ceadel, *The Origins of War Prevention* (Oxford, 1996), pp. 206–10.
[48] *Memoirs of Evan Rees: Consisting Chiefly of Extracts from his Letters* (Neath, 1853); Phillips, *The History of the Vale of Neath*, pp. 445–6.

fellow countryman Henry Richard. Although Iolo was never an active pacifist – he believed (as did Thomas Belsham) that self-defence was morally justifiable – he was glad to associate himself with this small group of peace-loving people who supported the weak and the underprivileged in every possible way. Indeed, as Elijah Waring readily confessed, the fountain of Iolo's own benevolence, in spite of his empty purse, was 'deep and perennial'.[49]

The busy market town of Bridgend, with its strong tradition of druidism, masonic activity and radical discourse, also had small groups of Dissenters and intellectuals who enjoyed the company of the craggy stonemason. Even though the inhabitants of Cardiff dubbed it 'a poor, starveling place',[50] Bridgend had ambitions of becoming the county town. Iolo was especially interested in the exploitation of the white lias limestone quarries in the area[51] and he befriended members of the well-known Bedford family. John Bedford, a colourful Birmingham-born ironmaster, had bought an 80-acre estate at Cefncribwr where he set up an ironworks and became well known for improving refining techniques before his death in 1791.[52] His son, also called John, was a brick-maker who reckoned that Bridgend offered Iolo far better prospects for his bookselling business than Cowbridge since it was more accessible and progressive.[53] Thomas Bedford, the youngest brother of the ironmaster John Bedford, also corresponded with Iolo. The Bedford family were Baptists, but Thomas was a Unitarian who greatly admired the venerable bard as 'a promoter of truth and the rights of contience in religious matters'.[54] So, too, did Robert Dare, whose woollen factory in Bridgend produced cloth for female members of the royal family as well as aristocrats and dealers in London, Bristol and Bath. A native of Ottery St Mary in Devon, Dare was a vegetarian, a bibliophile and a radical Independent.[55] He used to invite colourful conversationalists to his home near Bridgend and, being a shrewd theologian as well as a charming host, he enjoyed listening to the likes of Iolo and Richard Llewellyn of Ynysawdre, an extraordinary oriental scholar, indulging in vigorous bouts of 'verbal fencing'.[56] It may well be that Iolo's conversations

---

[49] *RAEW*, p. 128.
[50] T. J. Hopkins (ed.), 'C. C.'s Tour in Glamorgan, 1789' in Stewart Williams (ed.), *Glamorgan Historian, 2* (Cowbridge, 1965), pp. 129–30.
[51] NLW 13116E, pp. 346–59; Colin Baber, 'The Subsidiary Industries of Glamorgan, 1760–1914' in *GCH V*, pp. 218, 222.
[52] Philip Riden, *John Bedford and the Ironworks at Cefn Cribwr* (Cardiff, 1992).
[53] *CIM*, I, p. 841, John Bedford to Iolo Morganwg, 10 December 1796.
[54] Ibid., III, p. 345, Thomas Bedford to Iolo Morganwg, 26 April 1815; Neville Granville, *Cefn Cribwr: Chronicle of a Village* (Barry, 1980), p. 77.
[55] Glamorgan Archives, D/D X 182/1; NLW 13089E, p. 123; Davies, *General View of the Agriculture and Domestic Economy of South Wales*, II, p. 148; H. J. Randall, *Bridgend: The Story of a Market Town* (Newport, 1955), pp. 67–70.
[56] *RAEW*, pp. 14–15.

with Dare about the manufacture of woollen cloth, flannel and stockings prompted him to use part of the legacy bequeathed by his deceased brother John to set up his daughters Margaret and Ann as milliners at a general store in Cefncribwr, a place which he also registered as a Unitarian meeting house in May 1817.[57]

Cardiff, a modest market town of 1,870 inhabitants in 1801, was a less congenial place for a firebrand like Iolo. It was a bastion of high Toryism and the might of the Bute family meant that there was little to encourage supporters of Tom Paine or Unitarian proselytes.[58] Iolo avoided the town as much as possible. It brought back ugly memories of his incarceration in 1786–7 and of altercations with merchants and dealers who had lucrative interests in the slave trade in the Caribbean. Yet, he refused to abandon it as a lost cause and sought to establish friendly relations with incomers with the broadest sympathies. Among them were the Vachells of Devon. Charles Vachell (d. 1832), who had served as a surgeon in the Navy in the early 1790s, established a business as a druggist or an apothecary in Cardiff. His eldest son, Charles Vachell junior (d. 1859) was also a druggist. Born in Exeter, he acquired considerable land and properties in Cardiff and was mayor of the town in 1848 and 1855.[59] Iolo came to know him after he married the Quaker Margaret Redwood at Llan-maes in December 1811[60] and he greatly admired the manner in which he thereafter practised his Quaker principles by helping the poor. He played host to Iolo on many occasions and remained a loyal and generous friend.

Iolo also endeavoured to enlist the support of the prominent Whig and social reformer John Hodder Moggridge, who lived at Llanrumney Hall, a substantial estate on the banks of the river Rumney, some five miles from Cardiff. Having made a fortune in the woollen trade in Gloucestershire, Moggridge had settled in Llanrumney Hall in 1812.[61] Iolo stayed with him in August 1813 and had fruitful discussions about promoting Unitarian causes and alleviating poverty.[62] Moggridge had a strong social conscience and by attributing the social distress of the times to the excessive weight of taxation and other public burdens he provoked considerable public debate in *The Cambrian* and other

---

[57] NLW 21406E, no. 1.
[58] Philip Jenkins, 'The Tory tradition in eighteenth-century Cardiff', *WHR*, 12, no. 2 (1984), 180–96; Hywel M. Davies, 'Loyalism in Wales, 1792–1793', ibid., 20, no. 4 (2001), 693.
[59] Peter Thomas, 'Professor Theophilus Redwood (1806–1892)', *Llantwit Major: Aspects of its History*, 3 (2004), 25–6; Christine Young, 'The Vachell Family of Cardiff, and the Dispersal of the Wilkins' Land', ibid., 7 (2007), 50–61; *CIM*, III, p. 188, Iolo Morganwg to Taliesin Williams, 8 October 1813.
[60] NLW 109/76, Charles Vachell, Cardiff, and Margaret Redwood, Llan-maes, marriage bond, 4 December 1811; Glamorgan Archives, DD/SF; *RAEW*, pp. 19–20.
[61] David Williams, *John Frost: A Study in Chartism* (Cardiff, 1939), pp. 30–1.
[62] *CIM*, III, p. 163, Iolo Morganwg to Taliesin Williams, 4 August 1813; ibid., III, p. 171, Iolo Morganwg to Taliesin Williams, 16–17 August 1813.

newspapers.⁶³ During the 1820s he formulated the 'Village System', a social experiment which led to the founding of new settlements at Blackwood and Ynys-ddu in Monmouthshire. He became heavily involved in the work of mechanics' institutes and also as a promoter of the Society for the Diffusion of Useful Knowledge.⁶⁴ All this was deeply appealing to Iolo, as was Moggridge's audacity in unsuccessfully contesting the Monmouthshire borough seat against Henry Somerset, the Marquis of Worcester, son and heir to the 6th Duke of Beaufort, in March 1820. His nomination was seconded by John Frost, the future Welsh Chartist leader.⁶⁵ There is no doubt that engaging Moggridge's support lent lustre to Iolo's growing circle of influential Dissenters. He was always eager to seek the advice and guidance of progressive, enlightened figures of this kind and to use their ideas in promoting charitable work and reforming morals.

Iolo was also wise enough to realize that many roads were now leading to Merthyr Tydfil. This 'poor mountain village',⁶⁶ as he once called it, where the druido-bardic tradition had flourished in the hill country, had become a remarkable industrial town whose rapid growth threatened to leave every other urban rival in south Wales trailing far behind. Dissenting radicalism was deeply rooted in the town and Iolo struck up a friendship with Christopher James, a mercer and wine merchant who built the Bush hotel in Merthyr and became a significant influence on the growth of Unitarianism in the town.⁶⁷ In April 1815 James strongly urged Taliesin ab Iolo to further his career by opening a commercial school in Merthyr as an initial foothold before seeking a post as an accountant or a steward or a clerk in the burgeoning town.⁶⁸ By that stage the relationship between Taliesin and the volatile David Davis had mysteriously broken down, and in February 1816, thanks to the bequest made by Iolo's brother in Jamaica, the apple of his father's eye duly set himself up as master of a 'Mathematical and Commercial Academy' for young boys at Merthyr, where he later gained a reputation as a ferocious thrasher of errant pupils.⁶⁹ Taliesin's removal to Merthyr strengthened Iolo's links with the town, and especially with the ironworkers, colliers, artisans and craftsmen who belonged to the Cyfarthfa

---

[63] See 'Cambrensis', *Observations on the Present Difficulties of the Country* (London, 1816).
[64] Brian Ll. James, 'John Hodder Moggridge and the Founding of Blackwood', *Presenting Monmouthshire*, II, no. 5 (1968), 25–9.
[65] Williams, *John Frost*, p. 32; Margaret Escott, 'Parliamentary Representation' in Chris Williams and Sian Rhiannon Williams (eds.), *The Gwent County History. Volume 4. Industrial Monmouthshire, 1780–1914* (Cardiff, 2011), pp. 267–8.
[66] NLW 13089E, p. 121.
[67] Charles Wilkins, *The History of Merthyr Tydfil* (Merthyr Tydfil, 1867), p. 251.
[68] *CIM*, III, p. 347, Iolo Morganwg to Taliesin Williams, 27–29 April 1815.
[69] Brynley F. Roberts, 'Mab ei Dad: Taliesin ab Iolo Morganwg' in Hywel Teifi Edwards (ed.), *Merthyr a Thaf* (Llandysul, 2001), pp. 62–4; idem, '"The Age of Restitution": Taliesin ab Iolo and the Reception of Iolo Morganwg' in *Rattleskull Genius*, pp. 465–6.

Philosophical Society. As the success of the 'Iron Kings' unquestionably proved, Merthyr was the place to be for those bent on making money. But it was also a congenial home for inquisitive, thinking men who were thrilled by the thud of pistons, the hiss of engines and the blast of furnaces, and even more inspired by the flow of enlightened ideas and the talk of freedom.

The Cyfarthfa Philosophical Society had been set up in December 1807 by sixty founding members who assembled at the Dynevor Arms with a view to serving their community in the way the Lunar Society benefited intelligent and inventive people in Birmingham.[70] Each member subscribed a guinea to enable the Society to buy a telescope, a pair of globes, a microscope, a planetarium, an orrery and an equatorial. Many of those who listened intently to lectures and aired their views on scientific and philosophical topics were Arminians, Arians and Unitarians who admired Voltaire and Tom Paine and read their works 'with great unction'.[71] Iolo was thrilled to rub shoulders with intelligent stonemasons like himself, engineers, mathematicians and highly skilled puddlers, colliers and miners. Benjamin Saunders, a master-moulder at Cyfarthfa ironworks, was sufficiently gifted to build a planetarium and make a quadrant, a thermometer and a water-gauge.[72] When the mechanical genius Watkin George built an extraordinary wheel which worked four furnaces, a song was composed in honour of a machine 'the very best the world has ever seen'.[73] For Iolo, the most intelligent and agreeable family he encountered among these strong-willed Dissenters were the Williamses of Penyrheolgerrig. He described Morgan Williams (d. 1796) as 'a most Ex[cellen]t Character' and 'a great reader of our best philosophical works'.[74] His sons, John and William, were active members of the Cyfarthfa Philosophical Society, proud of their 'valuable Philosophical and mathematical Instruments'[75] and ready to exert political influence in dissident circles. William Williams was in fact the father of Morgan Williams (b. 1808), who became the most outspoken and prominent Chartist in Merthyr and who, in his dotage, wrote admiringly of Iolo.[76] Iolo liked nothing better than to launch, sustain and clinch an argument with such dissidents.

These were the individuals and groups whom Iolo courted, befriended and respected in the swiftly growing urban communities of Glamorgan. Many of them were incomers who were steeped in the Dissenting inheritance and had

---

[70] *CIM*, III, p. 151, Iolo Morganwg to Thomas Rees, 3 May 1813; Jenny Uglow, *The Lunar Men: The Friends who made the Future 1730–1810* (pbk. edn., London, 2003).
[71] Wilkins, *The History of Merthyr Tydfil*, pp. 269–70.
[72] Gwyn A. Williams, *The Merthyr Rising* (London, 1978), p. 74.
[73] Wilkins, *The History of Merthyr Tydfil*, p. 203.
[74] NLW 13151A, p. 69; *CIM*, III, p. 151, Iolo Morganwg to Thomas Rees, 3 May 1813.
[75] NLW 13151A, p. 69.
[76] Williams, 'Notable Men of Wales: Iolo Morganwg (Edward Williams)', 102.

the knowledge and, more importantly, the desire to improve society. The more heterodox and prickly they were, the more Iolo enjoyed their company, not least because their progressive ideas and radical stance made the ruling elite increasingly nervous. As he moved among them, speaking loudly, candidly and sceptically, he was a constant reminder that Unitarians were overwhelmingly concerned with burning issues and injustices relating to *this* world.

From the time of the founding of the Unitarian Society of South Wales in 1802 onwards Iolo invested considerable time and energy in placing it on a firm footing. He played a strategic role in formulating and implementing the rules and regulations of the Society and was also charged with the task of preparing a Welsh version.[77] He was acutely conscious of the fact that Unitarianism had many enemies, among them formidable prelates like Thomas Burgess and also influential Dissenters like David Peter, senior tutor of the Dissenting academy in Carmarthen. There was active hostility to contend with and no member of the beleaguered denomination, as Thomas Evans (Tomos Glyn Cothi) had discovered, could count on the protection of the law. Until 1813 Unitarianism was outlawed and its small and widely scattered congregations, even though they appeared to be more numerous and threatening than they actually were, hardly presented a major challenge to the Calvinist monopoly. The first register of these founding members who paid a subscription of five shillings contained just forty-nine names, the most important of whom were London-based luminaries such as Theophilus Lindsey, Thomas Belsham and William Owen Pughe, eleven ministers based in south Wales, and a strong representation from among the Rees family of Gelli-gron. Only three women were listed.[78]

Not surprisingly, of the five founding members appointed to serve on the executive committee of the Society, Iolo was the principal mouthpiece. To David Davis and others, his mere presence on this committee was inspirational. Apart from his knowledge of south Wales, Iolo was well placed to offer advice on Welsh nomenclature, devotional literature, mission fields and anything which might help to promote what he called the 'genuine truths of pure morality and unsophisticated Christianity'.[79] 'We can not dispense with your patronage',[80] wrote the doting Davis, and he and his colleagues gratefully entrusted to him the task of discovering, or more accurately, coining the Welsh-language equivalents for 'Unitarian' ('Dwyfundodwr'), 'Unitarianism'

---

[77] Edward Williams, *Rheolau a Threfniadau Cymdeithas Dwyfundodiaid yn Neheubarth Cymru* (Llundain, 1803). For drafts, see Cardiff 2.1020, p. 20, and NLW 13145A, pp. 159–74, 278–98, 366–84. Iolo claimed 'I had plan'd it [the Society] about a year and a half ago'. *CIM*, II, p. 440, Iolo Morganwg to William Owen Pughe, 25 October 1802.

[78] NLW 13145A, pp. 296–8; Williams, *Rheolau a Threfniadau Cymdeithas Dwyfundodiaid yn Neheubarth Cymru*, pp. 21–4.

[79] *CIM*, II, p. 441, Iolo Morganwg to William Owen Pughe, 25 October 1802.

[80] Ibid., II, p. 724, David Davis to Iolo Morganwg, 26 October 1805.

('Dwyfundodiaeth') and the 'Divine Unity' ('Dwyfundod') for the benefit of those who worshipped the 'one only Living and True God'.[81] These worshippers were mostly serious-minded shopkeepers, farmers, artisans and craftsmen (both in rural and industrial communities), people who had a stake in property and a desire to worship according to their conscience rather than the will of the state. Thomas Davies, Unitarian minister at Cefncoedycymer, believed that there was every prospect that Unitarianism would become 'the popular religion of Cambro-British Christians',[82] but its promoters were never likely to be as compelling to people as were Methodist zealots who made it their business to make windows into people's souls. Iolo and his acolytes preferred the company of thinking people who could cope with demanding theological and ideological concepts and who concerned themselves with the plight of poor, downtrodden members of society.[83]

Iolo served the fledgling Society in several ways. He made use of the *Monthly Repository* which, from 1806, became the house journal of the Unitarian movement in Britain. Founded and edited by Robert Aspland, it contained biographical sketches, biblical essays, theological disputes, political criticism and obituaries, all of which helped to bring liberally-minded congregations closer together in a common cause.[84] Iolo supplied its editor with regular reports on the progress of Unitarianism in south Wales and was warmly praised by Thomas Belsham for his 'meritorious efforts to promote the cause of truth & the great doctrine of the divine unity'.[85] In particular, he was prepared to travel considerable distances to counsel and encourage newly-constituted churches. One shining example was his efforts on behalf of beleaguered Unitarians in south Cardiganshire where two sharply contrasting figures were seeking to further the cause of anti-trinitarianism. One was Charles Lloyd, the son of David Lloyd, Brynllefrith, who was a notable classical scholar. In 1799 he returned to his native patch from Exeter in order to make a living as a progressive farmer. For all his brilliant gifts as a scholar, however, Lloyd was not an easy man to handle. Once famously described as 'of wonderful ability, bad

---

[81] NLW 13145A, p. 450; NLW 21366E, p. 12ᵛ; *Monthly Repository*, II (1807), 444. See also Geraint H. Jenkins, '"Dyro Dduw dy Nawdd": Iolo Morganwg a'r Mudiad Undodaidd' in idem (ed.), *Cof Cenedl XX: Ysgrifau ar Hanes Cymru* (Llandysul, 2005), pp. 65–100.

[82] *Monthly Repository*, I (1806), 492–3.

[83] John Seed, 'Theologies of Power: Unitarianism and the Social Relations of Religious Discourse, 1800–1850' in R. J. Morris (ed.), *Class, Power and Social Structure in British Nineteenth-Century Towns* (Leicester, 1986), pp. 108–56.

[84] *Memoir of the Life, Works and Correspondence of the Rev. Robert Aspland* (London, 1850); Francis E. Mineka, *The Dissidence of Dissent: The Monthly Repository 1806–1838* (Chapel Hill, N.C., 1944).

[85] *CIM*, III, p. 249, Thomas Belsham to Iolo Morganwg, 15 March 1814.

temper, jealous to a degree, and always in hot water of his own boiling',[86] he was evidently a man after Iolo's heart. He certainly shared Iolo's taste for furious arguments and it was at his bidding that two groups of worshippers seceded from the mother church at Llwynrhydowen and set up two strictly Unitarian churches at Pantydefaid and Capel-y-groes in 1802.[87] Iolo had no wish to jeopardize his cordial relationship with David Davis of Castellhywel, who was the Arian minister at Llwynrhydowen, but he felt obliged to lend support to the seceders who, in turn, warmly welcomed him on his arrival and enjoyed his companionship. Having bought his chisel and mallet with him, he carved pertinent scriptural inscriptions on each building: 'I ni nid oes ond unduw, y Tad' (To us there is only one God, the Father) at Pantydefaid and 'I'r unig wir Dduw' (To the only true God) at Capel-y-groes.[88] The latter church benefited from the largesse of David Jenkin Rees of Lloyd Jack in the Vale of Aeron, an extraordinarily generous benefactor and improver who gave liberally to Unitarian causes and did everything within his power to alleviate the lot of the poor. Iolo made a point of spending time in his company and their friendship was maintained until Rees fell victim to typhus in 1817.[89]

Although Iolo remained full of energy and endeavour in promoting Unitarianism in this way, not least because it enabled him to enjoy the cut and thrust of debate with antagonists, he was extremely glad when a Unitarian fund was established in 1806 to enable the movement to employ missionaries.[90] Benjamin Phillips, an unusually eloquent preacher from St Clears, and David Oliver, minister at Gellionnen from 1806, both advanced from Arminianism to Unitarianism and travelled extensively in south Wales in a bid to establish new causes and fortify the spirits of existing ones. Their labours were enhanced when James Lyons, an Irishman who also preached to large audiences in Scotland,[91] embarked on extensive tours in 1808 and 1811 in order to rescue worshippers 'lost in the mists of Calvinism and Sabellianism'.[92] Although Lyons suspected that Welsh Unitarians were less well-versed in theological minutiae than their counterparts in Scotland, he praised their liveliness and tolerance.[93] Of Iolo he wrote: 'He is a man of very extensive and varied information, of

---

[86] George Eyre Evans (ed.), *Lloyd Letters (1754–1796)* (Aberystwyth, 1908), p. xxx; D. Elwyn Davies, *'They Thought for Themselves'* (Llandysul, 1982), pp. 36–7. For Lloyd, see also *DWB*, *ODNB* and Davies, *Cewri'r Ffydd*, pp. 87–103.

[87] John Gwili Jenkins, *Hanfod Duw a Pherson Crist* (Liverpool, 1931), pp. 312–15.

[88] NLW 13141A, p. 236; NLW 21398E, no. 15.

[89] J. Jenkins, 'David Jenkin Rees o Loydjack', *Yr Ymofynydd*, new series, IX, no. 32 (1884), 90–2; *Monthly Repository*, XII (1817), 740–5; Davies, *Cewri'r Ffydd*, pp. 67–73. Iolo described him as 'our most worthy, good and energetic friend'. *CIM*, III, p. 280, Iolo Morganwg to John James, 1 September 1814.

[90] George Chryssides, *The Elements of Unitarianism* (Shaftesbury, 1998), p. 23.

[91] *Monthly Repository*, XIX (1824), 629.

[92] Ibid., V (1810), 463.

[93] Ibid., VI (1811), 692.

amiable manners, of great liberality, and of very great zeal for the promotion of rational religion.'[94] In 1816 Iolo was instrumental in drawing up an itinerary for Richard Wright, a labourer's son and formerly General Baptist minister at Wisbech, who spent ten weeks in south Wales.[95] A tiny, energetic figure, he thought nothing of walking thirty miles a day and Iolo, together with Benjamin Phillips, who acted as his interpreter, were the only ones who could keep up with him on his 800-mile itinerary. To his great pleasure, Wright was greeted by large congregations, especially in Carmarthen, Swansea, Neath, Aberdare and Merthyr. Although prone to exaggerate the number of hearers and what he had achieved, Wright was especially delighted by the reception Iolo had arranged for him at Merthyr. He preached to overflowing congregations on seven occasions and discovered 'more of the spirit of enterprise, of free inquiry and liberality, than in many other places'.[96] His overall assessment was that there was much still to be done and that the work of the Society would be greatly strengthened were it to appoint a permanent Welsh-speaking missionary and launch a Welsh-language journal. A bond formed between the two foot-sloggers and, in his review of the tour, Wright produced a shrewd and accurate sketch of Iolo in his seventieth year:

> Though we had not met before, we knew each other by character, and he now came twenty miles [to Neath] to meet me. He was old, and subject to a complaint which had prevented his being able to sleep in a bed, or to rest in a horizontal posture, for many years. He was a good poet and mineralogist, and possessed a great deal of genius and information. He had no small degree of eccentricity; his feelings were remarkably independent; and he was enthusiastically fond of liberty. He appeared to be universally respected. He traveled with me from place to place about a week, and I was much entertained by his conversation.[97]

Iolo had already sensed that an intellectual void lay at the heart of the Unitarian ministry in south Wales. At his instigation, in July 1813 the Unitarian Society had petitioned the Presbyterian Board of the Carmarthen academy, urging it to appoint a Unitarian to its complement of tutors.[98] Iolo was convinced that the Calvinist curriculum imposed by David Peter on young students

---

[94] Ibid., 685.
[95] Ibid., XI (1816), 680–4; Cardiff 4, 207, no. 4, Thomas Evans to John James, 5 September 1816; Richard Wright, *A Review of the Missionary Life and Labors of Richard Wright* (London, 1824).
[96] Wright, *A Review of the Missionary Life*, p. 375.
[97] Ibid., pp. 372–3.
[98] NLW 21406E, no. 8.

was spreading a 'thick and black darkness' ('tywyllwch dudew')[99] over the land. The supine response from Carmarthen angered him and prompted him to campaign vigorously in 1815–16 on behalf of a Welsh Unitarian seminary: 'I have warmth enough in this cause', he assured Thomas Belsham, 'and on the present occasion I feel that the ebullition of my national blood has not yet ceased though verging on three score years and ten.'[100] 'Hey! Plant the acorn!' ('Hai! Plannwch y fesen!'),[101] he urged John James, a promising Unitarian minister who had received a call from Gellionnen in August 1814. Iolo drew up plans for such a college, including designs for a lecture room, a common room, a school room, a chapel, a house for the principal tutor, a kitchen, a matron's apartment, bedrooms, pantries and a bowling green.[102] As for a suitable location, he favoured Swansea or Neath, though he also believed that Bridgend, Briton Ferry or Pyle would be entirely suitable. He also seriously contemplated setting up a Unitarian library in Bridgend which would include 'some of the best authors on the most important of Politics and Theology, and those on both sides of the several questions with that faithful impartiality that Justice, and the unprejudiced search after Truth, requires'.[103] Once more, Iolo had demonstrated his vision.

In a bid to make Unitarianism better known and more congenial to heads of households, Iolo also busied himself by translating helpful tracts into Welsh and honing his skills as a hymn-writer. In 1804 the Society published his translation of John Clarke's *An Answer to the Question, Why are you a Christian?*[104] and ten years later Iolo published in Merthyr his translation of John Prior Estlin's catechism *General Instructions in the Doctrines and Duties of Religion*.[105] He spent long hours preparing lists of extracts from the scriptures, in English and Welsh, to support anti-trinitarianism and sometimes grouped them together under headings such as 'Jesus Christ a Man' ('Iesu Grist yn Ddyn') and 'Divine Unity'.[106] One very pressing reason for this activity was the growing success of Calvinistic Methodism. Its numbers were increasing so swiftly that it could no longer feel comfortable within the established church.

---

[99] *CIM*, III, p. 281, Iolo Morganwg to John James, 1 September 1814. See also D. Elwyn J. Davies, 'Astudiaeth o Feddwl a Chyfraniad Iolo Morganwg fel Rhesymolwr ac Undodwr' (unpublished University of Wales Ph.D. thesis, 1975), pp. 452–3.

[100] *CIM*, III, p. 290, Iolo Morganwg to [Thomas Belsham], 13 October 1814.

[101] Ibid., III, p. 281, Iolo Morganwg to John James, 1 September 1814.

[102] NLW 21406E, nos. 27–8.

[103] NLW 21407E, nos. 11–12.

[104] Edward Williams (trans.), *Atteb i'r Gofyniad, Pa ham yr wyt ti yn Gristion?* (Llundain, 1804); Cardiff 2.1020, p. 20.

[105] Edward Williams (trans.), *Holiadur, neu Addysgiadau Cyffredin, Hawl ac Atteb, yn Athrawiaethau a Dyledswyddau Crefydd* (Merthyr Tydfil, 1814). For the manuscript copy, see NLW 13145A, pp. 230–57. Iolo also translated part of Thomas Belsham's *A Calm Inquiry into the Scripture Doctrine concerning the Person of Christ* into Welsh. NLW 21432E, no. 3.

[106] NLW 13145A, pp. 13–151. See also ibid., pp. 466–85, 490–3, 507–31.

From 1810 it became a denomination with an acute sense of its own history and destiny. But Iolo was singularly unimpressed by the 'horribly irrational' behaviour of 'the hell and damnation folks' who flocked to Bala or Llangeitho and he often called on God to protect him from 'Calvinistic rancour, fury & falsehood'.[107] He derived perverse delight from confronting and confounding Methodists, and making enemies of them. It was characteristic of him to have derisively dismissed William Williams, Pantycelyn, as a 'hymn carpenter'[108] and to have composed around 3,000 hymns, over three times as many as Pantycelyn had managed.[109] Indeed, it has been calculated that he composed on average a hymn every three days between 1802 and 1826.[110] Only one anthology – *Salmau yr Eglwys yn yr Anialwch* (1812) – was published during his lifetime and few of his hymns rise to great literary heights, even though David Davis of Neath gushingly claimed that they 'breathe enlightened and sublime devotion, often expressed in some of the finest strains and loftiest flights of a luxuriant-but-well-pruned imagination of any, I think, that I have ever read'.[111] But it needs to be borne in mind that the Bard of Liberty had no ambitions to become a 'Sweet Singer' like Pantycelyn or imitate his florid style or endorse his political conservatism. Whereas the eyes of Pantycelyn and his fellow hymnists were firmly fixed on heaven, Iolo focused on the challenges of the here and now. His stock of simple, intelligible hymns and psalms was designed to reflect Christian morals and obligations, highlight the power, wisdom and benevolence of God, and act as a counterblast against 'the most glaring wickedness of our own infernalized age'.[112]

There were other 'hymn coblers',[113] even within anti-trinitarian folds, of whom Iolo disapproved heartily. Chief among these was Thomas Evans (Tomos Glyn Cothi). Iolo's relationship with the mottled Carmarthenshire weaver had cooled considerably after 1803, and revelations of the latter's indiscretions in Carmarthen prison had left a bitter aftertaste. According to Timothy Davis, the second son of David Davis, Castellhywel, Evans 'did not

---

[107] *CIM*, III, p. 260, Iolo Morganwg to Taliesin Williams, 31 March 1814; ibid., III, p. 554, Iolo Morganwg to [?], 4 September 1820.
[108] NLW 13130A, p. 191. See also NLW 21419E, no. 41, and *CIM*, III, p. 108, Iolo Morganwg to William Howell, 23 June 1812.
[109] For Iolo's bulkiest collections of hymns, see NLW 21336A–21348A, 21352A. See also a valuable anthology, Cathryn A. Charnell-White (ed.), *Detholiad o Emynau Iolo Morganwg* (Aberystwyth, 2009).
[110] *'The Bard is a Very Singular Character'*, p. 203, n. 168.
[111] *CIM*, III, p. 118, David Davis to Iolo Morganwg, 26–29 August 1812. Elsewhere, he referred to Iolo's psalms as 'superlatively excellent'. Ibid., III, p. 140, David Davis to Iolo Morganwg, 28 February–1 March 1813.
[112] Ibid., III, p. 107, Iolo Morganwg to William Howell, 23 June 1812.
[113] NLW 21431E, no. 57.

come out of jail with credit'.[114] Bound over to keep the peace for seven years, he withdrew from radical circles and his correspondence with Iolo ceased after 1805. When Evans, probably inadvertently, stole a march on Iolo by publishing a collection of Welsh hymns in 1811[115] the latter accused him of plagiarism and betrayal.[116] Thereafter Iolo made no attempt to heal the breach. Indeed, he disowned Evans as a moral degenerate and 'a rank infidel'.[117] Yet, it was Iolo's hymns which lived on, at least within the Unitarian fraternity. His 1812 anthology ran to a second edition in 1827, a second volume appeared in 1834, and a bumper edition of both volumes was published in 1857. The best part of half of the hymns included in the popular Unitarian hymn-book *Emynau o Fawl a Gweddi* in 1878 were composed by Iolo.[118]

Iolo also used the Unitarian Society of South Wales as a vehicle for his wider humanitarian concerns. He remained greatly attached to the anti-slave trade campaign and maintained that humankind could not progress if slave-trading merchants and wealthy plantation owners were allowed to prosper. 'What injury have the poor Africans done to mankind?'[119] was a thorny question he often posed. He continued to play a significant role in turning public opinion in south Wales against what he called the 'diabolical traffic'[120] in slaves and made many high-sounding declarations on the subject. But Pitt's 'Reign of Terror' and the long war with France drained the abolitionist movement of popular support. Men of property warned against the consequences of free speech, democracy and French-style politics, and there were no local anti-slavery societies to support Iolo and other abolitionists until Swansea and Neath led the way in 1822.[121] Iolo was among a small minority who empathized with black slaves and championed those who were brave enough to resist. He was jubilant on receiving 'glorious news' in June 1802 of the rebellion of slaves in Saint-Domingue (Haiti): 'The blacks are soundly drubbing the white devils, nicknamed men, *llwyddiant iddynt* [success to them].'[122] He also yearned for the opportunity to liberate his brothers' negro

---

[114] NLW 5490C, unpaginated diary entry, 14 February 1833.
[115] Thomas Evans, *Cyfansoddiad o Hymnau* (Caerfyrddin, 1811).
[116] NLW 13145A, pp. 321–3; NLW 13159A, pp. 253–4; Edward Williams, *Salmau yr Eglwys yn yr Anialwch, Cyfrol I* (Merthyr Tydfil, 1812), p. vi.
[117] *CIM*, III, p. 539, Iolo Morganwg to [Thomas Davies], 27 January 1820.
[118] *Literary and Historical Legacy*, p. 123.
[119] *CIM*, II, p. 326, Iolo Morganwg to William Owen Pughe, 8 September 1800.
[120] Ibid., II, p. 63, Iolo Morganwg to Mary Barker, 26 March [1798].
[121] Chris Evans, 'Was Wales opposed to the Slave Trade?' in Huw V. Bowen (ed.), *A New History of Wales* (Llandysul, 2011), p. 109.
[122] *CIM*, II, p. 417, Iolo Morganwg to Walter Davies (Gwallter Mechain), 1 June 1802. See Laurent Dubois, *Avengers of the New World: The Story of the Haitian Revolution* (Cambridge, Mass., 2004).

slaves in Jamaica from 'their long miseries and captivity'[123] and shook with indignation whenever landowners and merchants mocked his efforts to influence public opinion. Pitt was so determined to vanquish the French that the abolition of slavery was low on his list of priorities. But his death in 1806 opened new doors for William Wilberforce and his supporters, and on 23 February 1807 the House of Commons voted overwhelmingly in favour of the Slave Trade Abolition Act.[124] Tears streamed down Wilberforce's cheeks on this poignant occasion and it is easy to imagine that eyes also moistened in a certain cottage in Flemingston when news arrived that royal assent had been gained on 25 March. To mark the occasion Iolo composed 'Cân Rhyddhad y Caethion' (Song on the Liberation of the Slaves) in which he expressed his great delight in witnessing the 'joyful day' on which the brutal trade in slaves was declared illegal:

> Dydd i agor drws pob carchar,
>   Dryllio'r gadwyn, torri'r iau,
> Dydd i sychu dagrau galar,
>   Dydd ein Duw sy'n ymneshau.[125]

> (A day to open all prison doors,
> Shatter chains, and break the yoke,
> A day to dry the tears of sorrow,
> The day of our God is drawing near.)

At a time when the bulk of the Welsh were indifferent to the plight of slaves and scornful of Iolo's dedication to their cause, it had not been easy to play even a small part in bringing about this historic event. David Davis of Neath was convinced that Iolo's tireless campaigns and timely interventions had sustained the momentum of the abolitionists in south Wales and warmly congratulated him on ending 'the nefarious traffic in human flesh': 'Is not this triumph of humanity over the most execrable cruelty a ten thousand times more proper subject of public thanksgiving to the benevolent "Father of all" than all the victories ever gained by the Nelsons of the world over their brethren in arms?'[126]

---

[123] *CIM*, II, p. 669, Iolo Morganwg to William Owen Pughe, 28 April 1805.
[124] William Hague, *William Wilberforce: The Life of the Great Anti-Slave Trade Campaigner* (London, 2007), p. 354.
[125] T. C. Evans (Cadrawd) (ed.), *Gwaith Iolo Morganwg* (Llanuwchllyn, 1913), p. 57.
[126] *CIM*, II, pp. 828–9, David Davis to Iolo Morganwg, 3 April 1807.

As Andrew Davies has shown,[127] the issue of slavery and the abolition of the slave trade posed an extraordinarily painful moral challenge for Iolo. Although he had already accepted relatively small sums of money from his rich Jamaican-based brothers, he had refused offers of an annual benefaction and had assured William Owen Pughe that his children would never be allowed to profit from the blood-soaked gains of their benighted uncles:

> God deliver my very poor children from ever having a single farthing from such estates. May the vast Atlantic ocean swallow up Jamaica, and all other slave-trading and slave-holding countries, before a boy or a girl of mine eats that single morsel that would prevent him or her from perishing of hunger, if it is the produce of slavery.[128]

But the scenario changed in December 1803 when his brother John died, leaving an estate worth £7,676, including thirty-six slaves valued at £3,880.[129] Iolo and his children were to receive a total bequest of around £400. But when John Williams's widow challenged the terms of the will, the matter lay dormant for several years. In the meantime the traffic in slavery ended in 1807 and many slaves were freed. By 1810 all his brothers had died and, after much heart-searching, Iolo eventually enlisted Alfred Estlin, a Bristol solicitor, to pursue his family's claim on his brother's bequest. By this stage he was falling ever deeper into the poverty trap and he knew that the Jamaican windfall would go a long way to remove his debts and improve the economic prospects of his children. Since the slave trade had now been abolished, he was able to argue that he could accept the money with a clear conscience. But, as his correspondence indicates, he had strong misgivings about the whole affair and it is hard to believe that he did not feel a lingering sense of shame in profiting indirectly from the labour of black slaves in the fields, mills and boiling houses of Jamaica. He continued to profess his hatred of slavery to friend and foe alike even as he helped his son to set up a commercial school in Merthyr and his daughters to establish a milliners' shop at Cefncribwr. Having watched over his beloved children's lives and fretted about what would become of them for so long, Iolo's decision to accept what could be construed as a tainted bequest was entirely understandable.

If 25 March 1807 was a red-letter day in Iolo's life, so too was 21 July 1813, when the Doctrine of the Trinity Act removed penalties against anti-

---

[127] Andrew Davies, '"Uncontaminated with Human Gore"? Iolo Morganwg, Slavery and the Jamaican Inheritance' in *Rattleskull Genius*, pp. 293–313. See also Geraint H. Jenkins, '"Diabolical Traffic": Iolo Morganwg, Slavery and Merthyr Tydfil', *MH*, 19 (2008), 7–17.
[128] *CIM*, II, p. 537, Iolo Morganwg to William Owen Pughe, 25 August 1803.
[129] NLW 21410E, no. 42; *CIM*, III, pp. 50–1, Iolo Morganwg to David Davis, 31 January 1811.

trinitarians and enabled Unitarianism to become a fully legal faith. He duly noted the passing of the bill by declaring in one of his notebooks that he and his fellow worshippers had become 'Freemen in their Native Land'.[130] This freedom led him to redouble his anti-war campaigns. Closely associated with his Quaker friends in Neath and Cardiff, he threw in his lot with the Peace Society and made it a habit to ask awkward questions of warmongers. Had anyone preached an anti-war sermon in the royal chapel, in Westminster Abbey or in St Paul's Cathedral?[131] Would Napoleon have come into existence as a perpetrator of 'war and blood, fire and sword' had it not been for the conduct of William Pitt and his associates in forcing the French to defend themselves against 'some of the darkest machinations that were ever inspired by the powers of darkness'?[132] He despised Nelson, Picton, Wellington and others who revelled in gaining military honours and within meetings of the Unitarian Society of South Wales he doggedly preached the merits of using the 'bloodless weapons'[133] of truth, reason and justice. His 'Quakerish' sentiments had convinced him that the day would soon dawn when nations would no longer learn war and that the 'wintry storms' which raged through Europe would be no more.[134] In one of his most intriguing drafts, written 'in the character of a Quaker', he urged Napoleon (as he had urged Pitt in 1796) to don the mantle of greatness by establishing a congress of nations committed to the cause of universal peace and toleration.[135]

Under the influence of the Quakers, Iolo became increasingly critical of the rigid structures favoured by the Unitarian Society. Such was his stature within the movement that his colleagues found him difficult to control at times. At the eleventh annual general meeting, held at Aberdare in June 1812, Iolo persuaded the executive committee to subject the Society to the principle of 'self-reformation' which would allow its rules and regulations to be revised triennially.[136] Fearful that Unitarianism was in danger of becoming a priest-ridden elitist 'conclave of cardinals', he favoured setting up 'priestless' societies sustained by itinerant ministers and heads of households.[137] He laid out plans for a new body called the 'Berean Society' which would set itself the task of

---

[130] NLW 21344A, note on inside cover of the notebook.
[131] NLW 13120B, p. 361.
[132] NLW 21319A, pp. 1, 3.
[133] Ibid., p. 2.
[134] *CIM*, II, p. 881, Iolo Morganwg to Benjamin Heath Malkin, 28 November 1809; NLW 21319A, p. 1.
[135] *CIM*, II, pp. 642–4, Iolo Morganwg to Napoleon Bonaparte [?1805].
[136] *Monthly Repository*, VIII (1813), 214–15. See also his observations on 'Unitarian Discipline and Polity' in NLW 13103B, p. 14, and his criticism of irregularities in NLW 13157A, p. 265.
[137] NLW 13145A, pp. 203–18, 310–14; NLW 21406E, no. 34; *CIM*, III, p. 355, Iolo Morganwg to Taliesin Williams, 26 July 1815; ibid., III, p. 367, Iolo Morganwg to the Revd John Jones, 29 September 1815; ibid., III, p. 406, Iolo Morganwg to [John Rowland(s)], 24 June 1816.

encouraging lay participation and scriptural debate.[138] But while marvelling at his ingenuity and persistence, his colleagues did not allow him to do as he pleased. The likes of Elijah Waring and Joseph Tregelles Price were not permitted to set the agenda in Unitarian circles and an internal crisis was averted.

Other issues in post-war Wales now attracted Iolo's attention. In 1818 he surprised everyone by intervening in the campaign for the county seat. A year earlier Sir Christopher Cole of Penrice Castle, a retired naval officer who had seen conflict in the American, French and Napoleonic wars but who was best known for his daring conquest of the Banda Islands in 1810, had been put up as a candidate by a landowning clique in order to prevent the seat from falling into the hands of John Edwards, an affluent, opportunistic London Welshman whose father had bought the Rheola estate, near Neath. Cole was the type of naval hero whom Iolo loathed with all his heart. He was returned unopposed in 1817, but Edwards had already begun plotting his electoral strategy as the future champion of the county's independent freeholders.[139] Cole's supporters were deeply divided in 1818, so much so that he decided to withdraw from the contest, only to change his mind at the last minute. Iolo was so furious when he heard of Cole's dishonourable behaviour that he sat down on the roadside on his way to Bridgend to compose a song in support of the independent yeomanry. Entitled 'Glamorgan Triumphant, or, Edwards for ever!', it was in many ways a reprise of songs circulated during the 1789 election.[140] Iolo thundered against the 'meritless' aristocracy who, 'with a high hand, wield tyranny's rod and our homage demand':

> Ye sons of Glamorgan be bold in the cause
> Of your dear native land, of your freedom and laws;
> Behold on your plains how the tyrant appears,
> In support of oppression his standard uprears.
> See the spawn of false greatness, like furies combin'd,
> Against merit and truth, with infernalized mind;
> Let them rave, let them strain in a fruitless endeavour,
> In spite of them all we shout 'Edwards for ever!'[141]

---

[138] NLW 13106B, pp. 49–52, 85–9; NLW 13128A, p. 188; NLW 21360B, pp. 26–32. One of his concerns was that many Unitarian ministers who preached and wrote in Welsh were guilty of 'the grossest anglicisms'. NLW 13129A, pp. 213–16.
[139] Roland G. Thorne (ed.), *The History of Parliament: The House of Commons 1790–1820. Volume III* (London, 1986), pp. 482, 675–6.
[140] NLW 21402F, nos. 11, 11b, 11c; *CIM*, III, pp. 477–9, Iolo Morganwg to John Edwards, 6 July 1818.
[141] *CIM*, III, p. 478, Iolo Morganwg to John Edwards, 6 July 1818.

The dispute provoked a flurry of correspondence in *The Cambrian*[142] and, under heavy pressure, 'Old Kit Cole' withdrew his candidature. To celebrate Edwards's victory, Iolo published *Vox Populi Vox Dei!*, a sixpenny pamphlet which also included songs entitled 'Edwards for Ever!' by his daughters Margaret (Peggy) and Ann (Nancy).[143] By ousting Cole, Iolo claimed that voters for 'Edwards y Cymro' had spared the county from further shame and embarrassment:

> We will no longer be controll'd by the domineerings of unconstitutional claims and influences. Vox populi vox Dei is an ancient adage, a very good one, and, I believe, but very little short of the Truth, which sooner or later will recover its own.[144]

In 1820, however, Cole re-entered the fray, prompting Iolo to depict him as a sturdy beggar, supported only by knaves and fools, who craved 'false honours, vain titles and pelf'.[145] His son Taliesin joined in by penning a song called 'The King of the Beggars',[146] but Cole's supporters were able to demolish Edwards's claim to be a proud Welshman by producing a baptismal certificate which betrayed his Lambeth origins. Cole regained the seat and held it, with little distinction, until 1830. With his proverbial prankster charm, Iolo promised to compose a new song in honour of Cole – to the tune of 'Mad Moll' – to be declaimed loudly at every annual commemoration of the conquest of Banda.[147]

Just as the language used by Iolo in *Vox Populi Vox Dei!* harked back to the 1790s, so did the emblems of Unitarianism revive memories of the Gorsedd of the Bards in the same period. The motto 'Y Gwir yn erbyn y Byd' (The Truth against the World) was incorporated by Iolo into the rules and regulations of the Unitarian Society of South Wales in 1802.[148] Ten years later the mystic sign (*nod cyfrin*) /|\ appeared on the title-page of his collection of Unitarian hymns.[149] Concerned lest the patriotic jubilation which followed the battle of Waterloo should undermine the morale of republican bards and Dissenting ministers, he presided over Gorsedd rituals at the Rocking-stone or *Y Maen*

---

[142] See extracts in NLW 6575E and NLW 21402F, no. 14.
[143] Edward Williams, *Vox Populi Vox Dei!* (Swansea, 1818). See also NLW 21402F, no. 11. Waring referred to him as 'launching the missiles of squibs and lampoons with no sparing hand'. *RAEW*, p. 136.
[144] NLW 21402F, no. 17a.
[145] Ibid., nos. 13, 13a.
[146] Ibid., nos. 10, 10a, 10b.
[147] NLW 21400C, no. 35.
[148] D. Elwyn Davies, 'Iolo Morganwg (1747–1826), Bardism and Unitarianism', *Journal of Welsh Religious History*, 6 (1998), 8.
[149] Williams, *Salmau yr Eglwys yn yr Anialwch, Cyfrol I*.

Chwŷf, as he liked to call it, at Pontypridd in 1814 and 1817.[150] The Gorsedd, he maintained, was the finest and most inspiring response to a world of 'warring Pride, of bloodful strife'.[151] He was already laying plans to use druidism as a conduit for his radical Unitarianism when a group of Welsh literary parsons persuaded him to assist them in promoting a series of eisteddfodau under the aegis of the newly-constituted Cambrian Society in 1818.[152] Iolo knew of course that the Society's president, Bishop Thomas Burgess, was a sworn enemy of radical Unitarianism and that his aim was to provide the established church with a more acceptable Cymricized public face and to act as a socio-cultural bulwark at a time when 'the signal of revolution is sounded over the land, and sedition and infidelity, treason and atheism stalk around us in all their naked deformity'.[153] In the event, Burgess came to rue the day when Iolo was invited to adjudicate at the Carmarthen provincial eisteddfod in July 1819. The old Glamorgan bard deeply embarrassed his host on the final day by holding a Gorsedd ceremony and initiating Dissenters of a distinctly radical hue. Iolo unapologetically refused to curtail the proceedings and loudly defended the principles of liberty and rationalism. In trepidation, Burgess sought the views of Edward 'Celtic' Davies about Iolo's true intentions and was told that the little republican stonemason was eager 'to root up every sound principle of Politics & religion'.[154] Burgess was apoplectic and Taliesin warned his father that the Bishop of St David's 'is more your enemy than friend'.[155] A Unitarian was still reckoned by civil and church leaders to be capable of fomenting strife. Iolo had always derided such views and continued to do so. 'Now, sir', he mused in a letter to Benjamin Malkin, 'what will be the term that may be properly applied to the poor Welsh bard of Flimston? Pop-gun, beyond a doubt.'[156]

---

[150] *CIM*, III, pp. 306–7, Thomas Williams (Gwilym Morganwg) to Iolo Morganwg, 6 December 1814; *HGB*, pp. 43–8; Huw Walters, 'Myfyr Morganwg and the Rocking-Stone Gorsedd' in *Rattleskull Genius*, pp. 402–3.

[151] NLW 13093E, p. 81.

[152] A printed prospectus of the Cambrian Society is in NLW 1949E. For the background, see Bedwyr Lewis Jones, *Yr Hen Bersoniaid Llengar* ([Penarth], [1963]); Hywel Teifi Edwards, *The Eisteddfod* (Cardiff, 1990), pp. 16–17, and Geraint H. Jenkins, 'The Unitarian Firebrand, the Cambrian Society and the Eisteddfod' in *Rattleskull Genius*, pp. 285–7.

[153] *Cambro-Briton*, I (1819), 71.

[154] Cardiff 3.86, Edward Davies to Thomas Burgess, undated.

[155] *CIM*, III, p. 583, Taliesin Williams to Iolo Morganwg, 26 January 1821. Iolo had previously informed Burgess that the gates of hell would never prevail against Unitarian congregations. Ibid., III, p. 321, Iolo Morganwg to [Thomas Burgess] [?1815].

[156] *CIM*, II, p. 880, Iolo Morganwg to Benjamin Heath Malkin, 28 November 1809. In this context Iolo wondered, having seen the poet Reginald Heber described in a review as 'of no ordinary calibre', whether all poets, like cannons, would henceforth be characterized by their calibre.

Again and again, however, it is Iolo the humanitarian who shines through in his papers. Following his return to Wales in 1795 right through to his death in 1826 he pledged to work on behalf of poor, underprivileged and oppressed people. He told Hannah More: 'I have commenced an odd kind of apostleship. It is to instruct those of my own class in the manners of the great, holding them up, not as examples, but as objects of detestation.'[157] To his lasting credit, he felt impelled to spend a large amount of his time persuading the rich and the powerful to be 'doers of justice'.[158] Cases of distress moved him personally and he deplored the tendency to ascribe poverty to the moral failings of the poor themselves. As an enlightened Christian, he felt duty-bound to support the sick, the infirm and the oppressed, and to shame others into doing likewise. Although he knew in his heart of hearts that a demanding faith like Unitarianism was never likely to become a religion of the poor, he still maintained that it had an important role to play in alleviating distress and exposing injustice.

Since Iolo spent most of his life in poverty, he was able to empathize with the lot of fellow sufferers. He prided himself on his 'invincible abstemious habits of living'[159] and for the most part subsisted on bread, butter, cheese, fresh vegetables from his garden, and copious cups of tea. He always travelled on foot and only very rarely caused discomfort to horses by mounting and riding them. 'I never had any taste for horse flesh', he assured Walter Davies.[160] Among his favourite proverbs and sayings were 'Living from hand to mouth' ('Byw o'r llaw i'r genau') and 'Living on the penny' ('Byw ar y geiniog').[161] Although he accepted that money, like nauseous medicine, was a necessary evil,[162] his pockets seldom jingled with many coins. His very public spat with Owain Myfyr meant that he could no longer expect fat cheques from London. Nor could he feed his family with the modest subventions from the Royal Literary Fund. As he got older and more infirm, stonemasonry became a grind, a painful trade for an asthmatic, and he was unable to depend on it for a regular income. By 1806 he was in such straitened circumstances that Llewellyn Traherne of Coedrhiglan and St Hilary rallied the local gentry in his hour of need. A fund was established by up to thirty benefactors who contributed an annual guinea or half a guinea per person between 1806 and 1824.[163] On

---

[157] *CIM*, I, p. 756, Iolo Morganwg to [Hannah More] [?May 1795].
[158] Ibid., I, p. 824, Iolo Morganwg to the Members of the Bath Agricultural Society, 19 July 1796.
[159] Ibid., III, p. 152, Iolo Morganwg to Thomas Rees, 3 May 1813.
[160] Ibid., II, p. 414, Iolo Morganwg to Walter Davies (Gwallter Mechain), 13 May 1802.
[161] NLW 21426E, no. 63.
[162] *CIM*, III, p. 89, Iolo Morganwg to David Davis, 6–11 January 1812.
[163] NLW 21410E, no. 45; NLW 21413E, no. 21; *CIM*, II, p. 798, Iolo Morganwg to [Llewellyn Traherne] [May 1806].

hearing of Traherne's intervention, Iolo was momentarily affronted – 'My independent spirit was a little wounded'[164] – but he was genuinely touched by this benevolence, especially at a time when his creditors were losing patience and his family was suffering many privations. Iolo thus had a better understanding than most of the miseries of poverty and of how the lower orders coped or failed to cope with grievous economic circumstances.

In an age of high sickness levels and chronic diseases, Iolo was a great believer in self-help and mutual help. Haunted by memories of his deceased child Elizabeth, he saw every ailment as potentially life-threatening and assiduously monitored the health of his family. His papers are also peppered with references to his own disabilities and illnesses. From time to time, to a greater or lesser degree, he was troubled by asthma, angina, dropsy, glandular fever, gout, migraine, pleurisy, rheumatism, sciatica, tinnitus and vertigo. From 1805 until his death, he could sleep only by sitting upright in a high-backed armchair. Preoccupied with his bowel movements, he prepared detailed accounts of his infirmities and discomforts. He had a low opinion of most physicians, surgeons and apothecaries, and he held quacks in utter contempt. A strong believer in self-medication, he built up a well-stocked medicine chest, dosed members of his family, nursed them, dressed their cuts and burns, re-set broken limbs, and plied them with a variety of herbal remedies, some of which were recommended by the widely admired Myddfai physicians of yore.[165] This saved him a good deal of money and reinforced his prejudices against professional medical men and mountebanks: 'What a scoundrelly profession is that of a doctor . . . As rascally a trade as that of a parson. In nothing better than that of a king.'[166] For short-term relief he used opium and purgatives as well as old favourites like Dr James's Powders, Bateman's Pectoral Drops and Daffy's Elixir. His neighbours and even needy travellers benefited from his medical knowledge and benevolence, and, according to Waring, he never thought of such acts of kindness as being anything more than 'the discharge of a moral and social duty'.[167] In a poem entitled 'The Wishing Cap', he championed the distressed and the disempowered:

> I wish to befriend the poor victims of grief,
> To hush the sore plaints of distress.
> To seek out for anguish the speedy relief,
> And the wrongs of the trampled redress.

---

[164] *CIM*, III, p. 268, Iolo Morganwg to John Herbert Lloyd, 1 July 1814.
[165] See NLW 13111B for medical texts transcribed by Iolo and NLW 13160A, p. 289, for nostrums by Meddygon Myddfai. Waring described Iolo as 'a good herbalist'. *RAEW*, p. 88.
[166] *CIM*, II, p. 482, Iolo Morganwg to William Owen Pughe, 29 March 1803. For the wider background, see Roy Porter, *Quacks: Fakers and Charlatans in English Medicine* (Stroud, 2000).
[167] *RAEW*, p. 128.

> I wish not for wealth, I would rather be poor,
> And on providence daily rely
> That knows all my wants, and to these at my door
> Affords an abundant supply.[168]

As a man of compassion, Iolo could no more ignore suffering on his own doorstep than he could defend the slave trade in the distant Caribbean islands. He was one of the few in the Cowbridge area who knew how to petition for help for widows, blind persons and disabled soldiers and seamen from a wide variety of charities and charitable groups in London and Bristol. He championed attempts by Nicholas James, a poor blind boy from Aberdare who had settled at Llancarfan, to secure assistance from a benefaction made by John Merlott, a former mayor of Bristol.[169] He urged William Owen Pughe to find employment as a clerk for William Spencer, a young midshipman and a friend of his son Taliesin, who had fallen on hard times following the death of his father John of Saers Farm, St Mary Church.[170] In a bid to secure compensation from the Chatham Chest, he intervened on behalf of one John Morgan who had been severely wounded at sea and discharged from the Navy as being medically unfit for service.[171] He applied to the Lloyd's Patriotic Fund, which assisted ex-servicemen and their widows and their dependants, on behalf of a poor woman from Cowbridge whose husband had died of fever.[172] By cultivating relationships with influential men he endeavoured to raise money to help Sarah Bedford, the widow of John Bedford, son of the ironmaster, and her six children.[173] Tireless in his efforts to mobilize support for such causes, Iolo was adept at pricking consciences and moving even the most obdurate people to pity.

Ever since he was a young man, Iolo had believed that the judicial system served the rich better than the poor and that its prejudices against religious deviants, notably Rational Dissenters, were a standing reproach. Echoing Clarendon, he railed against a legal system which enabled 'great men' to fly above the reach of justice at the expense of the poor.[174] 'I hate the law as I hate war',[175] he told John Prior Estlin and he believed that the procedures and

---

[168] NLW 21422E, no. 14.
[169] NLW 21411E, nos. 32, 32a, 32c.
[170] *CIM*, II, pp. 442–3, Iolo Morganwg to William Owen Pughe, 25 October 1802.
[171] Ibid., II, pp. 824–5, Leonard Harper to Iolo Morganwg, 14 January 1807.
[172] Ibid., II, p. 883, Iolo Morganwg to Benjamin Heath Malkin, 28 November 1809.
[173] Ibid., III, p. 422, Thomas Bedford to Iolo Morganwg, 16 February 1817. See also an account of his efforts on behalf of John Nicholas, a farmer from St Hilary whose house had been accidentally destroyed by fire on 30 January 1816, and who was unable to feed and clothe his pregnant wife and five children. NLW 21411E, no. 52.
[174] NLW 13147A, pp. 309–10.
[175] *CIM*, III, p. 418, Iolo Morganwg to John Prior Estlin [?1817].

language used in courts were 'the devil's language' ('iaith y diawl').[176] By regularly frequenting the proceedings of the Courts of the Great Sessions and, to a lesser degree, the Courts of Quarter Sessions, he learned a good deal about how judges, magistrates, lawyers and juries behaved, how poor, illiterate and sometimes monoglot Welsh speakers were treated, and how the law was used to paralyse calls for toleration and freedom. Had he not fallen out with Thomas Evans (Tomos Glyn Cothi) after his fall from grace, he would have published a book devoted to his exertions on behalf of his Unitarian colleague, to the glaring injustices suffered by him and to the vain efforts to petition for his release.[177] Iolo was deeply affected by individual cases of injustice and suffering, and waged vigorous campaigns on behalf of strangers as well as acquaintances. When Edward Jenkins, a maltster from Picketston in the parish of Llan-maes, was fined £400 by the Court of Exchequer in September 1813 for allegedly defrauding the inland revenue, he protested his innocence and refused to pay. Impressed by his luminosity, Iolo did everything possible to help him, including assembling and submitting a petition on his behalf to the Prince Regent, urging him to remit the penalty and save Jenkins from financial ruin.[178] A month later Iolo scurried around the Vale seeking signatures for a petition he had drawn up on behalf of William Morgan, a young labourer from Llantrisant, who had broken into an inn at Tonyrefail and stolen 25 shillings, a crime which was deemed punishable by death.[179] Executions were a popular spectator sport in Georgian times, but Iolo had always shunned such 'awful spectacle[s]'.[180] He managed to acquire 136 signatories by 6 October 1813, the most prominent of whom was John Wood, a Cardiff attorney, who ordered one of his clerks to write out the petition neatly and legibly on parchment.[181] It called on the Prince Regent to commute the punishment for that of transportation to one of the Crown's foreign plantations or colonies. After a nerve-shredding week in custody, the suitably contrite Morgan was informed that a

---

[176] Ibid., II, p. 279, Iolo Morganwg to William Owen Pughe, 15 April 1800.
[177] NLW 21373D, f. 10; National Archives, HO 47/27, pp. 297–301; Geraint H. Jenkins; '"A Very Horrid Affair": Sedition and Unitarianism in the Age of Revolutions' in R. R. Davies and Geraint H. Jenkins (eds.), *From Medieval to Modern Wales: Historical Essays in Honour of Kenneth O. Morgan and Ralph A. Griffiths* (Cardiff, 2004), pp. 175–96.
[178] NLW 21411E, nos. 48–51; *CIM*, III, pp. 162–5, Iolo Morganwg to Taliesin Williams, 4 August 1813.
[179] NLW, Great Sessions 4/633/8, nos. 16, 26, 64; *The Cambrian*, [18] September 1813; *The Cambrian Magazine*, 1 October 1813, 51; *CIM*, III, pp. 183–5, Iolo Morganwg to Thomas Redwood [?2 October 1813].
[180] *CIM*, III, pp. 188–90, Iolo Morganwg to Taliesin Williams, 8 October 1813.
[181] National Archives, HO 47/52; *CIM*, III, p. 188, Iolo Morganwg to Taliesin Williams, 8 October 1813.

conditional pardon had been received and that he was to be transported for life.¹⁸²

On several occasions Iolo gave advice to defendants regarding their pleas or the nature of their testimony, and he himself rather enjoyed being called to give evidence either as a witness or an expert in a certain field. When able to control his explosive temper and curb his sarcasm, he was more than a match for pettifogging lawyers. One of the highlights of his performances in the witness box occurred when he was seventy-six years old. In mid-April 1823 he was called to give evidence at the Court of the Great Sessions held in Cardiff on behalf of Robert and Evan Thomas, two illiterate farmers from Llantrisant, who were seeking to recover property from the estate of one of Iolo's great enemies, the late William Rees of Court Colman. In order to support the none-too-confident plaintiffs, Iolo practised his courtroom skills beforehand and spent several days in musty archives reading wills, marriage settlements and bonds, parish registers, deeds of indenture, leases, rent rolls and monumental inscriptions. The case lasted for four days, during which Iolo was minutely cross-examined for many hours by a brow-beating and increasingly exasperated barrister.¹⁸³ Iolo held his ground and his testimony was corroborated by William Illingworth, deputy keeper of the records in the Tower of London. Much to the disgust of the Rees family, the jury found in favour of the two bemused farmers. Iolo was jubilant:

> A completer victory at law was never yet obtained than ours. I thank God for it, for no testimony has ever been more the testimony of conscience than mine was, which was in the highest degree corroborated by that of Mr Ealingworth who, with myself, are branded . . . as the greatest scoundrels that ever existed!!! Whoever exerts himself to bring truth and justice to light will ever in this world be so branded . . .¹⁸⁴

Iolo's satisfaction on seeing the outraged response of relatives of his departed *bête noire* was further deepened from having outmanoeuvred several intimidating Methodist attorneys and 'some very zealous evangelicals'¹⁸⁵ who had used every possible ploy to rob the two farmers of their rightful inheritance.

---

[182] National Archives, HO 19/3; *CIM*, III, p. 195, Iolo Morganwg to Taliesin Williams, 12–15 October 1813.
[183] NLW 21397E, nos. 1–24; *The Cambrian*, 26 April 1823; *CIM*, III, pp. 656–9, Iolo Morganwg to Edward Williams, jun. I, 17 April 1823.
[184] *CIM*, III, p. 657, Iolo Morganwg to Edward Williams, jun. I, 17 April 1823. For other examples of Iolo using his legal expertise, see NLW 13157A, p. 28, and NLW 21411E, no. 21.
[185] *CIM*, III, pp. 553–8, Iolo Morganwg to [?], 4 September 1820.

Iolo also used other, more popular, venues to rail against the privileged few who were able to 'plunder the vast majority of what the Great Parent obviously designed for all' and to espouse the cause of those who wore 'tattered Garb' and lived in wretched poverty.[186] The influx of wealthy absentee landlords incensed him and, fortified by tea and laver-bread cakes, he regaled audiences in the inns and taverns of Cowbridge with his witty epigrams and satirical songs about 'plant Alis y biswail' (the dunghill English), prompting them to cry out: 'O boys! 'tis Iolo the Bard, Iolo the Bard, all along! How the old cock crows!'[187] Iolo believed that excessive wealth hardened people's hearts, ruined their morals, and 'render[ed] them poor, very poor indeed, in real happiness'.[188] He delighted local topers with his 'Heroic Song to Miss Tilney Long' who, from 1812, commanded the headlines for her enormous wealth. Catherine Tylney-Long Wellesley, known as 'the Wiltshire heiress', was the eldest daughter and co-heir of Sir James Tylney-Long and Lady Catherine Sidney Windsor. Following the death of her father in 1794 and her elder brother in 1805, she inherited the entire estates of the family in Essex, Hampshire and Wiltshire. In March 1812 she married William Wellesley-Pole, nephew of the Duke of Wellington and a notorious gambler who now boasted of having bedded the richest commoner in England.[189] Iolo's satirical song – an attack on 'immense riches' – was to be sung to the tune of 'old Daddy Cut-purse, My Grandmother's noddle, Mr Thingumbob's Nose, or all of them together', to the accompaniment either of Chinese gongs, Jews' harps and Scottish fiddles or of 'a Kentish Band of rough Music consisting of squawling cats, squealing Pigs, howling dogs, braying asses, and scolding wives':

> Miss Tilney Long! thrice wealthy maid!
> Great heiress of some wretch who said
>   'I'll have it right or wrong'
> Well-shear'd from many a shivering back,
> The golden fleeces fill thy sack,
>   O rare! Miss Tilney Long!
>
> Thee thus we praise, thus rather brand,
> The richest wench in all our Land.
>   And Strike the roaring Gong! (gong! gong! gong! gong! gong!)

---

[186] NLW 13151A, p. 106; NLW 13112B, pp. 273–85.
[187] Charles Redwood, *The Vale of Glamorgan: Scenes and Tales among the Welsh* (London, 1839), pp. 227–32. For Iolo's songs of the Cowbridge topers and their rivals, see NLW 21392F, no. 20, and NLW 21434E, no. 16b–c. For some trenchant *cywyddau*, see NLW 13134A, pp. 1–8, 149–53.
[188] *CIM*, II, p. 847, Iolo Morganwg to William Owen Pughe, 27 April 1808.
[189] For the estates of the Child, Tylney-Long and Wellesley families, see Essex RO, D/DCw T25.

> To slaves of wealth dwell on thy fame,
> 'All laud and praise unto thy name!'
> 'O great Miss Tilney Long!'[190]

But although Iolo enjoyed the knockabout stimulation of satirical songs and bawdry, he knew that the widening gap between the rich and the poor was a serious business. In a poem sent to David Jenkin, editor of *Seren Gomer*, in January 1814 he despaired of ever seeing equal justice for all:

> Dan draed y balch mewn llys a llan
>   Mae'r duwiol gwan yn gorwedd,
> Heb un i'r truan dan ei faich
>   Yn estyn braich amgeledd.

> (Under the feet of the proud in court and church
> The weak, godly ones lie,
> With no one extending to the wretch under his burden
> The arm of succour.)[191]

As the post-war depression deteriorated, he became not only genuinely distraught but also furiously angry about the condition of poor and helpless people. Successive harvest failures led to food shortages and famine.[192] People starved to death. The poor rate rocketed and unmarried mothers, the sick and the old were treated with gross brutality in many parts of Wales, not least by rich landowners who had no experience of the misery of poverty. Iolo railed against 'good for nothing' nobles 'whose dictates we are arrogantly called upon to obey, and for all this be thankful, and consider them as a superior order of beings'.[193] Having long ruminated on the subject of taxation, he wrote to Lord Sidmouth, chancellor of the exchequer, urging him to impose swingeing taxes on wealthy gentlemen who settled in France, Holland or America but who still gained enormous incomes from rents and mortgages in Britain.[194] By raising the profile of local victims of injustice, he very firmly reminded magistrates of their moral responsibility to relieve the condition of the poor and perform acts of mercy. He showered Cowbridge magistrates with hard-hitting missives calling on them to do their Christian duty towards

---

[190] NLW 21392F, no. 39.
[191] *CIM*, III, pp. 228, 229 (trans.), Iolo Morganwg to David Jenkin, 8 January 1814.
[192] David J. V. Jones, *Before Rebecca: Popular Protests in Wales 1793–1835* (London, 1973), p. 35.
[193] *CIM*, III, p. 544, Iolo Morganwg to [?John Edwards], 27 March 1820.
[194] Ibid., III, pp. 333–7, Iolo Morganwg to [?Henry Addington, 1st Viscount Sidmouth], 26 February 1815.

poor people in the 'infernalized parish of Flemston'[195] where he lived. Overseers in such small parishes were unable to raise the necessary sums to relieve the poor, but there was no excuse for their brusqueries. Iolo highlighted the case of William Williams, a farm labourer and a father of four who was prevented from working by a whitlow on his thumb, but whose weekly parochial allowance had been withdrawn by the overseers who insisted that he was fit to work, and the case of Alice John, a young servant from Iolo's parish whose sight was rapidly fading, but who was intolerably abused by the same overseer whose inhumanity, Iolo claimed, was 'driving the poor into madness'.[196] He also took up the case of Catherine Thomas (Cati Caerffili), a native of Caerffili whose parents came from Flemingston and had died young. Harshly treated by her employers, the wretched young woman rambled the countryside in search of food and work, stealing and selling her body in order to earn a few shillings and becoming such a nuisance that, so Iolo claimed, local farmers and overseers of the poor conspired against her so that 'she might be hang'd or transported out of the way'.[197] Iolo saw merit in her and admired her efforts to teach herself to read in Welsh and English. He managed to secure a place for her in a benevolent institution in London, only for her to abscond and sink into 'depths of depravity out of which nothing, I fear, but a miraculous interposition of divine providence can recover her'.[198]

The irony is that by his final years Iolo himself had never been so poor or in such pain. Enfeebled and hobbling around on a crutch, he was heavily dependent on opium and ether and, courtesy of his son, noggins of brandy. His wife was nearly blind, but his own failing eyesight did not dissuade him from calling for pen and paper as he prepared an edition of his hymns and psalms.[199] Even in his last year he was still railing against the 'great, wholly uninspired, blockhead Myfyr' ('y Myfyrgyff mawr llwyr diawen, llwyr egwan ei ymbwyll') and his old friend William Owen Pughe, 'the bill-hook craftsman of the great jack-o'-lanterns, Dr Southcott' ('saer bilwg yr hudlewyrn mawr, y Dr Sythgwd'),[200] as well as fulminating against landed gentry who 'resolve to set themselves up as examples in every feat which is judged improper in

---

[195] Ibid., III, p. 467, Iolo Morganwg to the Magistrates of Cowbridge, 13 March 1818. See also Jones, *Before Rebecca*, pp. 54–9.

[196] *CIM*, III, pp. 444–5, Iolo Morganwg to Robert Nicholl, 24 October 1817; ibid, III, pp. 465–7, Iolo Morganwg to the Magistrates of Cowbridge, 13 March 1818.

[197] NLW, Great Sessions 14/51, f. 247r; *The Cambrian*, 17 April 1819; *CIM*, III, pp. 505–9, Iolo Morganwg to William Wingfield, 8–9 April 1819.

[198] *CIM*, III, p. 529, Iolo Morganwg to David Rowland(s), 14 June 1819; Cathryn A. Charnell-White, 'Women and Gender in the Private and Social Relationships of Iolo Morganwg' in *Rattleskull Genius*, pp. 374–6.

[199] Edward Williams, *Salmau yr Eglwys yn yr Anialwch, Cyfrol II* (Merthyr-Tydfil, 1834).

[200] *CIM*, III, pp. 753, 759 (trans.), Iolo Morganwg to Taliesin Williams, 17 January–4 February 1826.

a man' ('ymroddant, yn hyttrach, i fod yn ddrychau nod (samplau) ym mhob camp a fernir yn anweddus ar ddyn').[201] He delighted in the occasional company of his charming grand-daughter Elizabeth and expressed heartfelt gratitude to his children as well as to the Quakers and Unitarians who rallied round in his hour of need. His piteous plight was expressed in his last letter to Taliesin on 9 November 1826: 'For the sake of the almighty God, hear the voices and cries of an aged & helpless father and mother.'[202] He died peacefully, aged seventy-nine, on 18 December and was laid to rest in Flemingston parish church.[203]

Iolo's renown as a brilliantly creative poet and writer is largely a posthumous construct. In his day he was better known as the 'Bard of Liberty' and he would sooner have been remembered as a champion of liberty and justice than for anything else. By nature he was argumentative and he proudly retained his prickly independence throughout his life. As Elijah Waring noted, his verbal flow was well-nigh unstoppable and Iolo himself confessed to being 'often out of etiquette'[204] in fighting his corner. Without for a moment condoning its excesses, he maintained his admiration for the French revolutionary tradition and involved himself heavily in furious oral and printed debates with enemies of liberty and toleration. Persecuting laws were as abhorrent to him as were handcuffs, shackles, thumbscrews and the gallows. His instinctive sympathy was with the underdog and with victims of injustice, be they political dissidents, common criminals, black slaves or peace activists. The word *dyngarwch* (humanity) figures prominently in his writings and whenever he saw a case of injustice he always expressed his sense of moral outrage. As Waring emphasized, Iolo would give his last shilling to someone in greater need than him,[205] and many unmarried mothers, the sick and the infirm, the unemployed and the destitute had good cause to be thankful to 'old Iolo'. The sufferings of other people mattered to him and his sense of compassion shines through in his correspondence and papers. 'No idea can be more grievous to me', he wrote, 'than that of quitting this life without having been in some degree the benefactor of mankind.'[206]

---

[201] Ibid., pp. 754, 761 (trans.).
[202] Ibid., III, p. 800, Iolo Morganwg to Taliesin Williams, 9 November 1826.
[203] *RAEW*, pp. 154–5. Iolo was buried in the floor of the church. NLW 21277E, no. 854.
[204] *CIM*, III, p. 515, Iolo Morganwg to Thomas Dale, Thomas Norton Longman and Evan Williams, 17–19 April 1819.
[205] *RAEW*, pp. 55–8. His daughter Margaret (Peggy) maintained that he had been 'blest with a heart benevolent and kind'. NLW 21377B, p. 4^v.
[206] NLW 21387E, no. 23.

Select Bibliography

Aarsleff, Hans, *The Study of Language in England, 1780–1860* (new edn., London, 1983).
Alden, Jeff (ed.), *Old Inns and Alehouses of Cowbridge* (Cowbridge, 2003).
Allen, Richard C., *David Hartley on Human Nature* (Albany, NY, 1999).
Allen, Richard C., *Quaker Communities in Early Modern Wales: From Resistance to Respectability* (Cardiff, 2007).
Anderson, Benedict, *Imagined Communities: Reflections on the Origin and Spread of Nationalism* (rev. edn., London, 1991).
Anthony, C. Robert, 'Seaport, Society and Smoke: Swansea as a Place of Resort and Industry, c.1700–c.1840' (unpublished University of Leicester Ph.D. thesis, 2002).
—— '"A Very Thriving Place": The Peopling of Swansea in the Eighteenth Century', *Urban History*, 32, no. 1 (2005), 68–87.
Armstrong, Alan (ed.), *The Economy of Kent 1640–1914* (Woodbridge, 1995).
Ashraf, P. Mary, *The Life and Times of Thomas Spence* (Newcastle upon Tyne, 1983).
Aspinall, Arthur (ed.), *The Correspondence of George, Prince of Wales, 1770–1812* (8 vols., London, 1963–71).
Baber, Colin, 'The Subsidiary Industries of Glamorgan, 1760–1914' in John and Williams (eds.), *Glamorgan County History, Volume V*, pp. 211–75.
Bailey, Brian, *Hangmen of England: A History of Execution from Jack Ketch to Albert Pierrepoint* (London, 1989).
Baines, Paul, *The House of Forgery in Eighteenth-Century Britain* (Aldershot, 1999).
Barker-Benfield, G. J., *The Culture of Sensibility: Sex and Society in Eighteenth-Century Britain* (London, 1992).
Barrell, John, *'Exhibition Extraordinary!!': Radical Broadsides of the mid 1790s* (Nottingham, 2001).
—— *Imagining the King's Death: Figurative Treason, Fantasies of Regicide 1793–1796* (Oxford, 2000).
—— *The Spirit of Despotism: Invasions of Privacy in the 1790s* (Oxford, 2006).
—— and Jon Mee (eds.), *Trials for Treason and Sedition, 1792–1794* (8 vols., London, 2006–7).
Basker, James G. (ed.), *Amazing Grace: An Anthology of Poems about Slavery, 1660–1810* (London, 2002).
Baycroft, Timothy, and Mark Hewitson (eds.), *What is a Nation? Europe 1789–1914* (Oxford, 2006).

Belanger, Terry, 'Publishers and Writers in Eighteenth-Century England' in Isabel Rivers (ed.), *Books and Their Readers in Eighteenth-Century England* (Leicester, 1982), pp. 5–25.

Bell, David A., *The First Total War: Napoleon's Europe and the Birth of Modern Warfare* (London, 2007).

Berg, Maxine, *Luxury and Pleasure in Eighteenth-Century Britain* (Oxford, 2005).

—— *The Age of Manufactures 1700–1820: Industry, Innovation and Work in Britain* (new rev. edn., London, 1994).

—— and Helen Clifford (eds.), *Consumers and Luxury: Consumer Culture in Europe 1650–1850* (Manchester, 1999).

Berger, Stefan (ed.), *Writing the Nation: A Global Perspective* (Basingstoke, 2007).

—— and Chris Lorenz (eds.), *The Contested Nation: Ethnicity, Class, Religion and Gender in National Histories* (Basingstoke, 2008).

——, Linas Eriksonas and Andrew Mycock (eds.), *Narrating the Nation: Representations in History, Media and the Arts* (Oxford, 2008).

Bewley, Christina, and David Bewley, *Gentleman Radical: A Life of John Horne Tooke 1736–1812* (London, 1998).

Black, E. C., *The Association: British Extraparliamentary Political Organization, 1769–1793* (Cambridge, Mass., 1963).

Bonnell, Thomas F., *The Most Disreputable Trade: Publishing the Classics of English Poetry 1765–1810* (Oxford, 2008).

Boorman, David, *The Brighton of Wales: Swansea as a Fashionable Seaside Resort, c.1780–c.1830* (Swansea, 1986).

Bowen, Geraint, *Golwg ar Orsedd y Beirdd* (Caerdydd, 1992).

—— 'Gorsedd y Beirdd – From Primrose Hill 1792 to Aberystwyth 1992', THSC (1992), 115–39.

—— and Zonia Bowen, *Hanes Gorsedd y Beirdd* (Cyhoeddiadau Barddas, 1991).

Bowen, Huw V., *The Business of Empire: The East India Company and Imperial Britain, 1756–1833* (Cambridge, 2006).

Boyns, Trevor, Dennis Thomas and Colin Baber, 'The Iron, Steel and Tinplate Industries, 1750–1914' in John and Williams (eds.), *Glamorgan County History, Volume V*, pp. 97–154.

Braithwaite, Helen, *Romanticism, Publishing and Dissent: Joseph Johnson and the Cause of Liberty* (Basingstoke, 2003).

—— 'From the See of St Davids to St Paul's Churchyard: Joseph Johnson's Cross-Border Connections' in Damian Walford Davies and Lynda Pratt (eds.), *Wales and the Romantic Imagination* (Cardiff, 2007), pp. 43–64.

Breuilly, John, *Nationalism and the State* (2nd edn., Manchester, 1993).

—— 'Historians and the Nation' in Peter Burke (ed.), *History and Historians in the Twentieth Century* (Oxford, 2002), pp. 55–87.

Brewer, John, and Roy Porter (eds.), *Consumption and the World of Goods* (London, 1993).

Brockliss, Laurence, and David Eastwood (eds.), *A Union of Multiple Identities: The British Isles, c.1750–c.1850* (Manchester, 1997).

Bromwich, Rachel, *'Trioedd Ynys Prydain' in Welsh Literature and Scholarship*, G. J. Williams Memorial Lecture (Cardiff, 1969).

—— *Trioedd Ynys Prydein: The Triads of the Island of Britain* (3rd edn., Cardiff, 2006).

—— 'Trioedd Ynys Prydain: The *Myvyrian* "Third Series"', *THSC*, (1968), 299–338; ibid. (1969), 127–55.

Bronson, Bertrand H., *Joseph Ritson: Scholar-at-Arms* (2 vols., Berkeley, Calif., 1938).

Brown, Roger Lee, 'Swansea Debtors' Gaol in the Nineteenth Century', *Morgannwg*, XVII (1973), 10–24.

Burford, Ephraim J., *Wits, Wenchers and Wantons. London's Low Life: Covent Garden in the Eighteenth Century* (London, 1986).

Butler, Marilyn, *Romantics, Rebels and Reactionaries: English Literature and its Background 1760–1830* (Oxford, 1981).

—— 'Romanticism in England' in Roy Porter and Mikuláš Teich (eds.), *Romanticism in National Context* (Cambridge, 1988), pp. 37–67.

Butterfield, Herbert, *The Whig Interpretation of History* (London, 1931).

Cannon, Jon, and Mary-Ann Constantine, 'A Welsh Bard in Wiltshire: Iolo Morganwg, Silbury and the Sarsens', *Wiltshire Studies*, 97 (2004), 78–88.

Capp, Bernard, *When Gossips Meet: Women, Family, and Neighbourhood in Early Modern England* (Oxford, 2003).

Carr, Glenda, *William Owen Pughe* (Caerdydd, 1983).

—— 'An Uneasy Partnership: Iolo Morganwg and William Owen Pughe' in Jenkins (ed.), *Rattleskull Genius*, pp. 443–60.

—— 'Bwrlwm Bywyd y Cymry yn Llundain yn y Ddeunawfed Ganrif' in Geraint H. Jenkins (ed.), *Cof Cenedl XI: Ysgrifau ar Hanes Cymru* (Llandysul, 1996), pp. 59–87.

Carruthers, Gerard, and Alan Rawes (eds.), *English Romanticism and the Celtic World* (Cambridge, 2003).

Castle, Terry, *The Female Thermometer: Eighteenth-Century Culture and the Invention of the Uncanny* (Oxford, 1995).

Ceadel, Martin, *The Origins of War Prevention: The British Peace Movement and International Relations, 1730–1854* (Oxford, 1996).

Chandler, James, and Kevin Gilmartin (eds.), *Romantic Metropolis: The Urban Scene of British Culture, 1780–1840* (Cambridge, 2005).

—— and Maureen N. McLane (eds.), *The Cambridge Companion to British Romantic Poetry* (Cambridge, 2008).

Charles-Edwards, T. M., and R. J. W. Evans (eds.), *Wales and the Wider World: Welsh History in an International Context* (Donington, 2010).

Charnell-White, Cathryn A., *Barbarism and Bardism: North Wales versus South Wales in the Bardic Vision of Iolo Morganwg* (Aberystwyth, 2004).

—— *Bardic Circles: National, Regional and Personal Identity in the Bardic Vision of Iolo Morganwg* (Cardiff, 2007).

—— 'Women and Gender in the Private and Social Relationships of Iolo Morganwg' in Jenkins (ed.), *Rattleskull Genius*, pp. 359–81.

—— (ed.), *Detholiad o Emynau Iolo Morganwg* (Aberystwyth, 2009).

Clark, Anna, *The Struggle for the Breeches: Gender and the Making of the British Working Class* (London, 1995).

Clark, Peter, *British Clubs and Societies 1580–1800: The Origins of an Associational World* (Oxford, 2000).

Clune, Frank, *The Scottish Martyrs: Their Trials and Transportation to Botany Bay* (Sydney, 1969).

Colley, Linda, *Britons: Forging the Nation 1707–1837* (rev. edn., London, 2009).

Collins, Henry, 'The London Corresponding Society' in John Saville (ed.), *Democracy and the Labour Movement* (London, 1954), pp. 103–34.
Constantine, Mary-Ann, *'Combustible Matter': Iolo Morganwg and the Bristol Volcano* (Aberystwyth, 2003).
—— *The Truth against the World: Iolo Morganwg and Romantic Forgery* (Cardiff, 2007).
—— 'Chasing Fragments: Iolo, Ritson and Robin Hood' in Sally Harper and Wyn Thomas (eds.), *Cynheiliaid y Gân / Bearers of Song: Essays in Honour of Phyllis Kinney and Meredydd Evans* (Caerdydd / Cardiff, 2007), pp. 51–7.
—— 'Iolo Morganwg, Coleridge, and the Bristol Lectures, 1795', *Notes and Queries*, new series, 52, no. 1, March 2005, 42–4.
—— 'Ossian in Wales and Brittany' in Howard Gaskill (ed.), *The Reception of Ossian in Europe* (London, 2004), pp. 67–90.
—— 'Songs and Stones: Iolo Morganwg (1747–1826), Mason and Bard', *The Eighteenth Century: Theory and Interpretation*, 47, nos. 2–3 (2006), 233–51.
—— '"This Wildernessed Business of Publication": The Making of *Poems Lyric and Pastoral* (1794)' in Jenkins (ed.), *Rattleskull Genius*, pp. 123–45.
—— 'Welsh Literary History and the Making of "The Myvyrian Archaiology of Wales"' in Dirk Van Hulle and Joep Leerssen (eds.), *Editing the Nation's Memory: Textual Scholarship and Nation-Building in Nineteenth-Century Europe* (Amsterdam, 2008), pp. 109–28.
Conway, Stephen, *The British Isles and the War of American Independence* (Oxford, 2000).
Cookson, J. E., *The British Armed Nation 1793–1815* (Oxford, 1997).
—— *The Friends of Peace: Anti-War Liberalism in England, 1793–1815* (Cambridge, 1982).
Corfield, Penelope J., 'Rhetoric, Radical Politics and Rainfall: John Thelwall in Breconshire, 1797–1800', *Brycheiniog*, XL (2009), 17–36.
—— and Chris Evans, 'John Thelwall in Wales: New Documentary Evidence', *BIHR*, LIX, no. 140 (1986), 231–9.
Cowbridge: Buildings and People. Sources and References (Cowbridge, 2000).
Crawford, Robert, *The Bard: Robert Burns, A Biography* (London, 2009).
Crowe, Richard M., 'Diddordebau Ieithyddol Iolo Morganwg' (unpublished University of Wales Ph.D. thesis, 1988).
—— 'Iolo Morganwg and the Dialects of Welsh' in Jenkins (ed.), *Rattleskull Genius*, pp. 315–31.
—— 'Thomas Richards a John Walters: Athrawon Geiriadurol Iolo Morganwg' in Hywel Teifi Edwards (ed.), *Llynfi ac Afan, Garw ac Ogwr* (Llandysul, 1998), pp. 227–51.
Daunton, Martin, and Matthew Hilton (eds.), *The Politics of Consumption: Material Culture and Citizenship in Europe and America* (Oxford, 2001).
David, Saul, *Prince of Pleasure: The Prince of Wales and the Making of the Regency* (London, 1998).
Davies, Andrew, '"Uncontaminated with Human Gore"? Iolo Morganwg, Slavery and the Jamaican Inheritance' in Jenkins (ed.), *Rattleskull Genius*, pp. 293–313.
Davies, Caryl, *Adfeilion Babel: Agweddau ar Syniadaeth Ieithyddol y Ddeunawfed Ganrif* (Caerdydd, 2000).
Davies, D. Elwyn, *Capel Gellionnen 1692–1992* (s.l.: [Capel Gellionnen], 1992).
—— *Cewri'r Ffydd: Bywgraffiadur y Mudiad Undodaidd yng Nghymru* (Cymdeithas Undodaidd Deheudir Cymru, 1999).

—— 'They Thought for Themselves': A Brief Look at the Story of Unitarianism and the Liberal Tradition in Wales and Beyond its Borders (Llandysul, 1982).

—— 'Astudiaeth o Feddwl a Chyfraniad Iolo Morganwg fel Rhesymolwr ac Undodwr' (unpublished University of Wales Ph.D. thesis, 1975).

—— 'Iolo Morganwg (1747–1826), Bardism and Unitarianism', *Journal of Welsh Religious History*, 6 (1998), 1–11.

Davies, Damian Walford, *Presences that Disturb: Models of Romantic Identity in the Literature and Culture of the 1790s* (Cardiff, 2002).

—— '"At Defiance": Iolo, Godwin, Coleridge, Wordsworth' in Jenkins (ed.), *Rattleskull Genius*, pp. 147–72.

—— and Lynda Pratt (eds.), *Wales and the Romantic Imagination* (Cardiff, 2007).

Davies, David, *The Influence of the French Revolution on Welsh Life and Literature* (Carmarthen, 1926).

Davies, Hywel M., *Transatlantic Brethren: Rev. Samuel Jones (1735–1814) and his Friends* (London, 1995).

—— 'Loyalism in Wales, 1792–1793', *WHR*, 20, no. 4 (2001), 657–716.

—— 'Morgan John Rhys and James Bicheno: Anti-Christ and the French Revolution in England and Wales', *BBCS*, XXIX, part 1 (1980), 111–27.

Davies, Iolo, *'A Certaine Schoole': A History of the Grammar School at Cowbridge, Glamorgan* (Cowbridge, 1967).

Davies, J. Barry, 'Flemingston Court: One of the Greater Houses of the Vale', *Meisgyn and Glynrhondda Local History Newsletter*, 118 (1997), 1–10.

Davies, J. H., *A Bibliography of Welsh Ballads printed in the 18th Century* (London, 1911).

—— (ed.), *The Letters of Goronwy Owen (1723–1769)* (Cardiff, 1924).

Davies, R. R., and Geraint H. Jenkins (eds.), *From Medieval to Modern Wales: Historical Essays in Honour of Kenneth O. Morgan and Ralph A. Griffiths* (Cardiff, 2004).

Davies, Thomas G., *Neath's Wicked World and Other Essays on the History of Neath and District* (West Glamorgan Archive Service, 2000).

Davies, Walter, *General View of the Agriculture and Domestic Economy of South Wales* (2 vols., London, 1815).

—— 'A Statistical Account of the Parish of Llanymyneich in Montgomeryshire', *Cambrian Register*, I (1796), 265–83.

Davies, William Ll., 'David Samwell (1751–1798): Surgeon of the "Discovery", London-Welshman and Poet', *THSC* (1926–7), 70–133.

—— 'David Samwell's Poem – "The Padouca Hunt"', *NLWJ*, II, nos. 3 and 4 (1942), 142–52.

Davis, Martin, 'Hanes Cymdeithasol Meirionnydd 1750–1859' (unpublished University of Wales MA thesis, 1987).

Davis, Michael T., 'The Mob Club? The London Corresponding Society and the Politics of Civility in the 1790s' in idem and Paul A. Pickering (eds.), *Unrespectable Radicals? Popular Politics in the Age of Reform* (Aldershot, 2008), pp. 21–40.

—— (ed.), *London Corresponding Society, 1792–1799* (6 vols., London, 2002).

——, Iain McCalman, and Christina Parolin (eds.), *Newgate in Revolution: An Anthology of Radical Prison Literature in the Age of Revolution* (London, 2005).

Dearnley, Moira, '"Mad Ned" and the "Smatter-Dasher": Iolo Morganwg and Edward "Celtic" Davies' in Jenkins (ed.), *Rattleskull Genius*, pp. 426–42.

DeLacy, Margaret, *Prison Reform in Lancashire, 1700–1850: A Study in Local Administration* (Manchester, 1986).
Denning, R. T. W. (ed.), *The Diary of William Thomas of Michaelston-super-Ely, near St Fagans Glamorgan, 1762–1795* (Cardiff, 1995).
Ditchfield, Grayson M., 'The Parliamentary Struggle over the Repeal of the Test and Corporation Acts, 1787–1790', *EHR*, LXXXIX (1974), 551–77.
—— (ed.), *The Letters of Theophilus Lindsey (1723–1808). Volume I: 1747–1788* (Woodbridge, 2007).
Donovan, P. J. (ed.), *Cerddi Rhydd Iolo Morganwg* (Caerdydd, 1980).
Dresser, Madge, *Slavery Obscured: The Social History of the Slave Trade in an English Provincial Port* (London, 2001).
Dubois, Laurent, *Avengers of the New World: The Story of the Haitian Revolution* (Cambridge, Mass., 2004).
Duffy, Michael, *The Englishman and the Foreigner* (Cambridge, 1986).
Dunn, John, *Setting the People Free: The Story of Democracy* (London, 2005).
Durey, Michael, 'William Winterbotham's Trumpet of Sedition: Religious Dissent and Political Radicalism in the 1790s', *Journal of Religious History*, 19, no. 2 (1995), 141–57.
Dybikowski, James, *On Burning Ground: An Examination of the Ideas, Projects and Life of David Williams* (Oxford, 1993).
—— 'David Williams (1738–1816) and Jacques-Pierre Brissot: Their Correspondence', *NLWJ*, XXV, no. 1 (1987), 71–97; ibid., no. 2 (1987), 167–90.
Dyck, Ian (ed.), *Citizen of the World: Essays on Thomas Paine* (London, 1987).
Dyer, George, *Memoirs of the Life and Writings of Robert Robinson* (London, 1796).
Eastwood, David, 'John Reeves and the Contested Idea of the British Constitution', *British Journal for Eighteenth Century Studies*, 16 (1993), 197–212.
Eaton, George, *A History of Neath from Earliest Times* (Swansea, 1987).
Edwards, Hywel Teifi, *The Eisteddfod* (Cardiff, 1990).
Ellis, Tecwyn, *Edward Jones, Bardd y Brenin, 1752–1824* (Caerdydd, 1957).
Emsley, Clive, 'An Aspect of Pitt's "Terror": Prosecutions for Sedition during the 1790s', *Social History*, 6, no. 2 (1981), 155–84.
—— 'Repression, Terror and the Rule of Law during the decade of the French Revolution', *EHR*, C (1985), 801–25.
Escott, Margaret, 'Parliamentary Representation' in Chris Williams and Sian Rhiannon Williams (eds.), *The Gwent County History. Volume 4. Industrial Monmouthshire, 1780–1914* (Cardiff, 2011), pp. 368–86.
Evans, Chris, *Slave Wales: The Welsh and Atlantic Slavery, 1660–1850* (Cardiff, 2010).
—— *'The Labyrinth of Flames': Work and Social Conflict in Early Industrial Merthyr Tydfil* (Cardiff, 1993).
—— *The Letterbook of Richard Crawshay 1788–1797* (Cardiff, 1990).
—— 'Was Wales opposed to the Slave Trade?' in Huw V. Bowen (ed.), *A New History of Wales* (Llandysul, 2011), pp. 107–12.
Evans, D. Silvan (ed.), *Gwaith y Parchedig Evan Evans (Ieuan Brydydd Hir)* (Caernarfon, 1876).
Evans, Evan, *Casgliad o Bregethau* (2 vols., Y Mwythig, 1776).
Evans, George Eyre, *Midland Churches: A History of the Congregations on the Roll of the Midland Christian Union* (Dudley, 1899).
—— *Record of the Provincial Assembly of Lancashire and Cheshire* (Manchester, 1896).

—— (ed.), *Lloyd Letters (1754–1796), being extant letters of David Lloyd, Minister of Llwynrhydowen* (Aberystwyth, 1908).
Evans, J. J., *Dylanwad y Chwyldro Ffrengig ar Lenyddiaeth Cymru* (Lerpwl, 1928).
Evans, Muriel Bowen, 'Sir Gaeriaid: Some Comments on Carmarthenshire and its People by Iolo Morganwg', *CA*, XXIV (1988), 33–55.
Evans, R. J. W., *Austria, Hungary, and the Habsburgs: Essays on Central Europe, c.1683–1867* (Oxford, 2006).
—— 'Wales and Oxford: Historical Aspects, National and International' in Charles-Edwards and Evans (eds.), *Wales and the Wider World*, pp. 118–38.
—— 'Was there a Welsh Enlightenment?' in Davies and Jenkins (eds.), *From Medieval to Modern Wales*, pp. 142–59.
Evans, R. Paul, 'The Flintshire Loyalist Association and the Local Holywell Volunteers', *FHSJ*, 33 (1992), 55–68.
Evans, T. C. (Cadrawd), *Gwaith Iolo Morganwg* (Llanuwchllyn, 1913).
Evans, Thomas, *Cyfansoddiad o Hymnau* (Caerfyrddin, 1811).
Finn, Margot C., *The Character of Credit: Personal Debt in English Culture, 1740–1914* (Cambridge, 2003).
Fishlock, Trevor, *In This Place: The National Library of Wales* (Aberystwyth, 2007).
Fitzpatrick, Martin, 'Enlightenment' in Iain McCalman (ed.), *An Oxford Companion to the Romantic Age: British Culture 1776–1832* (Oxford, 1999), pp. 299–311.
—— 'The "Cultivated Understanding" and Chaotic Genius of David Samwell' in Jenkins (ed.), *Rattleskull Genius*, pp. 383–402.
——, Peter Jones, Christa Knellwolf, and Iain McCalman (eds.), *The Enlightenment World* (London, 2004).
——, Nicholas Thomas, and Jennifer Newell (eds.), *The Death of Captain Cook and Other Writings by David Samwell* (Cardiff, 2007).
Foner, Eric, *Tom Paine and Revolutionary America* (Oxford, 2005).
Foulkes, Isaac, *Geirlyfr Bywgraffiadol o Enwogion Cymru* (Liverpool, 1870).
Foxcroft, Louise, *The Making of Addiction: The 'Use and Abuse' of Opium in Nineteenth-Century Britain* (Aldershot, 2007).
Frank, Joseph (ed.), *The Letters of Joseph Ritson, Esq.* (2 vols., London, 1833).
Franklin, Caroline, 'The Welsh American Dream: Iolo Morganwg, Robert Southey and the Madoc Legend' in Carruthers and Rawes (eds.), *English Romanticism and the Celtic World*, pp. 69–84.
Franklin, Michael J., *Sir William Jones* (Cardiff, 1995).
—— 'Sir William Jones, the Celtic Revival and the Oriental Renaissance' in Carruthers and Rawes (eds.), *English Romanticism and the Celtic World*, pp. 20–37.
—— 'The Colony Writes Back: Brutus, Britanus and the Advantages of an Oriental Ancestry' in Davies and Pratt (eds.), *Wales and the Romantic Imagination*, pp. 13–42.
—— (ed.), *Sir William Jones: Selected Poetical and Prose Works* (Cardiff, 1995).
Fulford, Tim, *Romantic Indians: Native Americans, British Literature, and Transatlantic Culture 1756–1830* (Oxford, 2006).
—— and Peter J. Kitson (eds.), *Romanticism and Colonialism: Writing and Empire, 1780–1830* (Cambridge, 1998).
Garrett, Clarke, *Respectable Folly: Millenarians and the French Revolution in France and England* (Baltimore, Md., 1975).
Gatrell, Vic, *City of Laughter: Sex and Satire in Eighteenth-Century London* (London, 2006).

Gellner, Ernest, *Nations and Nationalism* (Oxford, 1983).
Goodridge, John, *Rural Life in Eighteenth-Century English Poetry* (Cambridge, 1995).
Goodwin, Albert, *The Friends of Liberty: The English Democratic Movement in the Age of the French Revolution* (London, 1979).
Grafton, Anthony, *Forgers and Critics: Creativity and Duplicity in Western Scholarship* (London, 1990).
Grant, Raymond, *The Parliamentary History of Glamorgan 1542–1976* (Swansea, 1978).
Granville, Neville, *Cefn Cribwr: Chronicle of a Village* (Barry, 1980).
Griffith, John T., *Rev. Morgan John Rhys* (2nd edn., Carmarthen, 1910).
Groom, Nick, *The Forger's Shadow: How Forgery Changed the Course of Literature* (London, 2002).
Guibernau, Montserrat, and John Hutchinson (eds.), *History and National Destiny: Ethnosymbolism and its Critics* (Oxford, 2004).
—— and John Hutchinson (eds.), *Understanding Nationalism* (Cambridge, 2001).
Haakonssen, Knud (ed.), *Enlightenment and Religion: Rational Dissent in Eighteenth-Century Britain* (Cambridge, 1996).
Hague, William, *William Pitt the Younger* (pbk. edn., London, 2005).
—— *William Wilberforce: The Life of the Great Anti-Slave Trade Campaigner* (London, 2007).
Halliday, Stephen, *Newgate: London's Prototype of Hell* (Stroud, 2006).
Harris, Bob, *The Scottish People and the French Revolution* (London, 2008).
Harvey, Karen, *Reading Sex in the Eighteenth Century: Bodies and Gender in English Erotic Culture* (Cambridge, 2004).
Hayter, Alethea, *Opium and the Romantic Imagination* (rev. edn., Wellingborough, 1988).
Haywood, Ian, *Faking It: Art and the Politics of Forgery* (Brighton, 1987).
Hesse, Carla, *Publishing and Cultural Politics in Revolutionary Paris, 1789–1810* (Berkeley, Calif., 1991).
Hibbert, Christopher, *George IV* (Harmondsworth, 1976).
Hitchens, Christopher, *Thomas Paine's Rights of Man: A Biography* (London, 2006).
Hobsbawm, Eric, *Nations and Nationalism since 1780* (Cambridge, 1990).
Hochschild, Adam, *Bury the Chains: The British Struggle to Abolish Slavery* (London, 2005).
Holmes, Richard, *The Age of Wonder* (London, 2008).
Hone, J. Ann, *For the Cause of Truth: Radicalism in London 1796–1821* (Oxford, 1982).
Hopkins, T. J. (ed.), 'C. C.'s Tour in Glamorgan, 1789' in Stewart Williams (ed.), *Glamorgan Historian, 2* (Cowbridge, 1965), pp. 121–33.
Hostettler, John, *Thomas Erskine and Trial by Jury* (Chichester, 1996).
Howard, John, *The State of the Prisons in England and Wales* (Warrington, 1777).
Howard, Sharon, 'Riotous Community: Crowds, Politics and Society in Wales, c.1700–1840', *WHR*, 20, no. 4 (2001), 656–86.
Howell, David W., *Patriarchs and Parasites: The Gentry of South-West Wales in the Eighteenth Century* (Cardiff, 1986).
—— *The Rural Poor in Eighteenth-Century Wales* (Cardiff, 2000).
Hucks, Joseph, *A Pedestrian Tour Through North Wales, in a Series of Letters* (London, 1795).
Hughes, Stephen, *Copperopolis: Landscapes of the Early Industrial Period in Swansea* (Aberystwyth, 2000).

Hutton, Ronald, *Blood and Mistletoe: The History of the Druids in Britain* (London, 2009).
—— *The Druids* (London, 2007).
Huws, Daniel, *Caneuon Llafar Gwlad ac Iolo a'i Fath* (Cymdeithas Alawon Gwerin Cymru, 1993).
—— 'Iolo Morganwg and Traditional Music' in Jenkins (ed.), *Rattleskull Genius*, pp. 333–56.
Innes, Joanna, 'The King's Bench Prison in the Later Eighteenth Century: Law, Authority and Order in a London Debtors' Prison' in John Brewer and John Styles (eds.), *An Ungovernable People: The English and their Law in the Seventeenth and Eighteenth Centuries* (London, 1980), pp. 250–98.
Ireland, Richard W., *'A Want of Order and Good Discipline': Rules, Discretion and the Victorian Prison* (Cardiff, 2007).
Jacob, Margaret C., *Living the Enlightenment: Freemasonry and Politics in Eighteenth-Century Europe* (Oxford, 1991).
James, Allan, *Diwylliant Gwerin Morgannwg* (Llandysul, 2002).
James, Brian Ll., *Thomas Richards 1710–1790: Curate of Coychurch, Scholar and Lexicographer* (Coychurch, [1989]).
—— 'The Vale of Glamorgan, 1780–1850: A Study in Social History, with special reference to the ownership and occupation of land' (unpublished University of Wales MA thesis, 1971).
—— 'Cowbridge' in Stewart Williams (ed.), *South Glamorgan: A County History* (Barry, 1975), pp. 225–41.
—— 'John Hodder Moggridge and the Founding of Blackwood', *Presenting Monmouthshire*, II, no. 5 (1968), 25–9.
—— 'The Cowbridge Printers' in Stewart Williams (ed.), *Glamorgan Historian, 4* (Cowbridge, 1967), pp. 231–44.
—— 'The Welsh Language in the Vale of Glamorgan', *Morgannwg*, XVI (1972), 16–36.
James, E. Wyn, 'Caethwasanaeth a'r Beirdd, 1790–1840', *Taliesin*, 119 (2003), 37–60.
—— '"Seren Wib Olau": Gweledigaeth a Chenhadaeth Morgan John Rhys (1760–1804)', *TCHBC* (2007), 5–37.
—— 'Thomas William: Bardd ac Emynydd Bethesda'r Fro', *LlC*, 27 (2004), 113–39.
—— 'Welsh Ballads and American Slavery', *WJRH*, 2 (2007), 59–86.
James, Lemuel, *Hopkiniaid Morganwg: Being a Genealogical Biography of the Hopkin Family of Glamorgan with the Works of Hopkin Thomas Philip and Lewis Hopkin* (Bangor, 1909).
Janowitz, Anne, 'Amiable and Radical Sociability: Anna Barbauld's "Free Familiar Conversation"' in Gillian Russell and Clara Tuite (eds.), *Romantic Sociability: Social Networks and Literary Culture in Britain, 1770–1840* (Cambridge, 2002), pp. 62–81.
Jarman, Paul, '*Madoc*, 1795: Robert Southey's Misdated Manuscript', *Review of English Studies*, 55, no. 220 (2004), 355–73.
Jarvis, Branwen, 'Iolo Morganwg and the Welsh Cultural Background' in Jenkins (ed.), *Rattleskull Genius*, pp. 29–49.
Jenkins, D. E., *The Life of the Rev. Thomas Charles BA of Bala* (3 vols., Denbigh, 1908).
Jenkins, David, *A Refuge in Peace and War: The National Library of Wales to 1952* (Aberystwyth, 2002).
Jenkins, Elis, 'Artists in the Vale of Neath' in Stewart Williams (ed.), *Glamorgan Historian, 1* (Cowbridge, 1963), pp. 44–53.

—— (ed.), *Neath and District: A Symposium* (Neath, 1974).
Jenkins, Geraint H., *Cadw Tŷ mewn Cwmwl Tystion: Ysgrifau Hanesyddol ar Grefydd a Diwylliant* (Llandysul, 1990).
—— *Facts, Fantasy and Fiction: The Historical Vision of Iolo Morganwg* (Aberystwyth, 1997).
—— *Iolo Morganwg y Gweriniaethwr* (Aberystwyth, 2010).
—— *The Foundations of Modern Wales: Wales 1642–1780* (Oxford, 1987).
—— *Theophilus Evans (1693–1767): Y Dyn, ei Deulu, a'i Oes* (Adran Gwasanaethau Diwylliannol Dyfed, 1993).
—— '"A Rank Republican [and] a Leveller": William Jones, Llangadfan', *WHR*, 17, no. 3 (1995), 365–86.
—— '"A Very Horrid Affair": Sedition and Unitarianism in the Age of Revolutions' in Davies and Jenkins (eds.), *From Medieval to Modern Wales*, pp. 175–96.
—— 'An Uneasy Relationship: Gwallter Mechain and Iolo Morganwg', *MC*, 97 (2009), 73–99.
—— 'Clio and Wales: Welsh Remembrancers and Historical Writing, 1751–2001', *THSC*, new series, 8 (2002), 119–36.
—— '"Diabolical Traffic": Iolo Morganwg, Slavery and Merthyr Tydfil', *MH*, 19 (2008), 7–17.
—— '"Dyro Dduw dy Nawdd": Iolo Morganwg a'r Mudiad Undodaidd' in idem (ed.), *Cof Cenedl XX: Ysgrifau ar Hanes Cymru* (Llandysul, 2005), pp. 65–100.
—— 'Historical Writing in the Eighteenth Century' in Branwen Jarvis (ed.), *A Guide to Welsh Literature c.1700–1800* (Cardiff, 2000), pp. 23–44.
—— '"Horrid Unintelligible Jargon": The Case of Dr Thomas Bowles', *WHR*, 15, no. 4 (1991), 494–523.
—— 'Iolo Morganwg a Chaethwasiaeth' in Tegwyn Jones and Huw Walters (eds.), *Cawr i'w Genedl: Cyfrol i Gyfarch yr Athro Hywel Teifi Edwards* (Llandysul, 2008), pp. 59–85.
—— '"Peth Erchyll Iawn" oedd Methodistiaeth', *LlC*, 17, nos. 3 and 4 (1993), 195–204.
—— '"Taphy-land Historians" and the Union of England and Wales 1536–2007', *Journal of Irish and Scottish Studies*, 1, no. 2 (2008), 1–27.
—— 'The Bard of Liberty during William Pitt's Reign of Terror' in Joseph F. Nagy and Leslie E. Jones (eds.), *Heroic Poets and Poetic Heroes in Celtic Tradition: A Festschrift for Patrick K. Ford. CSANA Yearbook 3–4* (Dublin, 2005), pp. 183–206.
—— 'The Cultural Uses of the Welsh Language 1660–1800' in idem (ed.), *The Welsh Language before the Industrial Revolution*, pp. 369–406.
—— 'The Eighteenth Century' in Philip Henry Jones and Eiluned Rees (eds.), *A Nation and its Books: A History of the Book in Wales* (Aberystwyth, 1998), pp. 109–22.
—— '"The Taffy-land historians have hitherto been sad dogs for the most part": Iolo Morganwg the Historian', *Morgannwg*, LII (2008), 5–29.
—— 'The Unitarian Firebrand, the Cambrian Society and the Eisteddfod' in idem (ed.), *Rattleskull Genius*, pp. 269–92.
—— 'The Urban Experiences of Iolo Morganwg', *WHR*, 22, no. 3 (2005), 463–98.
—— 'Thomas Burgess, Iolo Morganwg and the Black Spot', *Ceredigion*, XV, no. 3 (2007), 13–36.

—— 'Wales in the Eighteenth Century' in H. T. Dickinson (ed.), *A Companion to Eighteenth-Century Britain* (Oxford, 2002), pp. 392–402.

—— 'Yr Eglwys "Wiwlwys Olau" a'i Beirniaid', *Ceredigion*, X, no. 2 (1985), 131–46.

——, Richard Suggett and Eryn M. White, 'The Welsh Language in Early Modern Wales' in Jenkins (ed.), *The Welsh Language before the Industrial Revolution*, pp. 45–122.

—— (ed.), *A Rattleskull Genius: The Many Faces of Iolo Morganwg* (Cardiff, 2005; pbk. edn. 2009).

—— (ed.), *The Welsh Language before the Industrial Revolution* (Cardiff, 1997).

——, Ffion Mair Jones, and David Ceri Jones (eds.), *The Correspondence of Iolo Morganwg* (3 vols., Cardiff, 2007).

Jenkins, J., 'David Jenkin Rees o Loydjack', *Yr Ymofynydd*, new series, IX, no. 32 (1884), 90–2.

Jenkins, John Gwili, *Hanfod Duw a Pherson Crist* (Liverpool, 1931).

Jenkins, Philip, *The Making of a Ruling Class: The Glamorgan Gentry 1640–1790* (Cambridge, 1983).

—— 'Jacobites and Freemasons in Eighteenth-Century Wales', *WHR*, 9, no. 4 (1979), 391–406.

—— 'The Creation of an "Ancient Gentry": Glamorgan 1760–1840', *WHR*, 12, no. 1 (1984), 29–49.

—— 'The Demographic Decline of the Landed Gentry in the Eighteenth Century: A South Wales Study', *WHR*, 11, no. 1 (1982), 31–49.

—— 'The Tory Tradition in Eighteenth-century Cardiff', *WHR*, 12, no. 2 (1984), 180–96.

—— 'Tory Industrialism and Town Politics: Swansea in the Eighteenth Century', *Historical Journal*, 28, no. 1 (1985), 103–23.

Jenkins, R. T., 'Bardd a'i Gefndir', *THSC* (1946–7), 97–149.

—— 'William Richards o Lynn', *TCHBC* (1930), 17–68.

—— and Helen M. Ramage, *A History of the Honourable Society of Cymmrodorion and of the Gwyneddigion and Cymreigyddion Societies (1751–1951)* (London, 1951).

John, A. H., and Glanmor Williams (eds.), *Glamorgan County History, Volume V: Industrial Glamorgan from 1700 to 1970* (Cardiff, 1980).

John, Llewelyn B., 'The Parliamentary Representation of Glamorgan, 1536 to 1832' (unpublished University of Wales MA thesis, 1934).

Johnston, David, 'Iolo Goch and the English: Welsh Poetry and Politics in the Fourteenth Century', *CMCS*, 12 (1986), 73–98.

Johnston, Kenneth R., 'Whose History? My Place or Yours? Republican Assumptions and Romantic Traditions' in Damian Walford Davies (ed.), *Romanticism, History, Historicism: Essays on an Orthodoxy* (Abingdon, 2009), pp. 79–102.

Jones, Alun R., 'Lewis Morris and "Honest Mr Vaughan" of Nannau and Corsygedol', *JMHRS*, XIII, part 1 (1998), 31–42.

Jones, Bedwyr Lewis, *Yr Hen Bersoniaid Llengar* ([Penarth], [1963]).

—— 'Lewis Morris a Goronwy Owen: "Digrifwch Llawen" a "Sobrwydd Synhwyrol"' in J. E. Caerwyn Williams (ed.), *Ysgrifau Beirniadol, X* (Dinbych, 1977), pp. 290–308.

—— 'Rhyddiaith y Morrisiaid' in Geraint Bowen (ed.), *Y Traddodiad Rhyddiaith* (Llandysul, 1970), pp. 276–92.

Jones, David Ceri, '"Mere Humbug": Iolo Morganwg and the Board of Agriculture', *THSC*, 10 (2004), 76–97.
Jones, David J. V., *Before Rebecca: Popular Protests in Wales 1793–1835* (London, 1973).
Jones, Dot, *Statistical Evidence relating to the Welsh Language 1801–1911 / Tystiolaeth Ystadegol yn ymwneud â'r Iaith Gymraeg 1801–1911* (Cardiff / Caerdydd, 1998).
Jones, E. H. Stuart, *The Last Invasion of Britain* (Cardiff, 1950).
Jones, Emrys, 'The Welsh in London in the Seventeenth and Eighteenth Centuries', *WHR*, 10, no. 4 (1981), 461–79.
—— (ed.), *The Welsh in London 1500–2000* (Cardiff, 2001).
—— and Dewi Watkin Powell, *The Honourable Society of Cymmrodorion: A Concise History 1751–2001* ([London], [2004]).
Jones, Ffion Mair, *'The Bard is a Very Singular Character': Iolo Morganwg, Marginalia and Print Culture* (Cardiff, 2010).
—— '"A'r Ffeiffs a'r Drums yn roario": Y Baledwyr Cymraeg, y Milisia a'r Gwirfoddolwyr', *Canu Gwerin*, 34 (2011), 19–42.
—— '"Gydwladwr Godi[d]og . . .": Gohebiaeth Gymraeg Gynnar Iolo Morganwg', *LlC*, 27 (2004), 140–71.
Jones, Gwyn, *The Oxford Book of Welsh Verse in English* (Oxford, 1977).
Jones, Huw, *Diddanwch Teuluaidd* (Llundain, 1763).
Jones, Owen, Iolo Morganwg and William Owen Pughe, *The Myvyrian Archaiology of Wales* (3 vols., London, 1801–7).
—— and William Owen (eds.), *Barddoniaeth Dafydd ab Gwilym* (Llundain, 1789).
Jones, Rowland, *A Postscript to the Origin of Language and Nations* (London, [1768]).
Jones, Thomas, *The British Language in its Lustre* (London, 1688).
Jones, W. Tudor, *The Rise and Progress of Religious Free Thought in Swansea* (Swansea, 1900).
Jones, Whitney R. D., *David Williams: The Anvil and the Hammer* (Cardiff, 1986).
Joyner, Paul, *Artists in Wales c.1740–c.1851* (Aberystwyth, 1997).
Keane, John, *The Life and Death of Democracy* (London, 2009).
—— *Tom Paine: A Political Life* (London, 1995).
Kidd, Colin, *British Identities before Nationalism: Ethnicity and Nationhood in the Atlantic World, 1600–1800* (Cambridge, 1999).
—— *Subverting Scotland's Past: Scottish Whig Historians and the Creation of an Anglo-British Identity, 1689–c.1830* (Cambridge, 1993).
Kinross, John, *Fishguard Fiasco: An Account of the Last Invasion of Britain* (Tenby, 1974).
Lake, A. Cynfael (ed.), *Blodeugerdd Barddas o Ganu Caeth y Ddeunawfed Ganrif* (Cyhoeddiadau Barddas, 1993).
Lamb, Robert, and Corinna Wagner (eds.), *Selected Political Writings of John Thelwall* (4 vols., London, 2009).
Lamont, Claire, and Michael Rossington (eds.), *Romanticism's Debatable Lands* (Basingstoke, 2007).
Langford, Paul, *Englishness Identified: Manners and Character 1650–1850* (Oxford, 2000).
Larkin, Edward, *Thomas Paine and the Literature of Revolution* (Cambridge, 2005).
Leask, Nigel, *British Romantic Writers and the East: Anxieties of Empire* (Cambridge, 1992).
Leathart, William D., *The Origin and Progress of the Gwyneddigion Society* (London, 1831).

Leerssen, Joep, 'Nationalism and the Cultivation of Culture', *Nations and Nationalism*, 12, part 4 (2006), 559–78.
Lewis, Aneirin, 'Tomos Glyn Cothi a'r Dr John Disney', *LlC*, 6, nos. 3–4 (1961), 219–20.
Lewis, Ceri W., *Iolo Morganwg* (Caernarfon, 1995).
—— 'Iolo Morganwg' in Branwen Jarvis (ed.), *A Guide to Welsh Literature c. 1700–1800* (Cardiff, 2000), pp. 126–67.
—— 'The Literary History of Glamorgan from 1550 to 1770' in Williams (ed.), *Glamorgan County History, Volume IV*, pp. 535–639.
Lewis, Frank R., 'Edward Davies, 1756–1831', *TRS*, XXXIX (1969), 8–23.
Lewis, Gwyneth, 'Eighteenth-Century Literary Forgeries, with Special Reference to the Work of Iolo Morganwg' (unpublished University of Oxford D. Phil. thesis, 1991).
Lewis, Tom, *The History of the Hen Dŷ Cwrdd, Cefn Coed y Cymmer* (Llandysul, [1947]).
Linch, Kevin B., '"A Citizen and not a Soldier": The British Volunteer Movement and the War against Napoleon' in Alan Forrest, Karen Hagemann and Jane Rendall (eds.), *Soldiers, Citizens and Civilians: Experiences and Perceptions of the Revolutionary and Napoleonic Wars, 1790–1820* (Basingstoke, 2009), pp. 205–21.
Linebaugh, Peter, *The London Hanged: Crime and Civil Society in the Eighteenth Century* (2nd edn., London, 2003).
—— and Marcus Rediker, *The Many-Headed Hydra: Sailors, Slaves, Commoners, and the Hidden History of the Revolutionary Atlantic* (London, 2000).
Llwyd, Humphrey, *Cronica Walliae*, ed. Ieuan M. Williams (Cardiff, 2002).
Löffler, Marion, *The Literary and Historical Legacy of Iolo Morganwg 1826–1926* (Cardiff, 2007).
Lord, Peter, *The Visual Culture of Wales: Imaging the Nation* (Cardiff, 2000).
—— *Words with Pictures: Welsh Images and Images of Wales in the Popular Press, 1640–1860* (Aberystwyth, 1995).
Lynch, Jack, *Deception and Detection in Eighteenth-Century Britain* (Aldershot, 2008).
McCalman, Iain, *Radical Underworld: Prophets, Revolutionaries and Pornographers in London, 1795–1840* (Cambridge, 1988).
—— (ed.), *An Oxford Companion to the Romantic Age: British Culture 1776–1832* (Oxford, 1999).
McCarthy, William, *Anna Letitia Barbauld: Voice of the Enlightenment* (Baltimore, Md., 2008).
McCue, Daniel L. Jr., 'The Pamphleteer Pitt's Government Couldn't Silence', *Eighteenth-Century Life*, 5 (1978–9), 38–49.
McIlvanney, Liam, *Burns the Radical: Poetry and Politics in Late Eighteenth-Century Scotland* (East Linton, 2002).
McKenna, Catherine, 'Aspects of Tradition Formation in Eighteenth-Century Wales' in Joseph F. Nagy (ed.), *Memory and the Modern in Celtic Literatures. CSANA Yearbook 5* (Dublin, 2006), pp. 37–60.
Mackenzie, Henry, *Julia de Roubigné*, ed. Susan Manning (East Linton, 1999).
Makdisi, Saree, *Romantic Imperialism: Universal Empire and the Culture of Modernity* (Cambridge, 1998).
Malkin, Benjamin H., *The Scenery, Antiquities, and Biography of South Wales* (2nd edn., 2 vols., London, 1807).
Manly, Susan, *Language, Custom and Nation in the 1790s* (Aldershot, 2007).

Martin, E., *Occupations of the People of Sandwich* (Sandwich, 1978).
Martin, Peter, *Samuel Johnson: A Biography* (London, 2008).
Marx, Karl, and Frederick Engels, *Collected Works 1864–1868, Volume 42* (London, 1987).
—— *Collected Works 1868–1870, Volume 43* (London, 1988).
Mather, F. C., *High Church Prophet: Bishop Samuel Horsley (1733–1806) and the Caroline Tradition in the later Georgian Church* (Oxford, 1992).
Matthews, J. H. (ed.), *Cardiff Records* (6 vols., Cardiff, 1898–1911).
Mee, Jon, *Dangerous Enthusiasm: William Blake and the Culture of Radicalism in the 1790s* (Oxford, 1992).
—— '"Images of Truth New Born": Iolo, William Blake and the Literary Radicalism of the 1790s' in Jenkins (ed.), *Rattleskull Genius*, pp. 173–93.
Miles, Dillwyn, *The Secret of the Bards of the Isle of Britain* (Llandybïe, 1992).
Millward, E. G., 'Merthyr Tudful: Tref y Brodyr Rhagorol' in Hywel Teifi Edwards (ed.), *Merthyr a Thaf* (Llandysul, 2001), pp. 9–56.
—— (ed.), *Blodeugerdd Barddas o Gerddi Rhydd y Ddeunawfed Ganrif* (Cyhoeddiadau Barddas, 1991).
Mineka, Francis E., *The Dissidence of Dissent: The Monthly Repository 1806–1838* (Chapel Hill, N.C., 1944).
Miskell, Louise, *Intelligent Town: An Urban History of Swansea, 1780–1855* (Cardiff, 2006).
—— 'The Making of a new "Welsh metropolis": Science, Leisure and Industry in Early Nineteenth-century Swansea', *History*, 88, no. 289 (2003), 32–52.
Mitchison, Rosalind, *Agricultural Sir John: The Life of Sir John Sinclair of Ulbster 1754–1835* (London, 1962).
—— 'The Old Board of Agriculture (1793–1822)', *EHR*, LXXIV (1958), 41–69.
Moore, Donald, 'Visions of the Vale', *Morgannwg*, L (2006), 77–119.
Moore, Patricia (ed.), *Glamorgan Sheriffs* (Cardiff, 1995).
Morgan, Gerald, 'Ieuan Fardd (1731–1788): "Traethawd ar yr Esgyb Eingl"', *Ceredigion*, XI, no. 2 (1990), 135–45.
Morgan, John E., *Hanes Pontardawe a'r Cylch* (Pontardawe, 1911).
Morgan, Kenneth, *Bristol and the Atlantic Trade in the Eighteenth Century* (Cambridge, 1993).
Morgan, Morien, and Thomas Morgan, *Hanes Tonyrefail* (Caerdydd, 1899).
Morgan, Prys, *Iolo Morganwg* (Cardiff, 1975).
—— *The Eighteenth Century Renaissance* (Llandybïe, 1981).
—— '"A Kind of Sacred Land": Iolo Morganwg and Monmouthshire', *The Monmouthshire Antiquary*, XXVII (2011), 127–33.
—— 'A Private Space: Autobiography and Individuality in Eighteenth- and Early Nineteenth-Century Wales' in Davies and Jenkins (eds.), *From Medieval to Modern Wales*, pp. 160–74.
—— 'Dyro Olau ar dy Eiriau', *Taliesin*, 70 (1990), 38–45.
—— 'From a Death to a View: The Hunt for the Welsh Past in the Romantic Period' in Eric Hobsbawm and Terence Ranger (eds.), *The Invention of Tradition* (new edn., Cambridge, 1992), pp. 43–100.
Morris, Marilyn, *The British Monarchy and the French Revolution* (Yale, 1998).
Morris, Norval, and David J. Rothman (eds.), *The Oxford History of the Prison* (Oxford, 1995).

Mugglestone, Lynda, *'Talking Proper': The Rise of Accent as Social Symbol* (2nd edn., Oxford, 2003).
Mullan, John, *Sentiment and Sociability: The Language of Feeling in the Eighteenth Century* (Oxford, 1988).
Nash, David, *Blasphemy in Modern Britain* (Aldershot, 1999).
Nicholas, W. Rhys, *Thomas William Bethesda'r Fro* (Abertawe, 1994).
Nichols, John (ed.), *The Miscellaneous Works, in Prose and Verse, of George Hardinge* (3 vols., London, 1818).
Norris, John M., 'The Policy of the British Cabinet in the Nootka Crisis', *EHR*, LXX, no. 277 (1955), 562–80.
Oddy, John (ed.), *The Writings of the Radical Welsh Baptist Minister William Richards (1749–1818)* (Lewiston, NY, 2008).
Okey, Robin, 'Wales and Eastern Europe: Small Nations in Comparison' in Charles-Edwards and Evans (eds.), *Wales and the Wider World*, pp. 184–217.
Orrin, Geoffrey R., *Medieval Churches of the Vale of Glamorgan* (Cowbridge, 1988).
Owen, Bryn, *The History of the Welsh Militia and Volunteer Corps 1757–1908. Volume 3, Glamorgan. Part 2, Volunteers and Local Militia, 1796–1816; Yeomanry Cavalry, 1808–1831* (Wrexham, 1994).
Owen, Geraint Dyfnallt, *Thomas Evans (Tomos Glyn Cothi)* ([Abertawe], 1963).
Owen, Gwynne E., 'Welsh Anti-Slavery Sentiments, 1795–1865: A Survey of Public Opinion' (unpublished University of Wales MA thesis, 1964).
Owen, Hugh, *The Life and Works of Lewis Morris (Llewelyn Ddu o Fôn) 1701–1765* (Anglesey Antiquarian Society and Field Club, 1951).
—— (ed.), *Additional Letters of the Morrises of Anglesey (1735–1786)* (2 vols., London, 1947–9).
Owen, Morfydd E., *Y Meddwl Obsesiynol: Traddodiad y Triawd Cyffredinol yn y Gymraeg a'r Myvyrian Archaiology of Wales* (Aberystwyth, 2007).
—— 'Royal Propaganda: Stories from the Law-Texts' in T. M. Charles-Edwards, Morfydd E. Owen and Paul Russell (eds.), *The Welsh King and his Court* (Cardiff, 2000), pp. 224–54.
Owen, William, *The Heroic Elegies and Other Pieces of Llywarç Hen* (London, 1792 [1793]).
Owen Pughe, William, *A Dictionary of the Welsh Language* (2 vols., London, 1803).
—— *Hu Gadarn, Cywydd o 111 Caniad* (Llundain, 1822).
Paine, Thomas, *Rights of Man*, ed. Gregory Claeys (Indianapolis, Ind., 1992).
—— *Rights of Man, Common Sense, and Other Political Writings*, ed. Mark Philp (Oxford, 1995; new edn. 2008).
Parry, J. Glyn, 'Stability and Change in Mid-Eighteenth Century Caernarfonshire' (unpublished University of Wales MA thesis, 1978).
Parry, Thomas, '*Barddoniaeth Dafydd ab Gwilym*, 1789', *JWBS*, VIII, no. 4 (1957), 189–99.
—— (ed.), *The Oxford Book of Welsh Verse* (Oxford, 1962).
Patton, Lewis and Peter Mann (eds.), *The Collected Works of Samuel Taylor Coleridge: Lectures 1795 On Politics and Religion* (London, 1971).
Pentland, Gordon, 'Patriotism, Universalism and the Scottish Conventions, 1792–1794', *History*, 89, no. 295 (2004), 340–60.
Percival, Arthur, *Old Faversham* (Rainham, 1988).

Phillips, D. Rhys, *A Forgotten Welsh Historian (William Davies, Cringell, Neath, 1756–1823)* (Swansea, 1916).
—— *The History of the Vale of Neath* (Swansea, 1925).
Phillips, Geraint, *Dyn heb ei Gyffelyb yn y Byd: Owain Myfyr a'i Gysylltiadau Llenyddol* (Caerdydd, 2010).
—— 'Bywyd a Chysylltiadau Llenyddol Owain Myfyr (Owen Jones), 1741–1814' (unpublished University of Wales Ph.D. thesis, 2006).
—— 'Forgery and Patronage: Iolo Morganwg and Owain Myfyr' in Jenkins (ed.), *Rattleskull Genius*, pp. 403–23.
—— 'Math o Wallgofrwydd: Iolo Morganwg, Opiwm a Thomas Chatterton', *NLWJ*, XXIX, no. 4 (1996), 391–410.
Phillips, Mark Salber, *Society and Sentiment: Genres of Historical Writing in Britain, 1740–1820* (Princeton, NJ, 2000).
Phillips, W. J., 'Iolo Morganwg and the Rees Family of Gelligron', *NLWJ*, XIV, no. 2 (1965), 227–36.
Philp, Mark, 'The Fragmented Ideology of Reform' in idem (ed.), *The French Revolution and British Popular Politics* (Cambridge, 1991), pp. 50–77.
—— 'Vulgar Conservatism, 1792–3', *EHR*, CX, no. 435 (1995), 42–69.
Pinfold, John, *The Slave Trade Debate* (Oxford, 2007).
Poole, Steve, 'Pitt's Terror Reconsidered: Jacobinism and the Law in two South-Western Counties, 1791–1803', *Southern History*, 17 (1995), 65–88.
—— (ed.), *John Thelwall: Radical Romantic and Acquitted Felon* (London, 2009).
Porter, Roy, *Flesh in the Age of Reason* (London, 2003).
—— *London: A Social History* (London, 1994).
—— *Quacks: Fakers and Charlatans in English Medicine* (Stroud, 2000).
—— 'Material Pleasures in the Consumer Society' in Roy Porter and Marie Mulvey Roberts (eds.), *Pleasure in the Eighteenth Century* (Basingstoke, 1996), pp. 19–35.
—— 'Mixed Feelings: The Enlightenment and Sexuality in Eighteenth-Century Britain' in Paul-Gabriel Boucé (ed.), *Sexuality in Eighteenth-Century Britain* (Manchester, 1982), pp. 1–27.
—— and Mikuláš Teich (eds.), *Romanticism in National Context* (Cambridge, 1988).
Pratt, Lynda (ed.), *Robert Southey: Poetical Works 1793–1810. Volume 5. Selected Shorter Poems, c.1793–1810* (London, 2004).
Prescott, Sarah, *Eighteenth-Century Writing from Wales: Bards and Britons* (Cardiff, 2008).
Priestman, Martin, *Romantic Atheism: Poetry and Freethought, 1780–1830* (Cambridge, 1999).
Probert, William (trans.), *The Ancient Laws of Cambria* (London, 1823).
Radcliffe, Evan, 'Revolutionary Writing, Moral Philosophy, and Universal Benevolence in the Eighteenth Century', *Journal of the History of Ideas*, 54, no. 2 (1993), 221–40.
Randall, H. J., *Bridgend: The Story of a Market Town* (Newport, 1955).
Raven, James, 'The Book Trades' in Isabel Rivers (ed.), *Books and Their Readers in Eighteenth-Century England: New Essays* (London, 2001), pp. 1–34.
Redwood, Charles, *The Vale of Glamorgan: Scenes and Tales among the Welsh* (London, 1839).
Rees, Eiluned, 'Developments in the Book Trade in Eighteenth-Century Wales', *The Library*, 5th series, 24 (1969), 33–43.
Rees, William, *Cardiff: A History of the City* (2nd edn., Cardiff, 1969).

Rendall, Jane, 'Feminizing the Enlightenment: The Problem of Sensibility' in Martin Fitzpatrick, Peter Jones, Christa Knellwolf, and Iain McCalman (eds.), *The Enlightenment World* (London, 2004), pp. 253–71.

Rhys, Hywel Gethin, *'A Wayward Cymric Genius': Celebrating the Centenary of the Death of Iolo Morganwg* (Aberystwyth, 2007).

Richard, David (Dafydd Ionawr), *Cywydd y Drindod* ([Wrexham], 1793).

[Richards, William], *Cwyn y Cystuddiedig* (Caerfyrddin, 1798).

Richardson, T. L., *Historic Sandwich and its Region 1500–1900* (Sandwich Local History Society, 2006).

Ridd, Tom, 'Gabriel Powell: The Uncrowned King of Swansea' in Stewart Williams (ed.), *Glamorgan Historian, 5* (Cowbridge, 1968), pp. 152–60.

Riden, Philip, *John Bedford and the Ironworks at Cefn Cribwr* (Cardiff, 1992).

Rigby, Brian, 'Radical Spectators of the Revolution; The Case of the *Analytical Review*' in Ceri Crossley and Ian Small (eds.), *The French Revolution and British Culture* (Oxford, 1989), pp. 63–83.

Rivers, Isabel, and David L. Wykes (eds.), *Joseph Priestley, Scientist, Philosopher, and Theologian* (Oxford, 2008).

Roberts, Brynley F., 'Mab ei Dad: Taliesin ab Iolo Morganwg' in Hywel Teifi Edwards (ed.), *Merthyr a Thaf* (Llandysul, 2001), pp. 57–93.

—— '"The Age of Restitution": Taliesin ab Iolo and the Reception of Iolo Morganwg' in Jenkins (ed.), *Rattleskull Genius*, pp. 461–79.

Roberts, Gomer M., *Bywyd a Gwaith Peter Williams* (Caerdydd, 1943).

—— *Emynwyr Bethesda'r Fro* (Llandysul, 1967).

Roberts, J. M., *The Mythology of the Secret Societies* (London, 1972).

Roberts, Peter, *Sketch of the Early History of the Cymry, or Ancient Britons* (London, 1803).

Roberts, Peter R., 'The Decline of the Welsh Squires in the Eighteenth Century', *NLWJ*, XIII, no. 2 (1963), 157–73.

Roberts, Thomas A., *The Concept of Benevolence: Aspects of Eighteenth-Century Moral Philosophy* (London, 1973).

Roe, Nicholas, 'Radical George: Dyer in the 1790s', *Charles Lamb Bulletin*, 49 (1985), 17–26.

Rogers, Nicholas, 'The Sea Fencibles, Loyalism and the Reach of the State' in Mark Philp (ed.), *Resisting Napoleon: The British Response to the Threat of Invasion, 1797–1815* (Aldershot, 2006), pp. 41–59.

Ross, J. E. (ed.), *Radical Adventurer: The Diaries of Robert Morris 1772–1774* (Bath, 1971).

Roth, Cecil, *The Nephew of the Almighty* (London, 1933).

Rousseau, Jean-Jacques, *Eloisa: or, a Series of Original Letters*, translated by William Kenrick, 1803 (facsimile repr., 2 vols., Oxford, 1989).

Rubel, Margaret Mary, *Savage and Barbarian: Historical Attitudes in the Criticism of Homer and Ossian in Britain, 1760–1800* (Oxford, 1978).

Russett, Margaret, *Fictions and Fakes: Forging Romantic Authenticity, 1760–1845* (Cambridge, 2006).

Rutt, J. T. and Arnold Wainewright (eds.), *Memoirs of the Life of Gilbert Wakefield* (2 vols., London, 1804).

St Clair, William, *The Reading Nation in the Romantic Period* (Cambridge, 2004).

Salmon, David, *The Descent of the French on Pembrokeshire* (Carmarthen, 1930).

Schama, Simon, *Citizens: A Chronicle of the French Revolution* (London, 1989).
Schonhorn, Manuel, *Defoe's Politics: Parliament, Power, Kingship, and Robinson Crusoe* (Cambridge, 1991).
Seed, John, 'Theologies of Power: Unitarianism and the Social Relations of Religious Discourse, 1800–1850' in R. J. Morris (ed.), *Class, Power and Social Structure in British Nineteenth-Century Towns* (Leicester, 1986), pp. 108–56.
Smiles, Sam, *The Image of Antiquity: Ancient Britain and the Romantic Imagination* (London, 1994).
Smith, Anthony D., *National Identity* (Harmondsworth, 1991).
—— *Nationalism and Modernism* (London, 1998).
—— *The Ethnic Origins of Nations* (Oxford, 1986).
—— 'The "Golden Age" and National Renewal' in Geoffrey Hosking and George Schöpflin (eds.), *Myths and Nationhood* (London, 1997), pp. 36–59.
Smith, Olivia, *The Politics of Language, 1791–1819* (Oxford, 1986).
Smyth, Jim, *The Making of the United Kingdom, 1660–1800* (Harlow, 2001).
Solkin, David H., *Richard Wilson: The Landscape of Reaction* (London, 1982).
Stone, Lawrence, *The Past and the Present Revisited* (London, 1987).
Stuchtey, Benedikt, 'Literature, Liberty and Life of the Nation: British Historiography from Macaulay to Trevelyan' in Stefan Berger, Mark Donovan and Kevin Passmore (eds.), *Writing National Histories: Western Europe since 1800* (London, 1999), pp. 30–46.
Suggett, Richard, 'Iolo Morganwg: Stonecutter, Builder, and Antiquary' in Jenkins (ed.), *Rattleskull Genius*, pp. 197–226.
—— 'Slander in Early-Modern Wales', *BBCS*, XXXIX (1992), 119–53.
Swaine, Anthony, *Faversham: Its History, its Present Role and the Pattern for its Future* (Faversham, 1970).
Sweet, Rosemary, 'Stability and Continuity: Swansea Politics and Reform, 1780–1820', *WHR*, 18, no. 1 (1996), 14–39.
Taylor, Clare, 'Edward Williams ('Iolo Morganwg') and his Brothers: A Jamaican Inheritance', *THSC* (1980), 35–43.
Thale, Mary (ed.), *Selections from the Papers of the London Corresponding Society 1792–1799* (Cambridge, 1983).
Thelwall, John, *Poems, Chiefly Written in Retirement 1801* (Oxford, 1989).
Thomas, D. O., *Ymateb i Chwyldro / Response to Revolution* (Caerdydd / Cardiff, 1989).
—— 'George Cadogan Morgan', *The Price-Priestley Newsletter*, 3 (1979), 53–70.
—— 'Richard Price's Journal', *NLWJ*, XXI, no. 4 (1980), 366–413.
—— and W. Bernard Peach (eds.), *The Correspondence of Richard Price. Volume I: July 1748–March 1778* (Cardiff, 1983).
Thomas, David (Dafydd Ddu Eryri), *Corph y Gainge, neu Ddifyrwch Teuluaidd* (Dolgelleu, 1810).
Thomas, Graham, 'Gwallter Mechain ac Eisteddfod Corwen, 1789', *NLWJ*, XX, no. 4 (1978), 408.
Thomas, Hilary M. (ed.), *The Diaries of John Bird of Cardiff: Clerk to the first Marquess of Bute 1790–1803* (Cardiff, 1987).
Thomas, J. E., *Britain's Last Invasion: Fishguard 1797* (Stroud, 2007).
Thomas, Peter, 'Professor Theophilus Redwood (1806–1892)', *Llantwit Major: Aspects of its History*, 3 (2004), 21–43.

Thomas, Peter D. G., *Politics in Eighteenth-Century Wales* (Cardiff, 1998).
—— '"Bill of Rights Morris": A Welsh Wilkite Radical and Rogue – Robert Morris (1743–1793)' in Stephen Taylor, Richard Connors and Clyve Jones (eds.), *Hanoverian Britain and Empire: Essays in Memory of Philip Lawson* (Woodbridge, 1998), pp. 267–87.
—— 'Glamorgan Politics, 1688–1790' in Williams (ed.), *Glamorgan County History, Volume IV*, pp. 394–429.
Thomas, Rhiannon, 'William Vaughan: Carwr Llên a Maswedd', *Taliesin*, 70 (1990), 69–76.
Thompson, E. P., *The Making of the English Working Class* (Harmondsworth, 1968).
—— *The Romantics: England in a Revolutionary Age* (Woodbridge, 1997).
Todd, Janet, *Sensibility: An Introduction* (London, 1986).
Trollope, Glynden, *The Cambrian and General Advertiser for the Principality of Wales, 1804–1930* (Berkhamsted, 2003).
Trumpener, Katie, *Bardic Nationalism: The Romantic Novel and the British Empire* (Princeton, NJ, 1997).
Turley, David, *The Culture of English Antislavery, 1780–1860* (London, 1991).
Turner, Sharon, *A Vindication of the Genuineness of the Ancient British Poems of Aneurin, Taliesin, Llywarch Hen and Merdhin* (London, 1803).
Uglow, Jenny, *The Lunar Men: The Friends who made the Future 1730–1810* (pbk. edn., London, 2003).
Walker, R. J. B., *Old Westminster Bridge: The Bridge of Fools* (Newton Abbot, 1979).
Walters, Huw, 'Myfyr Morganwg and the Rocking-Stone Gorsedd' in Jenkins (ed.), *Rattleskull Genius*, pp. 481–500.
Walters, John, *A Dissertation on the Welsh Language* (Cowbridge, 1771).
Ward, Ned, *A Trip to North-Wales* (London, 1701).
Waring, Elijah, *Recollections and Anecdotes of Edward Williams, the Bard of Glamorgan; or, Iolo Morganwg, B.B.D.* (London, 1850).
Warrington, William, *The History of Wales* (London, 1786).
Warter, John W. (ed.), *Southey's Common-place Book. Fourth Series* (London, 1850).
Watts, Michael R., *The Dissenters. Volume II. The Expansion of Evangelical Nonconformity* (Oxford, 1995).
Weinbrot, Howard D., *Eighteenth-Century Satire: Essays on Text and Context from Dryden to Peter Pindar* (Cambridge, 1988).
Western, J. R., 'The Volunteer Movement as an Anti-Revolutionary Force, 1793–1801', *EHR*, LXXI (1956), 603–14.
Wharam, Alan, *The Treason Trials, 1794* (London, 1992).
Whelan, Timothy, 'William Fox, Martha Gurney, and Radical Discourse of the 1790s', *Eighteenth-Century Studies*, 42, no. 3 (2009), 397–411.
White, Daniel E., 'The "Joineriana": Anna Barbauld, the Aikin Family Circle, and the Dissenting Public Sphere', *Eighteenth-Century Studies*, 32, no. 4 (1999), 511–33.
White, Eryn M., 'The Established Church, Dissent and the Welsh Language *c.* 1660–1811' in Jenkins (ed.), *The Welsh Language before the Industrial Revolution*, pp. 235–87.
Wilkins, Charles, *The History of Merthyr Tydfil* (Merthyr Tydfil, 1867).
Williams, A. H. (ed.), *John Wesley in Wales 1739–1790* (Cardiff, 1971).
Williams, D. Trevor, *The Economic Development of Swansea and of the Swansea District to 1921* (Swansea, 1940).

Williams, David, *John Evans and the Legend of Madoc 1770–1799* (Cardiff, 1963).
—— *John Frost: A Study in Chartism* (Cardiff, 1939).
Williams, Edward, *Dagrau yr Awen neu Farwnad Lewis Hopcin Fardd, o Landyfodwg ym Morganwg* (Pont-y-fon, 1772).
—— *Poems, Lyric and Pastoral* (2 vols., London, 1794).
—— *Rheolau a Threfniadau Cymdeithas Dwyfundodiaid yn Neheubarth Cymru* (Llundain, 1803).
—— *Salmau yr Eglwys yn yr Anialwch* (Merthyr Tydfil, 1812; 1834).
—— *Trial by Jury, the Grand Palladium of British Liberty* (London, 1795).
—— *Vox Populi Vox Dei!* (Swansea, 1818).
—— (trans.), *Atteb i'r Gofyniad, Pa ham yr wyt ti yn Gristion?* (Llundain, 1804).
—— (trans.), *Holiadur, neu Addysgiadau Cyffredin, Hawl ac Atteb, yn Athrawiaethau a Dyledswyddau Crefydd* (Merthyr, 1814).
Williams, G. J., *Iolo Morganwg – Y Gyfrol Gyntaf* (Caerdydd, 1956).
—— *Iolo Morganwg a Chywyddau'r Ychwanegiad* (Llundain, 1926).
—— *Traddodiad Llenyddol Morgannwg* (Caerdydd, 1948).
—— 'Brut Aberpergwm: A Version of the Chronicle of the Princes' in Stewart Williams (ed.), *Glamorgan Historian*, 4 (Cowbridge, 1967), pp. 205–20.
—— 'Bywyd Cymreig Llundain yng Nghyfnod Owain Myfyr', *Y Llenor*, XVIII (1939), 73–82, 218–32.
—— 'Daniel Walters', *Y Llenor*, XX (1941), 176–82.
—— 'Daniel Walters: A Poet of the Vale' in Stewart Williams (ed.), *Glamorgan Historian, 3* (Cowbridge, 1966), pp. 238–43.
—— 'Glamorgan Customs in the Eighteenth Century', *Gwerin*, 1 (1957), 99–108.
—— 'Gorsedd y Beirdd a'r Seiri Rhyddion', *LlC*, 7, nos. 3 and 4 (1963), 213–16.
—— 'Hanes Cyhoeddi'r "Myvyrian Archaiology"', *JWBS*, X, no. 1 (1966), 2–12.
—— 'Josiah Rees a'r *Eurgrawn Cymraeg* (1770)', *LlC*, 3, no. 2 (1954), 119.
—— 'Sabeliaid Aberthin', *Y Cofiadur*, 25 (1955), 23–8.
Williams, Glanmor, *Reformation Views of Church History* (London, 1970).
—— 'Gomer: "Sylfaenydd ein Llenyddiaeth Gyfnodol"', *THSC* (1982), 111–38.
—— 'The Earliest Non-conformists in Merthyr Tydfil', *MH*, I (1976), 84–95.
—— (ed.), *Glamorgan County History, Volume IV: Early Modern Glamorgan from the Act of Union to the Industrial Revolution* (Cardiff, 1974).
Williams, Gwyn A., *Madoc: The Making of a Myth* (London, 1979).
—— *The Merthyr Rising* (London, 1978).
—— *The Search for Beulah Land* (London, 1980).
—— *The Welsh in their History* (London, 1982).
—— 'John Evans's Mission to the Madogwys, 1792–1799', *BBCS*, XXVII, part 4 (1978), 569–601.
—— 'South Wales Radicalism: The First Phase' in Stewart Williams (ed.), *Glamorgan Historian, 2* (Cowbridge, 1965), pp. 30–9.
Williams, John Ab Ithel, *Barddas; Or, A Collection of Original Documents, Illustrative of the Theology, Wisdom, and Usages of the Bardo-Druidic System of the Isle of Britain. Volume 1* (Llandovery, 1862).
Williams, John, *An Enquiry into the Truth of the Tradition concerning the Discovery of America by Prince Madog ab Owen Gwynedd, about the year 1170* (London, 1791).
—— *Farther Observations on the Discovery of America by Prince Madog ab Owen Gwynedd, about the year 1170* (London, 1792).

Williams, Morgan, 'Notable Men of Wales: Iolo Morganwg (Edward Williams)', *The Red Dragon: The National Magazine of Wales*, II (1882), 97–104.

Williams, Taliesin (ed.), *Cyfrinach Beirdd Ynys Prydain* (Abertawy, 1829).

—— (ed.), *Iolo Manuscripts: A Selection of Ancient Welsh Manuscripts* (Llandovery, 1848).

Wilson, Ben, *What Price Liberty?* (London, 2009).

Wood, Marcus, *Radical Satire and Print Culture 1790–1822* (Oxford, 1994).

Woodfine, Philip, 'Debtors, Prisons, and Petitions in Eighteenth-Century England', *Eighteenth-Century Life*, 30, no. 2 (2006), 1–31.

Woodring, Carl, *Politics in English Romantic Poetry* (Cambridge, Mass., 1970).

Worrall, David, *Radical Culture: Discourse, Resistance and Surveillance, 1790–1820* (Hemel Hempstead, 1992).

—— *The Politics of Romantic Theatricality, 1787–1832* (Basingstoke, 2007).

—— *Theatric Revolution: Drama, Censorship, and Romantic Period Subcultures 1773–1832* (Oxford, 2006).

Wright, Herbert G., 'The Relations of the Welsh Bard Iolo Morganwg with Dr Johnson, Cowper and Southey', *Review of English Studies*, VIII, no. 30 (1932), 129–38.

Wright, Richard, *A Review of the Missionary Life and Labors of Richard Wright* (London, 1824).

Young, Christine, 'The Vachell Family of Cardiff, and the Dispersal of the Wilkins' Land', *Llantwit Major: Aspects of its History*, 7 (2007), 50–61.

Zigrosser, Carl, 'The Medallic Sketches of Augustin Dupré in American Collections', *Proceedings of the American Philosophical Society*, 101, no. 6 (1957), 535–50.

Index

Aber-cwm-y-fuwch 21, 136
Aberdare 22, 63, 70, 71, 135, 231, 237
Aberthaw 29, 50
Aberthin 156
Acts of Union (1536–43) 18, 165, 166, 192
Advancement of Learning (1605), Francis Bacon 16
Aikin, John 104, 108, 128, 215
Alawn 185
Allen, William 217
America 79, 82, 89, 97
  alleged discovery by Madoc 43, 83, 86
  American Philosophical Society 215
Ancient Laws of Cambria, The (1823), William Probert 205
Aneirin 187
Anstey, Christopher 107
Antichrist in the French Convention (1795) 119, 149
Ardudful 64
Arianism 70, 71, 135, 142, 214, 221
Arminianism 70, 224
Asiatick Researches 87–8
Aspland, Robert 223
Association for the Preservation of Liberty and Property against Republicans and Levellers 3, 101
Aubrey, Richard (d. 1820) 214
Aubrey, Richard (d. 1836) 214

Barbauld, Anna Letitia 104, 106, 215
  Sins of the Government, Sins of the Nation (1793) 106
Barclay, Robert 106
Bard, The, Thomas Gray 63
Barddoniaeth Dafydd ab Gwilym, Owen Jones and William Owen, eds. (1789) 64

bardic alphabet 185, 202
Barker, Mary 154–5
Bassett family of Bonvilston 75
Bassett family of Llaneley 11
Bassett, William, solicitor 27
Bath 81, 96, 107
Beaufort, Duke of 74, 75
Beaupré Castle 49
Beavan, Captain John 152
Bedford, John, brickmaker 130, 218
Bedford, John, ironmaster 218, 237
Bedford, Sarah 237
Bedford, Thomas 218
Bell, John 106
Belsham, Thomas 103, 218, 222, 223, 226
Berean Society 231–2
Bertie, Willoughby, 4th Earl of Abingdon 139
Betws Tir Iarll 22, 71
Bevan, Madam Bridget 6
Bill of Rights Society *see* Society of Gentlemen Supporters of the Bill of Rights
Binon (Beynon), William 83
Blades, Elizabeth (née Seys) 11
Blake, William 104, 117
Bleddyn ap Cynfyn 10
Blomberg, Revd Frederick William 107
Board of Agriculture 131–4, 143
Borlase, William 92
Boverton 11, 167
Bowdler, Elizabeth Stuart 84, 86
Bowdler, Henrietta (Harriet) Maria 84, 86
Bowles, General William Augustus 82, 84
Bradford, John of Betws Tir Iarll 22, 71, 135

Brân Fendigaid 184, 185
Bridgend 79–80, 130, 218, 226
Brissot, Jacques-Pierre 100
Bristol 96, 123, 125, 127, 128
Brothers, Richard 119–20
'Brut Aberpergwm' 188
'Brut y Tywysogyon' 187–8
Brutus 177, 184
Bulgin, William 123
Bull's Head in Walbrook ('Y Crindy') 33, 35, 37
Burgess, Thomas, bishop of St David's 198, 202, 222, 234
Burke, Edmund
    Reflections on the Revolution in France (1790) 89, 97
Burns, Robert 9, 41, 50, 81, 153, 198
Bute family 219

Cadwaladr the Blessed 10
Caerffili 242
Calvinistic Methodists 6, 7, 20, 37, 69, 70, 135, 142, 155–6, 198, 223, 226–7, 239
Cambrian, The 213, 217, 219, 233
Cambrian Register 130, 205
Cambrian Society 194, 202, 234
Cambro-Briton 205
Caradog of Llancarfan 4, 5, 178
Caradogion Society 91, 92
Caratacus 153, 185
Cardiff 29, 51, 218, 219, 238, 239
Carmarthen 18, 135, 138, 225
    dissenting academies 70, 138, 139, 157, 179, 222, 225
    eisteddfod (*c*. 1453) 65, 181
    eisteddfod (1819) 202–3, 234
Caroline, Princess of Brunswick 120
Catholicism 6, 200
Catwg Ddoeth 5, 187
Cefncoedycymer 142, 214, 223
Cefncribwr 219, 230
Charles, John 27, 46
Charles, Thomas 156
Chatterton, Thomas 52, 158, 174
Church, Revd William 27
Clarkson, Thomas 126
Coedrhiglan 53, 235
Cole, Sir Christopher of Penrice Castle 232–3
Coleridge, Samuel Taylor 86, 123, 161
Collins, William 43

Colville, Sir John 83
Combination Laws (1799 and 1800) 150
Cowbridge 29, 31, 48, 124, 128, 145, 240
    book club 39
    Cowbridge Book Society 124
    Cowbridge Volunteer Infantry 152, 153
    diocesan library 39
    grammar school 19, 52, 80
    magistrates 241–2
    politics 74–5
    town hall 50, 77
Cowper, William 105, 128
Coychurch 11, 23, 24
Crawshay, Richard 143–4, 159, 167, 168
Cruikshank, Robert 12
Cunnington, William 203
Cymmrodorion Society 33

Dafydd ab Edmwnd 65, 181
Dafydd ap Gwilym 15, 22, 25, 34, 40, 47, 52, 62, 64–5, 175, 187
    'Cywydd y Gal' 37
Dafydd ap Rhisiart 17
Dafydd Ddu Eryri *see* Thomas, David (Dafydd Ddu Eryri)
Dafydd Ionawr *see* Richards, David (Dafydd Ionawr)
Dafydd, Wiliam (Gwilym Glyn Ogwr) 136–7, 138
Dare, Ann 219
Dare, Margaret 219
Dare, Robert 218–19
Davies, David, Rhayader 156
Davies, Edward 'Celtic' 158, 234
Davies, Dr John, Mallwyd 24
Davies, Richard, bishop of St David's 184
Davies, Thomas, Cefncoedycymer 223
Davies, Walter (Gwallter Mechain) 18, 91, 132–4, 136, 212, 213, 235
    General View of the Agriculture and Domestic Economy of South Wales (1815) 134
Davies, William of Cringell 216
Davis, David ('Dafis Castellhywel') 70, 138, 140, 224, 227
Davis, David, Neath 160–1, 162, 216, 220, 222, 227, 229
Davis, Timothy 227
Dee, John
    'Title Royal' 83
Deere, Kitty 27
Deere, Matthew of Ash Hall 27

Deveson, John, stonecutter 32, 44
Diderot, Denis 176
Disney, John 103, 117, 156
Dissenting academies 7, 70, 135, 138, 139, 157, 179, 199, 222, 225
Doctrine of the Trinity Act 230–1
Drayson, Charles, stonemason and bricklayer 32
'Drive away Care Club' 35
Drych y Prif Oesoedd (1716; 1740), Theophilus Evans 40, 83, 177, 178
Dundas, Henry 111, 148
Dunraven, Countess Caroline of 9
Dupré, Augustin 90
Dyer, George 104–5, 117, 118, 120, 130, 136, 161, 215
   A Dissertation on the Theory and Practice of Benevolence (1795) 105
   Complaints of the Poor People of England (1793) 105
Dyfnwal Moelmud 183, 184, 205, 206

Eaton, Daniel Isaac 117
   Hog Wash 115
   Politics for the People (1793–5) 114
Edward I 92, 191, 192
Edwards, John, Rheola 232–3
Edwards, John (Siôn Ceiriog) 34, 37, 45
Edwards, Thomas (Twm o'r Nant) 173
Edwards, William, bridge-builder 214
Edwin family of Llanmihangel and Dunraven 11
Edwin, Charles Wyndham 74
Edwin, Lady Charlotte of Llanmihangel 7
Egerton, Thomas, bishop of Bangor 67
Einigan Gawr 182
eisteddfodau 21, 90–1, 147, 193
   see also Carmarthen; Gorsedd of the Bards of the Isle of Britain
Ellis, John, Llanbryn-mair 149
Emynau o Fawl a Gweddi (1878) 228
Erskine, Thomas 108, 117, 118
Essay on the Mechanical Fabrick of the Universe, An (1707), Conyers Purshall 16
Estlin, Alfred 230
Estlin, John Prior 158, 160, 237
Evans, David, Unitarian 139, 140
Evan(s), Edward, Aberdare 22, 63, 71, 135
   Afalau'r Awen (1816) 22
Evans, Evan (Ieuan Fardd) 25, 62–3, 66–7, 68–9, 170–1
   Specimens of the Antient Poetry of the Welsh Bards (1764) 62
   The Love of our Country (1772) 62, 67
Evans, Revd James, vicar of Marshfield 67–8, 69
Evans, John, Waunfawr 86
Evans, Joseph Priestley 140
Evans, Rees, Tonyrefail 137, 138
Evans, Theophilus 179
Evans, Thomas (Tomos Glyn Cothi) 15, 137, 140, 146, 156, 222, 227–8, 238
   The Miscellaneous Repository: Neu, Y Drysorfa Gymmysgedig 141
   trial 157–60
Evans, Thomas, Bromsgrove 139

Fanny Hill, John Cleland 36
Faversham 32, 35
Fenton, Richard 133, 203
Flemingston 7–8, 12, 27, 51, 53, 54, 137, 167, 242, 243
Flower, Benjamin
   Cambridge Intelligencer 141
Fox, George 69
Fox, John 131
Fox, William 106, 114
Franklin, Ben 141
French invasion of Pembrokeshire (1797) 150–1, 152, 206
French Revolution (1789) 3, 10, 47, 77, 79, 89, 90, 97, 100–1
Frend, William 106
Frome, Sarah 36
Frost, John 149, 220

Gair yn ei Amser (1798), Thomas Jones 156
Gellionnen 70, 123, 160, 214, 215, 216, 224, 226
Gentleman, Merchant, Tradesman, Lawyer, and Debtor's Pocket Guide, in cases of Arrest, The 58
George III 23, 107, 109–10, 117, 119, 128, 146, 149, 155, 160, 162
George, Prince of Wales 36, 107–8, 120
George, Watkin 221
Geraint Fardd Glas 187
Gibbon, Edward 177
Gibbs, Vicary 117, 118
Glamorgan 180–1, 212
   Blaenau 21, 22, 29, 70, 143, 167
   by-election (1789) 11, 72, 73, 74–7, 81
   by-election (1818) 213, 232–3

literary inheritance 63–4
Vale of Glamorgan 5, 7–8, 20, 21, 29
Glamorganshire Agricultural Society 124
Gloddaith, library 173
Godwin, William 1, 87, 104, 117, 141, 168
Gorsedd of the Bards of the Isle of Britain 91–5, 99, 112, 145–6, 152–3, 163, 170, 201–3, 210, 233–4
nod cyfrin (mystic sign) 182, 202, 233
Grenville, Lord 111
Griffith, Evan of Pen-llin 54
Griffith, John, Neath 149
Griffith, Samuel, Poyntz Castle 151
Gruffudd ap Nicolas 65
Guardian 16
Gurney, Martha 114
Gwallter Mechain *see* Davies, Walter (Gwallter Mechain)
Gweledigaetheu y Bardd Cwsc, Ellis Wynne 40
Gwilym Gam 64
Gwilym Glyn Ogwr *see* Dafydd, Wiliam (Gwilym Glyn Ogwr)
Gwron 185
Gwyneddigion Society 33–4, 35, 36–8, 46, 47, 90, 91, 147, 197, 209

Halhead, Nathaniel 119
Hanes y Bedyddwyr, ymhlith y Cymry (1778), Joshua Thomas 69
Hanes y Byd a'r Amseroedd, Simon Thomas 178
Hanes y Ffydd, Charles Edwards 178
Hardinge, George 60, 158–60, 203, 210
Nugae Antiquae et Novae (1782) 158
Hardy, Thomas, founder of the London Corresponding Society 116, 117, 118, 210
Harford, Fanny 76
Harris, Joseph (Gomer) 213
Bwyall Crist (1804) 213
Hengwrt, library 171, 173
Herald of Peace 217
Herder, Johann Gottfried 169–70, 186
Historia Regum Britanniae, Geoffrey of Monmouth 177
History of Brecknockshire, A (1807), Theophilus Jones 179
History of Wales, The (1584), David Powel 165, 178
History of Wales, The (1786), William Warrington 166, 178
Hoare, Sir Richard Colt 203

Holcroft, Thomas 117
Hollis, Brand 118
Homfray, Samuel 159
Honourable and Loyal Society of Ancient Britons, The 33
Hopkin, Lewis of Hendre Ifan Goch, Llandyfodwg 22, 71
Hornor, Thomas 216
Horsley, Samuel, bishop of St David's 138, 141
Howard, John 54, 55
Hu Gadarn 183, 184, 205
Huddy, William 139
Hughes, Robert (Robin Ddu yr Ail o Fôn) 34, 37, 45
Hywel Dda 183

Ieuan Fardd *see* Evans, Evan (Ieuan Fardd)
Ieuan Fawr ap y Diwlith 187
Ifor Bach 153
Ifor Hael 62, 173
Illingworth, William 239
Interesting Historical Events: Relative to the Provinces of Bengal (1766), J. Z. Holwell 88
Interesting Letters of Pope Clement XIV 41
Iolo ab Iorwerth Gwilym *see* Williams, Edward (Iolo ab Iorwerth Gwilym; Iolo Fardd Glas)
Iolo Fardd Glas *see* Williams, Edward (Iolo ab Iorwerth Gwilym; Iolo Fardd Glas)
Iolo Goch 191
Iolo Morganwg *see* Williams, Edward (Iolo Morganwg)
Iorwerth Fynglwyd 49
Ireland, William Henry 174

Jac Glan-y-gors *see* Jones, John (Jac Glan-y-gors)
Jacobitism 6
James, Christopher, Merthyr Tydfil 220
James, John, Gellionnen 226
James, Nicholas 237
Jansen, 'Citizen' Henri 101
Jenkin, David, Cowbridge carpenter 129
Jenkin, David, editor of *Seren Gomer* 241
Jenkins, Edward, maltster 238
John, Alice 242
John, Thomas, Little Newcastle 151
Johnes, Thomas of Hafod 171, 172
Johnson, Joseph, Unitarian bookseller 104, 204

Analytical Review 104
Johnson, Samuel 45, 59, 112, 168
Jones family of Fonmon 11, 75
Jones, David, 'The Welsh Freeholder' 138–9, 160
Jones, David, Llan-gan 69, 156
Jones, Edward ('Ginnico Jones') 144, 145
Jones, Edward, 'King's Bard' 112
   The Bardic Museum (1802) 175
Jones, Griffith, Llanddowror 6, 20
Jones, John (Jac Glan-y-gors) 144–5
Jones, John of Gellilyfdy 188
Jones, John Gale 149
Jones, Owen (Owain Myfyr) 25, 34, 40, 45, 53, 64, 90, 134, 144, 145, 175, 190, 209, 235, 242
   and *The Myvyrian Archaiology of Wales* 144, 171, 172, 173, 186, 188, 204
Jones, Robert (d. 1793) of Fonmon 11
Jones, Thomas, almanacker 169
Jones, William, Llangadfan 136, 170
Jones, Sir William 87–8, 158, 200
   Institutes of Hindu Law; or, the Ordinances of Menu (1796) 88, 148
   Principles of Government in a Dialogue between a Scholar and a Peasant (1782) 87
Joseph of Arimathea 184
Julia de Roubigné, Henry Mackenzie 41
Julie, ou la nouvelle Héloïse, Jean-Jacques Rousseau 41

Ketch, John 115
Kippis, Andrew 103
Kyrle, John 48

Leathart, William 119
Letters from Snowdon (1770), Joseph Cradock 45
Lhuyd, Edward 24, 170, 199
   Archaeologia Britannica (1707) 40, 171
Lindsey, Hannah 141
Lindsey, Theophilus 1, 103, 136, 140–1, 156, 160, 215, 222
literacy 6, 7, 39, 195, 204–7
literary forgery 3–4, 63–4, 163, 174–93
Llancarfan 4, 5, 20, 237
Llandough 10, 24, 27
Llandyfodwg 22, 145
Llan-gan 69, 156
Llan-maes 5, 238
Llantrisant 21, 238, 239

Llantwit Major 11, 167, 185
Llewellin, John of Coedrhiglan 53
Llewellyn, Richard of Ynysawdre 218
Lloyd's Patriotic Fund 237
Lloyd, Cati 53
Lloyd, Charles of Coedlannau Fawr 160, 223–4
Lloyd, David of Brynllefrith 138, 223
Lloyd, Gwenllian 53
Lloyd, John, chief justice 151
Lloyd, Richard of Esclus 193
Lloyd, Watkin 53–4
Llwyd, Humphrey 184
   Cronica Walliae 165
Llwynrhydowen 70, 138, 224
Llywarch Hen 187
Llywelyn ap Gruffudd 166, 191
Llywelyn, Morgan of Neath 64
Locke, John 40, 70, 73
London 30–46, 81–3, 96, 97, 127
London Corresponding Society 1, 98, 100, 116, 129–30, 201
London Philosophical Society 103
London Revolution Society 100
Lonsdale, Mark 82
Louis XVI 101
Lyons, James 224–5

Macaulay, Catherine 98
Macdonald, Sir Archibald 109
Mackworth, Sir Humphrey 50
Macpherson, James 52, 63, 92, 174, 200
Madog ab Owain Gwynedd 43–4, 83–5, 86
Maen Chwŷf, Y 233–4
Malkin, Benjamin 203, 234
Man of Feeling, The (1771), Henry Mackenzie 41
Margate 32
Marsh, Henry of Bristol 48
Matthew family of Llandaf and Radyr 11, 75
Matthew, Edward 11, 23
Matthews, William 132, 133
Merlott, John 237
Merthyr Tydfil 21, 70–1, 142, 165, 220, 225
   Cyfarthfa Philosophical Society 142–3, 220–1
   food riot 159
   Mathematical and Commercial Academy 220, 230

Metamorphoses, Ovid 15
Meyler, William, Bath bookseller 91
Milton, John 67, 128, 141
   Defensio pro Populo Anglicano (1651) 15
   Paradise Lost 15, 209
Moggridge, John Hodder 219, 220
Moll Flanders, Daniel Defoe 36
Montagu, Elizabeth 84
Monthly Repository 223
More, Hannah 10, 86, 235
   Village Politics 128, 147
Morgan ap Hywel 153
Morgan, Dr, surgeon of Llandaf 53
Morgan, George Cadogan 80
   Address to the Jacobine and other Patriotic Societies of the French (1792) 80
Morgan, John 237
Morgan, Thomas, Blaen-gwrach 216
Morgan, Thomas, gaoler 56, 59–60
Morgan, William, actuary 116
Morgan, William, Llantrisant 238–9
Morris brothers of Anglesey 170
   correspondence 36
Morris, John I 214
Morris, Sir John of Clasemont 214
Morris, Lewis 33, 36, 37, 40, 46, 177, 193
   'Celtic Remains' 40, 46
Morris, Richard 33, 40, 46, 193
Morris, Robert of Clasemont 43, 76
Mortimer, Sir Roger 191
Mountstuart, Lord 74, 75
Moysey, Abel 60
Murray, George, bishop of St David's 157
Myddfai physicians 236
Myrddin 187
Myvyrian Archaiology of Wales, The (1801–7) 144, 171, 173–4, 182, 185, 186, 187, 188–9, 202, 205
Myvyrian Archaiology of Wales, The (2nd edn., 1870) 206

Neath 216–18, 225, 228
Nelson, Horatio 144, 231
Newgate prison 1, 2, 119
Newton, Isaac 8
Nicholas, Jemima 151
Nicholl, Mary of Remenham 107, 112
Nicholls family of the Ham 11
Nootka Sound 85–6
Northmore, Thomas 117, 136

Observations on Man, his Frame, his Duty, and his Expectations (1749), David Hartley 103
Observations on Popular Antiquities (1777), John Brand 198
Oes Lyfr (1768), Thomas William 178
Oliver, David, minister at Gellionnen 224
Ossian 63
Owain Glyndŵr 166, 191, 192
Owain Myfyr *see* Jones, Owen (Owain Myfyr)
Owen, Goronwy 23
Owen, John, London bookseller 136

Paine, Thomas 87, 88–9, 91, 97, 99, 100, 101, 108, 109, 110, 115, 116, 128, 141, 142, 143, 147, 219, 221
   Age of Reason (1794–5) 118, 149
   Common Sense (1776) 89
   Rights of Man (1791, 1792) 14, 89–90, 97, 114, 128, 130, 145
Palmer, Thomas Fyshe 113
Panton, Paul of Plas Gwyn 171–2
Parry, John Humffreys 205
Peace Society 231
Peacham, Polly 36
Pen-llin 54
Penn, William 69, 106
Peter, David 157, 179, 222, 225–6
Phillips, Benjamin of St Clears 224, 225
Picton, Sir Thomas 231
Pindar, Peter 128
Pinkerton, John 78, 92
Pitt, William 1, 34, 85, 111–12, 117, 120, 128, 130, 141, 144, 146, 147, 148, 149, 155, 163, 164, 210–11, 229, 231
   'Gagging Acts' 148
Plennydd 185
Plymouth, Earl of 74
Pope, Alexander 39, 48
   The Dunciad 15, 116
Porson, Richard 117
Powel, David 184
   see also History of Wales, The
Powell, Gabriel 75
Powell, Revd Gervase 50
Powell, Vavasor 69
Price, Anna (née Tregelles) 217
Price, Deborah 217
Price, Joseph Tregelles 217, 232
Price, Lydia 217
Price, Peter 217

Price, Richard 79–80, 89, 99, 104, 116, 128, 139, 165
   Discourse on the Love of Our Country (1789) 80
Priestley, Joseph 87, 103, 104, 128, 137, 139, 140, 143
Pritchard, Edward 8
Pritchard, William 83
Probert, William 190
Prydain ab Aedd Mawr 183, 184, 205
Psalmanazar, George 174
Pughe, William Owen 12, 30, 53, 64, 83, 84, 90, 119, 120, 130, 133, 135, 136, 149, 151, 155, 158, 164, 171, 173, 176, 177, 190, 196, 200, 204, 209, 222, 230, 237, 242
   Cambrian Biography (1803) 205
   Coll Gwynfa 15
   The Heroic Elegies and Other Pieces of Llywarç Hen 205

Quakerism 69, 106, 212, 216–17, 219, 231, 243

Rational Dissent 1, 48, 61, 69–72, 82, 102–3, 136, 138, 209, 210, 214, 237
Redwood, Isaac 217
Redwood, Margaret 219
Redwood, William 217
Reed, John, Bristol 128, 130
Rees family of Gelli-gron 222
Rees, Abraham 215
   The New Cyclopaedia (1802–19) 215
Rees, David Jenkin of Lloyd Jack 224
Rees, Evan, Neath 217
   published *Sketches of the Horrors of War* (1818), Eugene Labaume 217
Rees, Josiah, Gellionnen 21, 70, 123, 160, 214
Rees, Owen, bookseller 123, 214, 215
Rees, Richard, publisher 215
Rees, Thomas, Gellionnen 215
   Racovian Catechism (1818) 215
Rees, William of Court Colman 51, 53, 239
Reeves, John 3, 101, 109, 113
Religio Medici, Thomas Browne 15–16
Rhita Gawr 94
Rhys Goch ap Rhicert 187
Rhys, Morgan John 80–1
   Cylch-grawn Cynmraeg (1793–4) 81, 141
Rich, Robert 130

Richard, Henry 218
Richards, David (Dafydd Ionawr) 144, 145
Richards, Thomas, Coychurch 23–4, 196
   Antiquae Linguae Britannicae Thesaurus 23
Richards, William of Lynn 101, 151–2
Riebeau, George 120
Ritson, Joseph 114, 197
Roberts, Elinor of St Mary Church 48
Roberts, Evan ('Y Crin') 33
Roberts, Peter 179
   Sketch of the Early History of the Cymry, or Ancient Britons (1803) 205
Roberts, Rees of St Mary Church 48
Robin Ddu yr Ail o Fôn *see* Hughes, Robert (Robin Ddu yr Ail o Fôn)
Robinson Crusoe, Daniel Defoe 16
Robinson, Robert of Cambridge 104
Rodney, George Bridges 126
Rosser, John, parish clerk 129
Rousseau, Jean-Jacques 70, 80, 176, 188
Rowlands, Henry 63, 92
   Mona Antiqua Restaurata (1732; 1766) 178
Rowlands, John, Unitarian Society of South Wales 214
Royal Literary Fund 80, 136, 175, 204, 235
Royal Society 33, 85
Rumney 50
Rutt, T[owill] 215

Śacontalá, Kalidāsa 88
St Athan 136, 167
St Cadog 4
St David 185
Saint-David for Wales (1781) 44
St David's College, Lampeter 198–9, 201
St Hilary 137, 235
St Illtud 185
St Mary Church 48, 50, 237
St Padarn 185
St Teilo 185
Salesbury, William 24
Samwell, David 84, 105
   'The Padouca Hunt' 84–5
Sandwich 32, 44
Saunders, Benjamin 221
Seren Gomer 213, 241
Shenstone, William 43
Sidmouth, Lord 241
Sinclair, Sir John 131, 132, 133, 134, 143
   The Statistical Account of Scotland (1790–7) 131

Siôn Ceiriog *see* Edwards, John (Siôn Ceiriog)
Skynner, Isaac 125, 127, 130–1
Society for Constitutional Information 43, 87, 100
Society for Effecting the Abolition of the Slave Trade 73
Society for the Diffusion of Useful Knowledge 220
Society for the Promotion of Permanent and Universal Peace 217
Society for the Publication of Welsh Manuscripts 171
Society of Antiquaries 33, 85
Society of Friends 106
Society of Gentlemen Supporters of the Bill of Rights 11, 43
Somerset, Henry, the Marquis of Worcester 220
Southcott, Joanna 119
Southey, Robert 1, 105, 154, 161, 195, 209
  Madoc 86
Spectator 16
Spence, Thomas 114, 115, 141, 162, 197
  Pig's Meat 114, 115
Spencer, John 237
Spencer, William 237
Sports and Pastimes of the People of England (1801), Joseph Strutt 198
Staley, Benjamin 117
Stanhope, Earl 116
State of the Prisons in England and Wales, The (1777), John Howard 54
Swansea 7, 18, 29, 127, 130, 139, 165, 213–16, 225, 226, 228
  industrialization 7
  politics 74, 75–6
Swift, Jonathan 39

Talbot, Thomas Mansel 49
Taliesin 187
Taliesin Tir Iarll 5
Talleyrand, Prince 101
Tate, General William 150
Tatler 16
Taynton, Colonel 12
Taynton, Francis, solicitor 131
Test and Corporation Acts 72, 103
Thelwall, John 116–17, 118, 149, 159, 210
Thomas, Catherine (Cati Caerffili) 242
Thomas, David (Dafydd Ddu Eryri) 91, 144, 164, 209

'Cân Twm Paen' 147
Thomas, Evan, Llantrisant 239
Thomas, George, shoemaker 157, 159
Thomas, Rhys, printer 39
Thomas, Robert, Llantrisant 239
Thomas, William of Michaelstone-super-Ely 20, 71, 75
Tir Iarll 12
Toleration Act (1689) 72
Tom Jones, Henry Fielding 36
Tomos Glyn Cothi *see* Evans, Thomas (Tomos Glyn Cothi)
Tonyrefail 137, 238
Tooke, Horne 116, 117, 118, 210
Toulmin, Joshua 136
Traherne, Llewellyn of Coedrhiglan and St Hilary 235–6
Traitorous Correspondence Acts 150
Treatise of Human Nature, A (1739–40), David Hume 40
Trioedd Ynys Prydain 188
Truman family of Pantlliwydd 150
Trysorfa Gwybodaeth, neu, Eurgrawn Cymraeg (1770) 21, 70
Turford, Hugh 106
Turner, Sharon 179, 195
  A Vindication of the Genuineness of the Ancient British Poems of Aneurin, Taliesin, Llywarch Hen, and Merdhin (1803) 205
Twm o'r Nant *see* Edwards, Thomas (Twm o'r Nant)
Twrch, Richard 49
Twrch, William 49, 75
Tydain 185
Tylney-Long, Sir James 240

Unitarian Society of South Wales 70, 124, 160, 209, 213, 214, 216, 222, 228, 231–2, 233
Unitarianism 1, 70, 103, 135, 136, 141, 157, 159, 160, 220, 222–3, 233, 235

Vachell, Charles (d. 1832) 219
Vachell, Charles (d. 1859) 219
Vanities of Philosophy and Physick, The (1699), Gideon Harvey 16
Vaughan family of Hengwrt 172
Vaughan, Robert of Hengwrt 183, 188
Vernon, Lord 74
Vocal Miscellany, The (1733) 13
Voltaire 80, 128, 136, 176, 221

Wait, Daniel Guildford 203
Wakefield, Gilbert 1, 104, 106, 117, 128, 136, 149
　Spirit of Christianity (1794) 106
Walker, Thomas 118
Walpole, Horace 158
Walters, Daniel 52, 53
Walters, John (1721–97), cleric and lexicographer 24–6, 50, 52, 94, 135, 196
　An English–Welsh Dictionary 24–6, 39
Walters, John (1760–89), headmaster of Cowbridge Grammar School 52, 53
　Poems with Notes (1780) 52
　Translated Specimens of Welsh Poetry (1782) 52
Walton, John, surgeon 53, 54, 60
Waring, Elijah 9, 13, 88, 103, 161, 164, 198, 217, 218, 232, 236, 243
Watkins, Richard 135
Wedgwood, Josiah 126
Wellesley, Catherine Tylney-Long 240
Wellesley-Pole, William 240
Wellington, Duke of 231, 240
Wentworth, William, 2nd Earl Fitzwilliam 139
Wilberforce, William 73, 106, 123, 126, 229
Wiliems, Thomas 24
Wilkes, John 11, 43
Williams, Ann (née Matthew) 5, 9, 11–12, 14–16, 17, 28
　death 26
Williams, Ann (Nancy) 51, 53, 219
　'Edwards for Ever!' 233
Williams, David 16, 80, 88, 100, 136, 165, 194, 203
　Letters on Political Liberty (1782) 80, 100
　Letters to a Young Prince (1790) 107
Williams, Edward (Iolo ab Iorwerth Gwilym; Iolo Fardd Glas) 137, 138
William(s), Edward, senior 5, 9–10, 11, 17, 120
Williams, Edward (Iolo Morganwg)
　admiration of Milton 15
　admiration of Shakespeare 14
　ancestry 10
　and a national library 193–4, 198
　and a Welsh Corresponding Academy 195, 196, 197, 198
　and Anglophobia 168
　and anti-slavery 7, 73, 105–6, 123–6, 133, 228–9, 230

　and Bristol 48, 123, 125, 127, 160, 212, 237
　and Freemasonry 75
　and Glamorgan 180–1
　and hymn-writing 227–8
　and Indian culture 87–8, 200–1
　and Kent 32, 35
　and Oliver Cromwell 10, 128
　and opium 31, 95, 175–6
　and politics of consumption 95–7
　and Rational Dissent 48, 61, 69–72, 82, 102–3, 155, 210, 214, 237–8
　and republicanism 79–121, 129, 161
　and the Board of Agriculture 131–4
　and the *Cambrian Register* 130
　and the Girondist movement 100–1
　and the Gorsedd 91–5, 99, 112, 145–6, 152–3, 163, 170, 193, 201–3, 210, 233–4
　and the Madoc legend 43–4, 83–5
　and the poor 237–42
　and the Welsh language 17–18, 20, 23–6, 192, 195
　and Welsh dialects 65–6, 196–7
　and Welsh nationhood 163–207
　applies for post of custom-house officer 50
　as Anglican 23, 66
　as 'Christopher Crabstick' 76
　'Bella! horrida Bella' 111
　birth 4
　'Blaendardd yr Awenydd' 25
　buys *Lion*, sloop 51
　'Cadair Morgannwg' 65
　'Callendar of all the Debtors now Confined in Cardiff Gaol, who in the Creditor's opinion deserve to be hanged, A' 57
　'Cân Gwenn' 53
　'Cân Morfydd i'r Gyllell Gîg' 38
　'Cân Rhyddhad y Caethion' 229
　'Cân y Maensaer' 49
　'Carmen seculare, or the Jubilant Song' 210
　'Castles in the Air' 81
　'Champions of Liberty, The' 77
　childhood 12–17
　Coelbren y Beirdd (1840) 206
　coining of new words 25–6, 196, 222–3
　'Cyfrinach Beirdd Ynys Prydain' 56, 65, 170, 204
　'Cywydd Gorymbil am Heddwch' 146

death 243
debts 47, 50, 53–4, 131, 170
'Detached Thoughts [on] Christianity and Religion' 71–2
'Devilish Good Thing' 35
'Diddanwch y Cymru' 27
'Divine Unity Asserted, The' 155
'Dywenydd Morganwg' 65
Fair Pilgrim, The 81
'Glamorgan Triumphant, or, Edwards for ever!' 232
'God save the King' 108, 110
'Gwŷr Cwm y Felin' 71
'Heroic Song to Miss Tilney Long' 240–1
'History of the Ancient British Bards or Druids, The' 145–6
'History of the British Bards, The' 170
'Hymn to the Devil' 52–3, 68
ill health 31, 53, 59, 95, 106, 144, 236
in gaol 13, 47, 54, 55–9, 158, 219
inherits farm 50–1
interest in horticultural improvements 51
'Invocation to Peace' 111
Iolo Manuscripts (1848) 206
Jamaican inheritance 219, 220, 230
'Jumper's Hymn' 69
'Learned Ignorants, The' 19
'Letters on Universal Legislation' 95–100
literary influences on 13–16, 23–5
'Marshfield Parson, or Parson of Parsons, The' 68
'Mesurau Morgannwg' 65
'My Own Life' 164
'Newgate Stanzas, The' 2–3, 210
'Ode, on converting a sword into a pruning hook' 102, 108
'Ode on the Mythology of the Ancient British Bards' 101, 108
'Ode to Benevolence' 42
'On first hearing the Cuckoo' 42
'On Historians of Wales' 178
'Padouca Gazette Extraordinary' 85
pastorals 42–3
Poems, Lyric and Pastoral (1794) 4, 8, 9, 11, 13, 26, 36, 42, 73, 81, 84, 89, 93, 100, 106–9, 112, 113, 116, 123, 158
publication 106
portraits of 12
Prospectus of Collections for a New History of Wales in Six Volumes, A (1819) 182

pseudonyms used 17, 35
Salmau yr Eglwys yn yr Anialwch (1812) 227, 228
sets out for London 26–8
shopkeeper in Cowbridge 124–31, 163, 210
'Song for the Glamorgan Volunteers' 153
'Stonecut[t]er's Song, The' 31, 38
stonemason 3, 10–11, 31, 49, 81
transcribed part of the introduction of Charles Wilkins's translation of the *Bhăgvătgēētā* 88
translates *An Answer to the Question, Why are you a Christian?*, John Clarke 226
translates *General Instructions in the Doctrines and Duties of Religion*, John Prior Estlin 226
translates the *Marseillaise* into English 141–2
triads 94, 102, 174, 188–91, 202, 205, 206
Trial by Jury, The Grand Palladium of British Liberty 118
'Triodd y Cymro' 190
views on Calvinistic Methodism 69, 135, 144, 155
views on Catholicism 200
views on Dissenters 23, 69–72
views on Quakerism 69, 106
views on the coming of Christianity 184–5
views on the established church 66–9, 110–11
views on the monarchy 90, 109–10
views on the University of Oxford 19
views on Unitarianism 103–5, 135, 155, 206, 224, 226, 231, 234, 243
views on war 43, 72, 102, 105, 106, 108–9, 110, 111, 148, 153, 155, 231, 237
Vox Populi Vox Dei! (1818) 213, 233
'War incompatible with the Spirit of Christianity' 111
'William the Cowardly Wretch' 27
'Wishing Cap, The' 236–7
Williams, Edward, Middle Hill, Llancarfan 20
Williams, Elizabeth (Iolo's daughter) 95, 102, 236, 243
Williams, Evan, London bookseller 130, 179, 204

Williams, John (Iolo's brother) 5, 48, 73, 105, 126, 219, 230
Williams, Dr John, Sydenham 84
Williams, Revd John 75
Williams, John, Llanrwst 144, 181
Williams, John of Penyrheolgerrig 221
Williams, Margaret (née Roberts) (Peggy) 48, 50, 53, 56, 59–60
Williams, Margaret (Peggy) 51, 53, 219
  'Edwards for Ever!' 233
Williams, Miles (Iolo's brother) 5, 48, 73, 105, 126, 230
Williams, Morgan, Chartist 221
Williams, Morgan of Penyrheolgerrig 221
Williams, Moses 170, 188
Williams, Peter 156
Williams, Taliesin (Taliesin ab Iolo) 56, 71, 144, 194, 205–6, 216, 220, 230, 237, 243
  'The King of the Beggars' 233
Williams, Thomas, bookseller 149
Williams, Thomas, solicitor 27
Williams, Thomas (Iolo's brother) 5–6, 31, 73, 105, 126
Williams, William, farm labourer 242
Williams, William, Pantycelyn 227
Williams, William of Penyrheolgerrig 221
Windsor, Lady Catherine Sidney 240
Windsor, Thomas 74, 76, 77
Winterbotham, William 1, 2–3, 119
Wollstonecraft, Mary 98, 104
Wood, John, attorney 53, 238
Wordsworth, William 9, 131, 161
Wright, Richard 225
Wyndham, Thomas Edwin 74, 77
Wynnstay, library 173

Young, Arthur 131
Ystradowen 27